Scotland Now: A Warning to the World

Scotland Now: A Warning to the World

By Tom Gallagher

Scotview Publications, Edinburgh

First published in the United Kingdom in 2016 by
Scotview Publications,
Edinburgh
© Tom Gallagher, 2015.
Printed in Bulgaria.

ISBN   978-0-9934654-0-6

For Jill Stephenson, Historywoman,
a capable exponent of the liberal Scottish spirit and a redoubtable foe of dreamy and now restrictive Scottish Nationalism.

SCOTLAND NOW

About the Author:

Tom Gallagher was born in Glasgow and currently lives in Edinburgh. He spent over thirty years teaching and researching on how to manage conflicts over identity and resources on the peripheries of Europe and is Emeritus Professor of Politics at the University of Bradford.

Previous Single-Authored Books

Portugal: A Twentieth Century Interpretation, Manchester: Manchester University Press, 1983.

Edinburgh Divided, Edinburgh: Polygon 1987.

Glasgow The Uneasy Peace: Religious Tension In Modern Scotland, Manchester: Manchester University Press, 1987.

Romania After Ceauşescu: the politics of intolerance, Edinburgh: Edinburgh University Press, 1995.

Outcast Europe: The Balkans From The Ottomans To Milosević, 1789-1989, London: Routledge 2001.
Theft of a Nation: Romania Since Communism, London: Hurst & Co, 2005, New York University Press 2006.

The Balkans Since The Cold War: From Tyranny to Tragedy, London: Routledge 2003.

The Balkans in the New Millennium, London: Routledge 2005.

Romania and the European Union: How the Weak vanquished the Strong, Manchester University press 2009.

The Illusion of Freedom: Scotland Under Nationalism, Hurst & Co, 2009, (revised US edition published by Columbia University Press in 2011).

Divided Scotland: Ethnic Friction and Christian Crisis, Argyll Publishing , Scotland, July 2013.

Europe's Path to Crisis: Disintegration Through Monetary Union Manchester: Manchester University Press, 2014.

SCOTLAND NOW

Contents

SCOTLAND NOW

Foreword

A year after the referendum, Scotland is more divided than ever. A two and a half year campaign designed in part to grind down opposition to independence took its toll. Worse, the campaign continues.

Tom Gallagher has provided a thoughtful and incisive analysis of what is going on in Scotland. He looks at the rise of politics based on identity and the rejection by half the population of what might be called 'traditional' politics.

This analysis is much needed.

Scotland does not have enough 'think tank' capacity: it seems to me that we have another choice to make in Scotland. Do we carry on debating whether or not there is to be another referendum or do we confront the problems facing our country today which afflict too many of our people?

A referendum, blaming 'the other', is an alibi for doing nothing.

Many nationalists won't like this analysis but the more thoughtful – and there are many – will want to contemplate what Prof Gallagher has to say.

Nor do his conclusions make comfortable reading for those of us who believe that we can be both Scottish and British, and that Scotland is better and stronger as part of the UK.

Many nationalists might want to consider where years of fomenting division and grievance will take us. Does it make sense to so polarise the country that one half becomes increasingly intolerant of the other?

At the time of writing, there seems sadly no end to it.

Nationalists often describe this process as a journey. If ever there was a case for believing that it is better to travel in hope than to arrive this is it.

Take the case for Scotland having what is called fiscal autonomy – that is raising all the money spent. True federalism if you like. The problem is that the gap between what Scotland spends and takes in by way of taxes will reach almost £10 billion by 2020.

We were told that had we voted Yes in 2014, splitting the union would be done and dusted by 2016. Fiscal autonomy it seems cannot possibly be delivered any time soon. The trouble is that travelling in hope is just that. Arrival means making hard choices and choosing priorities.

This means identifying winners and losers which would undermine a campaign that cannot afford to offend anyone.

Nationalists might also want to reflect on what is becoming a growing problem for them. Hubris can turn into nemesis. In many ways we live in a one-party state in Scotland.

The Scottish Parliament has no inbuilt checks and balances. The SNP's record in government is poor in key areas. There are still too many children who, no matter their intelligence, will never get to university because of their background.

The Scottish government has the power to build more houses but it is not doing it in anything like the number needed. And they have created a monster in the shape of a single police force.

Then there is the growing intolerance of those who oppose them. In the referendum campaign businesses and individuals who spoke out were shouted down. Pointing out inconvenient truths was 'scaremongering'. Suggesting that the oil price might not always remain high was 'spreading unnecessary fear'.

Universities in Scotland which should be a source of civic debate were told to shut up during the referendum. With a few honourable exceptions their leadership did.

Now the nationalists are trying to take over their governance. That must set alarm bells ringing. And the incessant bullying of the state broadcaster is worrying. The nationalists have long wanted to take hold of the BBC in Scotland and we know why.

There is much to think about here. But those who believe the opposite case need to ponder deep too. Today's politics are to a large extent driven by disillusion with politicians and institutions. We are living in the backwash of the financial collapse of 2008. Ironically, two Scottish banks played a starring role in this episode.

The economic case against independence is straightforward. But I think we need to do more than make that case, as Prof Gallagher observes. Scotland has contributed not just to the UK but to the world to an extent that is extraordinary for a small country.

From the Enlightenment, through the industrial revolution and in building the social revolution in the welfare state in the 20th century, we contributed so much. We can be proud of that. Today, the case for building on that, pooling and sharing, of both resources and intellect is as strong as ever.

I cannot see why we would throw over a 300 year old history for something that is uncertain.

It is fitting then that Prof Gallagher concludes with the view that we need a new conversation in Scotland. We need to confront the problems we face rather than seek alibis.

FOREWORD

I am very clear that last year's referendum was a one-in-a-generation chance to decide. That is what we were promised and promises should be kept. But if there is another referendum (and it's clear Scotland does not want one any time soon) there should be a specific proposition put in front of us, so that people can see precisely what is on offer and what is not. That is what happened in the referendum in 1997.

That way we could all reflect and ask ourselves whether or not what is proposed will help resolve many of our home grown problems.

There is not a country in the world that does not have to make choices. Unfortunately, in the mid part of this decade, we see far more disintegration and the creation of further problems. For a country that did so much to establish a new order over the past 300 years, we have the capability to do the same again.

Let's accept that both sides hold different views but let's see if we cannot begin to fix those things which have gone wrong, and don't condemn another generation to losing out while politicians squabble over constitutions. They are after all only a means to an end.

Prof Gallagher aims to stimulate a debate. I hope he succeeds. We all should.

Alistair Darling, October 2015

Preface

In the past quarter-of-a-century, the post-Cold War world has become one increasingly full of disappointment and growing menace. Many democratic countries, along with the global institutions which they influence and shape, have lost the ability to promote norms meant to strengthen a cooperative and peaceful international order. International relations are now marked by provocations and resentments which in some eyes ominously parallel the tensions that were apparent in the prelude to the First World War. Confrontation and crises have erupted in a range of countries from the Americas, North Africa, Southern Europe, and the Middle East due to failed economic experiments, religious extremism, ill-designed external interventions, or the violent collapse of personal rule. These are conflicts which world institutions and leading nations, shaped by liberal democratic norms, might have striven to contain but they now seem numb and ineffectual in face of them. The self-confidence and reach of the countries in the Euro-Atlantic security sphere was eroded by disastrous interventions in the Middle East following the 2001 terrorist attacks of 9/11 in the USA. Instead it is Russia which has returned to the centre of the global stage this time as an authoritarian nationalist state keen to keep repressive leaders in power and impose its will on neighbours even if it means re-writing the rules of international relations. A new generation of autocrats in middle-ranking states take their lead more from Russia (and at times from China also) than from an increasingly introspective USA in the era of President Barack Obama. The USA at least recovered from a deep financial crisis after 2008 while the European Union has become increasingly divided and dysfunctional due to its inability to escape from serious and prolonged economic difficulties that can be traced back to the impetuous acquisition of a single currency in 2000 for those countries in what has become the Eurozone.

Britain stayed out of the Eurozone and has followed the USA in enjoying a modest economic recovery after years of difficulty. But it also often seems introspective and reluctant to play a prominent role in seeking to anticipate and contain ominous international flare-ups.

PREFACE

Remarkably, its own survival as a unified state is now in open doubt. A referendum on whether Scotland, comprising the northern third of Britain, should become a separate country, was lost by the nationalists in 2014 but, if anything, the demand for secession has intensified since then.

This book asks how political separatism has gone from being a fringe force to a mass movement in a remarkably short period of time. It argues that the mood of disaffection in Scotland is not merely a local or parochial phenomenon but has parallels across different parts of the contemporary West. The SNP neglects to use substantial administrative powers to improve Scotland and it has no viable economic plan for independence but it is strong because of the emotional fervour it can rely on from a restive swathe of voters. If it succeeds in turning the island of Britain into two separate states it is likely to have a momentous impact on Western political affairs given the influential role that Britain has continued to exercise in global politics.

In the 1920s the Spanish philosopher José Ortega y Gasset argued that Western countries would become increasingly un-governable due to the rise of a 'mass man' whom cultural and educational changes had made increasingly volatile and short-term in his habits and outlook. He feared that populist movements offering simplistic solutions and seeking to manage a volatile society by appealing opportunistically to the emotions and heightened egos of numerous voters, would be the result and that immense turbulence would be hard to avoid.

His book *The Revolt of the Masses* appeared on the eve of the worldwide financial depression which was quickly followed by global war and two generations of confrontation between rival superpowers. Perhaps therefore it was only in the deceptive calm of the post-Cold War era that society could impose its own norms and expectations on Western countries which had for so long been on the front line in an armed confrontation which could have resulted in wholesale nuclear annihilation.

Today's mutinous conditions in Scotland were absent from the 1980s when it was well-known that the oil wealth lying in Scottish waters was sufficient to allow an independent Scotland to be economically viable. Voters there rejected political separatism when they had the chance to vote for their own autonomous parliament from 1999 onwards. Yet today, the British state in its southern English capital, London is assailed for wrongful policies in areas where, usually it is the Scottish government which enjoys responsibility and resources.

Separatists are evasive or reticent about how unpicking a 308-year-union and then providing alternative sources of economic viability could be accomplished without much dislocation and risk. But it has not prevented their principle vehicle, the Scottish National Party (SNP) from surging ahead after unexpectedly forming a minority government in 2007. Today one in fifty Scottish voters belong to the party and, in a remarkably quick period, it has established a grip on institutions across state and society which seasoned ruling parties across Europe are likely to envy.

The SNP has been in office for eight years but it operates and thrives essentially as a protest movement. After several generations of trying, it has succeeded in persuading several million Scots that the rest of Britain (and England in particular) is an alien 'other' in fundamental ways. It is usually not pressed by its clamorous new supporters on future policies, safeguards for vulnerable social groups or what the architecture of the new state will be like. Often they display an impatience with Scotland remaining part of NATO and hosting nuclear weapons and yearn for very different international relationships. There is also an absorption with the medieval centuries of Scottish history when a poor country enjoyed a precarious independence but had few achievements to its credit. By contrast, each of the three centuries of the post-1707 Union were shaped by major advances: an outburst of remarkable intellectual creativity in the 18th century which became known as the Scottish Enlightenment; a surge in economic enterprise which saw Scotland turn from being a mainly rural country to a heavily urbanised early centre of the industrial revolution in the 19th century; and a 20th century which saw major improvements in the living conditions of many of its people. But it is the downside of the Union which is emphasised in the nationalist worldview - class conflict, rural dispossession, involvement in base imperial adventures, and becoming the pawn of an America apparently drunk on its own post-World War II economic and military strength.

These themes, emphasising long-term grievances and current resentments have grown attractive to increasing numbers of Scots, especially men below the age of forty. They have their counterparts in other countries such as Germany and Spain where there is a turning away from identification with the intellectual and political features of a post-1945 Atlantic world influenced by the USA. But it is not just in these countries that there now a growing turn towards alternative models emphasising a multi-polar world with a central role for Russia or else radical economic models borrowed from Latin America despite their stark failure in Venezuela and Cuba.

A new climate favourable to experimentation and risk-taking has taken hold. In plenty of European countries, disaffection has been stoked by economic crisis leaving millions of young victims in its wake, people who have no hope of finding a place in the conventional labour market. In Scotland economic conditions are far more stable. It is not material hardship but a desire to experiment by psychologically restless Scots which has kindled a spirit of radical revolt. It has been manufactured by painting London as the bogey-man continuing to hold Scotland back.

Through inspired use of social media and the years of campaigning that occurred in the marathon referendum period, the political culture of Scotland was transformed. In the absence of a separate language or a distinctive Scottish culture or economic system, a preoccupation with England was the logical route to go down in order to discredit current political alignments. In England itself there was disaffection with an elite that was seen as dominated by career politicians tempted by cronyism and content to push policies such as intensifying European integration or mass immigration mainly to poorer urban areas, which are increasingly questioned. In 2015, the Labour Party even elected as its new leader a militant figure chiefly famous hitherto for his long-term backing for violent Irish nationalism. So political life across Britain was becoming increasingly turbulent due to mass disaffection and the ability of well-organized groups of determined radicals to achieve power-grabs in different areas of national life.

But in Scotland, it was a long smouldering national question which enabled opponents of the current political order to find the most successful outlet for their agitation. Insistence that external interference and malpractice were holding back Scotland became a passport to electoral success. The 2015 general election in Scotland was an issue-less one. What counted in the eyes of disaffected voters was who would stand up for Scotland. The party with the most emotion-laden approach to politics was bound to win hands down. Miscalculations by British Prime Ministers from Margaret Thatcher to Tony Blair and on to David Cameron allowed a party that had lurked in the shadows for decades finally to enjoy its place in the sun. But as I argue here, the main catalyst was the transformation in outlook of many Scots who as a group were impatient to be part of a vague but noisy liberation force in favour of creating a new state.

By the early 21st century, they had become prime candidates to be seduced by populism, the brand of politics which throws up leaders who insist they are uniquely qualified to discern the will of the people and carry it out even if it means interfering with fundamental elements of the democratic process. In 2009 I wrote *the Illusion of Freedom: Scotland Under Nationalism,* an early assessment of Scottish nationalism at a time when the SNP still lacked a majority at the Scottish parliament in Holyrood, Edinburgh. It argued that populism with an illiberal face would very likely be the direction of travel. It also contended that campaigning to loosen the fictional grip of London rather than building a better country able to handle the challenges of independence would be a vote-winner and was likely to pave the way for a restrictive regime. And it suggested that essentially old-style decision-making in which the SNP consolidated its grip by using state resources to win allies in the economic and cultural life of the country, would triumph.

In 2009, the era had yet to dawn when public broadcasters faced a demonstration by thousands of nationalists outside their offices with the SNP's leader Alex Salmond offering his benign approval. This was still a time when the SNP was largely believed when it claimed to be a civic nationalist force.

One of the book's weaknesses was a failure to imagine just how deeply and how fast Scottish society could fall under the influence of an unabashedly populist movement. But nevertheless, this particular book was treated as an alarmist tract even though it had been informed by several decades of academic teaching and research about how to manage nationalist tensions on the peripheries of Europe. So there was virtually zero interest in Scotland itself. Thanks to a publishing acquaintance having a relative who worked for a BBC morning news programme in London, I was interviewed about it in the autumn of 2009. Later, one of the programme editors remarked that the SNP had lobbied hard to prevent me appearing. Mine was apparently a hopelessly slanted voice and it was assumed that if nobody was put up against me in a debate, then the item would be cancelled. Perhaps the SNP's handling of the Scottish media had given it this degree of confidence, but the BBC in London held firm and the discussion went ahead.

Perhaps the book had also been shown to Alex Salmond because he later testily referred to me as 'the nutty professor'.[1] Today, the SNP is planning legislation which will vastly tighten the state's grip over Scotland's fifteen universities and presumably one not unwelcome side-effect (for the SNP) is that academics with inconvenient views will be less inclined to write or broadcast in ways that unsettle the powerful.

Alex Salmond's remark didn't rile me at the time because it was useful confirmation that he had limited patience with a pluralist spread of opinion in a country he was intent on transforming. Perhaps owing to his barely-concealed views about which were legitimate voices in current affairs broadcasting, I was largely overlooked by the Scottish media during the 2012-14 years of referendum campaigning. This proved fortuitous. Much of the BBC's coverage was narrow and unimaginative. It was often absorbed with arcane constitutional matters. Like the SNP itself, BBC Scotland was far more interested in process than in practical outcomes flowing from independence. It rarely if ever, explored the consequences for local communities dependent on British state jobs of a partition of the island and how the architects of independence could replicate them. It showed the determination of the SNP to have so many of Scotland's institutions dancing to its 'Yes' tune that this timid broadcasting channel nevertheless still fell foul of numerous nationalist activists.

So I had ample time to think of a book that tried to ask questions which were ignored in the cautious media coverage during the campaigning years stretching from 2012 to 2014. As the Introduction explains in detail, the book aims to show why the current absorption with dividing Britain in order to acquire a vestige of independence for Scotland is not good for most Scots or indeed beneficial for much of the rest of the world.

One of the first things attentive readers will spot is that it is self-published. For some it will merely confirm that the author is a fringe figure who found it hard to convince a regular publisher of the value of his work. There is a nugget of truth in such a view, albeit a small one. A detailed proposal was sent to two London publishers, an American university imprint with a long list of British titles, and a publisher in Middle Eastern hands with a similarly long list on modern nationalism. Three months elapsed without any response by which time I was well into the writing of the book and I decided the most practical course was to bring the book out myself. My previous twelve single-authored books had been published by university presses and academic publishers. So perhaps it was time for a new departure, however challenging it might prove.

I realised that in the eyes of many London commissioning editors and manuscript reviewers, it was likely that a critique of Scottish Nationalism would be seen as small-minded and even reactionary. The times had long passed when the rise of militant nationalist movements, ones determined to re-arrange existing territories, had been seen as parochial and retrograde in the liberal professions. Commentators in London newspapers like the *Times* and the *Financial Times* were soon hailing the arrival of the SNP and high-profile parliamentarians like 20-year-old Mhairi Black as a breath of fresh air in a stuffy and crony-ridden Westminster. Edgy voices calling for the creation of separate states on the island of Britain, were regarded as authentic cries of protest among radical professionals dismayed that the Conservatives continued to be in charge of Britain after the general election of May 2015.

If my manuscript was sent out for review I reckoned that the likelihood of academic readers recoiling from a critical account of the democratic world's most successful nationalist movement for its impracticality, methods of acquiring power and authoritarian temper were high. No longer was nationalism treated with disdain in higher education whose main trade-union often appeared to devote its main energies to advancing the cause of one particular form of nationalism, that of the Palestinians, and where populist regimes in Latin America and elsewhere enjoyed no lack of vocal sympathisers. I doubt if this book will be on too many reading lists at least in politics courses at Scottish universities but this does not unduly dismay me. It is meant for the general reader in Scotland, the rest of Britain and the wider world where there is puzzlement and sometimes incredulity at the ability of a movement like the SNP to develop such momentum in a country supposedly as calm and contented as Britain.

This book examines the nature of contemporary nationalism in Scotland, the reasons why its advance has been so rapid, and the extent the mood of disaffection is reflected in events elsewhere in Europe and beyond. It is meant for both a Scottish and a non-Scottish audience: it is important that people in the rest of the UK realise that just because devotees of nationalism are hyper-active in promoting their cause, this does not mean they constitute majority opinion. They still do not. There are plenty of voices in Scotland opposed to separation and prepared to offer detailed critiques of what is proposed by the SNP. The referendum years of 2012-14 witnessed the emergence of eloquent, well-informed and tenacious people, many ordinary citizens, firmly British-minded in outlook. They forensically examined the SNP's governing record in key areas of public policy, they tweeted, wrote blogs and letters to the press, and dissected the euphemistic and evasive documents sketching a post-British future emanating from the Nationalists. So the online media world was not overwhelmed by pro-independence 'Yessers' but the ability of the latter to harness the climate of disaffection on social media, helps to explain why many people who often spent many hours online, were converted to a political cause many had been completely numb to only a short time before.

I admire independent-minded Scots. Their intellectual curiosity, energy and idealism has had a remarkable impact on the world. But such Scots are very thin on the ground in the Scottish National Party. It relies on leader-worship and unthinking compliance with an agenda for separation that is based on emotional grievance rather than practical planning for the future. Under this party, Scotland is moving backwards. Science is distrusted, seats of learning need to be controlled, the state micro-manages the lives of Scots, preferring compliant subjects to free-thinking citizens.

Scotland's current drama is a reminder that a country can regress. The cultural achievements of the Scottish Enlightenment and the practical benefits of three centuries of shared endeavour with a cooperative and usually undemanding neighbour, can be rejected. The tussle between shrill, resentful, and present-orientated Scots and low-key, pragmatic and future-orientated ones, will not be settled soon. It will determine the fate of the second largest island in the world's temperate zone, one that has played an outsized role in human affairs, sometimes for ill but far more often for good.

The confrontation between egotistical and often angry romantics and citizens who embrace risk and experimentation only in the expectation that improvements are likely to flow that extend beyond themselves, has polarised Scotland. It is part of a wider struggle which will determine whether it is possible for Western countries to preserve the precarious balance of order, liberty and internal equilibrium which brought them considerable success and enabled them to be models for millions of

PREFACE

others elsewhere. So it just happens that the story of early 21st century Scotland is one of particular relevance to the rest of the world at a momentous and perhaps crucial turning-point in its affairs. This is the principal reason why, in early 2015, I resolved to sit down and write this book.

Tom Gallagher, 17 October 2015.

---

1. Derek Bateman, 'Making a difference', *Derek Bateman's Blog*, 22 April 2014, http://derekbateman.co.uk/2014/04/22/making-a-difference/

Introduction

The world surely has problems enough to contend with without worrying over-much about Scotland as it noisily awakens from a long political slumber. The un-wary deserve to be told to watch out for the treacherous Scottish weather, unruly football fans at a Glasgow soccer derby, or the midgy, a ferocious insect whose bites can turn an idyllic Highland holiday into a nightmare. But the world can surely cope with the emergence of a brand of nationalism with mass appeal that threatens to split the island of Britain in two. Perhaps it can or perhaps not. This book urges caution and advocates much closer attention to what is happening in Scotland. It offers an interpretation of recent events which will be viewed as hopelessly distorted by perhaps most Scottish nationalists. But this focus on the condition of the country is meant to inspire reflection and debate. Undoubtedly, it is the nationalist movement which stands to benefit the most if it decides to take stock even in the face of critical studies like this one. It might also be useful for readers with a British outlook: their perspective has failed to gain a proper outlet in public broadcasting and politicians opposed to separatism often struggled to articulate it when appearing on the media. Finally, the book is meant to raise awareness beyond this island about its current internal strains and tensions because they are bound to have a bearing on politics, international relations and indeed the outcome of territorial conflicts far and wide.

Scotland in the 18th century, when it had a population four times smaller than its present 5 million, managed to have a startling impact on the world, one that be-lied its size. It was at the forefront of a revolution of thought which helped lay the foundation for a modern world in which ignorance and superstition were forced to make way for rational modes of thinking and behaviour in many different places. The ruling Scottish National Party (SNP) usually has little to say about what has be-come known as the Scottish Enlightenment; it occurred during the first century of the political union between Scotland and England when allegedly Scotland entered a political eclipse.

In many ways, this territorial partnership was a model of power-sharing and recon-ciliation in a world of recurring conflicts similar to the ones which had pitted Scotland and England against one another for centuries. Scottish energies were released which had previously been dissipated in religious quarrels, cross-border warfare, and in factional strife at home. Scottish inventors and businessmen played a major part in driving forward the industrial revolution in England as well as Scotland. Scotland's role in establishing the British Empire far outweighed its size. Thrusting, hard-headed and also idealistic Scots were involved at all levels of this stupendous enterprise. Rapacious Scottish merchants engineered a war with China in 1840 so that they could continue to make enormous profits by dealing in opium there. Modern trends in education have ensured that such episodes have defined the British empire for recent generations. But alongside the exploitation, Britain strove to uphold constitutional freedoms, human rights and international law and Scots were often at the forefront of such progressive endeavours. The moral vision of anti-slavery campaigners, missionaries and those seeking better treatment for women and children in India, or creating democratic government in Canada and Australia, are not usually referred to by SNP politicians on their trips abroad. But such Scots helped to make the world a much better place and, on present trends, it appears unlikely that nationalists will accomplish even a fraction of their endeavours.

Back on the island of Britain energetic, ambitious and talented Scots helped to shape the boundaries and content of a British culture and disseminate its influence far and wide. It is unlikely that this cross-fertilisation of energies would have occurred unless many in Scotland had come to feel that a formal partnership with England was of lasting benefit to Scotland. The 1707 Act of Union initiated this new departure. A parliamentary union, voluntarily entered into, replaced a weak, introspective state with daunting policy failures with a union allocating Scotland major autonomy and enabling it to develop far more effectively than if it had remained aloof from the rest of the British Isles. Rather than being a check on Scottish capabilities, the union allowed hitherto dormant positive traits to flourish. Gradually expanding freedoms, secure property rights, and institutional autonomy provided the basis for an effective partnership.

Scots were also prominent in struggles for social reform at home. They played a central role in the 20th Century Labour Party. There was overwhelming acceptance in the rest of the UK when Scotland acquired its own parliament in Edinburgh in 1999 to manage large parts of its internal affairs. This had been an initiative launched by Scots in the Labour Party and in civic and religious bodies who bridled at the uncharacteristic centralisation being pursued in the 1980s during the premiership of Margaret Thatcher. Political autonomy became unavoidable because Scotland increasingly voted in a different way from some of the most populous regions of England. The great political beneficiaries of devolution have been the nationalists.

But it is easily forgotten that until the eve of its success, the SNP was hostile to the late 20th century campaign for a Scottish Parliament that was designed to oversee the work of the administration which had existed in Edinburgh for over a century.

Perhaps one of the best literary representations of Scotland and the Scottish character is *The Strange Case of Dr Jekyll and Mr Hyde* by Robert Louis Stevenson. A virtuous personality struggled to contain an evil double who achieved ascendancy during the hours of darkness. Ultimately, the good personality felt that in order to halt his diabolical alter ego, suicide was the only course to adopt.

Politically, Scotland also wrestled with two alter egos. During the heyday of the Union, many resented the subordinate role Scotland played in the Union. A lot of Scots bridled when English sporting commentators or decision-makers instinctively confused their English part of the Union with all of Britain. There was anger when the title adopted by the new monarch Elizabeth in 1953 was Queen Elizabeth II even though there had never been an Elizabeth I in Scotland. It suggested that the Union was being too easily taken for granted by its senior partner. This indignation was eclipsed by the burning resentment felt at the rule of Mrs Thatcher in the 1980s. Her Conservative Party enjoyed a fast shrinking presence in Scotland. But she pursued deflationary policies which proved disastrous for heavy industry in Scotland (and the north of England). It scarcely mattered that industries reliant on state protection from overseas competition would be on their way out nearly everywhere by the end of the century. Her Scottish ministers often tempered her free market zeal when it came to Scotland and worked hard to establish successor industries in Scotland, some of which have proved far more viable. But Margaret Thatcher became a dark star, a symbol of English arrogance and absolutism for whom there is no counterpart in the previous centuries of union.

Noisy indignation about the alleged role of Scotland's neighbour England in holding the country back, started to go mainstream. The former Labour MP Tom Harris recalls the astonishment of he and his colleagues in the early 1990s when opinion polls started to reveal that the SNP was by far the favoured option when people were asked which party do you think stands up best for Scotland?[1] It was a Labour Prime Minister, Tony Blair who agreed to deliver a Scottish parliament and during a decade at the helm, living standards improved for most Scots, as well as UK citizens elsewhere, faster than they had done for a long time. Yet Blair in his turn would be vilified in Scotland as well as in the UK particularly among former left-wing supporters appalled by his decision to ally with right-wing US President George Bush II and rush headlong into a disastrous military intervention in Iraq. By 2015, the Labour Party in Scotland was joining the Conservatives in the ranks of the political untouchables. A party which had won 41 of Scotland's 59 Westminster seats in 2010 was reduced to a mere one.

In a way it could be seen as poetic justice because Labour had been the one chiefly popularising the idea that the Tories were an anti-Scottish toxic force. Perhaps the party's strategists had never envisaged that the same tactics would one day rebound with such devastating force on them. But a much bigger blunder was Labour's failure to remake itself as a patriotic left-wing force confident in its management of the new institutions of self-governance. Dissatisfaction mounted particularly from the left. The hitherto noisy but usually irrelevant Nationalists had the presence of mind to exploit this crisis of credibility in Scotland's dominant party.

Populist parties, whose primary appeal is to the emotional instincts of people, usually don't get very far without a charismatic or at least bold and outspoken leader. After nearly sixty years in the electoral wilderness, the SNP finally struck lucky. Alex Salmond became leader in 1990 and for the next quarter-of-a-century led the party (except for a 4-year sabbatical early in the 2000s). Salmond has an easy manner and air of authority which enabled him to master the media and confront decision-makers in London. Nearly everywhere, leaders like Salmond, who portrayed himself as 'the people's friend', were being replaced by colourless machine politicians. Scotland was no exception. His opponents sometimes had limited experience of real life and did not speak the same language as the voters they were trying to attract.

Salmond is an arch-dissembler who has tried to promote himself as the 'Scottish Everyman' able to peer into the hearts of his countrymen and divine their hopes and dreams. In a 2014 memoir, he depicts himself as the paternalistic tribal chief, combining the warrior ethos with a popular egalitarian one. Such traits loomed large in the Scottish Highland culture and they gradually began to displace the lower-key and unadventurous Scottish Lowland mindset especially with the decline of industry. Salmond's often abrasive style unsettled women and the party's greatest triumph would only occur after he stepped down in 2014. But his uninhibited drive and single-minded commitment to realising his goal of separating Scotland from the rest of the United Kingdom (UK), helped to bring a fringe force to the centre of power.

Both he and his successor as SNP leader, Nicola Sturgeon had no hesitation about endlessly flattering the Scots: they are a special people who belong to an exceptional country with its own 'soft power' that can put England's in the shade. They have only been held back apparently because they have been imprisoned in an unjust union with an increasingly incompatible neighbour. Such rhetoric had usually fallen flat when there was powerful island-wide solidarity. This solidarity brought Britain through the Second World War and laid the basis for a wave of social reform. But the retreat of empire removed an important element of common ground. Elite mismanagement of industrial relations dented a British outlook as did several of the privatisation schemes of the 1980s and 1990s which removed well-known British symbols from public ownership.

The arrival of a Scottish parliament in 1999 inevitably meant that the central focus of politics switched from Westminster to Edinburgh. Society was also becoming more hedonistic and less resistant to risk-taking. Religious observance plunged. Casual relationships increasingly replaced marriage, especially in working-class communities. Scots became more self-centred and materialist and absorption in civic and community endeavours faded.

New authority figures also appeared. Business, religious, sporting or civic figures who enjoyed respect because of personal endeavour and were able to act as a counterweight to the large Scottish state, faded from the spotlight. They were replaced by celebrities who were famous for being radical in their tastes, lifestyles or views. A new celebrity culture offered approval for different forms of personal experimentation. In the newly restless and edgy Scotland an egocentric figure like Alex Salmond probably thrived far more easily than he would have done in the past.

These self-styled 'creative' Scots have offered a particular service by articulating a sense of grievance that a political force like the SNP needs to popularise in order to make crucial headway. It is regularly argued by the SNP that 'privileged', 'arrogant' and 'exploitative' Tories from England have held back Scotland and plundered its resources in order to augment their wealth. Its breakthrough came at the third election for the Scottish Parliament, held in 2007. The ruling Labour party was divided at the top in London and ill-led in Scotland. The SNP emerged just one seat ahead of Labour but nevertheless formed a government which survived a full term even though outnumbered by its rivals.

The SNP presented itself as the national defender, championing Scottish interests against a London power structure ready, it seemed, to trample Scotland underfoot. There were regular stage-managed confrontations with London. These enabled the SNP and a slick media machine to insist that Scots ought to re-endorse the party for standing up against a bullying territorial overlord. In 2011, the party's electoral manifesto made no mention of its central objective, independence. On the ballot paper, what caught the eye was not 'Vote SNP' but the part that followed: 'Re-Elect Alex Salmond as First Minister.' With 44 per cent of the vote, the SNP won an outright majority, 69 of the 129 seats in the Holyrood parliament.

In the long age of nationalism, the preference for identifying external sources for national failings is not confined to Scottish nationalists. It is rare to hear an admission that shortcomings may have internal origins and that they may not necessarily soon vanish upon the arrival of independence.

The SNP's confrontational stance caused mounting exasperation in London. The

Tory-Liberal Democrat coalition headed by David Cameron had not tried to claw back any powers from Edinburgh. Public spending in Scotland continued to be around £1200 per head more than in the rest of the UK and the reviled Tories made no effort to re-balance this proportion in a time of economic austerity.[2] But Cameron decided that the Scottish electorate must be given the chance to decide if it really wished to opt for separation from the rest of the UK. Under the 2012 Edinburgh agreement, the SNP government would be able to decide the referendum question, the size of the electorate and the duration of the campaign. These concessions were seized upon by the SNP and showed how a complacent government in London under-estimated the cunning and determination of a resourceful regional foe.

The cross-party Better Together campaign had trump cards in its bid to preserve the Union. It claimed that Scotland would run a massive deficit if deprived of the funding stream provided by the rest of the UK and most economists agreed. The campaign urging a 'Yes' vote to the question 'Should Scotland Be Independent' struggled to show what currency an independent state would have (with Salmond insisting on the retention of the pound to the private dismay of many in his own camp).

But major holes in practical planning for the future did not impede the pro-separation side. It embraced the opportunities for campaigning and conversion offered by the new tools of the social media. Without them it is hard to see how a process of mass radicalisation could have been accomplished. But this is what happened as the Yes side absorbed a legion of new recruits from middle-class professionals to ethnic minorities, (Irish-minded or else with roots in south Asia) in the remarkably long thirty months allowed for campaigning.

A popular front of 'Yes' enthusiasts sprang up whose members believed they could fulfil themselves via independence or were motivated by the struggle to achieve it. They included idealists and authoritarians as well as numerous intellectuals, entertainers and media folk who not long before had other political loyalties. In possession of often strongly socialist views, they reinforced the palpable sense of self-righteousness resting in doctrinaire nationalism. Two perspectives combined in 2012, the national one emphasising political sovereignty as a liberating force and the egalitarian one, promising social justice and a widespread re-distribution of resources.

They both possess an essentially benign view of human nature. The sense of evangelical fervour, the expectation that epic deeds were within the grasp of a people which had finally discovered its self-belief, were viewpoints articulated by many Scottish intellectuals who dropped their critical detachment and enthusiastically embraced what seemed like a cause poised to radically alter the face of Scotland. The atmosphere at campaign rallies had a quasi-religious aura with truths being simply confirmed rather than evaluated and debated. It meant that some sceptics were prepared to view the independence campaign more as a dreamy cult rather than as a conventional political movement for change.

In-depth debate about the kind of state, institutions and civic endeavour necessary for the self-governing experiment to flourish have never exactly been strong features of nationalist movements. But this form of calm deliberation was often difficult to spot in 2014. At times, it seemed that nationalism was what Alex Salmond said it was. His poor grasp of policy detail often proved to be his Achilles Heel. Nevertheless, his views on central issues were rarely if ever challenged within the Yes movement. The cause stood above policy matters however important some of them might be for the well-being of citizens in whose name the freedom journey was being undertaken.

The lacklustre 'No' side exploited these failings but a 30 point lead in the first half of the campaign shrank to a ten point one when the votes were counted on 18 September 2014. The campaign, especially in its closing stages, was bad-tempered and rowdy, marred by attacks on pro-Union speakers and the systematic defacing of pro-Union posters and placards even when on private property. Several polls taken one year later showed that a quarter of people had suffered abuse, got into arguments, or lost friends over their stance in the referendum.

It is not far-fetched to claim that the marathon referendum campaign succeeded in opening up divisions in Scotland almost as harmful as the ones that scarred French society for a generation after the 1940-44 Nazi occupation of France. If remarks made by Alistair Darling , the official leader of the victorious pro-Union side, are anything to go by, he believes such a comparison to be valid. In a television documentary broadcast in September 2015, he argued that Scotland had become more divided now than it was a year ago, saying: 'I have never come across some of the divisions, amongst friends, amongst family – people saying things to each other that I would have thought unbelievable. I think that it is corrosive, it won't go away – this is not something you can easily fix and it's almost being encouraged by the nationalists – this idea that if you're not for them you're against Scotland'.[3]

The 'No' side won the vote, but all the momentum remained with the 'Yes' side, which, instead of collapsing, went on to make the SNP perhaps the biggest political party per head of population in Europe, enabling it to win all but three of Scotland's 59 seats at Westminster in the 2015 British general election.

Scotland is a small country. Other small countries across the world have been beset by populist movements with vaulting ambitions. Once they occupy the seat of power they often have little idea how to turn their passionate rhetoric into practical policies. All too often the sole beneficiaries prove to be well-situated political insiders who may even turn into a new ruling class. If many Scottish voters join with their current leaders and decide to take a holiday from reality, will it ultimately count for that much in the scale of human affairs?

The secession of Scotland from the rest of the UK is likely to have far greater impact than say the break-away of Catalonia from Spain or the secession of parts of northern Italy from Rome-administered Italy. What happens in Britain is noticed all over the world not least because London is one of the main centres of global communications. In 2014, the 'demonstration' effect of a powerful state possibly on the verge of breaking up caused dismay even in countries like China which can hardly be described as an ally of Britain. Rulers with their own restive minorities were bound to be concerned at the example provided by Scotland. Scots appeared to have few outstanding grievances and seemed to get a good economic deal from being part of a Union state which was doing better than much of the rest of Europe in economic terms by 2014. What lessons would genuinely mistreated groups desiring autonomy or sovereignty derive from a Scottish revolt against Britain? And would ethnically dominant but insecure states (of which there are many) be as willing as before to offer concessions to restive minorities given the turmoil that has occurred despite the granting of increasingly extensive forms of autonomy to Scotland?

Leaving aside Russia and North Korea, the only vocal well-wishers the proponents of independence had were exponents of breakaway nationalism in some EU states. A successful 'freedom' bid by Scotland was obviously bound to increase the credibility of separatists in European countries like Spain and Italy but it caused dismay in perhaps most other countries, especially those based around an ethnic majority.

Surely, by gaining independence Scotland would merely be following in the footsteps of countries which Scots had helped to found ranging from the United States in the 18th century to Canada, New Zealand and Australia between 1840 and 1914? These were young countries in which a lot of preparation and thought was devoted to building the architecture of future states. They attracted a lot of energetic and self-reliant migrants whose outlook enabled new states based on well-ordered liberty to put down solid roots. Scotland is an old country both in terms of history and the demographic profile of its population. Its would-be state builders are driven by a mix of emotional resentment and personal ambition rather than an eagerness to create a new state qualitatively better than the one they hope to divorce from. Backing for independence has reached impressive levels in Scotland but, arguably there are insufficient independent-minded people to be found there. Instead there is a state which is very large even by western standards and which those organizing the freedom journey have allocated the task of building the new nation.

On the first anniversary of the 2014 referendum, it was virtually impossible to encounter any Scottish Nationalists keen to point out what they would have done to make Scotland a different place if only they had won. Instead, there were lamentations about a defeat apparently engineered by the sharp practice of the Union's defenders; and the SNP made no bones about flinging itself into permanent campaigning mode in order to reverse the defeat sometime in the future.

Does independence for Scotland really alter that much? After all, the European Union has increasingly drained much practical power from its 28 members and the SNP has made it plain how keen it is for Scotland to become the next one. Scotland in 2014 exported £47.6 billion worth of goods to the rest of Britain compared with just £12 billion to 12 European states nearly all of whom were EU members.[4] It is paradoxical that the SNP is so obsessed with renouncing the sovereignty of the UK and lodging much of it with the EU when it has relatively limited practical ties with the institutions in Brussels. They have acquired the profile of a semi-state and while the British state has increasingly been prepared to share power with different national components and regions, it is clear that the EU is ever more inclined to hoard power at the expense of national members.

Surely, if it decided to extend membership to Scotland, the EU would curb the populism of the SNP and it would settle down to govern within the policy framework being rolled out across the EU by a centralising bureaucracy? There are some grounds for accepting the likelihood of such a scenario. The SNP has few favoured policies which it jealously defends. It is mainly concerned with expanding the power of the local state and building up a strong patronage machine. These priorities can co-exist with a European state which wants local states essentially to act as conveyor belts for its decisions. The overriding appeal of the EU for the SNP is that it is an instrument that enables it to escape from Britain and venture into international affairs supposedly as a sovereign actor.

Of course these ambitions depend on the EU remaining a vigorous entity. The rise of the SNP has coincided with major crises, first over the single currency and then over the refugees and migrants fleeing wars in nearby countries (or driven by economic opportunity). These challenges have revealed the EU to be internally divided and a deeply ineffective crisis manager. What if the process of European integration goes into reverse or the EU shrinks in size or even breaks up altogether due to the strain of these challenges and the absence of a common resolve to overcome them? This scenario is not as far-fetched as once it seemed and leading EU decision-makers have delivered blunt warnings about the EU's survival being at stake.

Most of Scotland's neighbours would do their best to adapt to a Europe without the EU. They might seize new opportunities to manage their trading relations with the rest of the world better than the EU bureaucracy has been doing recently. The European Free Trade Association exists to act as hub for functional cooperation.

INTRODUCTION

NATO remains the key security agency promoting Euro-Atlantic cooperation. But how would Scotland cope if it was unable to join the EU or else the European project entered into an eclipse?

Under the 1997 devolution agreement, Scotland has no control over foreign policy. But the readiness of SNP governments to strike up ties with countries in East Asia and the Middle East, ones often with debatable records on human rights and their own territorial or religious ambitions, is bound to bring pause for thought among some neighbouring countries. Scotland's biggest international controversy in the devolution era occurred in 2009 when the SNP released a Libyan national, Abdelbaset al-Megrahi while he was still in an early stage of the life sentence he had received for blowing up an aeroplane mainly carrying US nationals in 1988. Many of the relatives of victims were shocked and top US government officials were deeply angry. It was a sign of the readiness of the SNP government to stand up to the power not only of London but also of Washington. But the grounds for picking a quarrel with the USA seemed flimsy and the affair suggested that there was impatience among nationalists with persevering with membership of an international alliance still dominated very much by the USA.

If a strong 'anti-imperialist' outlook influences the way that those in charge of an independent Scotland relate to the rest of the world, it is likely to place the country at odds with nearly all of its neighbours. It was noticeable that no prominent figures in the world of politics in France, Ireland, or the Scandinavian countries supported independence, while several warned about the geopolitical dangers, including one serving foreign minister. A preference in perhaps each of these countries for Britain remaining intact because of its past role as an anchor of stability in North-West Europe, is hard to disguise.

But perhaps fears about Scotland proving a wild card in north-west-Europe owing to its readiness to make unusual alliances, perhaps in order to obtain financial backing for its independence gamble, will be muted. After all, the country has been influenced by many centuries of attachment to a British liberal order.

Parliamentary government, the freedom of the press and assembly, the independence of judges, the ability of citizens to live free from undue state interference, and a vigorous civil society tempering the reach of the state are all parts of the British inheritance. These plural norms had developed early in the island story of Britain and had not been interrupted by conquest or violent revolution. They had influenced neighbouring states where the tradition was one of absolutist and sometimes arbitrary rule with centralising monarchies leaving little scope for citizens to challenge their authority.

It is a reasonable expectation that these liberal and plural values will still resonate in a Scotland even under firm nationalist direction. But during the past 4 years of outright SNP rule, there have been troubling occurrences. Nationalists have used the state to micro-manage the private lives of citizens and curb the autonomy of institutions. A 'Named Person' law gives the state the right to appoint guardians for every Scottish child up to the age of 18 who can supersede the rights of parents . Concerns have been raised about controversial measures taken by a hurriedly-centralised police force which are seen to threaten personal liberties. Major pillars of civic Scotland, the legal profession and academics in higher education have expressed alarm about attempts to alter Scottish law or else severely curb the autonomy of Scotland's 15 universities. Legal moves are proposed to alter the law of inheritance, thereby enabling the government to alter landholding patterns in Scotland.

By contrast, the government now run by Nicola Sturgeon, an avowed centraliser, shows little interest in tackling the poor performance of the health and education sectors which affect the life chances and conditions of nearly all of the population. A visit to rural communities as well as housing estates on the periphery of cities reveals a similar picture of state encroachment and even sometimes rigid oversight. Previously independent organizations that provided a free space between the individual citizen and the state are being colonised by a party-led state. Anyone unhappy with this situation and who prefers civic autonomy often encounters marginalisation and open scorn.

Creeping authoritarianism and a propensity for social engineering are often associated with populist movements once they reach power. Scotland now appears to be no exception. But it is still unusual for such a restrictive and forceful movement to arise in a relatively calm part of the world. It is also unusual to see so many Scots becoming addicted to the SNP's own constitutional obsessions when, only a short time before, they were of little interest except to hardcore political campaigners. If Scotland enters an era of 'Un-enlightenment' in which rulers turn their backs on past traditions of civility, moderation and belief in reason that flowered in the 18th century, it will be Scots living in Scotland who will chiefly be the poorer for it. But, as I have tried to suggest, it would be inadvisable to assume that the effects of such a regression will be largely confined to Scotland. In the wake of a united Britain, much of the democratic world would probably welcome a Scotland whose new rulers were keen to build an efficient and representative state ready to maintain alliances designed to uphold global peace and security in a democratic context. But there is insufficient evidence that Scotland's nationalist would wish to follow the calm and incremental nation-building experience of Canada for example where Scots had a pivotal role over several centuries. The rhetoric of the SNP suggests that neutralist or outright anti-imperialist stances might be favoured instead.

INTRODUCTION

So, on balance, the answer to the question whether what happens in Scotland really matters to the rest of the world has to be answered in the affirmative. If Scotland is indeed to become independent, then the new epoch would be beneficial for Scots and their neighbours if much greater external attention was paid to what is happening in Scotland now. Without displaying over-fondness for Britain, I believe that the unity of the second largest island in the world's temperate zone continues to benefit the overwhelming majority of its inhabitants (and particularly those in Scotland). Advocates of separation have failed to spell out how unpicking a 308-year-union and then providing alternative sources of economic viability could be accomplished without much dislocation and risk. Depressingly, during the whole referendum phase, not once was I plunged into doubt about my British unity stance by any compelling new argument or insight from the independence side.

Much of the rest of the world also viewed Scottish nationalism as too impractical and parochial. Success for its chief goal could have unwelcome side-effects in unexpected places. There was much rhetoric and endless flag-waving but few fresh ideas about how to make such a new departure work; nor were there sufficient reassuring signs that Scotland could avoid some of the pitfalls of small country nationalism over the past several centuries. All too often predecessor-movements assumed that freedom consisted of having control over a demarcated territory and that however well or badly its inhabitants were governed, ultimately didn't count.

There is a lack of elementary wisdom among too many powerful people in today's nationalist-run Scotland. They are too self-referential and complacent. They display little curiosity about how movements similar to their own came unstuck in the past not just due to adverse circumstances but also to major character defects. Scottish self-confidence and capacity to wield substantial powers of internal self-government will grow if autonomy is pursued in cooperation with the rest of the United Kingdom. Pursuing a Cold War with England on virtually each and every policy front is ridiculous and ultimately Scotland will end up the loser because it is weaker in too many ways and 'Braveheart' rhetoric will never alter that. Narrow and intransigent nationalism will make Scotland a dead-end country and quite possibly make any genuine independence a notional affair.

Those who worry about a world that is sliding towards ever greater discord and fragmentation, should take a closer look at Scotland. Benign attention and constructive engagement could save its rulers from becoming major losers through their impetuousness and introspection. Too many countries which ought to have had promising futures have become unstuck in a post-Cold War era full of disappointment and growing menace. Scotland has the potential to be a model (if perhaps not on the global scale of the 18th century) if it spurns irrational and short-sighted paths.

It did so when it was part of the British Union state especially at times when the rest of Europe was plunged into chronic turbulence. The Union legacy will never be undone and will continue to be recognised as a significant staging post in the creation of the modern world. Scottish nationalists can only attempt to surpass it if they cease trying to erase it and instead build a future where there is room for all citizens irrespective of whether a sense of Britishness or Scottishness defines their identity.

Chapter One: the Scottish National Cause.

If England was suddenly hit by an asteroid, it would be catastrophic for its inhabitants but it would also pose an awkward challenge for Scottish nationalism. A very considerable part of the national cause involves setting Scotland apart from its larger neighbour and delegitimizing what is seen as an English ruling order, one masquerading as a common British state. In the absence of a separate language or a distinctive culture or economic system, a preoccupation with England is perhaps understandable. But Scotland now enjoys considerable internal self-rule and even the prospect of outright independence. Yet adherents of the cause devote surprisingly little energy to trying to make current institutions of self-government the basis for a genuinely separate society. Nor is there much thought devoted to what a fully independent country will be like and what its priorities should be. Instead, the old SNP, the new mass membership force, and allied bodies in the 2012-14 Yes campaign, often seem to be bound up with identifying an alien 'other' in terms of class, territory, or political institutions. So much of the emotional energy which has been channelled into the cause is devoted to ventilating grievances against a former island partner from which Scotland has grown apart. Solidarity is expressed in devising public rituals and parading symbols which underline the cleavage. What the cause overlooks is more important than its fixation which makes it narrow and even superficial in its preoccupations. There is disinterest among its adherents in how power is exercised and resources allocated. This suggests that the cause bears more of the hallmarks of a cult than a conventional political movement and that if its core ambition of leaving Britain were to be fulfilled, it would struggle to know how to consolidate independence.

Chapter Two, The Party of Nationalism.

Scottish Nationalism has enjoyed dizzy acclaim and landslide victories during what has been a challenging time for parties right across the political spectrum in many other democracies. This chapter profiles the SNP as a political force. It identifies long-term core traits and asks to what extent it is directly responsible for a breakthrough, the scale and speed of which is perhaps unprecedented in British politics. The nature of its alliance with other pro-independence forces in the 2012-14 period is analysed as is the challenge it faces due to a massive increase in membership. An old established SNP is seeking to accommodate more militant newer party members based on those Scots radicalised in the referendum years. Writing in 2015, in no other democratic country is it possible to easily identify politicians who are regarded as champions even though most are unknown and are certainly yet to be tested. This is especially true of the large parliamentary group now operating at Westminster. The SNP has to juggle being a campaigning force, a party of patronage at Holyrood, an opposition force at Westminster while still in charge of a government at home. How well it can discharge these responsibilities will help to determine the degree to which it can extend its domination in to the future.

Chapter Three, British-Minded Scots in the Referendum and After.

This chapter explores the obstacles which prevented proponents of the Union launching a capable and self-confident campaign during the referendum and asks what shape are pro-Union forces in after the September 2014 vote. It examines the impact of the decision of the UK government to make concessions which enabled the SNP to manage a referendum process very much on its own separatist terms. The decision to emphasise the risks for ordinary citizens of secession rather than make a strong emotional case for the continuation of the Union is seen as the pivotal one by the Better Together camp. This caution and even negative approach threw the No side increasingly on the defensive. It failed to use the critical medium of social media effectively and the parties in charge of the campaign for the Union were unwilling, or simply unable, to mobilise pro-Union forces in Scotland in the wider society. The chapter suggests that the Labour Party, the central player in the No campaign found it hard to be enthusiastic about Britain and its historical legacy of cooperation, incremental progress, stability and democracy. Thus, what could have been the theme song of a successful campaign, that of a successful partnership in a remarkable political union, one arguably responsibly for more good than ill in the world, was left unsung.

Chapter Four, A Remarkable Election Deepens the Scottish Divide.

The British general election revealed that the strong nationalist performance in the referendum had been no temporary fluke. This chapter shows how the tectonic plates of Scottish politics perhaps decisively shifted. The spring 2015 contest was an occasion when the SNP was crowned as the voice of the people and Nicola Sturgeon, just five months, after taking charge, found herself, the leader with the strongest legitimacy in the 76-year history of her party. This was an issueless campaign when numerous voters looked for champions to suit their emotional mood rather than credible politicians ready to deliver beneficial policies. The chapter reveals the mood of populism and how a previously overlooked, but now highly professional, force catered for it. The opposition challenge was easily swatted aside because the

SNP-inclined voters were not interested in manifestos and programmes. Chronic SNP confusion over whether or not it wanted Scotland to be self-financing in an enhanced devolution scheme caused no wavering. Neither did the collapse in oil prices make any difference. There was no outcry over intimidation of candidates or attempts to prevent town-centre stump speeches. This was the moment when Scots cast off their long-held reticence about nationalism and at least half the nation converted to a bold and at times even militant form of it.

Chapter Five, Nationalist people.

Individuals stand out in nationalist parties especially if they are able to harness popular emotions. During its eight decades of existence, the SNP has been led by contrasting figures. This chapter starts with Nicola Sturgeon, both the newest and most successful leader. She has all-round qualities, being a hard-working minister and a remarkably effective campaigner, making history for her party in 2015. She is more long-term and conciliatory in her approach than her even more remarkable predecessor Alex Salmond. But her career in frontline politics is only probably in its early stages and firm judgments about her character and aims are probably inadvisable.

Alex Salmond led his party from the political wilderness to the centre of power and is likely to intrigue historians long into the future. He is charismatic, mercurial and partisan. Displays of impressive political artistry are sometimes followed by costly errors such as his stance on currency matters and his stormy relations with the media. He has greater appeal in his own party than in Scotland at large but by the time of his resignation, nearly one in 50 Scots were on the verge of joining the SNP. He is one of the most formidable insurgents seen in British politics for several centuries and it would be premature to assume that his career as a key figure in Scottish politics is over.

Middle-class professionals have dominated the party. Lawyers from the west of Scotland played an important role in forming it, securing a critical electoral breakthrough, and sustaining it through bleak times. Members of the liberal professions have not (so far) made their mark but medical doctors have at times been important. The party has been an arena for remarkable women, and two of them are compared, Margo MacDonald and Mhairi Black. Business figures have started to become more prominent which is not surprising in a state-led economy where the influence of the SNP is now manifest.

But the SNP political world is increasingly dominated by full-time politicians, some of whom are highly motivated. If the SNP is the expression of a belated middle-class revolution in Scotland, it is one whose leaders are bound up with the state rather than the wider society.

Chapter 6, the Cultural World and Nationalism.

Since the onset of devolution, intellectuals have become far *more* prominent in Scottish life. The magnetic pull of London which absorbed so much Scottish talent for centuries, has receded somewhat. An Edinburgh government now dispenses a lot of patronage to the arts and stimulating a Scottish cultural renaissance to re-inforce a parallel political upsurge, became an undisguised priority during Alex Salmond's years in charge.

This chapter dwells mainly on the 2-year referendum campaign. It asks how much of a pro-independence cultural mobilisation actually took place? How important was the contribution of 'Indy' writers, artists and musicians to the wider Yes cause? Were there any meaningful intellectual encounters and was new ground broken in exploring and charting the identity of the nation at such an eventful time? Or was the cultural side of the Yes movement just as evangelical and wary of deep-seated debate as its much larger political host?

A number of intellectuals absorbed with the nation (and sometimes their role within it) became more visible. But no cultural figure succeeded in becoming a major interpreter of the nation's mood at such an unsettled time. Political ferment is supposedly good for cultural innovation. However, it is tempting to conclude that intellectual agitation reinforced divisions rather than creating a new cultural paradigm for understanding Scotland and finding some basis for future common ground.

Original literature and arresting cultural productions largely did not materialise in 2012-14 perhaps because the political had such ascendancy over the cultural in the Indy cause. London's cultural shadow remained a perennial preoccupation but there were also numerous lower-profile cultural folk content with the British link for emotional as well as practical reasons and who worked to prevent it being severed.

Chapter Seven, the SNP and the World.

The world was largely numb to, or else unimpressed by the SNP's assertion that Britain was played out as a viable state and it was therefore time for Scotland to enter world affairs as a fully sovereign actor. For its part, the SNP and the Yes movement largely turned away from the world in the campaigning years from 2012-14. They strove to convert hitherto sceptical Scots to independence and present the world with a *fait accompli*.

The chapter identifies sometimes strained relations with major world players able to smooth Scotland's path to statehood. Both the European Union and the United States were courted but for different reasons these powerful entities failed to be accommodating to the SNP's aspirations, and relations soured. The EU remains as wary as ever of outspoken nationalism and the bellicose features of the Yes campaign at street level in 2014 will not have assisted the SNP's reputation. The USA is bound to be underwhelmed by Scottish Nationalism: too many vocal supporters of the party see challenging America as confirmation of their progressivism.

More energy has been devoted to forging ties with emerging powers in East Asia and the Middle East, Nationalists sometimes emphasising their independence from traditional western positions on defence and security. But most countries where a semi-official position has been adopted on Scottish independence appear to be wary of secession.

In order to boost its domestic credibility, the SNP has compared itself first with Ireland and then Scandinavia which it has claimed offer models of progressive independence that can be emulated in Scotland. But it plays down comparisons with movements in Quebec or in large mainland European states where the track-record of success for separatism has been far weaker. Ultimately, the SNP is chiefly interested in favourable PR images from places resonating with Scots that reinforce the case for acquiring independence now. Too often it ignores, or else conceals, awkward realities and shows a disinclination to learn from experiences of other parts of the world that may be directly relevant to Scotland. This opportunistic handling of the international dimension reveals a party that is introspective and some would even argue parochial in its approach to European affairs and wider global concerns.

The Conclusion argues that the SNP shrinks from encouraging independent-minded Scots. Its penchant for micro-managing their lives suggests that nationalist decision-makers are happier with a dependent population, one pushed and pulled by the state, rather than one possessing initiative and multiple ways of influencing planners and politicians between elections. It is also reasonable to ask whether the SNP itself really wishes to embrace the challenges of independence especially in the economic sphere or whether at heart it remains a protest party that finds itself in office due to the shortcomings of its rivals.

Doubts are concealed by the evangelical and festive zeal for independence displayed by many voters in Scotland. They disregard the risks which were laid out most starkly during the 2015 election campaign which coincided with a collapse in oil prices. The volatile mood of so many Scots rather than the SNP's record in government or the calibre and trustworthiness of its elected representatives, have turned a fringe cause into an electrifying movement.

The SNP is self-referential and it prefers to see its success in the Scottish context as the modern culmination of a slow-moving trend towards the recovery of sovereignty. But it is very much part of a Europe-wide movement of disaffection which has taken forms as varied as the ability of a hard-left politician to become leader of the British Labour Party and ruling parties in many countries to be rocked by new populist challengers. The SNP's advance has a particular dimension though. It has far more to do with a change in the collective outlook of Scots, making political culture far less risk-averse, than it does to troubled economic conditions, the shortcomings of its rivals, or its own particular qualities. Many Scots are now ready to bring their anger, restiveness, and impatience into the political arena. They see elections as an opportunity to express a territorial outlook rather than a time when to judge competing programmes and the differences these will make to their lives. The British state in its southern English capital London is condemned for wrongful policies in areas where usually it is the Scottish government which enjoys responsibility and access to plentiful resources.

The SNP has surged thanks to an upsurge in anti-elitism at grassroots level in Scotland even though it has been in charge of most aspects of Scottish policy-making for eight years. Many Scots yearn for an opposition to lead them against a British state which they believe is colluding against their best interests in numerous ways. It has become a bogeyman like the Pope of Rome used to be for militant Ulster Protestants or certain minorities were in previous ages of European history. To no small degree, this volatility may stem from a set of changes in behaviour and collective psychological outlook which have profoundly altered Scottish society in little more than a generation. The years of referendum campaigning allowed this new edgy, raucous and disputatious Scotland to fully emerge, greatly surprising fellow Scots and observers elsewhere who thought they had the Scots worked out as a level-headed and pragmatic people who confined their militant fury to sport or (in the past) to religion.

Populism now reigns supreme in Scottish politics. This means there is surprising disinterest in the way that the SNP rules Scotland or the personal ethics of its leaders. Politics has become a crusade that will enable Scots searching for autonomy and control in their own lives to hopefully achieve it in a territorial sense also. It is an impulse that has seemingly come from nowhere in just a few years and I do not know what staying-power it has. But the frustration and fury powering this thunderous change in Scottish outlook is a phenomenon deserving study at close quarters which is what is attempted here. There is a real likelihood that in a Western world where there is growing disaffection with established institutions, leaders, and customary ways of confronting problems, similar phenomena, morbid for some intoxicating and liberating for others, might also shake countries to their foundations.

---

1. Tom Harris, 'Jeremy Corbyn cannot save Scottish Labour from the SNP', *Daily Telegraph*, 17 September 2015.
2. Tom Peterkin, 'Scots public spending £1200 more than UK', *Scotsman*, 12 March 2015.
3. 'Scottish Television examines Scottish politics a year on from the referendum', STV, 14 September 2014, http://www.stvplc.tv/blog/2015/09/stv-examines-scottish-poli tics-a-year- on-from-the-referendum-with-documentary-scotland-what-next
4. *Daily Telegraph*, 14 September 2014.

CHAPTER ONE: THE NATIONALIST CAUSE IN SCOTLAND

Scotland's Biggest Family Firm

Nationalism has magnetism and staying power that few other modern political movements can claim. The cause had long lain dormant in Scotland until it burst forth as a real popular insurgency between 2012 and 2014. I and others of my acquaintance know family members, friends, and colleagues who were hardly preoccupied by Scottish Nationalism before 2013 but for whom the dream of Scottish independence became all consuming by 2014. In that year, dozens of Scottish children were named 'Indie' or 'Indy' and three others, two boys and a girl will grow up known as 'Freedom'.[1]

Most Scots rejected the offer of independence in the referendum held on 18 September 2014. But the cause of separation from a British state run from London had been promoted with such passion and flair that it had a catalytic effect on a population which, until a short time before, arguably had been mostly apolitical. Later Nicola Sturgeon, the leader of the SNP, claimed that a majority of Scots actually wanted independence in their hearts on referendum day.[2] Be that as it may, on 7 May 2015, the SNP captured all but 3 of Scotland's seats in Westminster in some of the biggest electoral swings seen in British political history.

This chapter argues that a potent cause has kindled a fresh interest in politics among numerous Scots. But the main changes are visible mainly at the emotional level. A long-established but suddenly wildly popular movement is able to operate as a surrogate family and it derives massive advantages in the process. There is powerful solidarity and the movement aligns itself sharply against forces which would jeopardise its existence. The cause stands for justice and, above all, equality but the means of its political deliverance is hierarchical and personal.

But nationalism often encourages a radical and non-negotiable approach to politics. This often means a dogmatic and self-righteous one which makes it very hard to bridge some of the numerous differences that have opened up both within Scotland and in its relationship with the rest of the UK.

Scottish Nationalism's new adherents are expected to be loyal and subservient. It is assumed that they will endorse and defend whatever steps the party takes to achieve its core aim of independence. There is no sign an organization that has suddenly turned into a mass movement will challenge top-down structures. The instinct to be followers of a virtuous cause remains the pre-eminent one. There is no hunger for pluralism and, on the contrary, respect for the differing view of others when presented in public often vanishes. The cause releases some inhibitions but is essentially superficial and conformist. A new orthodoxy indicating the direction Scotland ought to go in politically is staked out: it is vague on crucial details such as the means by which the new separate country will finance itself or the currency it will use. But there is no demand from its army of followers for clarification or reassurance. The new nationalists are not expected to think about surmounting these hurdles. Instead, they are expected to show vigilance and, at times hostility, towards 'enemies' against whom grievances and a sense of resentment over various assumed injustices can be kindled.

The emerging movement shows all the hallmarks of being a highly ritualistic one in which followers and leaders perform public roles asserting the virtue of their cause and the illegitimacy of those who still hold sway over Scotland's destiny. There is usually scant interest in how power is exercised and who are its beneficiaries. What counts is that leaders advance the fortunes of the cause and supply emotional gratification in the process to those who, in turn, are content to show subservience and agitate so as to bring closer the date of deliverance.

The picture of Scotland presented here is not an especially attractive one. But my intentions should not be misunderstood. One aim in writing this book is to suggest that Scotland, far from being an aberrant place, is only displaying in heightened form certain traits which are already strongly embedded in popular culture across much of the West. There is a search for rapid emotional gratification, superseding an approach to life that subsumes the ego and prefers incremental and well-signposted change.

Risk-taking had already started to outpace long-term prudence at least a generation ago. Scotland, has seen a surge in hedonistic personal behaviour in the last 30 years which means that for perhaps many citizens, only the SNP can display the characteristics of a conventional family based on trust, sharing, and obedience - since the real thing is melting away.

A cause which does not offer obvious solutions to a largely post-industrial country that would struggle to finance an extensive public sector nevertheless has blossomed. This, I believe, is due to changes in the organization of society, the nature of elites and everyday behaviour that have made Scottish society more uninhibited and volatile than it has been perhaps in any other moment of its recent history. Whether a territorial dimension exists in their politics or not, other countries with many economically under-active people, that may be encountering rapid secularisation, and where there has been an explosion in the use of the social media, could well also shift from calm continuity to sudden political turbulence as has happened in Scotland.

Nationalism's Fatal Charm

Until our own day Scots were spectators who observed nationalism coming alive and having different effects in other corners of the world. Unquestionably it is a political phenomenon which has thrived in contrasting social settings, historical epochs and geographical zones. It has dodged efforts to drain its influence or eliminate it altogether from the political arena. Moves to suppress nationalism were attempted by reactionary 19th century European monarchs, by Communists impelled to create a proletarian world order, and by the builders of a common European political order in the second half of the 20th century.

Nationalism has been far less successful in providing the basis for stable or enlightened rule in countries freed, or brought into being, by movements claiming inspiration from its ideas. Much of Latin America, different parts of Africa and Asia, and arguably even well-known European countries like Italy and Greece have experienced instability because of the limitations of nationalism. It is not a doctrine which always or even often, brings in its wake, responsible government. Too often nationalism has been manipulated by ambitious power-holders, sometimes with disastrous results. There is often a fixation with territory rather than the people who inhabit it. They can become pawns and sometimes spectacular victims as territorially-fixated rulers try to expand the physical size of the nation by subjugating neighbours. In the worst instances, nationalism can become a source of conflict and war.

Of course there are countervailing examples. Kemal Ataturk, in early 20th century Turkey, created a nationalist movement whose energies were directed inwards rather than outwards. It was concerned with transforming Turkey from a pious, rural and stagnant land to a modern, secular and economically successful one, capable of burying a historical reputation for backwardness and fanaticism. Similarly, Switzerland, located in the very heart of Europe, built a strong sense of national solidarity from combining the energies of three distinct ethno-linguistic components making up the population of the country. Even the cosmopolitan countries of Scandinavia have utilised national patriotism in order to promote the human solidarity needed to survive and progress in what can be an unforgiving physical environment.

Why was Scotland numb to nationalism for so long?

Alex Salmond, the chief architect of contemporary Scottish nationalism, entitled his 2015 book about the recent attempt to break away from the rest of Britain as 'The Dream Shall Never Die.[3] The title conveys emotional faith and solidarity. These characteristics enabled the Scottish National Party to endure in an electoral desert for nearly seventy years from its formation in 1934 until it finally emerged from the wilderness and, beginning in 2007, triumphed in elections with ever increasing majorities.

At least in democratic societies, it is unusual for any political movement to endure for so long without benefiting from real electoral success. The length of time that the SNP was required to wait before experiencing a breakthrough is striking for another reason.

Scotland had been one of the first places in Europe to acquire some of the major features of nationhood. However, it merged its destiny with that of its larger neighbour to the south following centuries of wars and contentions that even the rise of a Scottish king to the English throne in 1603 would not bring to an end. In 1707 near the dawn of the age of European nationalism, the two rivals joined to form one of the most enduring and successful political unions that the world has ever seen. Scotland was drawn into and, in turn reinforced, an extensive web of British associations. Peace and, in time, prosperity spread across the island. The Scottish economy benefited from free trade and access to Britain's growing empire which in time became an Anglo-Scottish undertaking. In the 1850s, middle-class Scots in a by now industrialised country, could make generous contributions to freedom struggles in Hungary and the Italian peninsula, hosting leaders like Mazzini and Kossuth, without feeling they were under the yoke of English oppression. Scottish patriotism was far from extinct though. Arguably it was flourishing in the 1850s given the appearance of an impressive 250 foot tower, the National Wallace Monument, erected near Stirling between 1859 and 1869. It commemorated the most celebrated medieval foe of English domination, William Wallace. But, in the third decade of Queen Victoria's reign, most nationally-minded Scots were at ease with a political order where central power resided in London. They did not feel under the yoke of English oppression. Discontented poorer Scots, of whom there were many, were more likely to resent exploitation and ill-treatment at the hands of industrialists who were nearly all Scots.

Such factors may explain why Scottish nationalism lay dormant and indeed was one of the last secessionist movements to burst forth in modern Europe. The 1707 Act of Union had given Scotland an unusual degree of autonomy at a time when rulers were usually bent on establishing absolute control over each corner of their realm. The Union may have brought into being a single state with one legislature, but there remained two distinct legal traditions, and two established churches, as well as educational and local governance institutions that retained broad autonomy in their respective spheres. The Union, in short, left intact local sources for the shaping of Scottish public life and the renewal of national identity and, in some ways, their influence outstripped that of the British parliament far to the south, perhaps for another century.

So apart from retaining a patriotic outlook, most Scots remained aloof from the cause of political nationalism which shook multi-national states with growing intensity from 1848 onwards. Up to the 1960s the ties that bound together two former rivals, locked in a political union, appeared durable ones. From 1939 to 1945, the war against the Axis powers would see Scots battling with, and working alongside other Britons to defend freedom against forces dedicated to wiping out most of the civilizational gains of previous centuries. The rise of the welfare state after 1945 simultaneously strengthened centralisation and allowed the British government to tap important new sources of social and economic legitimacy.

The SNP would not begin achieving electoral success until the 1960s as Britain hastily relinquished its empire and joined the Common Market (later the EU).

Elite mismanagement of industrial relations, and the deadly crisis which erupted in Ulster at the end of the 1960s, punctured a sense of deference towards politicians who had long operated on the basis of consensus. Socially conservative Scotland was slow to stir. But there was a reaction on nationalist lines against the unusually decisive rule of Margaret Thatcher in the 1980s. She wished to restore British competitiveness by trimming the influence of old and ingrown elites and releasing the entrepreneurial energies of citizens who shared her vision of a renewed free market Britain. But this spirit of revived capitalism was mainly located in the English south which provided her with three unprecedented electoral victories after 1979.

Scotland had relied disproportionately on a range of heavy industries, each of which went into decline from the 1920s. Especially from 1945, much of its industrial base had been kept going by the state subsidies which 'the Iron Lady' regarded as a drain on British productivity. Thatcher's 'shock therapy', involving high interest rates and a high value for sterling, decimated low performing manufacturing industry in Scotland. She was on a collision course not just with the proletarian left in Scotland but with large portions of the middle-class which preferred to retain the corporatist policies which Thatcher was sweeping away.

The Scottish National Party (SNP) continued to be a fringe force. But a powerful nationalist backlash against Conservative rule gathered pace. It involved all the anti-Tory parties which usually won most of Scotland's seats. Their goal became a Scottish parliament responsible for much of Scotland's internal administration and it had been realised in 1999 two years after Labour's return to office in London.

Harnessing the Emotional Wave

Territorial politics had finally arrived in Scotland after several centuries of limited autonomy. But its architects proved to be out of their depth in managing the new situation. Labour was slammed at UK level for its international misadventures and for forgetting that perhaps most of its core supporters expected it to remain wary of capitalism. In Scotland, the party suffered for its timidity, having failed to remake itself as a patriotic left-wing force confident in its management of the new institutions of self-governance. Dissatisfaction mounted particularly from the left. The hitherto noisy but usually irrelevant Nationalists had the presence of mind to exploit this crisis of credibility in Scotland's dominant party. Under a shrewd and forceful leader, Alex Salmond, restless Labour Scots were wooed from the left. They were promised the Labour package of social justice, state intervention and increasing equality but wrapped in tartan colours. Salmond proceeded to surf the wave of identity politics in spectacular fashion by building a new Nationalist power base in the most densely populated parts of west-central Scotland - the very places where the SNP had been spurned from its birth in 1934.

In 2010 the decision of the Liberal Democrats to agree to form a coalition with the Conservatives destroyed the credibility of that party among most of its Scottish supporters. They contributed to the outright victory achieved by the SNP in the 2011 elections for the Scottish Parliament. This political earthquake was only a small foretaste of what was to come. But it was enough to convince David Cameron that the Scots must be given the choice to vote on whether they still wished to be part of the United Kingdom.

By means of the Yes campaign, Scottish Nationalism, and its most high-profile leaders, cemented the goodwill and trust they had acquired by a skilful performance in government. There was an outpouring of emotion but also conformism as people (many of whom had previously only been lightly touched by it) absorbed the perspectives and arguments underling the cause. For some nationalism almost became a complete way of life as shown by their determination to keep the symbols of independence prominently displayed in the windows of their homes and cars. But shepherding ordinary citizens behind a political cause did not happen overnight. Eighteen months into the referendum campaign, the pro-Indy author and broadcaster Lesley Riddoch complained of an absence of 'general confidence about an independent future'. Scots were:

'not just assessing the plans of Alex Salmond. Consciously or unconsciously, they are also assessing the capacity of their fellow Scots. Are we mentally, physically and emotionally equipped for "going it alone?" Anyone on holiday with fellow Scots this summer will have seen first-hand what statistics can only assert. A fair chunk of us are smoking, eating and drinking ourselves into early graves – and that knowledge creates a deep-seated, little-discussed sense of foreboding'.[4]

As late as June 2014, 'Carl Le Fong', a frequent contributor to comments on the on-line letters page of the *Scotsman* newspaper was able to identify only four categories of people certain to vote Yes in September, comprising (in his view a mere 30 per cent of likely voters):

'THE ZEALOTS (600,000) - SNP hard -core members who want the independence 'badge', at ANY cost; who would quite happily see swathes of the ordinary working population thrown out of employment, interest rates rise, mortgage repayments soar, pensions be put in jeopardy, border controls being instigated, on top of having no currency and banking union.

THE ILL-INFORMED (130,000) - People that you hear saying, "oh we'll give it try", oblivious to the fact that it is a one-off decision that cannot be reversed. These are the kind of people who base their opinions on what they see on the TV e.g. Eastenders, Coronation Street, Jeremy Kyle, Big Brother and TOWIE.

THE TARTAN ARMY TYPE (50,000) - Predominantly men between twenty and fifty, with a "wha's like us' outlook, who like to shout "get right intae they English ba**ards"

SOME CELTIC SUPPORTERS (15,000) - Hard-liners who see the UK as a Rangers supporters domain, and because they hate Rangers, by definition, they hate the UK. These people are of course unaware of the SNP history and their hostility to anyone with Irish/Catholic roots; and also the fact that an independent Scotland would not be in their minority's interests.

THE SCOTTISH GLITTERATI (5,000) - Self-confident 'B' list celebs - actors, singers, TV presenters etc, who hope to become much bigger fish in a smaller Scottish pool - perhaps they could be 'A' listers in an independent Scotland. This category also includes many political journalists, who are licking their lips at the prospect of umpteen new political departments opening up, offering them more jobs, a bigger profile and more lucrative contracts.

So there you have it, somewhere in the region of 800,000 for YESNP, out of a total turnout of probably 2.6 million(65%)

This should see the Yes vote of 30% and the NO vote of 70%'.[5]

Yet by early September 2014, Scotland's top pollster, the academic John Curtice found among Lesley Riddoch's doubting everyday Scots an embrace of risk and a feeling that 'independence would bring about a better economic tomorrow'.[6] The No side, having been 22 points ahead in mid-summer polling by YouGov was actually overtaken by Yes in one of its polls published in the *Sunday Times* on 7 September, causing huge panic in pro-Union ranks.[7]

A magnetic message which had been projected in every Scottish neighbourhood for at least two years had dispelled self-doubt and had become the respectable option. Expressing caution or disdain was unpopular. Most sceptics fell silent in the face of the Yes bandwagon. They did not want to appear out-of-step, nor to court hostility.

In 1982, the influential German psephologist, the late Elisabeth Noelle-Neumann had 'traced shifts in public opinion to each individual's fear of isolation… people who held opinions that they thought were likely to make them unpopular, tended to fall silent'. Most No voters long before the climax of the referendum may well have felt like members of a despised majority who were best advised to keep their allegiances firmly secret.

Any movement which can acquire the moral legitimacy that had been tantalisingly out of reach for so long is in a very formidable position. The nationalists had advanced from hopeless underdogs to serious challengers by identifying and denigrating 'others' who could be portrayed not just as opponents of the movement but also of Scotland and its inhabitants. They were not just the ruling Conservatives in London with weak support in Scotland but also the Labour party, campaigning alongside this wretched foe in Better Together. From Alex Salmond down, many were convinced of the imminence of victory by the closing days of the marathon campaign. Defeat, when it came, was not only a sickening blow but an inexplicable one.

It was simply 'morally impossible' for the other camp to triumph. Such a claim had been made, using exactly this phrase, by the Mexican politician, Andrés Lopez Obrador who challenged the results of his country's presidential election in both 2006 and 2012. The candidate having lost by half of one percent in 2006, his supporters blockaded the centre of Mexico City for fifty days, refusing to recognise the result.[8] The same sentiment was widespread in Scotland in the autumn of 2014. The pro-Union side had won by ten per cent but 100,000 people signed a petition, claiming the result had been rigged.[9]

Soon '45' became the symbol of the defeated Yes side. 'Indy Scots' were moral victors just as the Stuarts were when they staged a rebellion in 1745 to regain the British throne which they had lost in 1688. The technical losers possessed the legitimacy to rule which had been denied them by the upstart Hanoverians from whom the present royal family originate.

If the attempts in 1715 or 1745 of this toppled dynasty to regain the British throne had been successful, many historians believe that they would almost certainly have turned the country into a satellite of France under its reactionary Bourbon monarchs. But these failed rebellions have been invested with a radical aura, Salmond ranking them as one of the long-term 'movement[s] for radical change' in Scotland.[10] Perceived historical injustice has long preoccupied doctrinaire Scottish nationalists. One of the most distinguished of their number is Paul Henderson Scott. He has, on occasion, shown a preoccupation with the English that resonates with many others in the movement. This veteran publicist observed in 2014:

'it is remarkable how the effects of shared historical experience last long after the events. Scottish sturdiness and readiness to help one another is perhaps the consequence of centuries of hard experience in the long war against a larger and wealthier neighbour'.[11]

In 2006, he used a well-tried metaphor to drive the point home: 'there is the story about God dispensing resources to parts of the world destined to become countries. To the future Scotland, he gave fine scenery, a temperate climate, coal and iron are in the land, fish and oil in the sea. "Don't you think you are being a bit too lavish" asked St Peter? "Just wait until you see who they are getting as a neighbour" was the reply'.[12]

The rise of nationalism in Scotland had been impeded due to the absence of powerful cultural or linguistic markers that separated Scotland from the rest of the Union state of Britain. From the 19th century onwards, identity politics had taken hold in countries where championing a language became a platform for cultural autonomy and later full-fledged separation. But nor had Scotland suffered obvious aggression at the hands of its dominant partner. The grievances necessary to generate a potent form of political nationalism were simply not present, so argued the late Stephen Maxwell, one of the few impressive intellects at the forefront of the SNP before its major breakthrough. In a 1981 pamphlet, *The Case for Left-Wing Nationalism,* he openly argued that 'the historic sense of Scottish political and cultural nationality is too weak to serve as the basis for modern political nationalism'.[13]

According to the academic Ben Jackson, 'This absence of despotism in the relations between England and Scotland...meant that a different sort of nationalism would need to be constructed, one that sought to channel the late twentieth-century social and economic grievances felt by the Scottish working class into a critique of the British state and a faith in the possibilities opened up by a Scottish state committed to socialism'.[14]

The Referendum Inaugurates a New Religion

Yet months of campaigning succeeded in creating the 'us and them' binary division which has become a basis of enduring success for powerful nationalist movements.

CHAPTER ONE: THE NATIONALIST CAUSE IN SCOTLAND

Scottish nationalism was paraded in raw populist form though neighbourhood rallies and raucous and emotional online propaganda. 'Labour' and 'Tory' became automatic expressions of abuse rather than the names of parties which stood for rival but still legitimate platforms. By contrast, a majority of supporters indicated to one pollster that they viewed criticism of the SNP as an insult directed at them personally.[15]

The fervour generated led, afterwards to concert halls being regularly filled up by new devotees to the cause. It was one that offered instant solidarity and fellowship with hundreds of thousands of other Scots who would probably never be encountered in real life. The Scottish variant was finally breaking through into the senior league of political nationalism at a time when technological innovation enabled the message to be spread to social groups who previously were unreachable. One online site, Wings over Scotland, through its combativeness and self-righteous fervour, had a catalytic impact on the Yes side. It acquired a cult following among many nationalists as few other political blogs anywhere in the English-speaking world have ever managed to do. A heavy investment has been made in media initiatives by the Yes side and arguably they have given a long-term boost to the nationalist movement that may well have two major consequences: increase its militancy and transfer its centre of gravity from rural and small-town Scotland to electorally more influential urban and post-industrial areas.

A form of political theology was now in play which I had argued, as early as 2010, had the makings of a cult when the SNP was only one-fifth of its later size.[16] The academic David Knowles later detected a form of 'political theology' in which emotion and blind faith were placed over reasoned argument.[17] The new recruits appeared not to be sceptical or demanding types but previously apolitical folk. An NHS privatisation move undertaken by the SNP government received no adverse comment from its supporters in late September 2014.[18] They were usually indulgent towards those at the top of the SNP; any signs of opportunism or inconsistency in the leadership did not unduly preoccupy members or supporters.

Huge trust was placed in powerful individuals, first Alex Salmond and then, almost overnight, Nicola Sturgeon, as champions of the cause. At the SNP conference in March 2015, to a wildly cheering audience, Salmond was introduced by his colleague Michael Russell as the 'man who will force the pace in London and make them wake up to Scotland's demands.'[19]

From Scots newly introduced to politics or else severed from their customary loyalties, Salmond and Sturgeon had helped create a tight-knit group who swept the SNP to a spectacular victory in the British general election of May 2015. Receptive voters were presented with Scottish and Westminster opponents who were blamed for almost everything that had gone wrong in the past even though the SNP's Scottish foes had been out of office for eight years. The SNP ensured that it became the repository for discontent with the political leadership and economic governance of the UK. Reminders of the iniquities of Thatcher's rule enabled the bonding effect between the post-British party and its new followers to be reinforced. The Yes side benefited from the claims of the former Chief Medical officer for Scotland Sir Harry Burns that Thatcher had driven a generation of men on Clydeside to drink and early deaths.[20] Statistics that showed Scottish children were getting a raw deal due to falling educational standards failed to stir any doubts about the SNP's competence or dedication to national improvement. None of its opponents even dared to argue that it might be unwise to grant the vote to Scots of this age group due to their poor education.

There was understandable indignation whenever a cause seen as eminently progressive was viewed in another light. Reiner Lukyen, a senior German journalist, with wide international experience, resident for 36 years in the West Highlands of Scotland, had an article published in the German newspaper *Die Zeit* on 8 May 2015 in which he wrote:

'Scottish Liberalism is Dead'. A majority of [Scottish voters] flung themselves into the arms of a party the ideology of which is modern national socialism light'.

'Populist, egalitarian, anti-elitist and glorifying the moral superiority of one's own nation'.

'Using their propaganda the party split the country into patriots and unreliable non-believers'.

'On one side the Yessers, faithful Scots who voted Yes in September, and on the other side unionists and quislings'.[21]

Understandably the SNP was indignant but Luyken maintained that he was certainly not calling the SNP 'Nazis': 'I never said Nazi, because Nazi is connected with something that turned into a completely different kind of historic phenomenon'. 'I say national socialism, and in the lower case, national socialism light, a modern form of national socialism light'.

He added 'If I tell my 93-year-old father some of the stuff the SNP come out with, he finds aspects of it very familiar. He remembers the time very well. It's the moral superiority, and the whole ideology of it. To have left-leaning ideology within a national context'.[22]

The SNP had convinced a lot of Scots now under its sway, that the country could experience a form of socialism in one country, a prospect that looked increasingly unlikely for the UK as a whole. Remarkably, this process of conversion was occurring while the collapse in the price of oil, the commodity meant to finance Scottish separation, was accelerating on the world market. Moreover the SNP struggled to show what kind of currency an independent Scotland would have. Yet there was none of the hesitation which had ensured that newly-enfranchised Scottish workers would wait several generations before endorsing the Labour party as a reliable driver of change.

Delegitimising Britain

The Yes campaign was replete with images and metaphors of national self-confidence and renewal. There was a quiet insistence that the solidarity and trust so many Scots had shown in the long referendum campaign could be harnessed to overcome whatever adversity Scotland might encounter on its ultimate freedom journey.

The future remained hazy but, from its new recruits, the SNP faced few demands to spell out in concrete terms how its plans could work. Perhaps earlier generations of Scots who realised that mistakes in high places could cost them and their families very dear, would not have been so taciturn and obliging. Even before the onset of militant forms of nationalism in continental Europe, there might have been some apprehension about the fixation with the past and with national symbols. Scotland's national colours were expropriated by the Yes side and would become an extension of the SNP's own appeal in 2015. Invariably, landmark historical events were pressed into service if they could boost national consciousness. The 700th anniversary of the 1314 victory over the English at Bannockburn was a natural symbol for a movement, so often pre-occupied with 'the English', to emphasise. Some years earlier, little had been done by the Scottish government about the 450th anniversary of the 1560 Scottish Reformation: arguably, it was a far more crucial formative event in the nation's history not least because it paved the way for a gradual reconciliation with England.

The SNP was very much bound up with itself and did not feel it was an offshoot of other movements, certainly not sinister ones hailing from a past age of nationalist excesses. Nationalist voices frequently argue that Scotland has banished discordant elements from its past more successfully than England has. There is no nostalgia for an imperial past or for Britain continuing to exercise an outsized role in world affairs. But the scant backing for Tony Blair's Iraq misadventure from *anywhere* in the UK suggests there is common ground about the preference for adjusting to being a country of middling influence primarily concerned with its own internal affairs. Even the ruling Conservatives are not keen on having a large military despite possible threats to British sovereignty posed by a newly-aggressive Russia. But naturally it pays for those with a post-British vision to portray the UK in other terms as a hyper power seeking to meddle in places where it has no cause to be engaged.

In 2012, while on a visit to Dublin, Alex Salmond tried to generate Irish backing for his separatist project by claiming that the people of Ireland would know that 'bullying and hectoring the Scottish people from London ain't going to work'. This particular interpretation of history was rebuked by Seamus Mallon, a former leader of Northern Ireland's moderate Irish nationalist party, the SDLP, who reminded Salmond that the Scots had been to the fore as perpetrators of British bullying in Ireland.[23]

Exaggerating Differences

There is scant evidence to suggest that Britain's neighbours (most likely Ireland included) would welcome the geo-political upheaval occasioned by the emergence of a separate Scotland (possibly in fairly acrimonious circumstances given the passions whipped up in 2014-15). But the direction of world politics over the last fifty years suits the SNP's cause rather well. The party's emergence from the political wilderness had probably been hastened by the occurrence of several pro-independence waves in world affairs. Firstly, there was the acquisition of independence for numerous former European colonies in Africa and Asia during the 1960s. Later, after 1989, a string of East European countries regained effective independence, or else became fully-fledged states for the first time, following the collapse of the Soviet Union. The idea that independence was a natural condition for Scotland was bound to gain some momentum in the face of countries, often with fewer advantages than Scotland, acquiring statehood.

Of course, an alarming number of these states failed to mature into successful independent countries and some even became failed states. But the direction of travel for much of the world, despite the excesses periodically committed in the name of political nationalism, has been towards territorial self-rule. After 1999, those who asserted that their primary loyalty was to Scotland and not to Britain inevitably grew in confidence as a Scottish parliament in Edinburgh replaced Westminster as the body overseeing the public service in Scotland. It was axiomatic in nationalist circles that Scotland deserved to complete the journey towards absolute sovereignty due to being a distinctive territory with its own legal personality and many of the ingredients of a nation.

Besides, it was felt that Britain was not a natural union but an artificial entity. After 2007, those who argued that the people of the island are simply too different from each other to share political institutions, acquired a growing audience. Put rather crudely, the nationalist contention is that a bus driver in Glasgow has more in common with the Scottish capitalist owning his firm than with a bus driver in Manchester.[24] So, much greater solidarity reputedly binds together people within Scotland irrespective of urban-rural, class, regional, or religious cleavages.

'Britishness is a virus that infects everyone in this room', the former BBC Scotland talk-show host Lesley Riddoch was reported as saying at a publishing event in Edinburgh in August 2015.[25] Three weeks later, the government announced financial backing for the promotion of the Scots language in schools. Sceptics view Scots as a dialect of English similar to northern English variants of the language. It is, however, seen as necessary to draw up a 'National Scots Language Policy'. Messages in public places will be written in English, Gaelic and Scots. There will be a Scots language ambassadors scheme in which well known people such as the novelist James Robertson and the children's group Singing Kettle will seek to disseminate Scots more widely.[26] Such a scheme is being rolled out after it had been reported in 2013 that the number of pupils in state schools studying a foreign language had fallen by nearly a quarter in the previous four years.[27]

Critics see this move and the much more heavily-financed promotion of Gaelic (or Gallic) language, an important and distinctive language once spoken widely in the mainland and islands of north-west Scotland, as part of a new cultural make-over. But in the summer of 2015, it was reported that the new head of the board promoting Scottish Gaelic could not even speak the language.[28]

Perhaps naturally enough, during its years in power, the SNP has looked for other ways to deepen the wedge between Scotland and the rest of the island. Charges were dropped for medical prescriptions and university education. Council tax was frozen. Private-sector involvement in public services, permitted in England, was ruled out in Scotland. These measures did not necessarily enhance equality or boost the access of poorer Scots to higher education. But they enabled the SNP to proclaim that Scotland was more humane and less heartless than reputedly class-ridden England. Yet polls taken at the height of the referendum ferment showed what previous ones had usually revealed: Scots had broadly similar views to the rest of the UK when it came to welfare, immigration, benefits, unemployment, public spending and membership of the EU.[29] Scotland was to the left of England but the degree was relatively small. The evidence to suggest that there was a fundamental gulf of social values on either side of Hadrians Wall remained elusive.

Delegitimising Britain and asserting that decoupling Scotland from an unsatisfactory political union was the best route to follow, were assumptions that brought mixed results for the SNP. Not enough Scots shared its post-British outlook, otherwise the Yes cause would have been victorious in 2014. But one belated victory for the SNP was gained in the aftermath of the referendum. Increasing numbers of Scots made it clear, by their responses to polls and by their voting behaviour, that economic impediments no longer made them allergic to independence. Backing for the SNP reached a historic high just as the price of oil slumped, potentially leaving an independent Scotland with a huge budget deficit; this sense of daring had eluded Scottish voters in the

1980s when peak oil production could easily have financed separation.

Nor was there any electoral cost for the SNP when its leaders made it clear after its May 2015 triumph that fiscal autonomy, in other words economic self-government, would need to be delayed until Scotland was able to stand on its own two feet and dispense with subsidies from the rest of the UK: a poll published on 10 June 2015, showed that 60 per cent of voters were poised to back the SNP in the forthcoming elections for the Scottish Parliament after this admission.[30] But within days the SNP had changed its mind and a pro-fiscal autonomy amendment to the Scotland Bill being debated in the UK Parliament was lodged in the name of 6 of its MPs.[31]

Land Stirs the Blood

Perhaps most strikingly of all, the Sturgeon government faced little adverse reaction when flaws in its scheme for a radical alteration in land ownership were revealed .

The ownership of much of the land in Scotland is concentrated in comparatively few hands. Some 400 individuals or trusts (family or commercial) are said to own much of the land surface. Yet much of the country is mountain and moorland. It was pointed out by Allan Massie that a 500-acre chunk of arable land in, say, Berwickshire, is far more profitable than 5,000 or even 15,000 acres in the Highlands.[32] It was the intention of the SNP to put a million acres in 'community' ownership by 2020. Yet such a venture had already been tried out on the Hebridean island of Gigha, requiring the state to intervene with aid.[33]

Legislation was announced in early 2015 designed to break up large estates and reduce concentrations of private ownership. The SNP even planned to overhaul the law of succession, which allowed wealth to pass to one single family member. The nationalists intended to give a greater number of relatives a right to inherit a share in a family farm. Countryside groups warned that such a measure would cause some holdings to be broken up into units too small to be economically viable.[34] The Royal Institution of Chartered Surveyors delivered a warning that the proposals had overlooked the threat to Scottish food production despite it arguably being a crucial factor; in other countries, state interference with property rights had caused land usage to decline. When pressed, the Sturgeon government confirmed that it has conducted no analysis of the impact of its radical land measures on the output of Scotland's food sector despite stating it was worth £790 million per year.[35]

Yet there was no dent in the SNP's credibility when such obvious negligence was exposed through a Freedom of Information request. Several thoughts are prompted by such nonchalance. These reforms are very much driven by the worldview of the urban central belt of Scotland and it may be that many of its inhabitants no longer see the connection between full supermarket shelves and the origins of much of this produce on the land. Not a few of those on the radical left may feel that belatedly seizing land from owners, some of whose ancestors may have acquired it through doubtful means, is merely delayed justice and that any disruption to food production is a small price for a famous victory over the forces of privilege. Certainly this episode is yet more evidence indicating how high are the numbers of Scots who believe in an existential form of nationalism: total self-government is justified on its own merits. What follows in economic terms, whether benign or harmful, is of secondary importance. Accordingly, risks should be assumed since the prize of freedom ultimately makes most costs bearable.

A much greater acceptance of risk is probably one of the key developments in Scottish life facilitating the Nationalist breakthrough. The historian Tom Holland scoffed on Twitter in August 2014 about Alex Salmond as 'a secessionist campaigning to have his currency dictated by the bank of the country he wants to secede from'.[36] It was a 'weird' attitude according to Holland but to Salmond's friend, the media magnate Rupert Murdoch it was the receptive national mood that counted. Four days before the referendum, he tweeted: 'Scottish economy may or may not be ready for independence, but country is ready emotionally and politically'.[37]

Unavoidably, for much of the time the referendum struggle focused on economic arguments. But the Yes side was not particularly interested in the economic dimension. Few plans were prepared to respond to the economic challenges. However, there was a recognition of the necessity to create a platform, or stage-set, showing interest and competence in economic issues (however contrived the exercise may have seemed to sceptics). 'Business for Scotland' was launched by the SNP, suggesting that it could draw on a solid bloc of entrepreneurs to argue for independence. It turned out that very many of its acolytes were in business in a very modest sense as landlords renting property or as providers of social services.[38] One member only came to wider fame as a result of his involvement in the disruption of a May 2015 Labour event in Glasgow which led to his suspension from the SNP.[39]

Alternative Online Reality

The case made for independence was often driven by assertion and inventive use of figures. Much the same could be said of the *Wee Blue Book*, published by the influential online site Wings over Scotland in the early autumn of 2014. It had a catalytic effect on Yes supporters, being seen as an unanswerable compendium of economic facts taking the case for independence to new heights of plausibility. It became a bible for campaigners: perhaps not since the publication of the pamphlet *Full Employment in a Free Society* by William Beveridge, the architect of the welfare state has an economic tract enjoyed such an immense electoral hold on people. Beveridge's pamphlet had resonated across the globe as a document offering the promise of freedom from misery and want. The *Wee Blue Book*'s impact was more localised. But it remains the most illustrious campaign emblem of 2014 at least for nationalists. Even though its claims about oil as a commodity that would under-write a separate future were cruelly undermined by the plunge in its price world-wide, the document continued to be referred to as a credible source even by SNP parliamentarians into 2015.

The science fiction writer Isaac Asimov once observed that 'Anti-intellectualism has been a constant thread winding its way through our political and cultural life, nurtured by the false notion that democracy means that *my ignorance is just as good as your knowledge.*" Douglas Alexander, the head of Labour's election strategy in 2015, confessed early in the campaign which would lead him to a crushing defeat in the Paisley constituency that it was getting harder for politicians to campaign in elections because of the grip of the social media on the popular consciousness. He observed that voters were increasingly getting their information from the 'echo chamber' of Facebook and Twitter:

'We are used to a politics where we share facts, but diverge on opinion,' he said. 'We are confronting increasingly, because of the rise of social media, a politics where people's social media feeds can be an echo chamber for, at best, their own opinions and, at worst, their own prejudices'.[40] To illustrate his point, he recalled a conver-sation with 'an intelligent woman' in a supermarket in his constituency. A senior social worker, she told him that she did not believe the results of the independence referendum, and that she thought there has been a conspiracy. She also thought the oil companies were involved in a global conspiracy to keep oil prices low, he said. Alexander said: 'Do you mind if I ask where you get your news?' And she said, 'I get if off Facebook every night'.[41]

The electoral earthquake in Scotland on 7 May 2015 led to Alexander being defeat-ed by a 20-year-old politics student on a 32.87 per cent swing to the SNP. No lon-ger were even voters in prestigious occupations scared off by impractical proposals, radical voices urging vague but fundamental change, or street agitators who might even turn on their opponents when electioneering.

In vain had Labour banked on authority figures steering its former loyal support-ers away from adventurous ideas. A poster published in September 2014 by Better Together proclaimed: '93 per cent of senior doctors are voting No. You will not get a second chance'. But in a land where traditionally education was the path to high social status and professionals enjoyed much deference in the wider society, such appeals seem to have fallen flat.

Certainly in much of Europe it had become a taboo subject for academics or me-dia figures to assert that, in particular circumstances, the people could emerge as dangers to the functioning of pluralist politics. In the United States, there were fewer inhibitions about spelling out the danger volatile majoritarian sentiment could sometimes pose for democratic life.

Writing in the *New York Times* in 2012, the influential columnist David Brooks pointed out that some of the more farseeing pioneers of democratic government in Europe and North America:

'had a low but pretty accurate view of human nature. They knew that if we get the chance, most of us will try to get something for nothing. They knew that people generally prize short-term goodies over long-term prosperity.'

He derived solace from the fact that America's Founding Fathers built checks and balances to avert the worst excesses of the popular will. Unlike in Europe, 'they also dispersed power to encourage active citizenship, hoping that as people became more involved in local government, they would develop a sense of restraint and responsibility'. Still, for a long time, 'the democracies in Europe and the United States were based on a similar carefully balanced view of human nature: People are naturally selfish and need watching. But democratic self-government is possible because we're smart enough to design structures to police that selfishness.'

He believed that the USA's fourth President James Madison put it well: 'As there is a degree of depravity in mankind, which requires a certain degree of circumspection and distrust: So there are other qualities in human nature, which justify a certain portion of esteem and confidence.'

But Brooks warned that such wisdom had deserted many contemporary democratic leaders. Their role was to satisfy the appetites of voters or else to flatter them if the former could not be achieved. In some cases, they became addicts of polls in order to be best placed to follow the crowd. Flattering the populace meant it was less easy to restrain the popular will and restraints keeping demagogy in check were sometimes overwhelmed.[42]

Religious Decline and the Cause

The restless and edgy Scotland that has emerged in recent decades has become a favourable terrain for politicians who sound as if they are uniquely equipped to peer deep into the nation's collective soul and interpret collective aspirations which they duly attempt to fulfil. Perhaps a Scotland in which the general will is expressed in emotive and sometimes raucous terms, with politicians at hand to act as deliverers, has sprung to life thanks to one overriding factor. That is the collapse of religious belief and worship in Scotland.

Scots used to be more religious than English people but now they are even less so. The Scottish Social Attitudes Survey found that the number of people who identify with the national (Presbyterian) church had fallen to just over 20 per cent in 2012 from 35 per cent in 1999; while those who professed "no religion" had risen from

40 to 54 per cent.[43]

For a long time, belief in God and participation in religious services, as well as their civic offshoots, were seen as customs which underpinned stability and encouraged a more frugal and longer-term outlook among members of Western societies. The Bible encouraged self-examination which often meant that really devout people viewed their lives as preparation for a more significant passage to a Heavenly afterlife. Such a perspective had a great hold on Scottish society for over four centuries. It may well have disinclined many Scots to throw in their lot with political nationalism. One Scottish Protestant writing in April 2015 was convinced that a retreat from biblical values had made much of the population defenceless before the siren cry of nationalism:

'There is an eternal morality and a universal ethical system. When we depart from the biblical standard we no longer have the categories as a society to evaluate what is and is not true. Scottish Nationalism would not have emerged were Scotland to have remained a Reformed, Presbyterian and Calvinist country. The acceptance of the depravity of the human condition and a view of the super-exalted glory of the Lord Jesus Christ between them leave no space for the worship of nation. I suppose in saying that I have broken another taboo. And I weep that it has come to this.'[44]

In 2015, it was revealed that membership of the Church of Scotland had fallen from 535,834 in 2004 to 380,163 in 2014.[45] Boosted by emigration from Poland, the health of Scottish Catholicism looked superficially brighter. The numbers of Scottish Catholics rose slightly according to the 2013 census. Some 72 per cent of Scots Catholics said religion was 'an important part of who they are' against 45 cent of Protestants believing this.

Catholics as a group had shown one of the sharpest swings to the SNP in 2015 and had backed the Yes side disproportionately in the earlier referendum (attracting much comment). At first glance this adherence of numerous members of a religious group to nationalism weakens the argument that the advance of secularism is a prerequisite for SNP success. But a strong sense of anti-British nationalism had existed among that segment of Scots Catholics mainly preoccupied with Ireland, a place from which many of their ancestors had originated. For many years, Celtic football club in Glasgow has been the main repository for that Irish consciousness. A large segment of the fan base cultivated Irish nationalist symbols. The magazine *Not the View*, published in the 1990s, was one of the most eloquent outlets for this perspective.[46] It is not altogether surprising that a generation later, its editor, Brendan O'Hara materialised as one of the most outspoken of the raft of new SNP MPs elected in 2015.

Arguably, the Catholic church has, at times in the past encouraged members to cultivate detachment from the wider society where there was perceived hostility to Catholics.[47] So the persistence of atavistic folk traditions may partly explain the swing towards the SNP among a group remnants of which could be roused by militant nationalist rhetoric of a kind which no other significant political force in Scotland had previously used.

Moreover, much of the Catholic backing for the SNP may have come from individuals whose allegiance to the church was superficial or merely declaratory. I took this argument further in 2014 when I argued that 'nationalism has become a comfort blanket for Catholics whose identity is no longer anchored in religious faith'.[48] Later the *Economist* noticed my claim that 'Working-class Catholic men who have drifted away from the church are more likely to make radical or experimental political choices because neither religion or a sense of responsibility to the family is holding them back as it might have done in the past'.[49] Two readers proceeded to gloomily observe: 'They use themselves as their subjective standard of what "good" is'. 'And that leads to arrogance and ultimately the downfall of one's self'.

Falling Madly in Love with Scotland

Attachment to country can lead to a sharpened sense of self-awareness. People may overcome a previous sense of marginality or inferiority. They may convince themselves that they are surmounting personal misfortune, even ill-health, by identifying their own fate with a bigger and more fundamental struggle. Joyce McMillan, the media columnist wrote in 2010 of the potential 'to transform Scotland's view of itself – to reframe the nation not as a problematic, provincial backwater but as a powerhouse of 21st century creativity, generating work that is recognised at the global level for its ability to articulate the current human condition'.[50]

On 21 August 2014 Michael Gray who came to prominence in the referendum as a young evangelical purveyor of nationalism, could barely conceal his delight on Twitter that 'In exactly 4 weeks time Scotland will be the biggest story in the world. Let's vote to stay centre stage'.[51] He posted this tweet a few hours after speaking at an Edinburgh book event in which he informed the audience about the phenomenal number of tweets mentioning the referendum and Scotland that had appeared across the world during the course of the event. (I was in the audience). Such runaway excitement about Scotland's political journey was a far cry from the self-effacing and under-stated image of the Scots which the world had long been used to.

A preoccupation with a sense of Scottishness had begun, several decades earlier, among celebrities as well as a few high-profile academics. Tom Devine, a historian justly famous for interpreting Scotland's modern story to the world, had co-edited a book called *Being Scottish*, as early as 2002.[52] Initially, the SNP had not been a major part of this national self-affirmation; Derek Bateman, formerly a well-known BBC presenter in Scotland, has argued in his pro-independence blog that so all-encompassing was the radical mobilisation by 2015, that the party of Scotland might still only be a small part of it:

'It isn't just an SNP surge we're experiencing – that's just the chosen vehicle. It's a release, a freedom from restraint, a re-discovery of self. We didn't wait to be led by a party... we went out and did it ourselves, on doorsteps and keyboards. We found solidarity of spirit and ambition. We researched and challenged'.[53]

Amidst the hue and cry, one element was missing. There were very few projects unfurled designed to make a difference to life in Scotland. Instead, it was flags that were being unfurled and patriotic postures adopted. Neil O'Brien, a journalist who, as an adviser to George Osborne in the UK government, played an important role in devolving practical power from central government to Manchester in the north of England, noticed this as early as 2010. In an article entitled 'Scots should forget about flying the flag and fix their country', he pointed out:

'The Scottish Parliament controls 61 per cent of public spending, equivalent to 29 per cent of GDP. The Scottish Executive has de facto control over a range of taxes, not just the power to vary income tax by 3p – in fact, it has far more latitude to increase or decrease taxation than it is ever likely to wish to use.

Holyrood has unlimited leeway to reform public services, including health and education. It has powerful tools to accelerate economic growth: it controls higher and further education, the planning system, and finance for transport and infrastructure. Thanks to public-private partnerships, it can borrow vast amounts'.[54]

Perhaps the nationalists would have been more project-orientated if their movement had included individuals from a public policy and academic background, at least some of whom possessed a practical outlook. Individuals with expert knowledge in specific areas might have thrown their energies into forming think-tanks committed to clear-cut policy objectives. But so far, in a party with vaulting ambitions for Scotland, such initiatives have been conspicuous by their absence. In the past several academics held elective office who enjoyed respect across party lines because of their public spirited reputation. They included two former members of the European parliament whose services the SNP was robbed off due to their early deaths. Dr Allan Macartney, an international relations expert, was an SNP MEP from 1994 until his death in 1998. Even better-known was Professor Neil MacCormick a distinguished constitutional law professor who was an MEP from 1999 until his death in 2009. Happily still with us at the time of writing is the modern historian Christopher Harvie who was an MSP at Holyrood from 2007 until 2011. He has developed original ideas on Scotland's transport needs in particular, an area of policy which in government after 2007, the SNP lacked conspicuous interest in.

A Disguised Middle-Class Revolution

Intellectuals, many of whom self-styled themselves as Scotland's 'creatives', formed the National Collective in 2012 but it had been wound up by the spring of 2015, its chief organiser accepting a full-time position in the SNP. It gave voice to Alex Salmond's dream of perennial Scottish freedom in evangelical rallies but failed to play a catalytic role in the post-2014 independence drive. Its failings were alluded to by Robin McAlpine who, during this period, emerged as an articulate and bold popular tribune who was independent of the SNP.[55] He formed Commonweal, a movement dedicated to the memory of the much admired communist trade-unionist Jimmy Reid. Reid, who had led shipyard workers on Clydeside to a famous industrial victory in 1972, eventually joined the SNP. He could be seen as a prophetic figure who prepared the way for growing numbers on the radical left to renounce their fidelity to a British path to socialism and embrace Scottish independence instead. McAlpine possessed some of Reid's charisma but he was a more self-referential figure who, in his speeches and articles, frequently drew on his own rather humdrum life and experiences to offer a personal interpretation of Scotland's freedom struggle.

He argued in the wake of the referendum that the Yes side would not have got so close to achieving a vote for independence if it had been reliant just on the SNP which, in his eyes was a pallid political force.[56] Probably, there were detached and clear-sighted figures in SNP ranks who recognised that agitation from below was necessary to enable their cause to make decisive strides. This breakthrough did occur after 2012 and it was figures like McAlpine, often with an uncompromising anti-elitist message, who gave the pro-independence far-left important traction.

In November 2013, shortly after he had been one of the stars of a Radical Independence Conference, attended by more than 1000 people, he issued a clarion call demanding that the radicals present show iron resolve and go out and humble a disorientated UK elite so that Scotland could be detached from its grasp. He recalled arguing on that occasion:

'First, we must prepare to write a constitution. The opportunity to build Scotland's future on the basis of a written statement of what citizens may expect from their state, a constitution which ensures that as far as possible it is the citizen who shapes the future, that decentralises power, that sets out a path on which we can travel, this is a great opportunity.

So second, we must take control of process of negotiating the separation of the states of Scotland and whatever the rest of the United Kingdom chooses to call itself. ....

Of course, one might well ask if those Whitehall mandarins are really as all-powerful as they would have us believe. One might wonder whether people who negotiate unbreakable deals for aircraft carriers which have no aircraft to carry are really so masterful that we should shake in our boots. I have worked with civil servants for many years and I personally feel no fear whatsoever at our ability to negotiate. ....

And of course Sterling is one of our assets. I have no doubt we'll easily be able to secure Sterling for our currency for as long as we want – despite the endless bluster from Westminster types...

Of course, I doubt we'll still want to be in Sterling for long since it is a very badly managed currency, but negotiation won't be difficult'.[57]

It is only through reading between the lines that it is possible to sense who McAlpine thinks will be these new assertive insurgents. It is not radicalised working-class folk, who he sees as having a largely passive 'walk-on' role. This became clear (at least to me) upon reading the article urging that a movement called Hope over Fear a vehicle for Tommy Sheridan, (a divisive figure on the Scottish far-left), be accepted as a full part of the independence movement:

'Does it matter that they are excluded from our usual narrative? Yes, for three crucial reasons. Like it or not, Hope Over Fear is the only really truly working class part of our wider movement. They are exuberantly, unashamedly gallus. They dress up, dress up their kids (often in kilts nearly dragging along the ground so outsized are they), bring flags and banners, paint their faces. They sing and dance, shout and cheer – and smile. A lot. They pop over to the pub for a pint and come back. They hug you, take selfies of themselves with whomever they can find. This is not grim workerism, this is a joyful, carnivalesque celebration of who we are. And it is enormous, infectious, contagious fun. We need that. We can't afford to cut ourselves off from that. The world of the independence movement cannot and must not start and finish at wish trees'.[58]

The son of a maverick SNP politician Isobel Lindsay, long distrusted by the party leadership for her outspoken criticism of capitalism and identification with several militant anti-imperialist struggles McAlpine was a middle-class Scot preaching radical change.[59] Ultimately, if the events of this time come to be seen as properly revolutionary, it may well be viewed as a movement driven by large segments of a radicalised middle-class and not a working-class phenomenon.

Pat Kane, a rock musician now in his fifties who shared much of Lindsay's philosophy, described McAlpine in 2010 as a 'one time publicity officer of Universities Scotland and a film-maker, and now director of Jimmy Reid's think tank'. This information was shared in an article where he endorsed the views of a more cerebral voice of SNP radicalism, Stephen Maxwell for writing, as early as 1981 'about the necessity of bourgeois leadership for Scottish independence'. (Kane's words)

He approvingly quoted Maxwell's 1981 argument that:

CHAPTER ONE: THE NATIONALIST CAUSE IN SCOTLAND

'It is improbable that any distinctively working class formation will be able to act as a determining force in the affairs of a Western democracy for the foreseeable future. The live issues in the politics of the 21st century are likely to reflect middle class not working class concerns. Of course the issues themselves – the environment, the centralisation of power, cultural autonomy in an age of mass communications, relations between developing and developed states – affect working class people as much as middle class people.'[60]

Writing over 30 years later, Kane drew attention to the absence of formidable trade unions and important manufacturing industries. Like the rest of the UK, he recognised that Scotland was now largely a service economy with a sprawling finance sector. Kane was one of the most conspicuous advocates of what would be a revolution from above directed by an elite of technically savvy professionals who believed that online technology and networking skills enabled them to circumvent the retreat of proletarian radicalism. In some quarters, the meteoric rise of an SNP dominated by lawyers, journalists and small entrepreneurs who had been unable to find a comfortable place in Scotland's economic hierarchy, suggested that a middle-class revolution was welling up against a public sector alliance of trade-unionists and town hall bureaucrats. An assault on the old order was being waged through radical patriotic sloganeering. It was being directed by frustrated middle-class professionals who had failed to get far up the ladder of power and for whom the SNP was a battering-ram to effect rapid change.

These new anti-elitists who sometimes struggled to break free of bourgeois conventions (the media noted that the children of Pat Kane had been schooled privately) sometimes swung behind populist measures whose chief significance was the way they tightened the grip of the state over hitherto autonomous or private Scottish bodies.[61]

Thus there was backing on the pro-Indy left for a 2015 government bill at Holyrood to have university chairs of court elected by a wider electorate than the court itself and to oblige universities to include representatives from particular interests groups on their the governing councils. Even the Scottish Labour Party backed the first reading of the bill because the influence of trade-unions was set to expand in the higher education sector. Louise Richardson, the outgoing Principal of St Andrews University, was the chief academic voice warning of the harm that could be done by the government interfering in the running of Scotland's universities.[62] But she was joined by others, notably Dame Jocelyn Bell Burnell, the President of the Royal Society of Edinburgh.

This was one of the shrinking number of professional bodies that the SNP could not easily influence. It was a forum for independent intellectual thought that had its roots in the 18th century Scottish Enlightenment. Scotland's thinkers were then rela-tively free from state control perhaps because political authority was centred in dis-tant London. But after 1999 this had ceased to be the case. The SNP was seeking to influence the internal governance of Scottish universities at a time when the party was embarrassed by revelations about favouritism in government contracts and the allegedly unethical business dealings of a prominent politician who renounced the SNP whip when these reached the light of day. In democratic countries where one party enjoys major sway, it has often been the academic world which is able to tell truth to power when it behaves in over-worldly ways. Attempts to gag universities or restrict their autonomy frequently led to uproar and major protests in Southern Europe and Latin America even bringing down governments and ending military rule. Perhaps this context may explain why Dame Jocelyn, an astrophysicist who discovered the first radio pulsars, remarked to Scottish MSPs in October 2015:

'When I'm abroad I find people saying to me, "What's happening to the Scottish university? What's the government there doing?", with the implication that there is interference – not quite articulated – the implication that there is suppression of critical thought'.[63]

The SNP's other populist proposal at this time was to use the law to fundamen-tally alter Scotland's system of land ownership.[64] Altering the law of succession was even proposed just as had occurred in France after 1789 in order to break up aris-tocratic land holdings by preventing wealth being bequeathed to one descendant. The priorities of urban elites on the rural world had already been imposed in Latin America, Africa and Eastern Europe by ruling populists sometimes through out-right expropriation.[65] The results had often been baleful in terms of food production and effective use of the land. In Scotland, warnings that state-led social engineering in the countryside would slash the numbers employed in the rural economy were likely to fall on deaf ears;[66] the SNP probably knew that attempts to alter property laws would resonate even with some of their opponents on the Scottish Left. These included people influenced by ancestral memories of past injustices committed towards rural-dwellers by powerful elites. Liberal voices which argued that it was wrong to clumsily reverse history especially if the modern custodians of the land had usually acted responsibly and strengthened precarious communities by provid-ing employment and other injections of cash in the local economy, were out on a limb in the Scotland of 2015.

A certain credulity and conformism at the bottom of Scottish society towards na-tionalist measures meant to undo the alleged wrongs of history, may have encour-aged the SNP in its attempt to establish the kind of dominance which few other parties hope to acquire at least in a democratic society.

CHAPTER ONE: THE NATIONALIST CAUSE IN SCOTLAND

Landowners joined other groups who were viewed as belonging to 'a foreign factor' doing Scotland down. Andreas Papendreou, in many ways the chief architect of the political and economic mess which delivered Greece into the hands of the far-left in 2015, had branded the 'foreign factor' (defined by American overlordship in Cold War times) as a humiliating imposition. After 1980 he succeeded in uniting much of society behind his avowedly anti-imperialist movement, Pasok. The Greek political scientist Takis S. Pappis saw this movement as a force standing for democratic illiberalism which he believes is the central feature of modern populism. His definition of a confrontational brand of politics singling out adversaries and highlighting grievances which they are responsible for, may contain contemporary Scottish echoes.

For him, populist parties 'simply fail to abide by the three most fundamental principles of political liberalism, namely, the acknowledgement of multiple divisions in society; the need to try reconciling such divisions via negotiated agreements and political moderation; and the commitment to the rule of law and the protection of all minority rights. Populist parties, instead accept that societies are divided by one single cleavage, ostensibly separating the simple people from their elites; pursue adversarial, rather than moderate, politics; and abide by majoritarianism and the idea that the officials should serve the people, rather than that the people should control officials'.[67]

'Westmonster'

For Scotland's populists, England is 'the other' which Scotland must define itself against whether London is blocking greater self-government, as in the time of Margaret Thatcher and John Major, or else conceding a substantial degree of home rule under a British Labour administration. It was the central organs of government in London which played the role of America (though the USA was criticised by the SNP in 2009 for refusing to endorse the early release of the man convicted for the 1988 Lockerbie bombing). The 2014 claim of Tom Devine that Britain was a 'failed state' no longer fit to rule over Scotland was an endorsement for such an outlook from a prestigious figure. It was challenged (among others) by fellow academic Michael Collins in 2015:

'Far from being [a] failed state... the United Kingdom is a liberal polity evidently capable of reform: witness the whole project of devolution since 1997. The scope for the British state to devolve further powers to Scotland is still large, and the willingness to do so palpable across Westminster'.[68]

However, Rupert Murdoch, the emperor of tabloid media populism, saw Westminster as a slippery, busted entity. He tweeted on 7 September 2014: 'Scotland. Now southern parties all promising much new autonomy if vote is No. Problem for them now is credibility. Also too late'.[69] His populism blended in with the grassroots campaign to rebrand the UK parliament as 'Westmonster'.[70]

It was a place where it was easy to convince restive Scottish voters that there had been 'thieving on industrial scale.[71] Any attempts to suggest that SNP MPs may have availed of the opportunities to benefit unduly from the expenses system, made little impact.[72] Indeed, an ICM poll released in mid-September 2014 found cutting ties with Westminster to be the single biggest attraction for Yes voters.[73]

A defence of Westminster, unusual in its robustness, came from the Aberdeenshire academic and blogger Effie Deans. She acknowledged that 'some people think that our politicians are corrupt' but she believed that [i]n fact we have some of the most honest politicians in the world'.

She grasped the nettle of the 2012 parliamentary expenses scandal which to her was 'a lot of nonsense':

'How much did these expenses cost the government? At most a few million. In an economy the size of the UK, this is a quite trivial sum. The whole problem stems from the fact that MPs are grossly underpaid. Someone involved in running a country should be paid a competitive amount, yet they don't even earn what a GP earns. This is silly. Pay MPs an index linked sum that is the equivalent of a director of a small company and then say they must have no expenses whatsoever. Problem solved'.

She was not cowed in her critical endorsement of Westminster as an effective polity by complaints emanating from 'Some SNP supporters [who] complain about paedophilia in Westminster'.

'I find it morally degenerate', she wrote, to try to use child abuse for political purposes. Child abuse exists everywhere in every country including in Scotland. There have been cover ups in Britain. People have been protected who ought not to have been protected. But the fact that we know about these things, the fact that the police are investigating is a demonstration of how little we are corrupt. In a country that is really corrupt you never hear about corruption and no-one dares mention it anyway'.[74]

She further believed that it was 'the blind hatred of the Tories that is behind the hatred of Westminster and any Westminster party'. This was ironic because as a former leader of the party in Scotland, Annabelle Goldie revealed there had been a close relationship with Alex Salmond during his spell at the head of a minority government between 2007 and 2011 when he needed Tory votes in Holyrood to get annual budgets (and other laws) passed.[75]

The *Times* columnist David Aaronovitch was intrigued about how the SNP had got so far by disqualifying opponents in the eyes of the people through simply branding them 'Tory'. Indeed he tweeted on 11 June 2015: 'One aspect of SNPery fascinates me - intelligent people thinking that simply labelling something as "Tory" settles all arguments forever'.[76]

After 2014, Only Nationalist Voices on the Streets

The SNP had come a long way by stigmatising opponents rather than winning arguments. It saw the *people* as a prize whose loyalty could easily be won and kept by encouraging core assumptions about which forces were holding Scotland back and how they were to be thwarted. In some eyes, this involved the spread of mass group think. The Scottish media columnist Chris Deerin was appalled by the break-through enjoyed by the SNP in the referendum period by treating the people as a passive herd rather than an alert electorate:

'The ...Yes campaign treated voters like infants and offered an unforgivably shoddy prospectus on which to base the creation of a new state. It was a case built on empty assertions and shifting goalposts rather than hard facts and considered projections. Since September, the oil price estimates used by the 'oil economist' Salmond as the underpinning for his financial calculations have fallen by more than half, but still, there is no humility to be found'.[77]

But nor was there any sign of a critical awakening among voters, almost 50 per cent of whom backed the party in the subsequent UK general election.

Salmond sought to retain confidence by using various populist tricks meant to suggest he was a mere servant of a cause much greater than himself. Thus, in August 2014, just as a poll suggested he might be deterring some Scots from voting Yes, he invoked a 17th-century Scots prophet, saying: ' If...the Brahan Seer said to me, 'Listen, you retire from politics tomorrow and I guarantee you Scotland will be an independent country in the spring of 2016', I would shake hands on that right away – absolutely.[78]

In ruefully acknowledging how the SNP continually appears capable of defying po-litical gravity, commentators flinch from conceding that there might be something deeply amiss with Scottish popular culture itself: in other words with the composite Scottish voter. In other countries this inhibition has been overcome.

In 2013, the Spanish writer Jaime Pozuelo-Monfort claimed: 'The Spanish masses have been historically incapable of recognizing and identifying excellence in lead-ership and as a result to elect representatives based on merit for the management of their affairs. The Spanish blindness or myopia impedes the differentiation of the better from the mediocre with binding consequences. The better man, the better woman is as a result annihilated...'[79]

Arguably such an annihilation was evident in Scotland on 7 May 2015 where not a few talented politicians, both veterans and newcomers, were passed over in favour of relatively unknown faces who won on 25 per cent swings and upwards solely due to being nominated by the SNP.

The perceptive Effie Deans expressed alarm at the hold of a partisan spirit over so many voters, alarm perhaps reinforced by the realisation that it was control of territory and not the common Scottish good which spurred on the party:

'It's the inability of Yes supporters to see any other position than their own that makes them so dangerous. They have reached the stage where democracy to them only means their side winning and they are unwilling to accept any other result... They campaign in the name of democracy, but don't believe in it'.[80]

Eric Joyce, the Labour MP for Falkirk from 2000 to 2012 may have lost some credibility due to his involvement in alcohol-related incidents but, writing as an independent MP, he was able to offer occasional sharp insights about the Scottish political condition.[81]

Thus on 29 April 2015, when the likely scale of the SNP's general election triumph was clear, he wrote:

'Perhaps it's time for people in Scotland to start wondering if they want to live in a place where it can be seriously projected that a single party might take all of the seats at a general election, and where well-educated and intelligent people would actually celebrate such a state of affairs. Or maybe it'll take a few years of independence before Scots are prepared to face up to reality'.[82]

But there was usually little heart-searching among the victors or media and academic well-wishers about the democratic implications of such a clean sweep.

In 2014 Chris Bambery, a Scottish Marxist analyst insisted that 'the 45 per cent vote for independence was overwhelmingly not for nationalism but for greater democracy'.[83] The pro-nationalist commentator Iain MacWhirter was delighted over how the 'festival of democracy' that was the referendum debate 'defied the conventional wisdom of political scientists and opinion pollsters who say that we live in an age of comfort, political apathy and retail politics'.[84]

Four days before the referendum, he had shown little patience with other commentators, such as the Edinburgh-born playwright and authority on Irish nationalism Kevin Toolis who were growing alarmed at the street militancy of SNP supporters. On the day that a large pro-government rally had been held in protest outside the BBC's Glasgow studios, he had tweeted 'Darkness visible. How long before the burning of books'? MacWhirter chided Toolis for being unable to 'tell diff[erence] between a street demo and Kristallnacht' and went on to state that 'the language you use compounds the stupidity of your observation. You know nothing about what's happening here'.[85]

Toolis's responded: 'Iain you r being both an arse + a fool. How do democracies die- one socalled 'street demo' at a time- 1 day it will be u'.[86]

MacWhirter replied in similar fashion to David Aaronovitch of the *Times* on 18 May 2015 when they debated whether Scottish Labour should swing to the radical left in a bid to outflank the SNP: 'With the greatest respect you don't understand the first thing about Scottish politics'.[87]

But his impressive serenity about the progressive character of SNPism had briefly cracked in December 2014 over the tactics of the party's online militants: He wrote in the *Herald* that '...the vehemence of the language used by some independence supporters may even have cost the Yes campaign the ultimate prize [on 18 September] as switherers reared back in the closing days and hours'.[88]

At times the energy and optimism of the Nationalists, so appealing to hitherto apolitical Scots, could very quickly spill over into self-righteousness. The feeling that Scotland's destiny was in the SNP's hands gripped not only party stalwarts but some of its media champions. Too often there was an impatience towards debate which made a mockery of MacWhirter's 'festival of democracy' claim. This was well illustrated on the BBC radio *Today* programme on 8 September 2014. Its veteran presenter John Humphries said to Angus Robertson, the SNP's leader at Westminster: 'you've got all these powers and have done nothing with them. Do you really want independence?' Instead of a reasoned answer, Robertson hit back: 'Its that kind of patronising attitude the people of Scotland object to... it's the tone I'm objecting to'.[89]

England 'the other'

Here was a political figure claiming that an entire nation would be offended by a particular question. The SNP was able to get away with the claim that it was this representative due to perhaps one overriding fact. There had been diminishing contact between many Scots and people resident elsewhere in the UK. Institutions which had a unifying role, allowing people from geographically varied backgrounds to share experiences, were perhaps diminishing in importance. Even in their own Scottish towns and cities, people got out less and enjoyed more private existences. They were more dependent on social media for information and views which enabled a party that had acquired mastery over this medium, to speak as if it was a national tribune. Perhaps most Scots still struggled with the view that Edinburgh was their national capital other than in the administrative sense. Except perhaps during the Edinburgh Festival, the city lacked the amenities which enabled it to exercise this magnetic pull. London was still recognised as a multi-facetted city which combined a strikingly varied number of roles. But increasingly left-wing SNP figures in particular depicted London as a kind of capitalist Babylon, a symbol for an unjust economic order which was grinding Scotland down. Hugh Reilly, a teacher who had a regular column in the *Scotsman* for many years insisted that if any Londoner was asked his nationality, he would answer 'English'. This article appeared 48 hours before the referendum vote and this history teacher invoked the spirit of Robert Bruce who 'heralded freedom for the Scots' thanks to his 'square-go' (fight) with an English king. He was disabused by a London reader who said that in his experience, most Londoners, when this question was put to them, would not answer English. But this pedagogue insisted that there had been 'three centuries of trying to weld four distinct peoples into one homogeneous race', a view that very few historians would agree with.[90]

In Place of Failure, the combative book by Jim Sillars which appeared on the first anniversary of the 2014 referendum, delivered a slashing attack on Britain's historical record.[91] It had been a trouble-maker and looter of other countries while ensuring that life at home was marked by injustice except for the privileged few in the 'metropolitan elite'. There was no mention of the fact that Britain had striven to uphold constitution freedoms, human rights and international law even during the heyday of empire. Lapses there had undoubtedly been. But without the huge expense and naval effort which Britain had invested in ending the slave trade, this practice is likely to have flourished into the 20th century and is already making an ominous comeback. The leading 19th century political figure, William Gladstone an Anglo-Scot, whose ancestors had indeed been involved in the slave trade, considered Britain to be 'the centre of the moral, social and political power of the world'.[92] No other power came close to it before 1914 in seeking to promote peace and it may not be a coincidence that the century of relative peace in Europe from 1815 to 1914 coincided with the British empire's chief period of ascendancy.

Gladstone was revered among many ordinary Scots in a way that perhaps no other politician has been until the flowering of nationalism. This Victorian Liberal sought to tame some of the worst effects of industrialisation which Sillars dwells upon in his book. He joins with the historian Tom Nairn in seeing Britain as a state in relentless decline, whose arrogant and often clumsy elite has lost authority not just over Scotland. He disparages its efforts to remain a balancing force in international relations through its contribution to NATO. Sillars is scornful of this defensive alliance. He equates its only offensive action, stopping the forced deportation of Albanians in Kosovo in 1999, when it was ruled by Slobodan Milošević, with Russia's occupation of Crimea and armed action elsewhere in Ukraine.[93]

Sillars used to criticise Alex Salmond for excessive negativity when he launched forceful assaults on British institutions. But in his 2015 book he displays much of his rival's past belligerency as when he describes the economic forecaster, the Institute for Fiscal Studies (one unafraid to discomfit governments in the past), as 'part of the metropolitan elite' after it failed to endorse the SNP's own predictions for an economically viable independent Scotland.[94]

SNP leaders of varying hues have struggled to lay out a practical vision for a future sovereign Scotland forged by their party. England continues to be a major fixation. Not just the party of independence but other Scottish bodies and personalities have often sought to define themselves by their alleged differences with England. England is central to Scottish identity more than any Scottish historical, religious , cultural, geographical, or economic factor is. The SNP has recently revealed a growing obsession with England which is not reciprocated towards Scotland by any party or institution in the rest of the UK. Previously, the party adhered to the convention that it kept out of parliamentary debates on matters that did not concern Scotland. But under the supposedly more pragmatic Nicola Sturgeon, this stance has been reversed. In July 2015, when the Conservative government announced that it would be introducing a law on fox-hunting that brought the law in England into line with the milder Scottish one, not only did the SNP announce that it would be opposing the bill but it would be changing its own law so as to tighten up on fox-hunting. At the time of writing, the SNP appears desperate to find reason to block the Scotland bill perhaps so that it won't have to demonstrate what it will actually do with the extra powers for Scotland that it contains.

In 2015, the Sturgeon government announced plans to ban independent schools from employing teachers not registered in Scotland. Arguably, this is a barely disguised move to heighten territorial barriers by preventing teachers trained in the rest of Britain from teaching in independent schools in Scotland and presumably distorting the minds of young Scots. Without such recruits, many independent schools would struggle to continue. Rod Grant, the head of Clifton School in Edinburgh, told MSPs that the new law posed a major threat to the quality of education that is offered to his pupils and the International school in Aberdeen was similarly alarmed. It was, according to Grant 'very anti-English' and a ludicrous waste of talent', meaning that Scottish independent schools would in theory be banned from employing even Stephen Hawking to teach physics.[95]

Some feared that the SNP would regard the acquisition of new powers primarily as an opportunity to deepen differences with the rest of the United Kingdom on multiple fronts. This might produce a backlash among Scots inconvenienced in their everyday lives by a party with such an ideological approach to governing. It was noted that in the 2014 Scottish Social Attitudes survey, people with mixed identity were up from 15 to 23 per cent and the percentage who felt more Scots than British, at 26 per cent was the lowest since the survey had started in 1992. The largest number of people, 32 per cent, self-defined themselves as both Scottish and British. But these nuances are sometimes overlooked by Conservative MPs who assume, as in the case of Crispin Blunt when interviewed by the BBC about the upgrading of the Faslane naval base, that most Scots are likely to be opposed to such a step because there is a common Scottish perspective on this and other issues.[96] Currently, very few Conservative MPs closely follow Scottish affairs, so they are sometimes hard-pressed to deal effectively in the Commons with SNP arguments.

The SNP is struggling to manage a highly emotional throng of Scots, often absorbed by 'others' who can be portrayed not just as foes of the movement but of the country and its inhabitants. Democracy was not a pressing concern for it or for its growing volume of supporters. Neither was there any visible outcry from society against menacing pro-SNP protests or attacks on opposition figures .

A patriotic cause had acquired mass appeal and united a party with large swathes of a population which for generations had been rather sceptical about politicians. The SNP had broken through, aided crucially by social media, just as the 'mass man', whose inexorable rise was predicted by the Spanish philosopher Ortega y Gasset in 1929, was perhaps finally making his true mark in Scotland. Absorbed with his and her comforts and emotional needs and favouring paternalistic leadership, this *Homo Caledonius* has grown increasingly unaccustomed to solving problems but demands instead, that an interventionist State tackles them.

Even before the appearance of his classic work, *The Revolt of the Masses*, Ortega had warned in 1922:

'This is the gravest danger that today threatens civilization: State intervention, the absorption of all spontaneous social effort by the State; that is to say, of spontaneous historical action, which in the long-run sustains, nourishes and impels human destinies.'[97]

The novelist and commentator Allan Massie had enumerated the drive towards a big state in SNP-led Scotland.[98] Measures to curtail the autonomy of the family, to create a centralized police force, to force through involuntary sales of country estates, and to override local objections to wind farms dominated the SNP's legislative agenda from 2011 to 2015. There was opposition but it was fragmented and these 'big brother' moves made absolutely no difference to the 2015 electoral result.

Very few commentators on the rise of Scottish nationalism really reflected much about the brooding presence of one of the world's largest public sectors in Scotland. The SNP was keen to concentrate as much (if not more) political power in Edinburgh than there had been in London during the Thatcher era. Managerialism and the imposition of top-down norms were bound to thrive in such a climate.

How could the cause avoid becoming a cliché-ridden fossil deprived of any beneficial application or role in Scottish life? Arguably, nationalism's reversal to being a shibboleth had occurred in Ireland after just one generation of independence.[99]

Once the nationalist cause had been a vehicle for even more passion and hope than it would be later in Scotland. Of course, there is a disinclination among exuberant and optimistic nationalists to take to heart lessons from the much-delayed modernisation of independent Ireland and try to apply them to Scotland. Such a blasé and self-referential outlook suggests that those Scots who have embarked on a journey of political self-exploration are in danger of creating a new order where power is hoarded rather than widely distributed. In such an outcome, there would be more continuity than change and whatever change that occurred might not necessarily be an improvement on previous British-influenced norms.

Conclusion

Very belatedly, the SNP has exhibited the prowess which can make political nationalism an irresistible force. It has mobilised for political ends emotions and attitudes that have far more to do with collective identity than with how the country is governed. A set of adversaries has been identified, residing chiefly in the 'foreign' capital of the British state: Scotland can only attain its true worth if they are repudiated and UK-wide institutions cease to have any meaningful hold on Scottish life.

Incredibly, the SNP has imposed this embattled perspective on several million Scots at a time of relative stability in the lives of perhaps most of them. Compared with the rest of Europe, there is no economic crisis, with Britain growing faster than most large Western economies. Under the Barnett formula, Scotland since the late 1970s has received a far more generous allocation of public spending than any other component part of the UK. Elsewhere in the world, it is easy to find conflicts of identity, pushed to the level of furious strife, whose origins may have been as modest as the ones that have flared up Scottish resentment.

Yet, perhaps around half of Scots appear to wish to overlook their material conditions in comparison to the rest of the world. They show little interest in assessing how well or poorly they have been governed by the SNP. Instead, they have enthusiastically linked up with the party in its crusade to create a separate state irrespective of the level of resources it will have at its disposal. Many adherents of the cause are existential nationalists who believe passionately in creating a sovereign Scottish state irrespective of its material conditions. Others are civic nationalists who are convinced that independence is likely to usher in a more democratic country in which the voices of ordinary citizens can influence decision-making by elites. Others argue that what the SNP stands for 'isn't really nationalism at all but an expression of progressive solidarity that happens to be culturally Scottish'.[100]

But the 21st century *nationalist* cause in Scotland is a classically nationalist one however artfully it is presented. There is an emphasis on ancestry, grievances directed externally, myths that sustain the national spirit, the need to liberate the people from alien and inauthentic power structures, and also an insistence that 'our' national project is qualitatively different than others because of the special vocation of the Scots or the circumstances in which they find themselves.

The belief in the intrinsic originality of what is happening in Scotland makes Scottish Nationalism a late arrival in the pantheon of nationalist movements. Given the temper of many of the adherents to this cause and their insistence that the SNP ought to follow an intransigent political course, it will be no surprise if the Scottish latecomer commits some of the mistakes, but hopefully not too many of the excesses of its predecessors. But it is impossible to be sure of the SNP's ultimate trajectory and it is prudent to warn of harmful pathways that it can easily be tempted down however jarring such observations are for the SNP's numerous fervent believers.

Notes for Chapter 1

1. 'Scottish Baby Names: Dozens of children named Indy or Indie', *Independent*, 11 March 2015.
2. *Daily Telegraph*, 15 September 2015.
3. Alex Salmond, *The Dream Shall Never Die*, London: William Collins, 2015.
4. Lesley Riddoch, 'Independent-mindedness missing', *Scotsman*, 7 October 2013, http://www.scotsman.com/news/lesley-riddoch-independent-mindedness-missing-1-3129034
5. Comment, Allan Massie, 'Brown is right on case for Union', *Scotsman*, 11 June 2014, http://www.scotsman.com/news/allan-massie-brown-is-right-on-case-for-union-1-3439834#ixzz3ldMnIAoR
6. John Curtice, 'Scottish independence: What will it take to persuade Scots to say no?' *Daily Telegraph*, 3 September 2014, http://www.telegraph.co.uk/news/uknews/scottish-inde pendence/11070471/Scottish-in dependence-What-will-it-take-to-persuade-Scots-to-say-no.html#disqus_thread
7. Isabel Hardman, 'Shock poll: Scotland's 'Yes' campaign pulls into lead. It's 51% to 49%', *Spectator*, 6 September 2014, http://blogs.spectator.co.uk/coffeehouse/2014/09/yes-cam paign-pulls-into-lead/
8. Paulina Echoa Espejo, 'Power to Whom: the people between procedure and populism', in *The Promise and perils of Populism: Global Perspectives*, edited by Carlos de la Torre, Lex ington, Kentucky, University of Kentucky Press, 2014, p.p. 79-83
9. Tomas Hirst, 'An Independence Vote-Rigging Conspiracy Theory Is Sweeping Scotland', *Business Insider*, 24 September 2014, http://uk.businessinsider.com/independence -vote-rigging-conspiracy-theory-sweeping-scotland-2014-9
10. Salmond, *The Dream Shall Never Die*, p. 11.

11. P.H. Scott, *Scotland: A Creative Past, an independent future*, Edinburgh, Luath press, 2014, p. 10.

12. 'England: A Difficult Neighbour' [from *Scotsman*, 4 July 2006], republished in P.H. Scott, *The Age of Liberation*, Edinburgh: Saltire Society, 2008, p. 183.

13. Maxwell, S. (2013) [1981] *'The case for left-wing nationalism'*, in Maxwell, S. *The Case for Left-Wing Nationalism and Other Essays*, Edinburgh, Luath Press., 2013.

14. See Ben Jackson, 'The left and Scottish nationalism', *Renewal*, Vol 22, No '1\2, 2014.

15. James Dennison, 'The Loser takes all – THE SNP after the referendum', *LSE Election Blog*, 13 April 2015, http://blogs.lse.ac.uk/generalelection/the-level-and-fervency-of-snp-support/

16. See Tom Gallagher, 'the Scottish Piazza echoes to the Liberation Beat', *Harry's Place*, 26 September 2009, http://hurryupharry.org/2009/09/26/the-scottish-piazza-echoes-to-the-liberation-beat/

17. David Knowles, 'The SNP's Political paradise', *Huffington Post*, 20 May 2015, http://www.huffingtonpost.co.uk/david-knowles/the-snps-political-paradise_b_7340854.html

18. Daniel Sanderson, 'Anger at outsourcing of staff survey at a greater cost', *Herald*, 20 October 2014, http://www.heraldscotland.com/news/health/anger-at-outsourcing-of-staff-survey-at-a-greater-cost.25625901

19. James Cusick, ' Alex Salmond unwittingly steals the show at SNP conference', *Independent on Sunday* 29 March 2015

20. Kevin McKenna, 'In the poor heart of Glasgow, political loyalties melt away', *Guardian*, 7 February 2015, http://www.theguardian.com/uk-news/2015/feb/08/poor-glasgow-safe-seat-cranhill-labour-snp-election-voters

21. Reiner Luyken, 'Der schottische Liberalismus ist tot', *Die Ziet*, 8 May 2015, http://www.zeit.de/politik/ausland/2015-05/schottland-wahlergebnis-grossbritannien-snp-nationalismus

22. Martin Little, 'Top German journalist living in Highlands accused of comparing SNP with Hitler', *Press and Journal*, 20 May 2015, https://www.pressandjournal.co.uk/fp/news/highlands/585307/top-german-journalist-living-highlands-compares-snp-hitler/

23. Nigel Biggar 'Independence will do nothing for Scots', *Standpoint*, May 2014.

24. Stephen Daisley, 'Essay: What is Scottish nationalism, what is it not, what could it be?' STV, 12 June 2015, /scotland-decides/analysis/1322184-essay-stephen-daisley-on-the-snp-and-the-politics-of-nationalism/

25. Aidan Kerr on Twitter, 23 August 2014, accessed 20 September 2015.

26. Tom Peterkin, 'Holyrood launches drive to promote Scots language', *Scotsman*, 10 September 2015.

27. Rory Reynolds and Jackie Kemp, '"Worrying" dip in foreign languages at Scots schools', Scotsman, 29 April 2013.

28. 'Gaelic board chief executive does not speak the language', STV News, 10 July 2015,

http://news.stv.tv/highlands-islands/1324480-interim-gaelic-board-chief-executive-joe-moore-does-not-speak-language/

29. John McDermott, 'Scotland and the Wish Tree', *Financial Times*, 31 August 2014.

30. *Scotsman,* 10 June 2015.

31. Adam Tomkins, 'Full Fiscal detriment', *Notes From North Britain*, 13 June 2015, https://notesfromnorthbritain.wordpress.com/

32. Allan Massie, 'The Tartan Stalinists; *Daily Mail,* 7 February 2015, http://www.dailymail.co.uk/news/article-2943915/The-Tartan-Stalinists-Forced-sales-country-estates-Snooping-state-guardians-child-Contempt-wealthy-Britain-Fantasy-No-s-stark-reality-SNP-landslide.html

33. Judith Duffy, 'A tale of two islands as Gigha dream turns sour', *Herald,* 23 November 2014, http://www.heraldscotland.com/news/home-news/a-tale-of-two-islands-as-gigha-dream-turns-sour.25940843

34. Simon Johnson, 'Family farms 'broken up' under SNP land reforms', *Daily Telegraph*, 30 November 2014.

35. Simon Johnson, 'SNP land reforms '"forget about food production"', *Daily Telegraph*, 19 May 2015, http://www.telegraph.co.uk/news/politics/SNP/11614062/SNP-land-reforms-forget-about-food-production.html#disqus_thread>

36. Tom Holland, Twitter, 9 August 2014, accessed 10 August 2014.

37. Rupert Murdoch, Twitter, 14 September 2014, accessed 15 September 2014.

38. Kevin Hague, 'Who do "Business for Scotland" represent', *Chokkablog* 17 June 2014, http://chokkablog.blogspot.co.uk/2014/06/who-do-business-for-scotland-represent.htm

39. David Clegg, ' Nicola Sturgeon under pressure to get a grip on SNP's extremist fringe as two party members are suspended over Glasgow protest', *Daily Record,* 5 May 2015, http://www.dailyrecord.co.uk/news/politics/nicola-sturgeon-under-pressure-grip-5642348

40. Frances Perraudin, 'Online rumours damage British democracy, says Douglas Alexander', *Guardian*, 17 March 2015, http://www.theguardian.com/politics/2015/mar/17/online-rumours-damage-british-democracy-says-douglas-alexander

41. Perraudin, 'Online rumours'.

42. David Brooks, 'The Age of Innocence', *New York Times,* 17 May 2012.

43. http.www.natcen.ac.uk/news-media/press-releases/2015/February/ssa2014_sectarianism_pr

44. Lily of St Leonards, We no longer even share the truth in Scotland', *Effie Deans Blogspot,* 25 April 2015, letter from m'athair .

45. 'Church of Scotland Blues – What the May 2015 Assembly Reports tell us about the State of the Kirk', *The Wee Flea,* <https://theweeflea.wordpress.com/, 17 April 2015

46. This connection is mentioned by Alex Salmond in the 2nd edition of his referendum memoir *The Dream Shall never Die*, London: Collins, 2015.

47. See Tom Gallagher, *Glasgow the Uneasy Peace: religious tension in modern Scotland,*

Manchester: Manchester University Press, 1987, chapters 2 and 3.

48. Tom Gallagher, 'Catholic Church silent as Scotland prepares to vote on independence', *Catholic Herald,* 12 August 2014, http://www.catholicherald.co.uk/features/2014/08/12/catholic-church-silent-as-scotland-goes-to-vote-on-independence/

49. Erasmus, 'Faith in the flag', *Economist,* 8 May 2015, http://www.economist.com/blogs/erasmus/2015/05/scotland-nationalism-and-religion?fsrc=nlw|newe|11-05-2015|

50. *Scotsman,* 24 July 2010.

51. Michael Gray, on Twitter, 21 August 2014, accessed 14 September 2015.

52. Tom Devine, *Being Scottish*, Edinburgh: Polygon, 2002.

53. Derek Bateman, 'Dim and Dimmer', Derek Bateman Blog, 25 May 2015.

54. Neil O'Brien, 'Scots should forget about flying the flag and fix their nation', *Daily Telegraph,* 13 July 2010, http://www.telegraph.co.uk/news/uknews/scotland/7888795/Scots-should-forget-about-flying-the-flag-and-fix-their-nation.html

55. Robin McAlpine, 'Hope over Fear', *Bella Caledonia*, 28 April 2015, http://bellacaledonia.org.uk/2015/04/28/hope-over-fear/

56. Robin McAlpine,' So Far So Good. British Unionism's Review of 2014', *Bella Caledonia*, 30 December 2014, http://bellacaledonia.org.uk/2014/12/30/so-far-so-good-british-unionisms-review-of-2014/

57. Robin McAlpine, ' the architects of a new nation', *Open Democracy,* 26 November 2013, https://www.opendemocracy.net/ourkingdom/robin-mcalpine/architects-of-new-nation

58. McAlpine, 'Hope over Fear'.

59. See 'Tom McAlpine – an appreciation', Scotsman, 1 March 2006, http://www.scotsman.com/news/obituaries/tom-mcalpine-an-appreciation-1-1107887

60. Pat Kane, 'On Stephen Maxwell (1): The Missing Million', 4 November 2013, *http://www.thoughtland.info/2013/11/on-stephen-maxwell-1-the-missing-million.html* for the above two quotes

61. Paul Hutcheon, 'Pat Kane: if there is a No vote Scotland will be a depressed place for quite a while', *Sunday Herald,* 10 August 2014, http://www.heraldscotland.com/politics/referendum-news/if-there-is-a-no-vote-scotland-will-be-a-depressed-place-for-quite-a-while-.24967605

62. Andrew Denholm,; Principal Louise Richardson criticises 'interfering' SNP as she leaves St Andrews for Oxford', *Herald*, 29 May 2015, http://www.heraldscotland.com/news/13215788.Principal_Louise_Richardson_criticises__interfering__SNP_as_she_leaves_St_Andrews_for_Oxford/

63. Scott McNab, 'Scots universities 'have reputation for Holyrood interference', *Scotsman*, 7 October 2015.

64. Simon Johnson, 'SNP to target landowners' property rights "for public good", *Daily Telegraph,* 20 May 2015,

http://www.telegraph.co.uk/news/earth/country side/11616876/SNP-to-target-land-owners-property-rights-for-public-good.html

65. See Catherine Boone, 'Electoral Populism Where Property Rights are Weak: Land Politics in Contemporary Sub-Saharan Africa', *Comparative Politics*, Vol. 41, no 2, 2009; also Henry L. Roberts, *Rumania: Political Problems of an Agrarian State*, New Haven: Yale University Press, 1951.

66. Massie, 'The Tartan Stalinists'.

67. See Takis S Pappas 'Carry on Sisyphus: short answers on Greece's post-electoral politics', *Open Democracy*, 26 January 2015

68. Michael Collins, 'Agenda: Recidivist nationalism is outdated in a union of shared resources and pooled sovereignty', *Herald*, 13 May 2015.

69. Rupert Murdoch on Twitter, 7 September 2014, accessed 15 September 2015.

70. 'Westmonster IndyRef Bumper Sticker', http://www.zazzle.co.uk/westminster_monster_indyref_bumper_sticker-128011545798501570

71. Donald MacLeod, 'Vote Yes, Scotland – we will survive', *Sunday Post*, 14 September 2014, http://www.sundaypost.com/news-views/columnists/donald-macleod/donald-ma-cleod-vote-yes-scotland-we-will-survive-1.574690

72. 'Complete MP's Expenses Guiide : Angus Macneil', *Daily Telegraph*, http://parliament.telegraph.co.uk/mpsexpenses/expense-microsite/mp-details/An-gus-Macneil/mp-12004)accessed 15 September 2015).

73. Paul Cairney, Politics and Public Policy, *Scottish Independence: a rejection of West-minster politics?* 14 September 2014, http://paulcairney.wordpress.com/2014/09/13/scottish-independence-a-rejection-of-westminster-politics/

74. Lily of St Leonards, 'What's so great about Britain?', *Effie Deans Blogspot*, 1 May 2015.

75. David Clegg, 'Former Scots Tory leader Annabel Goldie: Alex Salmond was happy to work with Tories but SNP U-turn reeks of posturing and hypocrisy', *Daily Record*, 17 February 2015.

76. David Aaronovitch on twitter, 11 June 2015 (accessed 15 September 2015).

77. Chris Deerin, 'Scotland has gone mad', *Cap_X*, 7 April 2015, http://www.capx.co/scotland-has-gone-mad/

78. Kevan Christie, 'Salmond would quit if it meant a Yes vote', *Scotsman*, 20 August 2014, http://www.scotsman.com/news/politics/top-stories/salmond-i-would-quit-if-it-meant-a-yes-vote-1-3514731

79. Jaime Pozuelo-Monfort , 'We Need Ortega y Gasset Back', *Economonitor*, December 2013, http://www.economonitor.com/blog/2013/12/we-need-ortega-y-gasset-back/#idc-container>

80. Lily of St Leonards', 'There's something rotten in the state of Scotland', *Effie Deans Blogspot*, 1 November 2014.

81. Falkirk MP Eric Joyce escapes jail after admitting assault charges in Commons brawl', *BBC News* (BBC). 9 March 2012.

82. Eric Joyce, 'Scotland's one-party state', 29 April 2015, http://ericjoyce.co.uk/2015/04/scotlands-one-party-state>

83. Chris Bambery, 'The referendum: winners & losers', *The International Socialist,* September 2014, http://internationalsocialist.org.uk/index.php/blog/the-referendum-winners-losers/#sthash.yfEJDAUQ.dpuf.

84. Iain Macwhirter, /*Disunited Kingdom: How Westminster Won a Referendum but Lost Scotland,* Glasgow: Cargo, 2014, p. 14.

85. Iain MacWhirter on twitter, 14 September 2014 (accessed 15 September 2015).

86. Kevin Toolis on Twitter, 14 September 2014 (accessed 15 September 2015).

87. Iain MacWhirter on twitter, 18 May 2015, accessed 15 September 2015).

88. Iain MacWhirter, 'The cybernats are playing into Labour's hands', *Herald*, 16 December 2014, http://www.heraldscotland.com/comment/columnists/the-cybernats-are-playing-into-labours-hands.114657748

89. Jim Murphy MP on twitter, 8 September 2014 (accessed 8 September 2014).

90. Hugh Reilly, 'A chance to end artificial alliance', *Scotsman,* 16 September 2014.

91. Jim Sillars, *In Place of Failure: Making it Yes Next Time...Soon,* Glasgow: Vagabond Voices, 2015.

92. See Robert Tombs, *The English and their History,* London: Penguin, 2015, p. 540.

93. Sillars, *In Place of Failure,* p.p. 61-62.

94. Sillars, *In Place of Failure,* p. 100.

95. Simon Johnson, 'SNP teacher ban for independent schools is "anti-English"', *Daily Telegraph,* 16 June 2015

96. World At one, BBC 28 August 2015.

97. Philip J. Clarke, ' José Ortega y Gasset's The Revolt Of The Masses', *Musings on Life and Literature,* 31 October 2014, http://philiphclark.com/jose-ortega-y-gassets-the-revolt-of-the-masses

98. Massie, 'the Tartan Stalinists'.

99. See among other works, R.F. Foster, *Vivid Faces: the Revolutionary Generation in Ireland, 1892-1923,* London: Penguin, 2014; also Terence J. Brown, *Ireland: A Social and Cultural History 1922-2002,* London: Harper Perennial, 2010 edition.

100. Rafael Behr, 'Cameron knows the risks of nationalism – but doesn't care if he splits the country ', *Guardian,* 28 April 2015, commentisfree/2015/apr/28/cameron-nationalism-split-country-national-identity-ory-english-grievance#img-1

CHAPTER TWO, THE PARTY

Finally at the Summit

Often in democratic politics it is far easier to campaign than to govern. The SNP, although in office since 2007, has been in campaigning mode for a great deal of this time. It has succeeded in creating an image of a plucky and embattled Scotland pitted against a difficult and larger partner, one which now resonates with plenty of Scottish voters. The party sometimes comes across as querulous, indignant, and ready to automatically place the blame for mistakes committed during eight years of insubstantial governance, on its predecessors or else on London. In 2015, this rhetorical militancy converted much of the electorate in the wake of the two-years of campaigning time gifted to the SNP by David Cameron. Arguably this event has heightened the immaturity of the party even while strengthening its hold on the emotions of a large portion of the Scottish people. It is ill-equipped to take charge of a relatively manageable country like Scotland even if independence does fall into its lap. But it has won several famous victories, perhaps none greater than the one at the UK general election held on 7 May 2015. This chapter explores the nature and outlook of a party with outsized ambitions and which until the early years of this century arguably was a fringe force.

The SNP emerged from the 2015 contest, having rewritten several of the rules that had shaped two hundred years of British electoral history. After a higher turnout than in the rest of the UK was confirmed, the party achieved record swings across Scotland. One resulted in the election in Paisley East of Mhairi Black, a student who, at the age of twenty, turned out to be the youngest MP returned anywhere in Britain since 1667[1]. The SNP, from having six MPs, suddenly found itself with 56. Its three main unionist rivals were left with a token single member each.

The SNP was now the third largest party in the House of Commons. Because of its haul of seats, it was entitled to perhaps as much as £6 million during the life of the new Parliament. Each year, it would receive between £1 and £1.2 million from the Treasury in what is known as *short money*[2]. It would also enjoy influence on parliamentary select committees and the party would be entitled to a much greater say in shaping the life of the Commons.

Since 2011, the SNP had already exercised the dominance at Holyrood of a kind which it was rare for any party to have enjoyed in the House of Commons. It was the majority government with 64 MSPs, and it had more than 400 councillors in local government. A membership which had swelled to over 105,100 members since September 2014 meant that such dominance appeared set to remain quite far into the future.

The 30-month long referendum campaign had given members unlimited opportunities for campaigning, an exercise which has had a bonding effect at all levels of the party however fickle the rewards in times past. It enabled them to feel part of a cause and a movement that was pushing the nation towards irrevocable change. The normal gulf between party chiefs and mass membership dissolved in this common endeavour. The SNP's dual command of Alex Salmond and Nicola Sturgeon issued messages about the virtues of independence which were absorbed and repeated on social media in appealing formats. An old idea previously seen either as fancifully utopian or as a tired cliché suddenly gripped the collective Scottish imagination as no other had done perhaps for generations. The success in reaching out and converting disengaged Scots to their previously derided cause was a mightily satisfying experience. The glorious referendum era had surely built up a store of capital and credit that is likely to enable the party to endure even if it falls a long way short of the goal it has set itself of being the architect of national independence.

For nearly all of its previous history, modern Scottish Nationalism had been stuck in the wilderness. Its oxygen supply just came from an electoral force whose support was spread thinly and which often seemed non-existent in Scotland's largest populated centres. Unlike other European nationalist movements, it was unable to project its appeal through language, sporting or cultural associations. A common British culture and an economy which shed most of its remaining distinctive Scottish features in the second half of the twentieth-century, just appeared to highlight the immensity of the political task it had set itself. The arrival of devolution in 1999 appeared to be a false dawn.

Coming From Behind

Nevertheless, the SNP suddenly had 35 Members of the Scottish Parliament (MSP). In 1999, it was actually not that far behind the still-dominant Labour Party in terms of votes. But the party failed to spring to life as a fresh and innovative force. Its leader Alex Salmond quit after one year, preferring Westminster to the Holyrood stage. The SNP was hampered by unsightly factionalism as MSPs returned as list members concentrated on internal politicking so as to be ranked in an eligible position on the party slate.[3] The leadership of John Swinney turned out to be a failure leading to the return of Alex Salmond in 2004. Quite possibly, Salmond would have spent the rest of his political career chipping away at Labour's ascendancy without achieving a decisive breakthrough for his party. But the SNP's cause was aided by the spectacular mistakes made by its chief foe: involvement in a controversial series of conflicts in southern Asia which divided the Labour Party and alienated many supporters;[4] a debilitating and decade-long personal feud at the top of the party; a failure to realise that Labour could not simply translate its dominance of Westminster and local government in Scotland to the arena of devolved politics without substantially raising its political game and adapting to Scottish identity politics.

Labour frittered away a strong hand through indolence or misfortune while the SNP after 2004, under a re-energised Alex Salmond, played a modest hand supremely well and made the most of whatever luck came its way. Recurring setbacks had made it dogged and stoical. It also had one guiding principle or *idée fixe*, that of independence. Besides 'the furtherance of Scottish interests', the party's constitution sets out only one aim:

'Independence for Scotland; that is the restoration of Scottish national sovereignty by restoration of full powers to the Scottish Parliament, so that its authority is limited only by the sovereign power of the Scottish People to bind it with a written constitution and by such agreements as it may freely enter into with other nations or states or international organisations for the purpose of furthering international cooperation, world peace and the protection of the environment'.[5]

The party's leaders have been permitted much latitude as long as they offer sufficient proof that their policies and manoeuvres are meant to draw nearer the realisation of that very goal. The SNP has acquired radically different policies on issues such as the European Union, the currency of a future Scotland, and the retention of any 'social union' with the rest of the UK with remarkably little internal turmoil because the core aspiration did not seem to be placed in question. To what extent the SNP should accommodate itself to devolution within the United Kingdom proved a more troublesome issue at times in the 1980s and 1990s but unity held.

The SNP was prepared to invest great authority in any leader who succeeded in throwing the British state opponents of Scottish independence onto the defensive whether or not it resulted in dramatic electoral headway. This was at no times truer than under the leadership of Alex Salmond. Gordon Wilson, his predecessor as leader, recounts that it soon evolved into a form of imperial rule under a wilful and resourceful individual.

By 1999 (he related in his history of the SNP):

'Alex Salmond had become the dominating figure within the SNP and only his decisions counted. I recall being at one of the planning meets called for a Sunday to set the themes of the campaign. Alex was nearly an hour late. The meeting had reached agreement on most of the policy and campaign issues. When Alex arrived, these proposals were abandoned and he dictated what he thought should take place'.[6]

There were occasions when benevolent autocracy could turn into despotism. One of these may have been in 1999-2000. In the first Holyrood election campaign, 'there had been a horrendous overspend' which led to an unedifying tussle between Salmond and the national treasurer, Ian Blackford. Salmond and his campaign manager Michael Russell had spent an estimated £200,000 on a newspaper in order to counteract hostile media coverage. Afterwards, Blackford tried to take control of costs and a plan to reduce the party overdraft of £419, 672 was agreed unanimously at the national executive. This involved cutting back on the leader's huge bill for taxis. But the issue became personalised as Salmond accused the treasurer of being a minion of his then arch-rival Jim Sillars. But at a subsequent meeting of the national executive (and in the absence of Blackford), Salmond 'moved a motion of no confidence in him on the twin bases of his competence and destabilisation of the Party.' According to Wilson, 'this led in turn to a threat of legal action by Blackford against Salmond for defamation on the grounds that the decision would adversely affect his reputation as an investment banker. Blackford's refusal to resign led to his suspension from membership of the SNP'. Soon afterwards, on 17 July Salmond announced that he was quitting as party leader.[7]

Sillars and Salmond made up in the referendum campaign and Salmond spoke for Blackford at an election rally in the Highland seat which he won in 2015. The SNP has always had tempestuous personalities, but the romantic beauty of its territorial cause, and the presence of an enemy whom each of the potential rivals dislike, have proven to be powerful incentives for nipping conflicts in the bud. There has been nothing remotely like the feud between Gordon Brown and Tony Blair which turned the Labour party from a force capable of establishing a lasting sway over British politics into a party divided into two hostile camps and therefore unable to unite in the face of the inevitable difficulties which periodically confront every government.

Globalisation, and the embrace of a radical version of multiculturalism as a means of managing an increasingly complex urban society, had led to strains within the Labour Party; ambitious Oxbridge-educated politicians, imbued with an elitist Fabian outlook, lost touch with many natural grassroots supporters. In 2015, the year the SNP finally stormed the ramparts of its chief foe not just in Clydeside but right across Scotland, a different from of insurgency occurred in England and Wales. The United Kingdom Independence Party (UKIP) succeeded in winning over many ex-Labour supporters in working-class areas.

Culture of Complaint

UKIP's impact in Scotland (where it had picked up a European seat in 2014) was negligible. For at least twenty years, the SNP had been seeking to popularise a new multicultural Scottish nation divorced from an ethnic base.[8] It sought to promote certain ethnic identities reconciled by a patriotic overlay. Critics (I being one) argued that such an approach was bound up with the quest for votes from particular ethno-religious groups.[9] On the economic front, it was embracing pro-immigration policies in order to make up for skills shortages in the workforce. Overall, it sought to lure world economic players to invest in Scotland with policies (such as a low corporation tax) that a globalist like Tony Blair would probably have admired.

The SNP got away with this *legerdemain* due to the strength of its core doctrine. The espousal of nationalism gives SNP leaders more room to manoeuvre and be flexible in practical policy terms than Labour socialism does. Arguably, nationalism is a more adaptable ideology and has less to prove in office than purveyors of socialism do; barring the kind of trauma seen in post-British Ireland nearly a century ago, where the birth of the country was accompanied by civil-war and partition, it does not usually provoke major schisms.

In early 21st century Europe, party unity has been far harder to preserve when the guiding ideology has been based on an economic model or formula. Socialists, doing badly in elections across much of Europe, find that voters lose patience if promises are not turned into policies which bring tangible material improvements. Certainly, the difficulty of achieving concrete progress in expanding state control over the economy, or reducing inequality in the face of hostile markets, sceptical media, and restive trade-unions has created recurring strains within the ranks of the Labour movement. In Scotland, the style, rhetoric and presentation of the ruling SNP seems to matter more than making clear progress in policy areas that matter to many citizens. The rhetoric is idealistic. But the SNP has not used the levers of power it wields to promote the redistribution of wealth.

The grant allocation it receives from central government for spending has not been cut, meaning Scotland has more to spend than many of the English regions. Yet in recent years the proportion spent on health and education has been lower than in England and Wales. Alex Bell, former head of policy under Alex Salmond, remarked in 2015: 'I absolutely get what they sound like – but there is almost no evidence that they are progressive in what they do'.[10]

The readiness of London to correct the imbalance between the tax revenue raised in Scotland and the country's rather larger spending needs, relieves a lot of pressure on the ruling nationalists. According to Alex Bell, John Swinney, Scotland's finance minister has a fairly easy job: 'he just has to divide up the pie'.[11] Quite possibly, it would have been a very different story if Scotland had voted 'Yes' in 2014. Early in the campaign, Alex Salmond had forecast that a future oil boom would underpin a surge in productivity and national wealth after a Yes vote.[12] Later, his government's 2013 independence white paper, which based its forecasts on a $113 a barrel oil price, claimed oil revenues for Scotland could hit £7.9bn in the financial year 2016/17 alone; its oil and gas bulletin in March 2013 predicted a range of revenues in Scotland's waters of between £31bn and £57bn for the five years from 2012/13 to 2017/18. Yet, the oil and gas bulletin published by Swinney on 25 June 2015 revealed that revenues were expected to plummet to well under a quarter of these forecasts, falling to as low as £2.4bn in total over the 2015-19 period.[13] Perhaps not unexpectedly, Swinney blamed the UK government's alleged poor management of the (largely private) oil industry for these disappointing figures.

The existence of a mistrusted central government, has been an invaluable foil for the SNP. But the timing of their release suggests that this pretext has limitations even in the eye of the SNP. Not only was the release of the figures postponed until after the general election but they were only divulged on the last day on which the Scottish parliament was sitting before its lengthy summer recess.[14] Thanks in part to plummeting oil prices, a Scotland poised to become independent would be facing a deficit of over £10 billion according to the Institute for Fiscal Studies, figures acknowledged by the SNP as broadly correct. However much the laws of political gravity currently favour the SNP, it is unlikely that any rulers of a newly independent country could easily withstand the backlash that would ensue from the unavoidable austerity measures. The acquisition of the power long desired by the SNP would automatically impose the economic pressures that made most of UK Labour's periods in office stormy and largely unsuccessful.

But as long as unpopular spending measures are seen as coming from distant London, the ruling SNP can present itself as an oppositional force which is 'Stronger for Scotland' (its 2015 electoral slogan). Its years in government have been dominated by campaigning and then establishing political control over the machinery of the Scottish state. Progress in these respects usually dominates the proceedings of its spring and autumn conferences. These are showcases for the emotionalism of Scottish nationalism which remains its dominant feature. Projecting Scotland as a quasi-religious cause creates the political mortar that binds together the various elements making up the party.

The conference provides a surge of emotional solidarity by emphasising how the nation still under-achieves due to being imprisoned in a state which has narrow southern English priorities. The looming shadow of the English colossus enables ranks to be closed. The numerous misfortunes Scotland faces can be attributed to this nearby overlord or to its local political accomplices.

Invariably, the party takes to its heart leaders who can articulate these grievances and promise resistance. A blame culture, in which the only domestic force which needs to examine its conduct is the Labour party, does not prepare the party to face up to troublesome issues like Scotland's multi-facetted social crisis which is unlikely to go away if and when the English retreat across the border. The party has largely remained a vast comfort zone unwilling to place a mirror in front of the nation's pock-marked face. It is unlikely that many of its devotees will wish to subject the party to any close examination as revelations about the conduct of ministers and MPs in the autumn of 2015 shows how much in reality it stands for the continuation of the 'old politics'. The only new innovation has been the barely-subdued personality cult that has grown up around Alex Salmond but also Nicola Sturgeon since at least the year of the 2007 party conference.

Until the 1990s the SNP's leaders were usually restrained figures. But an air of hysteria surrounds the duopoly that has reigned within the SNP since 2004. Especially once power was tasted, Alex and Nicola were treated at conference events by mature Scots virtually like rock stars. Their ability to torment Unionist rivals and throw the British establishment onto the defensive made them stellar performers who soon had no equal at the United Kingdom party conference season.

SNP Housekeeping

For 14 years as chief executive, Peter Murrell has choreographed the party conference. He was once Salmond's constituency assistant and in 2010 he married Nicola Sturgeon after a longstanding relationship. Since 2001, his salary has risen from £35,000 to more than £100,000. But he is self-effacing and does not hog the media as his arguably rather less successful Labour counterpart, Peter Mandelson, did from the mid-1980s onwards. At the typical SNP conference, one journalist has described him as 'usually standing in the shadows to the side of the stage.

He whispers instructions to Cabinet ministers as they prepare to make keynote speeches and is more powerful than anyone watching Mr Salmond's tub-thumping performances on the TV could possibly realise.

Only after Miss Sturgeon's speech, when he kisses his wife, does he appear in the spotlight'.[15]

Writing after the spring 2015 conference, another journalist stated that:
' the [SNP] folk who have spoken to me believe there must be distance between the posts of party leader and chief executive.

Insiders believe it is inevitable that a married couple in this situation will privately chew the fat on crucial party matters – finance, strategy, personnel – which could create problems for the SNP's democratic structures'.[16]

But the crucial point is that 'supporters credit' Peter Murrell 'with creating one of Europe's most formidable election machines'.[17] Much can be overlooked or forgiven if any political operator delivers success for the party troops to the degree that he has done. He is patient, disciplined and (apparently) collegiate. Even though married to the party leader, he only became the story in October 2015 when details of his role in supervising the pro-independence group Business for Scotland emerged. Overall, his burdens have been greatly eased by the availability of an unlimited flow of party finance during the years of SNP domination in Scotland.

Scottish Nationalism's benefactors have been a couple from Ayrshire, Chris and Colin Weir. These long-time SNP supporters enjoyed a huge £160 million lottery win in 2011. They donated a total of £4.5m to the SNP and the Yes campaign since their win. It means almost 80 per cent of £4.9 million funding for the independence campaign emanated from just one source.[18]

The Sturgeon-Murrell combination does not appear unusual in an era of pluralist politics where husband and wife, siblings, and other close relatives have swopped, or been in contention for, senior office in the democratic West from France to the USA. The hapless British Labour Party arguably allowed family politics to go too far when a less talented figure Ed Miliband stood against his more senior and better-rated sibling David for the leadership and beat him narrowly with the help of trade-union votes in 2010. It is hard to see this happening in the SNP only because it is a more disciplined party. But family politics is alive and well practically at all levels of the SNP perhaps to a greater degree than in any other major UK party. It undermines recurring complaints from the Nationalists that Westminster is an inbred Parliament full of coteries and cabals.

Dynastic Politics

Tom Johnston, one of the pre-1945 Scottish Labour heavyweights, wrote a book called *Our Noble Families*, exploring the dubious origins of leading aristocratic families in Scotland.[19] Perhaps the time may be fast approaching when the family politics of the SNP might be the subject of a slimmer and more upright book. Winnie Ewing, the first SNP figure to make a lasting breakthrough in electoral politics, has spawned a political dynasty. She is the mother of the MSP and minister Fergus and of Annabelle also an MSP. Fergus was the husband of the late Margaret Ewing, a Westminster and later Holyrood parliamentarian and a leadership contender in 1990.

In November 2014 when there was a contest for the deputy leadership involving three SNP politicians, it was instructive to see the family dynamics. Stuart Hosie, the winner, MP for Dundee East, is the husband of Shona Robison who was promoted to being Health secretary later in the same month. The runner up Keith Brown is the partner of the MSP Christina McKelvie.[20]

In third place was Angela Constance, the newly-appointed Education secretary. Her husband is a seasoned SNP activist and her father-in-law was an SNP deputy provost in East Lothian. A sizeable number of SNP parliamentarians, in both chambers where the SNP sits, employ close relatives in political roles. Nicola Sturgeon used to employ her mother and her sister at Holyrood. Both she and Salmond are childless which means that a dynastic succession is unlikely for the two best-known figures. But even if their emblematic names were to be carried forward to another generation of political office, it is unlikely if it would cause dismay among many voters. Many Scots dislike the Labour practice of sending its political warhorses to the House of Lords but only a minority would appear to believe that nepotism may have crept into the SNP, given the huge numbers now prepared to vote for the party. From 2015, much of north Ayrshire was represented by a husband and wife team, Kenny Gibson in the Scottish parliament and now his wife Patricia at Westminster. The new MP for Glasgow North-West Carol Monaghan joined her husband Feargal Dalton who represented part of the constituency on Glasgow city council.

A close-knit and tribal party like the SNP, often struggles to have a rich inner life. There are few think-tanks given the scope of its ambitions to remake the face of Scotland. Fringe meetings in which party thinkers or specialists in a specific policy area float new ideas are conspicuous by their absence (certainly compared with the SNP's rivals at UK level). Radical figures such as the late Stephen Maxwell or Isobel Lindsay, holders of the view that independence is only one step in the drive to transform Scotland, often failed to convince SNP selection committees for elective office. Even a former leader like Gordon Wilson disqualified himself from making a comeback at Holyrood in the late 1990s because of his scepticism that devolution would lead to independence. After this view was argued by him in print, he relates that he got a phone call 'from my former protégé John Swinney in which he expressed his regret that my long years of service would now be over....the message was clear. I was in the cold. It was not unexpected. Independent views were frowned upon in the prevailing orthodoxy'.[21]

Kicking Salmond Upstairs

Another way of looking at it was that Wilson had simply outlived his usefulness as a front-rank politician. His successor Salmond bowed out with a far more impressive electoral track-record. But Salmond had failed to secure a victory in the 2014 referendum arguably with so much going for the party. At least one major miscalculation over the currency union was clearly down to him. Before he voluntarily quit on 14 September, the press picked up internal rumblings of discontent about his *ad hominem* and impulsive style of leadership.[22] The timing of his departure was adept, however, knocking the shine off the No side's victory and helping to turn it into a pyrrhic one. But after the transfer of power, he showed signs of wishing to prolong his influence. In March 2015, he claimed that as the best-known figure of a much-reinforced SNP line-up at Westminster, he would act as the kingmaker and install Ed Miliband in Downing Street. 'I'm leading the SNP campaign' he said which brought the response from his successor that he was a member of her team.[23]

SNP elders also hardly bothered to conceal their determination that he would not automatically become leader of the parliamentary party at Westminster; potentially this would have enabled him to overshadow Nicola Sturgeon and it would have meant that Angus Robertson's long service as the SNP's Westminster leader would be rudely tossed aside. The previously low-profile Robertson was hailed in different SNP quarters for his qualities. Thus Peter Curran, a fluent SNP blogger wrote in March 2015: 'Angus Robertson, the modest hero of the SNP, the architect of so much of its success - our leader in Westminster. We owe so much to this man'.[24] It was even claimed that Stuart Hosie had prompted a BBC interviewer to ask him about the leadership of the SNP Westminster in order to be able to assert that there was certainly no vacancy.[25]

The Fixers who made Alex Box Office

There had been no recognisable group of Salmond loyalists in the parliamentary party to whom he could turn to in difficult moments. But he did promote figures whose authority derived from their closeness to him and not from any status or office they enjoyed within the party. He built up a team of advisers who came to form a nerve-centre of backroom staffers loyal to him. Perhaps the most durable one was Kevin Pringle, the son of a Perth milkman and a graduate of Aberdeen University, who joined the SNP at the age of 18. Nearly thirty years later, in June 2015, it was announced that he was stepping down as the strategic communications director for the SNP. Soon after, he joined Charlotte St Partners, a public relations firm that advises private clients on relations with government, having honed a communications strategy for the SNP which had enabled it to retain the initiative against a hostile and sceptical media.[26] He had rescued the at times over-confident Salmond from potentially severe difficulties thanks to poorly-thought-out gestures or statements. Above all, he had pioneered the party's online media strategy which perhaps was the main explanation for the mastery it had acquired over the Scottish political scene by 2014-15. As early as 1998, Sturgeon said that he was the SNP's 'biggest asset'.[27]

Another figure whose influence steadily grew was Stephen Noon. He wrote the SNP's 2011 manifesto and became the chief strategist at Yes Scotland. He exemplifies Salmond's knack of choosing talented if slightly unconventional figures who might have risen far more slowly under a more staid leader. A Jesuit-educated former Young Conservative, he was sacked as press secretary to the head of the Catholic Church in England for being gay and was very quickly taken on board by Salmond.[28] He promoted an optimistic image for the party designed to reach out to liberal, modernising citizens in a nation rapidly forsaking traditional loyalties in term of religion, lifestyle and attitudes. Many of those 'post-modern' Scots would vote for an independence choice for the first time ever in 2011.

Alex Bell was another outsider promoted to be head of policy in Salmond's office but he proved to be more radical in his thinking than the First Minister. He quit in July 2013 over the cautious approach of his boss to the flagship document on independence. He wrote in September 2013: 'The SNP must decide if the point of the white paper is to give a tactical answer that will win hearts or a more profound assessment that will persuade minds. So far it has opted for the former, with polls suggesting it has yet to pay off'.[29]

Geoff Aberdein, Salmond's Chief of Staff was another hard-driving figure whose career had flourished thanks to being an able and loyal lieutenant to the chief rather than a party regular. But for a large part of the marathon campaign, these attractively Machiavellian figures (who would have no counterparts on the No side) kept out of sight.

A broadly-based campaign had been launched on 25 May 2012 which saw the Green Party and the Scottish Socialist party working with the SNP to secure a 'Yes' vote when the time came for voters to answer the referendum question, 'Should Scotland be an Independent country'? It expanded to include groups representing intellectuals and professionals in the creative industries, while reaching out to women and restive Labour voters. The Radical Independence Campaign (RIC), the left-leaning National Collective, Women for Independence and Labour for Independence sought to win over groups hitherto numb to independence. Their leading lights spoke at thousands of 'Yes' rallies across Scotland. Niche groups were formed meant to show a well-spring of backing from occupational groups and from civic Scotland. An unmistakeably left-wing vision of the future was rolled out at rallies and meetings where the language of class conflict could be heard, especially in lower-income areas. But there was also 'Business for Scotland', a grouping of mainly small business figures supposed to indicate that plenty of entrepreneurs believed that there was also room for them in the Yes side's state-led vision for change.

The SNP appeared to be dwarfed by these new forces. When balance sheets were being drawn up after the referendum, it came in for some uninhibited criticism for its lack of martial spirit. Thus Robin McAlpine, of Commonweal, one of the most visible of the new nationalists, publicly accused it of caution and passivity:
'...the SNP spent a year being dragged around behind a much more vibrant non-par-

ty campaign that did most of the groundwork. It wasn't the SNP that changed the discourse in Scotland – in the early stages of the campaign the "don't rock the boat" message was the gospel. It was when the public responded to campaigns by RIC or Women for Indy or NHS Yes or Business for Scotland or National Collective that the SNP appeared almost forced to come in behind a campaign that was distinctly more radical and imaginative than anything it itself anticipated – or seemed to want'.[30]

Not just McAlpine himself but well-known journalists (in an age when a struggling media profession was increasingly defined by celebrity writers), were usually far more prominent than SNP parliamentarians on the campaign trail. But it was a combative and often aggressively personal online blog, 'Wings over Scotland', which became the most visible exponent of a Yes vote. The brainchild of a video games expert, Stuart Campbell, from his base in the Somerset town of Bath this expatriate Scot created a powerful online hub for cyber nationalism. Its fiery and demagogic attacks on the No side', allied to a self-righteous fervour, soon gave it a cult following among many Scots who were being drawn to the nationalist cause. Campbell's belligerency and undeniable talent for deconstructing the claims of pro-Union media, made this irascible and enigmatic figure the darling of Scots who wanted their champions to shoot from the hips and take no prisoners.[31]

By the summer of 2014, it was acquiring 4.5 million page views a month. Few, if any, political blogs elsewhere in the English-speaking world have ever managed to wield so much influence in a political struggle. For this alone, Wings is likely to be a subject of great attention in the academic field of media studies, perhaps for years to come. It produced, a pocket sized guide, the *Wee Blue Book,* arguing in favour of the viability of independence, which was freely distributed across Scotland in the closing stages of the campaign. In some eyes, without this booklet and the often razor-sharp assaults on the credibility of the NO camp, the Yes vote would have been unable to get above 40 per cent on 18 September. Campbell had created an autonomous branch of the Scottish nationalist movement in cyberspace which in certain respects was more vigorous than its terrestrial counterpart.

Many supporters saw Wings, and not the SNP, as their political family. On 31 December 2014, when Campbell was reviewing the impact of Wings, one admirer went online to tell him: 'I would give you one of my kidneys if you needed it. Huge gratitude for all your magnificent work'.[32] Its online crusade for independence engendered an ardent sense of solidarity more reminiscent of the comradeship among soldiers returning from the World War 1 front who threw themselves into political battles at home.

This was high octane propaganda which the SNP's own worthy publication, the *Scots Independent*, and indeed the Yes campaign in the demure hands of the former television executive, Blair Jenkins (until kicked upstairs in early 2014), never came near to emulating. Yet the SNP, or at least it's artful and determined leader, Alex Salmond never actually lost control of the campaign. Important political tasks had been franchised out to new allies. But the party's priorities remained central drivers of the Independence effort.

A sign of the SNP's anxiety to give the Yes campaign greater depth and direction was the arrival in its midst in May 2013 of Mark Shaw, a young Aberdeen-based property developer. Initially, he may only have had a part-time consultancy role but he was already talking in an authoritative manner about the need for the Yes campaign to raise its performance. He observed that 'People are not engaged yet. Next year they will get engaged'. He was also one of those who believed that 'we only get one shot at this', remarking also that 'everyone needs to be at the top of their game'.[33] He would later contribute £50,000 to the Yes side but perhaps Shaw's greatest service was to help ensure that tough hiring and firing decisions were not shirked so as to ensure that the Yes campaign maintained a vigorous campaigning advantage and did not grow complacent.[34]

Polls were showing that little more than one-third of voters were backing independence when Kevin Pringle, 'Salmond's most trusted adviser' was installed at the Glasgow headquarters of Yes Scotland in September 2013. In a press article announcing the step, an SNP source was quoted as saying that there was 'widespread concern' in the party's parliamentary ranks about the performance of Blair Jenkins.

SNP figures talked admiringly of Shaw as a no-nonsense figure who had shown an ability to 'cut through the flannel' in political campaigning in previous involvement with the party.[35] But some of the party's referendum allies found it hard to adapt to vigorous campaigning. After being dropped from the executive of Yes Scotland in early 2014, the Green Party's Stan Blackley complained that Yes Scotland no longer fully reflects the wider groups of people and parties seeking independence. There may have been a great deal of truth in his claim that:

'The wider Yes campaign has become a movement of the people, become cross-party and non-party with those without party affiliation now vastly outnumbering those with it...It has moved away from political identities to become something more diverse and more convincing than the SNP, and in doing so has left Yes Scotland behind'.[36]

But it may have been a tribute to the SNP's strategic planning that the Yes movement had attained such dimensions. Its poll ratings rose as the new professional touch became more apparent. The SNP had issued a statement after Blackley's departure saying that it was a time for a new emphasis in grassroots campaigning.[37] By September 2014, the claim by the chief strategist on the Yes side Stephen Noon that 'the biggest grassroots campaign in Scotland's history' had been rolled out was eminently believable. Andrew Gilligan of the *Daily Telegraph* in the same month wrote that 'the SNP ground operation, the best in Britain, was the first in the world to use the precision voter-targeting software that swept Obama to power in 2008, and has honed it since behind most "grassroots" street-stalls there's a Yesser with a smartphone'.[38]

Churchillian Salmond

The parallel may prove fanciful or even offensive for some but it is possible to offer a tentative comparison between the way the British government mobilised in 1940 to repel Hitler and the impact of the separatist campaign in Scotland in 2013-14. To mount effective resistance, Churchill reached far beyond his own Conservative Party and offered a common front based on the upholding of patriotism and freedom. He also reached out to talented, unconventional and hardnosed figures in different walks of life who would have been unlikely to attain political influence in more normal times. Arguably Salmond displayed some of this Churchillian flair for improvisation. The Weir's fortune meant that he had more resources than the cash-strapped British state could claim in 1940. But he made good use of these resources and helped ensure that inspiring symbolism and rhetoric enabled the cause to reach out to many previously quite numb to its charms. His own usefulness to the cause, especially in reaching out to undecided voters, was at times highly doubtful just as there were points when Churchill's conduct of the war was plainly erratic. Only five months before the referendum, in a poll of 1003 Scottish voters, 36 per cent said the thought of Salmond running an independent Scotland was pushing them towards a No vote in September's referendum. The findings came just days after the SNP leader was branded a liability to the Yes campaign by senior nationalist Jim Sillars.[39] Churchill's own wartime popularity levels were not as high as might have been expected and he went down to defeat in the 1945 election. Salmond turned his own defeat into a potential victory by quitting before he faced calls from within his party's ranks to allow his capable deputy to lead the assault on the Union.

One of those swept up in the patriotic fervour of Scotland in 2014 was Lauren Reid from Bathgate in West Lothian. Afterwards, she wrote eloquently about her 'journey from No to Yes':

'I'm a true convert, and once I crossed over I got busy – I leafleted and canvassed and worked my socks off as most activists do. I never joined the SNP because on the doorsteps I liked being able to say "it's not all about the SNP, I'm not a member". But after the referendum I did join. I joined because I knew that I could still be actively involved in campaigning for independence. Within a few months I was chosen to be Branch Organiser in my hometown of Bathgate. Every time a new leaflet came out I counted 10,000 leaflets into their individual runs and delivered them to volunteers and I delivered the ones that that no one else wanted to do after I'd done my own.

I organised training days and visited new members, encouraging them to get involved. Wednesday nights and Friday afternoons were spent on canvassing sessions. For the by-election in nearby Armadale I'd get up on a Saturday morning, leave the kids with my partner and chap doors. On other Saturdays I manned street stalls.

Monday and Tuesday were spent building the constituency website where each of the branches could have space to communicate outside the confines of internal emails but in private. I went to constituency meetings and was also made Political Education Officer. I was actively campaigning full-time while having a job, four young children and a house to run.

I didn't mind that I had very little time to see my friends, I didn't mind that I had to give up our family time at the weekends, I didn't mind that my petrol budget doubled, I didn't mind that I missed my wee girl singing solo at a school opening ceremony because I was out canvassing. It was all for the cause, for a better Scotland'.[40]

Anecdotal evidence suggests that Lauren Reid's journey from disengagement to intense commitment was repeated numerous times over in plenty of Scottish cities and towns. It suggests that the planning of Stephen Noon and others to create 'a groundswell of support, with Yes supporters and volunteers engaging with people in their social circles to move them closer and closer to a Yes vote', paid off. He wrote a month before the referendum: 'That effect – the power of the social network – has been part of a slow-burn as we nudge people up the support scale. It is working and the pace is gathering.

Across the movement, our focus is on Scotland's wealth of talent and resources and the firm belief that there is so much more that our nation can achieve. We know there are challenges ahead and that independence, while not a magic wand, gives us the powers we need to meet those challenges head on, and overcome them'.[41]

But such opportunities for political mobilisation would not have been so easily available if those directing the No strategy at the heart of British government had not (very early on) made blunders perhaps similar in scale to those committed by the losing side in the Second World War. Allowing a party already known for its campaigning prowess a period of over two years to campaign for its core goal, knowing that it had the ample resources of the Scottish state to draw upon, was a massive blunder on the part of David Cameron. It was only matched by his agreement to a question which had the forces of separation campaigning for a positive 'Yes' vote and their pro-British adversaries thrown onto the defensive, urging a 'No' vote.

The SNP and its Post-Referendum Lottery Win

CHAPTER TWO, THE PARTY

Thanks to reliance on a Canadian polling company, by September 2014 Salmond was convinced that his side would pull off a shock 8 point victory.[42] No held on but there was a massive consolation prize for Yes. The SNP managed to convert independence supporters to SNP supporters. Tens of thousands of people, energised by the campaign, refused to be stood down; many of them refused to meekly accept the referendum result and preferred resistance by other means via the SNP. Robin McAlpine, a stormy petrel of the campaign, warned in the referendum's aftermath that the SNP would not be able to contain the army of Scottish radicals pouring into the party.

He was sharply critical of the leadership for suspending councillors who had publicly burned copies of the report on devolution chaired by Lord Smith (which the SNP had endorsed). He expressed scorn for the caution of old guard figures vetting parliamentary candidates. He warned that 'if the leadership can't understand that politics has changed it will suffer'.

Writing at the start of 2015, he was convinced that two SNPs were now in existence. There is, 'a pre-referendum party ' led by 'a manager class; which perhaps unkindly McAlpine believed 'would have lost the referendum in a dispiritingly weak manner'.[43] Emerging alongside the existing party and already dwarfing it in size, is a new SNP. Not only the rhetoric but the dedication and activism shown by many of the new members shows that they wish to be architects of a new nation. They could be described as independence revolutionaries and they are in a party dominated by independence gradualists whose predecessors expelled members, and proscribed groups, which wished to flirt with extra-parliamentary politics.

McAlpine believed that the pre-referendum SNP establishment simply must realise that a changed Scotland has emerged from the crucible of the referendum campaign. The party must embrace the new politics instead of assuming that the referendum was an exceptional event and that the energy of members old and new must be channelled into predictable fields.

But the SNP did not behave in the defensive and unimaginative way McAlpine assumed it would. There was indeed a managerial party which under Nicola Sturgeon would make it clear that boundaries needed to be placed around militant behaviour especially online and in the street. But the rules of the party were modified so as to allow new members the right to vote in the selection meetings for Westminster seats being held in the winter of 2014-15. New candidates, such as Tommy Sheppard and Mhairi Black, had already shown proof of their radicalism. But there was a high-profile casualty, Craig Murray, a member of the SNP since 2011. This former British ambassador had acquired fame for exposing human rights abuses in Uzbekistan and noisily leaving the diplomatic service. He had been a prominent independence campaigner and had been asked by SNP activists in three central Scotland seats to stand for Westminster. Hugh Kerr, an SNP activist and a former Labour MEP, stated that 'he would make an excellent MP and could be the SNP foreign affairs spokesperson after all he knows where the bodies are buried![44] However, he unexpectedly failed the SNP's internal vetting process in December 2014.[45]

56-year-old Murray said that he was spurned for lacking 'commitment on group discipline' after being asked if he would vote for the bedroom tax if told to by the SNP leadership as part of a Westminster deal with another party. His answer was No. He said the question was absurd given it was clear SNP policy to reject this tax. It was a ploy to find an excuse to eliminate him as a possible candidate, 'classic Labour.. political management', he alleged in his blog. He wrote about being 'astonished by the hostility of the appeals board', chaired by an SNP MEP, Ian Hudghton who was also the party President, and two MSPs.[46]

Like McAlpine, he observed 'a conflict between the existing party hierarchy and the energy of the Yes campaign'. He was frank about the temporary lowering of the spirit it had caused him just as he moved to begin a new life in Scotland: 'I'm really sad, because like many people from the Yes movement I believed we were building a new kind of politics in Scotland. Instead, the SNP just seems to be trying to replicate classic Labour Party Tammany Hall political management'.[47] The issue played out on his blog with SNP members and supporters commiserating with him or else pointing out that there might be grounds to see him as a stranger to institutional discipline.[48]

Conservative MSP Murdo Fraser said the exclusion of Murray showed the SNP was only prepared to select candidates for the election who showed "slavish" loyalty to the party leadership.[49] But the ex-diplomat got short shrift from *Scotland on Sunday*. An editorial found his complaints about the SNP exaggerated suggesting 'a fondness for a conspiracy theory [rather] than any rational analysis about the state of the SNP leadership. The more sensible conclusion is Murray has misunderstood the nature of the modern SNP – and the SNP has understood the nature of Craig Murray all too well'.[50]

Old Guard Determined to Stay in Charge

Several months later, the SNP announced a loyalty test for its Westminster MPs which Murray might have had difficulty in adhering to. Under the proposed changes to internal rules, all of the party's MPs would be required to sign up to a code of conduct pledging they would not 'publicly criticise a decision, policy or another member' of the SNP's Westminster group, either in parliament or in other venues such as the media.

The proposals were drawn up by the SNP's Westminster leader, Angus Robertson

MP, and fellow MP Pete Wishart. They were included in the draft list of motions for the party's spring conference. So were further changes that would give the party's National Executive Committee (NEC) the ability to exercise some control over both constituency and regional MSP candidate selection for the 2016 Scottish parliament elections.[51] For the last 12 years, local SNP branches had selected candidates on a one member one vote system.

The SNP was not lacking would-be parliamentarians content to be managed. A few days after the proposed changes were announced, Brendan O'Hara said in his address to SNP party members during his successful bid to be selected to represent his party in the contest for the Argyll and Bute seat: 'In this next Parliament LOY-ALTY and DISCIPLINE will be essential. After 33 years of SNP membership I will not break ranks with the parliamentary group when the going, as it surely will gets tough.'[52] Such an expression of orthodoxy would not have been out of place from a Scottish Labour loyalist during the heyday of the autocratic Willie Ross in the 1960s. But the conference endorsed these and other leadership-directed changes without demur. Craig Murray attended the conference and he did not hide his dismay about further evidence that the SNP remained a highly managed force even against a background of the radical tumult which had swept over Scotland:

'The entire first day there was not a motion that was passed other than by acclaim, and there was not a single speech against anything, though there were a couple of attempts at referral back. The only item permitted on to the conference agenda, in closed session on day 2, that was in the least likely to cause controversy was the adoption of all women shortlists – and the only reason that was on the agenda was that the leader made it abundantly plain she wanted it. I incline to the view that as a short term measure it is justified, but I abstained because I did not like what I saw of the way it was managed.

It was the only debate the leader sat through, and it was very plain she was watching carefully how people were voting. There was a definite claque of paid party apparatchiks and organised feminists occupying front centre of the hall. There was a strong suspicion, voiced by Christine Grahame, that deliberately weak and left field speakers had been chosen against women shortlists. And for the vote, party functionaries including Angus Robertson and Ian McCann stood at the side of the hall very ostensibly noting who voted which way and making sure that the payroll vote performed. I was right next to where Angus Robertson stood as he did this. He moved into position just before the vote, made it very obvious indeed what he was doing, and left immediately after. I found myself regarding the prospect of a whole raft of new MPs, their research assistants and secretaries providing 200 more payroll votes, as depressing'.

I had intended to speak against the new standing orders for Westminster MPs, which contain eleven draconian clauses on whipping and discipline, as against three more liberal ones in the old standing orders. I confess I did not get to speak because the item was called at 9.05 on Sunday morning, on the morning the clocks went forward, and I was commuting from Edinburgh. The spirit was willing but the flesh is pretty knackered'.[53]

In recent times, the only occasion when the leadership ever faced a real struggle in getting a critical motion passed was in 2012. Supporting NATO was seen as crucial if Alex Salmond's hope of allaying the fears of moderate Scots hesitant about independence were to get anywhere. Therefore, a motion to overturn the SNP's long-standing opposition to membership of NATO was tabled that year. But conference delegates were split and they voted by 394 to 365 to back a new policy to support this policy change. Severin Carrell of the *Guardian* related: 'The result was far narrower than SNP leaders had expected, after numerous delegates said it would be hypocritical to join Nato while upholding the party's historic opposition to nuclear weapons, with the UK's nuclear arsenal based on the Clyde near Glasgow. To boos, Angus Robertson, the SNP's defence spokesman, said that 75% of Scots wanted the country inside NATO and their support was essential if the SNP wanted to win the referendum'.[54]

Soon after, two MSPs, John Finnie and Jean Urquhart, quit the party in protest and in late 2014 another one John Wilson, cited his dissatisfaction with the policy for his decision to sit as an Independent.

Manacling the Far-Left

The SNP had become the only real nationalist show in town by the spring of 2015. A year before, as the journalist Peter Geoghegan pointed out, it had been impossible not to collide with many people at Yes events who would declare, often quite solemnly, 'I am not a nationalist but...', only to quickly extol the virtues of independence. 'Energetic, opinionated, often youthful', these non-SNPers 'provided the most irreverent and interesting moments of the campaign'. Yet they appeared to have been scooped up by the party whose membership had risen five fold since September 2014. Other parties in the Yes alliance had registered membership growth but it was tiny compared with the transformation in the size of the SNP. As Geoghegan related: 'rather than a thousand flowers blooming, a single tall poppy has dominated the post-referendum garden. The much-vaunted Yes Alliance never got off the ground, in large part because the SNP had nothing to gain from an electoral pact when they could expect the overwhelming majority of Yes voters to rally behind the party'.[55]

Any alliances which the SNP made with its radical left allies of 2013-14 were very much on the party's terms. Thus some party figures such as deputy leader Stewart

Hosie reached out to Hope over Fear very much the vehicle for Tommy Sheridan, the leader of Solidarity.[56] He had organised a series of Hope Over Fear events during the referendum and had urged voters on the far-left to back the SNP in the 2015 general election. He had, however, been frozen out of the official Yes campaign by the leaders of Yes Scotland. Other prominent pro-yes groups, such as Radical Independence and Women for Independence, refused to share platforms with him.[57]

Sheridan had become a divisive figure ever since a deeply acrimonious split in the Scottish Socialist Party (SSP). He had been its lone MSP from 1999 to 2003 when it won another six seats. But the party soon split over his style of leadership. In 2006, he managed to defeat the publishers of the *News of the World* newspaper in a defamation case over allegations he was an adulterer and swinger. However, five years later Sheridan received a three-year jail sentence for perjuring himself in the initial trial. His conviction was largely based on testimony from former SSP colleagues who were branded by Sheridan as liars, an allegation they emphatically denied.[58]

In June 2015, it was announced that the SNP would be entering into an electoral pact with the SSP and others who had formed an electoral alliance called Rise. If it gains seats at Holyrood in 2016, almost certainly this would be at the expense of the Labour Party now in desperate trouble after its rout in the general election.

The SNP appeared capable of acting as a grand political overlord able to shape the fate of its once feared rival. A fierce barrage of invective directed at Jim Murphy had undermined his 5-month leadership of Scottish Labour. SNP online backers, and those writing for the new daily paper the *National*, repeatedly denounced the party for having a leader with such a British orientation. SNP politicians joined with these media allies in demanding that Labour select a leader who would cut its historic ties with the party across Britain and work closely with indigenous forces defending Scottish interests at Westminster and Holyrood. At times, the SNP appeared to be acting as if it had the prior right to define the orientation of its opponents. It was a paramount force under whom a 'saltire has been draped across the entire electorate...' Scotland's voters have all been claimed for the SNP', wrote one dazzled commentator in late 2014: 'We're all Alex Salmond's bairns'.[59]

The veteran Scottish commentator Gerry Hassan had frequently extolled mass engagement in Scottish politics but he noticed a 'palpable evasiveness in talking about some of the big issues Scotland faces' in the wake of the SNP's 2015 electoral triumph. A reader pointed out to him that:

'We increasingly seem to live in a society (in Scotland) where you just don't ask too many awkward questions, don't put your head above the parapet, don't rock the boat - whether you're in business wanting government contracts, in academia, in broadcasting, or in the arts wanting government grants.

I think a lot of this tendency towards [the] authoritarian "you'll do what's good for you and keep your mouth shut" is a Scottish cultural thing - part of our centuries-old heritage that we prefer not to acknowledge while we constantly big up our supposed "egalitarianism".[60]

The evidence that the SNP wished to keep tight hold of a battery of controls in a managed democracy was mounting. The parliamentary party had few independent–minded figures wishing to stand up for citizens rights against an over-mighty state. In 2014, the educationalist professor Walter Humes expressed his fears that an 'authoritarian drift' would be the outcome of such a total ascendancy by one party. He wrote:

'It is not difficult to construct a narrative of recent political developments which suggest an alarming centralist drift in a number of policy areas.

First, we have had the restructuring of important organisations (Police Scotland, Creative Scotland, Education Scotland), all with a similar "brand" which seems to imply that "Scottishness" in itself is a guarantee of quality. ...

'One of the lessons of history' which he believed only too applicable for Scotland 'is that movements which advance under the banner of freedom often soon reveal an oppressive agenda of control'.[61]

Moves to impose intrusive state direction on Scotland's universities in 2015 perhaps confirmed Professor Humes's fears rather earlier than even he himself had anticipated.

Harnessing Ethnic Passion

The SNP's rise to such a level of electoral domination meant a new challenge: the party had to engage with the politics of ethnicity. The pace of migration into Scotland had been smaller than in urban England since the 1960s but by 2015 there was a South Asian (and mainly Pakistani Muslim) community, a growing number of Poles and a community drawn from mainly pre-1914 Irish Roman Catholic immigrants to Scotland which had held aloof from the rest of the population in important respects and had encountered prejudice over a long period.

The depth of divisions had been revealed in an acrimonious by-election in the Lanarkshire seat of Monklands East in 1994. Afterwards, as a historian of the SNP relates:

'the party established an ad hoc committee comprised of Catholic-SNP supporters to discuss initiatives to build links to the Catholic community. The committee met informally for several months under the leadership of...Mike Russell. Its main role was to encourage the party leadership in giving prominence to campaigning against the Act of Settlement..it was an important symbol of anti-Catholic discrimination in the UK which was sanctioned by the state. By focusing on it determinedly in the

1990s, the SNP did itself no harm among Scotland's Catholics.[62]

Before his death in 2001, Cardinal Thomas Winning had offered a public endorsement to the SNP and his successor Cardinal Keith O'Brien would be even less inhibited in doing so.[63] In time the Catholic church acquired senior office-holders with an SNP background as parliamentary candidates or else with quite overt nationalist sympathies. Archbishop Philip Tartaglia of Glasgow made headlines in 2014 by being outspoken in his praise for Alex Salmond when he stepped down from his political offices and in effusively welcoming a successor who was firmly secular in outlook.[64]

By the autumn of 2014, the evidence was growing that people of ethnic Irish background had been to the fore in Scotland embracing the 'Yes' cause. Within weeks of the referendum, Glasgow had a near five-fold rise in membership and nearby Motherwell and Coatbridge had six-fold increases.[65] These are the heartlands of a community once defined by deep Catholic loyalties.[66] But by 2011 Lowland Scotland's Catholic community was in the process of dumping old orthodoxies, not just once strong Labour ties but also any meaningful connection with the faith of its fathers: attendance at Mass has collapsed in many areas and many nominal Catholics disdain marriage in favour of un-consecrated relationships. It was perhaps understandable that some clerics wished to preserve links with a rapidly secularising community by identifying with some of their ethnic emblems which included passionate backing for the Glasgow-based Celtic football club. Thus a cultural if not a devotional brand of Catholicism could be preserved.

Economic inactivity had also encouraged restiveness especially among middle-aged and male Catholics. Sometimes amounting to outright alienation with Britain,[67] it meant that the SNP's message of defiance was likely to strike a chord with people who may never move very far from their areas or have many links with the rest of Britain. Alex Salmond's image as a rule-breaker and agitator was bound to go down well with such mutinous voters. His movement had popularised anti-British sentiment not just among Clydeside Scots with a rebel Irish background but also among others whose background might even be Orange and Protestant. In that sense the rise of the SNP had created an overlay across an enduring fault-line in west of Scotland.

As well as online sites promoting anti-British themes, Scotland's oldest minority also had a number of prominent commentators who were urging them to embrace change. Perhaps the best-known was Kevin McKenna.

A seasoned journalist from a family steeped in Glasgow Labour politics who writes (unfashionably) about his Catholic faith, he has an excellent record in promoting respect for rival religious traditions (including the Orange Order). In 2014-15, McKenna used his visibility in the Scottish as well as the London media to play up the SNP's radical credentials and disparage Labour's fitness to rely any longer on the votes of working-class Scots. Jim Murphy was disparaged as 'a man who has pocketed a small fortune in legitimately claimed expenses from Westminster'.[68] But he usually passed over in silence the lavish expenses of Alex Salmond and his ministers at home and abroad whose publication the Scottish government sought to prevent over many months.[69]

In often stirring prose, McKenna has done nothing to stifle the anti-British mindset of many Clydeside Catholics thanks to withering invective about 'old Etonians' and 'their midnight horse-trading in the Westminster gin palace'.[70] The appearance of British tanks and artillery in Glasgow's George Square in January 1919 is a theme regularly invoked in his columns with the implication that the British state is prepared to be ruthless if it is crossed by those who fail to recognise their place.[71]

During the 2015 election campaign The *Times* (owned by the pro-SNP Sir Rupert Murdoch), gave McKenna a regular column as 'Glasgow man' to articulate the restive mood of the city.[72] In September 2014 the prestigious *Scottish Field* magazine also gave him a spot where he interviewed Sir Tom Devine, 'the rock star of Caledonian historians' who had already played a role, both in his writings and regular public talks, in smoothing the path of fellow Catholics towards political nationalism.[73] Both these talented figures from a previously submerged community defined a rebellious message which is likely to have influenced some of its most discontented members but may also have had a wider impact.

Constituencies in which Scottish Catholics were numerous registered some of the biggest swings towards the SNP in May 2015. The same was true for ones with a sizeable Asian Muslim community. But this community was more volatile and unpredictable than the Hibernian Catholics who had given several generations of quiet loyalty to the Labour Party. The only upset for the SNP in the entire spring 2015 election campaign was the defection of Muhammad Shoaib, a former trusted aide of Nicola Sturgeon. He had led 'Asians for Independence' and claimed that 'nobody campaigned harder for a Yes vote than I did'. But on 6 April 2015 he announced his defection to Labour due to 'shock' at the number of senior SNP figures who he claimed secretly backed a Tory election victory.[74]

Sturgeon would have known that this was a quixotic gesture unlikely to halt the surge towards the SNP from Scotland's Muslims. But it was perhaps a sign that the community was less easily managed than the older Irish Diaspora one usually was. A Muslim community largely centred around Glasgow had seen more upward mobility than the proletarian Irish, it had an influential business sector, and there was little sign of domination by obscurantist clerics.[75] It had well-known professionals such as the defence lawyer Aamer Anwar who had defended numerous celebrity clients and who announced that he was joining the SNP shortly after the referendum. If he had hopes of gaining the nomination for the Glasgow Central seat where many Asians lived, these were disappointed as this went to Alison Thewliss, a low-profile councillor nevertheless elected on a 35 per cent swing.

In a controversial decision, the SNP rejected the choice of party members in the Coatbridge and Airdrie constituency when they chose sitting councillor Dr Imtiaz Majid as the SNP candidate.[76] New rules allowing the central party a final say in the selection of candidates were utilised and Phil Boswell, active in the oil sector, was selected.

It is quite likely that in a constituency with the strongest Catholic emigrant profile in Scotland, the Muslim candidate would have been comfortably elected so strong was the tide in the SNP's favour.[77] But, armed with new powers, the SNP had shown it was prepared to intervene forcefully in a constituency where in the past there had been ethnic tensions (on an intra-Christian basis). The Labour Party had been reticent about doing so in some urban English areas, thus allowing its local organization to acquire a communal flavour where patriarchal politics caught on.

The modern and decisive image of the SNP which impressed so many, convinced the young Glaswegian academic Amanullah de Sondy, senior lecturer in contemporary Islam at the University of Cork, to announce that he was voting for the SNP in 2015.[78] His blog 'Progressive Scottish Muslim' had, for some years promoted a liberal and inclusive Islam, one that in particular was sensitive to the contribution that Muslim women could play in enabling the West to be a successful place for inter-faith encounter. In 2008, de Sondy had offered words of criticism after the SNP had sponsored a Scottish Islamic Foundation which had a short-lived existence despite receiving ample government funding.[79] He wrote:

'The real issues that are hampering progress amongst the Muslim communities will not be resolved by politically motivated foundations but through a deep spiritual awakening and reasoning with Islamic theology where we realise that the beauty of Islam can live in us all as Muslims and quite comfortably in our beloved Scotland.'[80]

In May 2015 his blog featured a photo of Tasmina Ahmed-Sheikh, a cosmopolitan Asian woman, a former actress and now a lawyer, and the new MP for Ochil and Perthshire South. She had been nominated for a constituency with very few co-ethnics but was returned with a 10,000 majority (though in a swing noticeably smaller than what the SNP would get in most other seats).

The SNP 56 at Westminster

Publically, the prospective SNP contingent of Westminster MPs expected that there would be a hung parliament. Labour as the largest party, would be in government dependent on SNP backing for the passage of much of its legislation. This was the trajectory of many of the polls. But they turned out to be spectacularly misleading.

It didn't turn out that way. There was to be a single Conservative administration. Divested of the Liberal Democrats, David Cameron remained as Prime Minister with an overall working majority of 12 for his party. It was changed times for the SNP. Peter Curran, the SNP blogger had written on 28 March about the party's Westminster encampment as if it had been surrounded by predatory elements:

'Angus Robertson MP and Stewart Hosie MP, the two stalwarts of the lonely advance guard of six SNP MPs, who have spent years as a tiny embattled group on the Commons benches, surrounded by the hostile forces of unionism, alternately abused and patronised, facing the full wrath and hostility of all unionist parties, including abuse from their fellow Scots in Labour, Lib Dems and Tory ranks, exhausted by commuting to and from their constituencies and demanding party duties in Scotland.'[81]

The main initial task of the SNP's Westminster leaders would be to prepare 50 newcomers to act effectively in the interests of Scotland in the citadel of the ancestral foe. According to the pro-SNP commentator Derek Bateman, it had been alleged that one of the first acts of several of the newcomers was to visit the William Wallace Memorial at Smithfield, scene of his execution in 1307.[82] In her oratory-fuelled maiden speech on 14 July, Mhairi Black left her listeners in no doubt about the fact that 'William Wallace was born in my constituency.'[83]

Among the 56 were MPs with a social profile which, at first sight, a lot of ordinary citizens could relate to. Margaret Ferrier, who overturned a 21,000 Labour majority in Rutherglen and Hamilton West, was a 54-year-old working mother who had worked since the age of 16 and was a commercial sales manager.[84] But John McNally, a barber who was elected for Falkirk, was the only SNP MP *without* some kind of white-collar background. (At least four of Scottish Labour's 2010-15 MPs had been manual workers).

The most common occupations of the 56 SNPs at Westminster were in business and finance. 15 of the SNP's 50 new MPs had experience of business or had worked in the financial or corporate worlds. Seven had worked in the legal profession and eight had come from the media. One in six of Scotland's 59 MPs had been political professionals (three being part of the third sector).[85]

Several of the younger MPs had ample political experience, such as 30-year-old Callum McCaig, a former leader of Aberdeen city council, but several were virtually new to politics. Lisa Cameron, an NHS mental health consultant elected for East Kilbride, Strathaven & Lesmahagow, had only joined the SNP on 19 September 2014. Carol Monaghan, newly elected for Glasgow North-West on a 39 per cent swing, and a physics teacher at a secondary school, only became active in the SNP after the referendum.[86]

The SNP was given a group of 30 offices in a shiny new building on Parliament Street which Angus MacNeil, one of the veteran MPs, soon dubbed 'Jockalypse House', after a pun made by the Conservative Boris Johnson during the campaign.[87]

Contrary to the earlier prediction of Mure Dickie of the *Financial Times,* the background of the Scottish MPs was *not* 'sharply different from most incumbents' drawn from the rest of the UK.[88] But some did swiftly draw attention to themselves by their irreverent behaviour. Roger Mullin who won Gordon Brown's Kirkcaldy seat, took a 'selfie' standing at the dispatch box. There was clapping during early debates which breached unwritten protocol. A stand-off occurred with veteran Labour MP Dennis Skinner, after the SNP attempted to take prime spots on the Opposition front benches of the Commons occupied by the Labour Party. At least SNP members were successful in taking over what had been Labour's favourite bar, the Sports and Social Club, sometimes known as the Sports and Socialist.[89]

One *Daily Telegraph* journalist argued that the SNP had every right to throw its weight around at Westminster given the scale of its triumph.[90] But several of the Nationalist intake insisted that they would be a benign presence. Tommy Sheppard, who ran a successful Edinburgh comedy club and had been a councillor in Hackney and later assistant secretary of the Labour Party in Scotland, was at pains to point out:

'We are not a bunch of people coming down on the Megabus with claymores... We are all fundamentally reasonable and constructive people and we would go there … to work constructively with other people in the House... Don't expect us to be in the corner of the bar by ourselves'.[91]

Callum McCaig, the victor at Aberdeen South concurred: 'We have a responsibility to Scotland but also to the wider United Kingdom to act in reasonable manner... It's not in our interest to disrupt the workings [of the UK] because that will disrupt Scotland'.[92]

But the radicalism of many became apparent upon being sworn in as MPs. Hannah Bardell, the MP for Livingston who had previously managed Alex Salmond's private office, omitted to mention the Queen's title and had to repeat the process. According to one journalist, Natalie McGarry of Glasgow East suggested she had been less than sincere when she took the vow to protect and serve the Queen and her heirs. She tweeted: 'As long as in your heart and your head you believe sovereignty lies with the people, doesn't matter what comes out your mouth'. The message was promptly deleted and replaced with one in which she explained: 'I will keep my oath to respect the parliament, but I am a republican. It's not a secret.'[93]

Perhaps unsurprisingly, several of the most radical-sounding MPs were former journalists. John Nicolson, one of many nationalists who previously worked for BBC Scotland, the supposed bastion of Unionism, startled English MPs on Radio 4's the World at One on 2 July by eloquently questioning the need for any UK military intervention in Syria. In his inaugural Common speech, the MP for East Dunbartonshire had invoked Thomas Muir, the 18th century son of a local laird who had sought to dethrone British power and align with the French revolution.[94]

Another ex-BBC journalist, 29-year-old Neil Gray, the new MP for Airdrie & Shotts, had no hesitation in branding the ruling Tories as 'absolutely ruthless. It is disgusting especially as I'm walking up through the streets of London and I see the money that's flowing through this place; there is clearly a need to redistribute some of the wealth in certain parts of the country'.[95]

65-year-old George Kerevan, the MP for East Lothian and a former staffer on the *Scotsman* newspaper, made headlines in the campaign when it was revealed that in his election address he had written: 'After Home Rule, independence will follow as the UK economy implodes [..] I would relish the chance to take Scotland's fight to the enemy camp.'[96]

It is perhaps not surprising to learn that 'the SNP not only has a higher percentage of gay MPs than any other parliamentary party in Europe, but, according to John Nicolson, 'because of our presence', Westminster is 'the most gay parliament in the world'.[97] The SNP's message of resisting established power structures was perhaps bound to draw plentiful left-wing gays into its ranks. The parliamentary party includes Martin Docherty, an ex-seminarian now in a civil partnership who is the MP for West Dunbartonshire and who campaigned against the nearby Trident nuclear base.[98] Catholics in general make up around 15 per cent of Scotland's population and those who at least proclaim a cultural or folk Catholicism, perhaps laced with Irish associations, are well-represented in SNP parliamentary ranks.

Claims that the SNP's MPs, especially those who came to the fore in the raucous referendum campaign, would prove hard for the party to manage, were not realised. This was perhaps revealed in an incident in June 2015 when four of the newcomers sent identical tweets claiming that Labour had voted with the Tories that included the mis-spelled phrase 'on mass'. The next day identical 'apologies' were issued on account of mistake made in this claim. There are a higher percentage of lightweight MPs with picaresque backgrounds in the SNP (who, in some cases, are already starting to make headlines) than in other parties which have enjoyed a surge in representation. This may not trouble the SNP leader. Not only does she currently shy away from confrontation with Westminster but she shows no underlying wish to move the party in a left-wing direction. It helps a centralist leader in Edinburgh if her Westminster contingent are largely composed of individuals unlikely to challenge her direction of travel.

Due to the importance of Westminster and the media attention devoted to it, the 56 SNP MPs will stand out far more than any of their Holyrood counterparts have ever done. The presence among them of the ebullient and pugilistic Alex Salmond is virtually a guarantee of that. If the 56 have one task it is to demonstrate to voters back home that an accommodation between Scotland and the rest of Britain is impossible while they belong to the same state. Under a Labour government, it would have been harder to demonstrate such incompatibility because there was bound to be much government legislation that it would be hard for the SNP not to support. The debates on the proposals for further devolution that had been contained in the Smith report on devolution was the first opportunity for this polarised view to be clearly set out. The Law Society represented an institution which had been a pillar of Scottish self-rule since the 1707 Act of Union and it felt that the proposed Scotland Act matched the provisions contained in the Smith report of 2014 (where there had been cross-party agreement). The Act proposed to devolve income tax on earnings to the value of £15 billion as well as VAT revenues and a range of welfare powers. But Angus Robertson warned that perceived shortcomings made it a distinct likelihood that the SNP would press for a second independence referendum within the next 5 years.[99] The party's preference was for full fiscal autonomy though different spokespersons had offered varying assessments of its viability and the speed with which it could be implemented. Tommy Sheppard MP had declared on 8 June that going for fiscal independence 'overnight...would be a disaster'. His party leader the next day said that Scotland could successfully 'shoulder' the cost.[100]

Until there is evidence to the contrary, it can be assumed that all of the 56 Scottish Nationalists at Westminster hope that their stay there will be temporary. Mhairi Black, the youngest, has complained about her working conditions (see chapter 5) but was soon singled out by Nicola Sturgeon as a future leader of the SNP. The SNP leader perhaps admired her determination to convert sceptical older Scots to independence even though her life experience was a fraction of most of theirs.[101] Perhaps her endorsement of Ms Black is a conscious admission that she also sees the need for a campaigning party long into the future rather than one dedicated to building a new nation. So, perhaps the London stay of the SNP parliamentarians won't be so shortlived after all. But as long as they are a sizeable and conspicuous presence in London, their behaviour will help to define their movement and its goals before a world audience.

Nationalism for 'Our People': Patronage and the Party

Less observed are the workings of Holyrood where, thanks to its domination, the SNP has complete control over the machinery of a parliament originally designed to be one where there would be a balance of power between different political forces. Through its decision-making in Edinburgh, the SNP has made it plain that preferment should be given to whosoever promotes Scottish values and interests in the arts, education and elsewhere. So, rather as the experience of numerous other freshly created states has shown, the desire to promote allies who share many of its core objectives is an explicit one.

In other places seeking to replace external influence or control with native governance, it quickly emerges that the politics of nationalist assertion often turns out to be a screen for patronage politics involving restricted coteries of interest groups and barely-concealed nepotism. In Scotland, there is little appetite for learning lessons from elsewhere not just in the SNP; and pro—independence commentators who warn that liberation politics could go sour due to the desire to siphon off public resources for private benefit, are virtually unheard of.

Some might argue that as part of a meritocratic British state, Scotland is shielded from influence-peddling and irregular use of public resources for political or private gain. Australia, Canada and New Zealand can be pointed to as relatively un-corrupt countries run on basically transparent principles, ones where Scots sometimes had a major role in creating the ground-rules for governance.

But people of Scottish descent – influenced to some degree by Scottish mores – also had a considerable role in maintaining the closed and discriminatory politics that gave a certain notoriety to the *post-bellum* American South and to Northern Ireland from 1920 to 1972. In west-central Scotland itself, there was a tradition of excluding a section of the population from high status or good-earning jobs on account of their perceived alien characteristics when it was an emphatically Protestant-dominated land – I refer to Catholics of Irish immigrant background.[102] It is ironic, although not completely surprising, that members of this community who are strong backers of Scottish independence now despise their Unionist opponents and wish to eradicate their influence.

For most of its existence Scotland has been a poor country which has seen sometimes intense competition for limited resources. Independence is unlikely to quickly usher in an era of abundance. Candid SNP politicians have admitted that the initial acquisition of full sovereignty is likely to be a period of tough adaptation and sacrifices. That surely means ambitious career-minded people are likely to look for protection for a public post, or else for a business breakthrough, from politicians able to influence the allocation of state resources. A system of political appointments and allocation of contracts based on informal criteria, exists in a lot of countries whose politics have been far more sedate than those of Scotland in recent times.

There is the case of Austria, a central European country not much larger in population than Scotland. (It is one that the SNP's parliamentary leader Angus Robertson is familiar with since he was based in Vienna during the 1990s, working for the country's national broadcasting service). After severe polarisation in the inter-war period, left and right after 1945 decided to promote stability by introducing the *proporz* [proportional] system. Klaus Kastner, a retired Austrian financier and one of the country's best-known bloggers in English has written candidly about this arrangement:

'The distribution of jobs in all public sector companies (as well as in public administration) followed the principle of 'proporz', i. e. jobs were assigned based on the proportionate results of the last election. The going saying was that 'for every job in the public sector you need 3 people: one Black, one Red and one who does the job'. Even at the lowest level of a public sector company, one needed a party book (or at least party support) to get a job. The two large parties had pervaded all life in public sector companies (and much of society's life in general). [Bruno] Kreisky's successor as Chancellor, Fred Sinowatz, once coined that famous phrase: "Without the party I would be nothing!"'

Nobody has yet displayed such candour in Scotland but if the SNP comes to exercise the domination that has sometimes led to the allocation of jobs on a discretionary basis in one-party municipal fiefdoms in Britain, then it is only a matter of time before someone will describe its approach to patronage, perhaps in extremely unflattering terms. Kastner went on to write:

'Every time a career step came up, the party book mattered. The miracle word had become "protection". If one had "protection" (that is support of a party or of a prominent politician), nothing could go wrong'.[103]

It is not difficult to imagine a situation emerging in Scotland where one of the sources of strength for a powerful political party is its ability to extend its success and survival through deft use of the public purse. Arguably the foundations for a politics of patronage have already been laid especially since the SNP became the first party in the devolution era to acquire an outright parliamentary majority. The centralisation of decision-making now involves ministers having major influence over public appointments. Accusations have been made in the regular media and in Holyrood that at least one minister had made appointments influenced by political favouritism.[104]

In a country as small as Scotland, citizens can (in theory) have good access to elected representatives but these office holders can also throw their weight around, influencing decision-making by personalised interventions. This indeed was shown when Alex Salmond, still first Minister, personally telephoned the principal of St Andrews University Louise Richardson to ask her to tone down her concerns about the impact of independence on Scottish higher education,('a loud and heated' discussion ensuing).[105]

Scottish politics could revolve around a distribution of favours (and an extraction of penalties) from citizens based on political criteria. If politics does pivot around what the state can take from some citizens and give to others, it may well produce a cleavage between those in a relatively protected state sector and less advantaged salary earners (or owners of capital) in the private sector. Arguably, Greece and Venezuela are two countries which have been thoroughly destabilised by such a cleavage. In Greece populist or negligent governments have often failed to collect taxes on a regular basis; in Scotland one of Salmond's last acts in government was to order an amnesty for citizens with historic council tax debts. Many went back on to the electoral register so as to be able to vote in the referendum but with this amnesty, councils were prevented from pursuing over £500,000 of debt.[106] In Venezuela, the *chavista* regime has penalised owners of private wealth with expropriations and harassment and some fear that the move against private landowners in Scotland is a sign that a confident SNP believes it can derive advantage from pursuing overt class warfare in Scotland.[107] Closed professions, administrative and bureaucratic impediments to entrepreneurship, and the politics of patronage have tipped both Greece and Venezuela into systemic crises. Per head of population, Scotland has one of the West's largest public sectors as a proportion of GDP.[108] The SNP has been highly interventionist, for instance keeping open an airport at Prestwick in Ayrshire (8 miles from Nicola Sturgeon's home town of Irvine) even though it has very few flights and runs at a steep loss.[109]

Labour shrunk from embracing a coherent programme of building an achievement-orientated Scottish state. But so has the SNP. Nevertheless, it now completely dominates Scotland both politically and in numerous other ways too. The party's doctrine has been able to adapt to the restive outlook of an unsettled generation of Scottish voters. It has made adept use of social media technologies to communicate its often populist message to irreverent, young people, newly risk-orientated women, and disgruntled males (often economically under-active). The SNP appears unconcerned that its plans for ensuring the economic viability of independence are sketchy and often need to be corrected in the face of unhelpful macro-economic realities. But many of the voters are similarly relaxed and appear ready to shoulder the risk. The thrill of the independence journey and the desire to break away from England which is increasingly a foreign land for many Scots, are now central desires. The SNP has managed to impose its worldview on many Scots, not yet it would seem a majority of them. Nevertheless, this is a singular victory for any party operating in the field of political nationalism. It is an outright triumph for the SNP when right across the democratic world, citizens are determined to trust parties with less and less. By contrast, in Scotland, the SNP appears to be only at the start of possibly a marathon period in office with little chance of it being replaced any time soon.

Notes for Chapter 2

1. BBC News, 7 May 2005, http://www.bbc.co.uk/newsbeat/article/32642208/meet-the-snps-mhairi-black-the-youngest-mp-elected-since-1667
2. Michael Settle, 'SNP in line for multi-million pound windfall', *Herald*, 26 March 2015. http://www.heraldscotland.com/politics/wider-political-news/snp-in-line-for-multi-million-pound-windfall-if-it-becomes-third-force.121738345
3. David Torrance, *Salmond: Against the Odds*, Edinburgh: Birlinn, 2012, p. 215
4. David Maddox, 'Scottish Labour's "downfall" began with Iraq war', *Scotsman*, 22 June 2015, http://www.scotsman.com/news/politics/top-stories/scottish-labour-s-downfall-began-with-iraq-war-1-3808644
5. Constitution of the Scottish National Party, (accessed 21 September 2015), http://www.snp.org/sites/default/files/assets/documents/constitutionofthescottishnationalparty.pdf
6. Gordon Wilson, *Scotland: the Battle for Independence, A History of the Scottish National Party 1990-2014*, Stirling: Scots Independent, 2014, p. 52.
7. Wilson, *Scotland: the Battle for Independence*, p. 59.
8. Peter Lynch, *The History of the Scottish National Party*, Cardiff: Welsh Academic Press, 2002, p. 212.
9. See Tom Gallagher, *The Illusion of Freedom: Scotland Under Nationalism*, London: Hurst, 2009, p.p. 139-41.
10. John McDermott, 'A veneer of competence', *Prospect*, July 2015, p. 37.
11. McDermott, 'A veneer of competence'.
12. Severin Carrell, 'Salmond provokes row by predicting £57 billion oil boom', *Guardian*, 11 March 2013, http://www.theguardian.com/uk/2013/mar/11/alex-salmond-scotland-oil-boom
13. 'Oil and Gas Analytical Bulletin', *The Scottish Government*, June 2015, http://www.gov.scot/Topics/Economy/Publications/oilandgas/OilGas4
14. Severin Carrell, 'Scottish government accused of trying to bury report', *Guardian*, 25 June 2015, http://www.theguardian.com/politics/2015/jun/25/scottish-government-accused-of-trying-to-bury-report-on-falling-oil-revenues
15. Tom McTague, 'Revealed: The secretive SNP chieftains helping Alex Salmond break the

Union', *Daily Mail*, 16 September 2014 .

16. Paul Hutcheon Blogspot, 'Holding power to account', 11 November 2014, (accessed 21 September 2015), http://paulhutcheon.blogspot.co.uk/2014/11/holding-power-to-account.html

17. McTague, 'Revealed'.

18. Katrine Bussey, 'Euro Million Lottery winners, *Daily Record*, 29 May 2015, http://www.dailyrecord.co.uk/news/scottish-news/euromillions-lottery-winners-colin-chris-5783011

19. Tom Johnston, *Our Noble Families* was first published in 1909.

20. Robbie Dinwoodie, 'Brown favourite to take over as deputy party leader', *Herald*, 26 September 2015.

21. Wilson, *Scotland: the Battle for Independence*, p. 43.

22. Simon Johnson and Ben Riley-Smith, 'Alex-Salmond's leadership of independence campaign under pressure after TV debate loss', *Daily Telegraph*, 7 August 2014.

23. Simon Johnson, 'Nicola Sturgeon I'm SNP leader not Alex Salmond', *Daily Telegraph*, 25 March 2015.

24. Peter Curran [Moridura] on twitter, 28 March 2015, accessed 28 March 2015.

25. Private information.

26. Iain MacWhirter, 'SNP facing their toughest scandal test', *Herald*, 1 October 2015.

27. McTague, 'Revealed'; Cameron Brooks, 'SNP chief spin doctor bows out to join PR firm', *Press and Journal*, 23 June 2015.

28. McTague, 'Revealed'.

29. Simon Johnson, 'Alex Salmond on course for defeat in independence referendum', *Daily Telegraph*, 18 September 2013.

30. Robin McAlpine, 'So far so good, British Unionism's review of 2014', *Bella Caledonia*, 30 December 2014, http://bellacaledonia.org.uk/2014/12/30/so-far-so-good-british-unionisms-review-of-2014/

31. Stephen Daisley, 'Wings over Scotland and the Changing face of the Scottish Media', STV, 20 June 2014, http://news.stv.tv/scotland-decides/analysis/279941-analysis-wings-over-scotland-and-changing-face-of-scottish-media/>

32. Rev. Stuart Campbell, 'That was a year that was', 31 December 2014, http://wingsoverscotland.com/that-was-a-year-that-was/

33. Eddie Barnes, 'Mark Shaw: the Aberdeen-based property developer will liaise between the Yes campaign and the SNP', *Scotsman*, 19 May 2013 .

34. Tom Peterkin, 'Who are the donors behind the Yes and No campaigns', *Scotsman*, 13 July 2014, http://www.scotsman.com/lifestyle/who-are-the-donors-behind-yes-and-no-campaigns-1-3474863

35. Barnes, 'Mark Shaw'.

36. 'Former executive Stan Blackley slams Yes Scotland', *Scotsman*, 20 April 2014,

http://www.scotsman.com/news/politics/top-stories/former-executive-stan-blackley-slams-yes-scotland-1-3382434#comments-area>

37. 'Former executive Stan Blackley'.
38. Andrew Gilligan, 'Scottish independence: 'Yes campaign every bit as dodgy as Iraq dossier', Sunday Telegraph, 14 September 2014.
39. David Clegg, 'Independence Poll: Our bombshell survey shows one in three Scots will vote No due to dislike of Alex Salmond', Daily Record, 15 May 2014.
40. Lauren Reid, 'A backwards step', http://wingsoverscotland.com/a-backwards-step/, 30 March 2015 .
41. 'Yes and No campaigns reveal September battle plans', Scotsman, 10 August 2014.
42. David Clegg, 'Revealed – Secret Poll Convinced Alex Salmond he would pull off shock victory', Daily Record, 24 September 2014,
   http://www.dailyrecord.co.uk/news/politics/revealed-secret-opinion-poll-convinced-4313922
43. McAlpine, 'So far so good'.
44. 'The Way Forward', Craig Murray Blog, 9 November 2014,
   http://www.craigmurray.org.uk/archives/2014/11/the-way-forward/>
45. Andrew Whitaker, 'SNP blocks Craig Murray's general election candidacy',
   Scotsman, 28 December 2014, http://www.scotsman.com/news/politics/top-stories/
   snp-block-craig-murray-general-election-candidacy-1-3645014#comments-area>
46. 'Disbarred', Craig Murray Blog, 27 December 2014,
   https://www.craigmurray.org.uk/archives/2014/12/disbarred/
47. Tom Gordon, 'Torture whistle blower anger at SNP "stitch-up"', Herald, December 2014,
   http://www.heraldscotland.com/politics/scottish-politics/torture-whistle-blowers-anger-at-snp-stitch-up-after-election-block.26155630
48. Whitaker, 'SNP blocks Craig Murray's'.
49. Whitaker, 'SNP blocks Craig Murray's'.
50. Editorial, Scotland on Sunday, 28 December 2014.
51. SNP To Introduce Tough New Rules Requiring Strict Loyalty From MPs', Buzzfeed, 1 March 2015.
52. 'SNP candidate for Argyll and Bute in major own goal', For Argyll, 4 March 2015,
   http://forargyll.com/2015/03/snp-candidate-for-argyll-bute-in-major-own-goal/>by
   newsroom <http://forargyll.com/author/newsroom/
53. 'Thoughts on the SNP conference', Craig Murray Blog, 30 March 2015,
   https://www.craigmurray.org.uk/archives/2015/03/thoughts-on-the-snp-conference/
54. Severin Carrell, 'Alex Salmond gains slim SNP vote for joining Nato', Guardian, 19 October 2012.
55. Peter Geoghegan, 'Yes Alliance has been consumed by the SNP's rigid   nationalism', Sunday Mail, 29 March 2015 .

56. http://www.thecourier.co.uk/news/local/dundee/stewart-hosie-brushes-off-criticism-for-yes-dundee-event-appearance-with-tommy-sheridan-1.712338

57. http://www.heraldscotland.com/politics/referendum-news/sheridan-frozen-out-of-yes-campaign.24489722

58. 'Sheridan frozen out of Yes campaign', *Herald*, 14 June 2014, http://www.heraldscotland.com/politics/referendum-news/sheridan-frozen-out-of-yes-campaign.24489722

59. 'Jacobites and Jacobinism: the problem with left fundamentalism', *Promised Joy*, 29 November 2014, https://faintdamnation.wordpress.com/2014/11/29/jacobites-and-jacobins-the-problem-with-yes-fundamentalism/#comments>

60. 'The SNP ascendancy is changing Scotland and the SNP', *Gerry Hassan Blog*, 15 June 2015, http://www.gerryhassan.com/blog/the-snp-ascendancy-is-changing-scotland-and-the-snp/#more-3629 (response of mac48)

61. Walter Humes, 'How can we curb authoritarian drift in Scotland', *Scottish Review*, 9 April 2014, http://www.scottishreview.net/WalterHumes153.shtml

62. Peter Lynch, *The History of the Scottish National Party*, Cardiff: Welsh Academic Press, 2002, p. 213.

63. Tom Gallagher, *Divided Scotland: Ethnic Friction and Christian Crisis,* Glendaruel, Scotland: Argyll Publishing, 2011, p. 213.

64. Damian Thompson, 'The Scottish Catholic Bishops and the nationalists: A scandal is coming to light', *Spectator,* 23 September 2014, http://blogs.spectator.co.uk/damian-thompson/2014/09/the-scottish-catholic-bishops-and-the-nationalists-a-scandal-is-coming-to-light/; see also 'church pays tribute to first minister', *Scottish Catholic Observer,* 26 September 2014, http://www.sconews.co.uk/latest-edition/40331/church-pays-tribute-to-first-minister

65. Gerry Braiden, 'Labour face battle to save heartlands from SNP surge', *Herald*, 12 October 2014, http://www.heraldscotland.com/politics/scottish-politics/labour-face-battle-to-save-heartlands-from-snp-surge.25569018

66. See Tom Gallagher, *Glasgow, the Uneasy Peace: religious tension in Modern Scotland*, Manchester: Manchester University Press, 1987.

67. Tom Gallagher, 'Catholic Church silent as Scotland prepares to vote on independence', *Catholic Herald,* 12 August 2014, http://www.catholicherald.co.uk/features/2014/08/12/catholic-church-silent-as-scotland-goes-to-vote-on-independence/

68. Kevin McKenna, 'Labour in Scotland is dying: Does anybody care', *Observer,* 27 September 2014, http://www.theguardian.com/commentisfree/2014/sep/27/labour-in-scotland-dying-does-anyone-care

69. Andrew Picken, '5-star fury over SNP junkets', *Sunday Post*, 20 July 2014,

http://www.sundaypost.com/news-views/politics/holyrood/5-star-fury-over-snp-jun-
kets-1.481315>.

70. Kevin McKenna, 'Jim Murphy gets Labour's problem, albeit too late in the day',
Observer, 11 April 2015, http://www.theguardian.com/commentisfree/2015/apr/12/
jim-murphy-scotland-labour-problem-nicola-sturgeon

71. Kevin McKenna, 'Scotland's Iron lady fomented revolution too', *Observer*,
14 April 2015, http://www.theguardian.com/commentisfree/2013/apr/14/radical-scot
land-has-iron-lady-too

72. Kevin McKenna, 'Can Labour do enough to woo Glasgow Man back to the fold',
Times, 19 March 2015.

73. Kevin McKenna, 'Devine inspiration', *Scottish Field,* September 2014.

74. David Clegg, 'Key SNP figure defects to Labour', *Daily Record,* 6 April 2015,
http://www.dailyrecord.co.uk/news/politics/key-snp-figure-defects-labour-5469873

75. Daniel Sanderson, 'SNP lawyer will not stand for Westminster', *Herald,* 4 December 2014,
http://www.heraldscotland.com/politics/scottish-politics/snp-lawyer-will-not-stand-
for-westminster.114015459

76. Daniel Sanderson, 'Election 15: the battle for the heart of Labour's heartland', *Herald,*
1 April 2014, http://www.heraldscotland.com/politics/scottish-politics/election-2015-
the-battle-for-the-heart-of-labour-s-heartlands-nears-a-fra.1427895887

77. See Peter Geoghegan, *The People's Referendum: Why Scotland Will never be the Same
Again,* Edinburgh: Luath Press, 2014, chapter 1.

78. Amanullah de Sondy, ' A Stronger and Progressive Scotland', *Progressive Scottish
Muslim*, 8 May 2015, http://progressivescottishmuslims.blogspot.co.uk/2015/05/a-
stronger-and-progressive-scotland-for.html

79. Tom Gordon, 'Islamic lobbying group with links to SNP faces closure', *Herald,* 30 Sep
tember 2012, http://www.heraldscotland.com/news/home-news/islamic-lobbying-
group-with-links-to-snp-faces-closure.1

80. 'Scottish Islamic Foundation: Cronyism, Pounds and the Media', Progressive Scottish
Muslim, 9 August 2008. http://progressivescottishmuslims.blogspot.co.uk/2008/08/
scottish-islamic-foundation-cronism.html

81. 'Nicola versus the Union mob', *Moridura Blogspot*, 12 April 2015,
moridura.blogspot.com/search/label/SNP%2FLabour%20deal

82. 'We did this', *Derek Bateman Blog,* 15 May 2015,
http://derekbateman.co.uk/2015/05/15/we-did-this/

83. Kashmira Gander, 'Mhairi Black speech in full', *Independent,* 15 July 2015,
http://www.independent.co.uk/news/uk/politics/mhairi-black-speech-in-full-snp-mp-
tears-apart-conservative-government-and-labour-opposition-in-maid-

en-speech-10389334.html

84. Meet your new Scottish MPs: 13 Margaret Ferrier', the *National,* 27 May 2015.

85. David Leask, 'Majority of MPs can boast middle-class occupations on CVs', *Herald,* 18 May 2015.

86. Marc Champion , 'Only the Scots Are Popular in This Election', *Bloomberg View,* 4 May 2015.

87. Rosa Prince, 'Ten things we've learned from the SNP's first week in parliament', *Daily Telegraph,* 24 May 2015, http://www.telegraph.co.uk/news/politics/SNP/11624189/Ten-things-weve-learned-from-the-SNPs-first-full-week-in-Parliament.html

88. Mure Dickie, 'Wave of SNP wins to bring culture shock to Westminster', *Financial Times* 22 April 2015.

89. Prince, 'Ten things we've learned'.

90. Dan Hodges, 'why are SNP MPs strutting around like they own the place, Because they do', *Daily Telegraph,* 29 May 2015, http://www.telegraph.co.uk/news/general-election-2015/politics-blog/11638541/Why-are-SNP-MPs-strutting-around-Westminster-like-they-own-the-place-Because-they-do.html

91. Dickie, 'Wave of SNP wins'.

92. Dickie, 'Wave of SNP wins'.

93. Prince, 'Ten things we've learned'.

94. House of Commons, *Hansard,* 17 June 2015, Column 299, http://www.publications.parliament.uk/pa/cm201516/cmhansrd/cm150617/debtext/150617-0001.htm

95. The *National,* 14 May 2015.

96. Kevin Hague, 'George Kerevan, my new SNP MP', *Chokka Blog,* 10 May 2015, http://chokkablog.blogspot.co.uk/2015/05/george-kerevan-my-new-snp-mp.html

97. Carole Cadwalladr, 'The SNP 56: a breath of fresh air', *Guardian,* 12 July 2015, http://www.theguardian.com/politics/2015/jul/12/snp-mps-at-westminster-scotland

98. National, 4 June 2015, http://www.thenational.scot/politics/meet-your-new-scottish-mps-19-martin-docherty-west-dunbartonshire.3698

99. Toby Helm, 'SNP warns Scotland could still vote for independence', *Observer,* 28 June 2015.

100. Lucy Fisher, 'Fiscal autonomy would ruin us, admits SNP MP', *Times,* 9 June 2015, http://www.thetimes.co.uk/tto/news/uk/scotland/article4464569.ece

101. 'Mhairi Black tipped to be future keader of the SNP', *Scotsman,* 8 October 2015; Mhairi Black, 'We need to help the elderly see through the Tories' scare stories', *National,* 10 October 2015.

102. See Gallagher, *Glasgow, the Uneasy Peace.*

103. For both quotes, see Yanis Varoufakis, 'On Bruno Kreisky's legacy: A Reply by Klaus

Kastner', *Notes for the Post-2008 World*, 8 December 2012, http://yanisvaroufakis.eu/2012/12/08/on-bruno-kreiskys-legacy-a-reply-by-klaus-kastner-with-a-rejoinder-from-me/

104. Tom Gordon, 'Health secretary in cronyism row about health position', *Herald*, 11 June 2013, http://www.heraldscotland.com/politics/political-news/health-secretary-in-cronyism-row-about-quango-position.21308879; Tom Gordon, 'Alex Neill in cronyism row after appointing official', *Herald*, 14 March 2015, http://www.heraldscotland.com/politics/scottish-politics/alex-neil-in-cronyism-row-after-appointing-official-from-his-local-snp-br.120661341

105. Ben Riley-Smith, 'Revealed: Alex Salmond personally pressurised St Andrews University head over independence concerns', *Daily Telegraph*, 16 September 2014, http://www.telegraph.co.uk/news/uknews/scottish-independence/11100754/Revealed-Alex-Salmond-personally-pressurised-St-Andrews-University-head-over-independence-concerns.html

106. Severin Carrell, 'Alex Salmond to ban councils from chasing historic debt', *Guardian*, 2 October 2014, http://www.theguardian.com/uk-news/2014/oct/02/alex-salmond-ban-scottish-councils-chase-historic-poll-tax-debts

107. For the respective nature and impact of populism in Venezuela and Greece, two blogs can be recommended *Caracas Chronicles*,: http://caracaschronicles.com/; and *Observing Greece*, http://klauskastner.blogspot.co.uk/

108. The Centre for Economic and Business Research went as far as claiming in 2008 that due to the public wage bill having reached a third of Scotland's then £33 billion annual spending budget, it was on course to become the third most state-dependent country after Cuba and Iraq. See Scotland edition of the *Sunday Times*, 11 January 2009.

109. http://www.scotsman.com/news/transport/prestwick-airp

CHAPTER THREE

British-Minded Scots in the Referendum and After

Any history enthusiasts absorbed with how empires and great states stumble and fall, might have been intrigued by events in north Britain in 2014. Some parallels exist between the collapse, on the one hand, of the Aztec and Inca empires in the Americas of the 16th century and the determined attempt to break-up Britain in that year. Alex Salmond amassed a coalition of adventurers ranging from far-left militants to property developers and transport tycoons who bear some comparison with Hernan Cortes and Francisco Pizarro who led the Spanish *conquistadores* on the successful assault of empires in Mexico and Peru. They were intrepid and not daunted by being outnumbered against established and heavily armed empires. Two crucial advantages narrowed the military odds in their favour: the possession of horses and their access to guns.

If there were any counterparts in the Scottish power-struggle, it was the access to the latest social media instruments of Facebook and twitter which enabled the anti-British insurgents to fan the flames of revolt in the northern territory they were intent on conquering. But unlike Montezuma and Atahualpa in Tenochtitlan and Cuzco, Britain's Prime Minister David Cameron already had access to the very tools which enabled his challenger to come rather close to inflicting a humiliating defeat on him. However, he disdained to use them and assumed that he could easily prevail. His advantage over the doomed New World empires was that at least he spotted that there was a challenge to the sovereignty of his state far enough ahead

Head over Heart

In January 2012, in the wake of the surprisingly large electoral victory for Salmond's SNP Cameron announced his intention to hold a referendum on Scottish independence. Most polls in Scotland showed that the pro-Union side enjoyed a two-to-one lead over advocates of separation and this would continue for at least 18 months. But in order to obtain agreement for a referendum, he made a series of concessions which it soon turned out strengthened the Nationalist side. The question on the ballot paper, the duration of the campaign, and the size of the electorate, eventually were seen to give Salmond and his allies major advantages; and at key moments, Cameron proved to be complacent and tactically inept.

In 2011, he had easily won a referendum on electoral reform which was one of the conditions for the Liberal Democrats entering a coalition with his Conservatives in 2010. Perhaps he felt the battle in Scotland would be won with hardly more effort. It is still unclear with whom he consulted as the referendum decision was taken and plans were drawn up. It is a fair surmise that nobody had pointed out that a referendum campaign, especially one lasting over 30 months, would be a gift for a populist movement like the SNP, indifferent towards governing but a highly-motivated campaigning force. It had been a fringe player until 2007 when it unexpectedly won the elections to the 8-year-old Scottish parliament. Perhaps there was simply nobody with the breadth of experience of more turbulent forms of politics beyond Britain's shores and close to Cameron able to tell him that unless the referendum was handled very carefully, it could destabilise the island of Britain's previously serene territorial order whatever the result would be.

The opposition Labour party was not surprised by Cameron's 2012 initiative. One of its leading figures in the referendum campaign revealed in June 2015 that he had approached his then leader Gordon Brown, in the last phase of his 2007-2010 UK Premiership, urging him to call a swift referendum. The SNP still appeared containable, living standards had grown after 13 years of Labour rule, the party could point to various social reforms that had benefited its long-term supporters in Scotland, and the Prime Minister was one of them, a Scot. But the indecisive Brown, troubled on numerous other fronts, was not persuaded by the idea.[1]

Two political rivals, indeed political enemies, Labour and the Conservatives, would be required to work together in a protracted campaign against their common foe of nationalism. Better Together would be the name of the cross party alliance thrown together in order to foil a break-up of the United Kingdom. The title implied that Scotland somehow stood apart from the rest of Britain but that for pragmatic reasons this distance should not become outright separation. Certainly there would only be a halting effort to show that Britain in totality counted for more than its individual parts. A campaign title expressing qualified commitment would appeal to the bank balances of voters rather than their hearts and minds.

Cameron left the running of the campaign very much to the Labour party. This was a logical decision. His party had only one of Scotland's 59 Westminster seats while Labour had 41 and was still dominant in local government. But the level of coordination between the two parties appears to have been remarkably limited in face of the magnitude of the challenge which they were soon to face. Alastair Darling, the leader of the Better Together campaign to preserve the Union, was a genuinely consensual figure, but even within the Labour Party, it looked at times as if groups were operating in silos with little real coordination. No major clashes appear to have erupted between these two uneasy and temporary allies. That may well have been part of the problem. They appeared to have a very limited idea of what was needed to accomplish victory. The Better Together symphony for union only had one register which was endlessly repeated. Scotland benefited from membership of the Union and, in current economic conditions, many of its inhabitants would confront major risks if placed outside it.

There was the failure to wage a multi-level campaign that could have taken different forms. One approach certainly would have been to focus not just on what was the value for Scotland but also the value for Britain and the Western world overall in a Union that had been a model for constructive cooperation between former enemies at its inception in 1707. Scotland had pioneered something remarkably valuable in a violent Europe and it would be foolish to discard the Union when it was hard to point to any group of Scots being oppressed or exploited by it.

The pro-independence 'Yes' side with its multiple communication outlets was able to paint a vivid picture of a fulfilling new future awaiting Scotland if it decided to become master of its own fate. It appeared to grasp that the collective personality of the nation had been changing and that many Scots were no longer proverbially cautious and risk-averse. Labour assumed that its own supporters could be kept in line by primarily emphasising that the Union stood for social and economic well-being. There was no need to underscore the importance of partnership and, the strength of Britain in a Europe which was being haunted by disorder and internal strife. Nor was there any need to galvanise Union supporters to be active campaigners in a political duel that would last over several years. Better Together may have committed an error by conceding that the core loyalty was to Scotland and not the UK which 're-cast the debate in SNP terms psychologically'.[2]

The trouble was that by the early 21st century many in the Labour party may have found it hard to be enthusiastic about a British legacy of cooperation, incremental progress, stability and democracy because they themselves were numb or suspicious towards such a composite image. During Tony Blair's 1997-2007 premiership, Britain had been redefined as a world society that should embrace globalisation. This ranged from promoting multiculturalism as a model for managing disparate urban communities to selling familiar British utilities to overseas companies. 'Cool Britannia' one of the themes of his time in office was a kind of repudiation of the apparently stuffy, homogenous and parochial country which he had inherited. But it would only be in the final weeks of the marathon campaign that it dawned on some of the smarter defenders of the Union that their short-sighted and anaemic strategy opened up the possibility of a stunning reverse.

Better Together was formally launched, on 25 June 2012, by a pair of normally highly adversarial parties with the Liberal Democrats having a secondary role. It was an undoubted achievement that the campaign remained intact while sometimes ferocious inter-party warfare continued at Westminster. Much credit should go to the politician who agreed to be its head, Alistair Darling. Having served in senior positions throughout Labour's thirteen years in power at Westminster, he was regarded as pragmatic and trustworthy beyond Labour ranks. He proceeded to work closely with Labour's erstwhile enemies, coming to the defence of senior Conservatives when they were denounced as 'alien' voices by the SNP.

Better Together had one message which dominated its conversation with the Scottish electorate from the start of the campaign to the day of voting in the referendum on 18 September 2014. The economic case for Britain staying united was overwhelming. Scotland got a very good deal from being part of the United Kingdom (UK). Staying in was very much in the immediate and long-term interests of most Scots; the advocates of separation were unable to make a credible economic case for Scotland going it alone.

This was a sober and utilitarian message with little space for the emotional case for the continuation of the Union state. The unflashy Alistair Darling, who had reached the pinnacle of his Westminster career as Chancellor of the Exchequer, was admirably suited to extol the virtues of economic prudence. He stuck, limpet-like, to this primary theme even as a rising chorus of voices (some finally from within his own campaign) demanded that a more emotional defence of a 307-year Union was imperative.

But he resisted any concerted attempt to depict the Anglo-Scottish union as a remarkable success story and disparage the 'pro-Indy' Yes side for portraying it in negative terms. Only late in the day would eloquent defences of the Union come from major public figures in politics and the media once it was clear that the economic case for the status quo was being dangerously undermined by the emotional one for secession.

The appeal to head over heart was the course followed due in large part to in-depth voting analysis provided by Andrew Cooper, one of Britain's most experienced pollsters. Two in-depth surveys involving 4,000 voters each were carried out first in May 2012, and again at the end of 2013. Focus groups were also done with floating voters. Two main voting blocs were found. The largest, comprising nearly 40 per cent of Scotland's 4 million voters, were committed No voters. They were split into two segments, 'mature status quo' and 'hard-pressed unionists'. They were followed by committed yes voters who, in 2012, made up just fewer than 30 per cent of voters. They were existential nationalists who 'would vote yes even if it impoverished the country', and 'blue collar Bravehearts', those working class, largely male, voters who identified themselves as Scottish, not British.[3]

In the second survey, the Yes vote was found to have gone up to 40 per cent. Undecided voters by the end of 2013 comprised one-third of the electorate according to Cooper's findings, so it was decided to concentrate resources on winning them over. They comprised two groups, 'comfortable pragmatists' and a smaller one of 'uncommitted security seekers', both of whom were somewhat numb to Britain but who would recoil from nationalism if it was shown that the risks were too great. Cooper is on record as saying that 'these people were only willing to [vote Yes] if they felt it wasn't associated with very strong risk. Therefore the campaign strategy was to keep those people focused on the risk'.[4]

White Paper

For much of the campaign, the energy of the Yes side was also devoted to wooing these cautious undecided voters. Before setting up the Yes campaign, the SNP had spent at least a year arguing that a 'Social Union' would persist after formal separation. Angus Robertson, the party's leader at Westminster, along with Salmond, sought to claim that independence and a continuity Britain could somehow operate in tandem. Scotland would not move into a post-British future at all but, through the crown, the armed forces, the BBC, and the National Health Service, there would be a durable social union.[5]

This theme would resonate through the grassroots campaigning of the Yes side until 2014. Indeed the SNP's desire to suggest that a pain-free independence could be acquired without any noticeable disruption to people's lives, sparked the resignation in July 2013 of Alex Bell whom Alex Salmond had employed as his chief political strategist.[6] Bell had argued that Britain's failure as a viable entity, as shown by intensifying austerity measures and a low-grade political elite remote from everyday society, should have been the central campaigning plank. In August 2014, when the Yes side appeared to be faltering, others spoke up for 'the Broken Britain' approach. Jamie Maxwell, an SNP supporter and frequent commentator in the London media, argued that it was 'all going wrong' for the Yes side; ground had been needlessly conceded by playing down the current state of Britain in favour of the future state of Scotland.[7]

'The White Paper' on *Scotland's Future* launched by the Scottish government on 26 November played down 'separation', emphasising continuity rather than break-up. This 650 page, 170,000 word blueprint for the future contained the case meant for the Scottish public. Copies would be available free-of-charge (at an eventual cost of £1.25 million) to anyone who requested one.[8] It set out the policy priorities of an independent Scotland but detail was scant, leading one pro-Union newspaper to describe it as 'a soufflé of half-truths and guesswork'.[9]

Social justice was emphasised. Scotland would be able to continue as a member of the EU on the same terms as Britain. Other institutions, such as NATO, would show understanding for a Scotland free of nuclear weapons continuing as a full member. Nor, according to the White Paper, would Scotland abandon the British pound and devise its own banking system; as 70 percent of Scotland's trade is with the rest of the United Kingdom, the acquisition of a Scottish currency would turn this market from a domestic to a foreign one overnight. Moreover, in the challenging times of early statehood, there was a reasonable likelihood that the value of the new currency would drop below the British pound. This would have unavoidable consequences for interest rates, debt financing and deficits. So there was a compelling case for financial coordination. The Bank of England would be the lender of last resort for Scotland. It would be in the best interests of both countries given their close economic links which meant that many of the terms and conditions concerning Scottish borrowing, spending and taxation levels would continue to be shaped by London. It raised questions about what was the point of going through the upheaval of unpicking a three centuries old union if the divorced couple were to remain entangled with one another in such key ways.

Alex Bell, while continuing to campaign for independence, argued later that: 'The SNP's strength does not lie in policy' and that Salmond's pound plan is 'arguably not independence'.[10] A highly euphemistic case had been made for economic viability in the White Paper with estimated revenue from oil fourteen times larger than such revenue would actually be by 2015. There was little real light shed on the economic direction, political structures and international links of a new country.

It is not surprising that few Yes campaigners, when asked to recall inspiring symbols or turning-points for their cause, bothered to refer to the White Paper. For the rest of the referendum campaign, Salmond was unclear what the currency of a self-governing Scotland would be. As late as August 2014, he refused to rule out sterlingisation, that is keeping the pound whether the rest of the UK approved or not.[11] A number of small countries, Ecuador, Panama, and Montenegro use major international currencies due to the fact that there is more confidence in the Federal Reserve or the European Central Bank than in their own financial regulatory bodies.[12] But economists warned that this option would lead to a flight of money from Scotland as it would have no central bank or lender of last resort. Deep spending cuts to build up reserves of sterling and ensure there is enough money in circulation, would also likely be required.[13]

Currency Tussle

On 13 February 2014, Chancellor of the Exchequer George Osborne visited Edinburgh to say definitively that a currency union was not going to happen. He declared: 'The pound isn't an asset to be divided up between two countries after a break-up like a CD collection... If Scotland walks away from the UK, it walks away from the UK pound.'[14] He was immediately endorsed by the chief financial spokesmen for the other main British parties.

Media commentators initially assumed that Salmond and his cause had been scorched by their seemingly amateurish approach to economics. 'Westminster dynamites Alex Salmond's currency union, causing Scottish nationalist meltdown' was the headline above the article by the right-wing journalist Iain Martin that was published in the *Daily Telegraph* immediately after Osborne's visit to Edinburgh.[15] On the political left, Martin Kettle who had previously written with a degree of admiration about the SNP's rise, a week later published a piece in *the Guardian* entitled 'Alex Salmond and co are acting like spoilt children'. He wrote: 'I know a serious argument when I hear one, and Osborne and the others have been making serious arguments in the past few days. It is simply mischievous to pretend that they are not dealing with major issues which, if mishandled, could be seriously destructive to ordinary lives, communities and standards of living'.[16]

But if Better Together hoped that Osborne's *demarche* would prove a defining moment of the campaign, it was mistaken. Kettle had branded Salmond's anger over attempts 'to dictate from on high' by people who do not understand Scotland' as 'a reputation destroying performance'. Scottish commentators disagreed however. As early as 17 February, two academics Gerry Hassan and James Mitchell, published an article in the *Guardian,* predicting that 'Osborne's High Noon approach to Scotland will backfire'.[17] One day earlier, Iain MacWhirter, a journalist who had shed his Labour sympathies for active endorsement of the independence cause, was in no doubt that an event had occurred which would 'resonate through history; a milestone in Scotland's relations with the rest of the UK'.

He wrote: 'A Tory Chancellor, George Osborne, riding into town, laying down the law, and then riding out again without giving any TV interviews, made even many Unionists feel they had been slapped in the face. You shall not use the pound, end of. Scots always knew they were the junior partners in the UK, but it was a shock nevertheless to have it confirmed in such a blunt way'.[18]

A poll released on 20 February 2014 found that only slightly more than one- third of Scottish voters believed that the Westminster parties were serious about denying an independent Scotland membership of a sterling zone.[19] Salmond appeared to be in harmony with the national mood when he claimed that the London elite were bluffing. He obtained astonishing ammunition in March 2014 when an unnamed minister, later revealed to be the defence secretary Philip Hammond (promoted a few months later to the job of foreign secretary) told a journalist in an off-the-record briefing, 'Of course there would be a currency union'.[20] Hammond's identity was divulged by the *Daily Telegraph*'s Scotland editor at the end of 2014.[21]

As late as August 2014, Salmond sought to recover lost ground after a poor debating performance with Darling by proclaiming: 'It's our pound and we're keeping it'.[22] For months, numerous economists had been making the point that the pound is not an asset like gold reserves or public infrastructure, but is a means of exchange. Adam Tomkins, one of Better Together's most effective campaigners, chided the journalist Iain MacWhirter for insisting that 'the pound is common property'.[23]

But whatever the underlying impracticalities of the SNP's position, the Yes side received a poll boost after Osborne's poorly calibrated intervention, one which had not occurred after the publication of the much hyped White Paper. Better Together seemed to be taken unawares. Not enough Scottish voters had listened to warnings about how a vulnerable post-Union currency position could impact on the cost of mortgages or interest rates for borrowing. Perhaps it had been assumed that the 'shock and awe' tactics from Britain's finance chief would have a sobering impact. Salmond proceeded to have a good two months of campaigning in which the Yes side crept up on its rival in the polls. His refusal to divulge what was his alternative currency strategy, his 'Plan B', did not do his cause serious harm. In mid-February a Scottish newspaper had been told by an SNP parliamentarian: 'Alex's line won't hold. We should have sorted an alternative proposal months ago'.[24]

It was widely assumed that Salmond's unvoiced intention was to use the currency of a foreign state without entering into a monetary union. 'It would mean', according to Tomkins that 'the Scottish Government would have no *input* into the governance of the monetary framework'.[25] In other words, Scotland would have its currency dictated by the bank of the country that he wanted to secede from. For Mark Carney, the Canadian in charge of the Bank of England, currency union would be incompatible with sovereignty.[26]

The currency episode showed that the pro-Union campaign had under-estimated the power of emotion and the way that it could be manipulated by a seasoned populist. Salmond understood the resentment that could be generated among undecided Scots about being patronised; it put in the shade, at least for a period, their economic fears. Ultimately, the currency union ploy would be a liability for the Yes side as some figures admitted when *post-mortems* were being undertaken. The occasion of Osborne's Edinburgh speech was arguably the end of the phoney war and the debut of a far more formidable Yes campaign able to operate at different levels and with contrasting sources of support. It was one which Better Together would increasingly struggle to compete with.

Unionists at Bay

Until the winter of 2013-14 it had been easy to scoff at the Yes Scotland campaign. Its launch, in May 2012, in a darkened Edinburgh cinema on a rare day of sweltering weather had been dominated by figures from the worlds of Scottish media and entertainment. They had been rather unkindly dubbed B division figures, but more worrying was the fact that some of the better-known ones had chosen to live far away from Scotland and could easily be branded in the media as tax-exiles.[27] Salmond even declared that the intellectuals among them could help make the impending White Paper 'resonate down through the ages' thanks to their literary contributions.[28] But in the end the pro-Indy wordsmiths either backed off or their services weren't required since most of the 670 pages read very much like a civil service boilerplate draft.

A more purposeful Yes campaign had sprung up by late 2013. It was increasingly highly visible in the poorer parts of Glasgow and several of its satellite towns. In a prescient article, Ewen McAskill, a Glasgow-born journalist back in his native city at the start of 2014 after a 7-year absence in the USA, noticed the change of mood.[29] The momentum was provided by the far-left which emerged greatly strengthened from the referendum period after years of scandal, infighting, and poor election results. Regular canvassing and evening meetings awoke interest in the campaign in increasing numbers of downscale areas of west-central Scotland. Cameron's willingness to leave the referendum timing to the SNP government allowed a long conscious-raising process to occur. Nobody in the pro-Union side seems to have anticipated that the length of the campaign would be exploited so effectively by the Yes side. The often pedestrian SNP is at its best in electioneering. But it was eclipsed in many areas by new activists, many of whom participated in the post-referendum explosion of membership which saw its size surpass 100,000. Thousands of Yes rallies were held in which the platform was often composed of people from beyond the SNP. They were billed as health service professionals, trade-unionists, women's activists or ethnic minority figures. This gave the impression that the Yes campaign was a united front of Scots eager for change rather than a narrow political construct. Social media played a vital ancillary role in promoting the image of a powerful social movement, even a national family in the making. Campaigners were able to emphasise the positivity of a potential new beginning without needing to unveil the architecture of a post-British Scotland. They were greatly helped by the referendum question, 'Should Scotland be an independent country'? It was far easier to make a

'Yes vote' appear positive and even momentous than a 'No' one and the scope for campaign slogans around the Yes motif was also far greater.

It is unclear how much thought Cameron and his advisers had given to the question, the length of the campaign, the decision to allow 16-18 year olds to vote, and the decision to disbar the up to 800,000 Scots living in the rest of the UK from voting. These were concessions made to the SNP in the run-up to the Edinburgh agreement on 15 October 2012 in return for its agreement to keep a second question on enhanced devolution off the ballot paper. Under this agreement, the Westminster government temporarily ceded legal authority to hold such a referendum to the technically subordinate parliament in Edinburgh.

For part of the time Better Together treated the campaign like an extended by-election. Its chief executive Blair McDougall, had previously worked for Ian McCartney and Douglas Alexander, two Scottish Labour figures whose careers were very much focused on London and Lancashire politics. He had also run the doomed campaign for the Labour leadership in 2010 of the victor's much better-known brother David Miliband.

McDougall was a stolid figure able to balance the various party perspectives. He remained very much in the background compared to his Yes counterpart Blair Jenkins, a former Scottish media executive. But there was no attempt to broaden the base of the No side by strengthening a presence at grassroots level and in the social media. In post-industrial Lanarkshire, which would vote Yes despite a historically weak SNP presence, the No camp appeared to write off many working-class Yes supporters. Many of these were Irish-orientated Catholics, previously a pillar of Labour support. One very senior Better Together figure told me that they were a lost cause. It was better conserving energy on undecided voters and re-affirming the economic case for rejecting separation. This individual represented a district which had been shaken in the past by intra-religious tensions. They were a pale version of the fiercer quarrel that had almost torn nearby Ulster apart. But the presence of figures from socially tense Labour heartlands may well have ensured that BT was not going to tap into British-minded grassroots feeling. Neither the Liberal Democrats nor the Conservatives (keen to appear a technocratic and sensible pillar of the centre-right which had banished any sectarian taint of the past) was prepared to push Labour into setting up grassroots affiliates. It meant there was no effort to promote a passionate defence of Britain, as a country with a history that was more virtuous than dishonourable and was worth keeping together; in contrast, the Yes side was only too keen to proselytize and recruit in areas where, outwardly, its prospects appeared uninviting.

McDougall compared the pro-Union campaign to 'the safe, solid but rather dull

Volvo' car.[30] Better Together was relying on the common sense of the majority of Scots asserting itself owing to the impracticality of the Yes side's economic plans. Following Osborne's intervention, it got further ammunition for its assertion that an un-costed drive to statehood was a hazardous course for Scotland. The European Commission ruled in late March 2014 that cross-border pension schemes would have to be fully-funded whereas single-country ones could go into deficit as long as members continued to be paid out. The SNP's finance minister John Swinney had hoped for a more flexible approach despite the mood of caution in Brussels arising in large part from a Eurozone crisis caused by poor regulation of the single currency. Provision for Scottish pensions was wrapped in uncertainty if firms had to ensure that they were fully- funded.[31]

Business Muzzled

At the start of February 2014, Brian Quinn, honorary professor of economics at Glasgow University and a former deputy governor of the Bank of England, had expressed misgivings that the multi-billion pounds Scottish financial services industry had not revealed its stance on independence with the campaign already into its second year. He argued that neutrality was an untenable position since many Scottish banks, pension firms and insurance companies had a majority of their customers living elsewhere in the UK, and might therefore have to consider moving their head offices out of an independent Scotland.[32]

By early March 2014, the list of companies which had expressed concern about the economic consequences of Scotland leaving the UK was growing. It included: BP, Shell, Standard Life, RBS, Lloyds Banking Group, Sainsbury's, Asda, as well as numerous Scottish companies and British trade bodies.[33] But their views were expressed in low-key terms. A programme, 'The Great British Break Up?', broadcast by the Channel 4 in July presented evidence that the SNP was using forceful means to keep business out of the independence debate.

It was claimed by Gavin Hewitt, former chief executive of the Scotch Whisky Association, that Angus Robertson, the SNP leader in the Commons, tried to tell the organisation to 'stay out' of the debate. Mr Hewitt said members of staff had met Mr Robertson at least six times in the past two years, adding: 'He and the SNP have regularly tried to get the message to the Scotch Whisky Association that the Scotch Whisky industry should stay out of the independence debate. He was, I think, trying to neuter business comment'. The programme claimed to have been told by nineteen firms that they were aware of threats of 'retribution down the track' for those who support the Union. It was stated: 'the intimidation is alleged to have come from the highest levels of the SNP, including from the office of Alex Salmond, the First Minister'.[34]

Salmond had made at least one highly belligerent statement on the economic front which was bound to worry business figures concerned with Scotland's credit worthiness and attraction as a source of inward investment. He had warned, even before Osborne's intervention, that if a currency union was denied to an independent Scotland, its rulers would feel under no obligation to honour any payment of the share of the UK debt which would accrue to Scotland.[35] He seemed to assume that investors might forgive any repudiation of debt and Scotland would avoid pariah status in international markets.[36]

The Centre for Public Policy for Regions (CPPR), a think tank not normally associated with political nationalism, published a paper after these threats began to be issued, setting out figures showing 'how dumping a share of the UK's debt would be worth twice as much to an independent Scotland as North Sea oil' (at mid-2014 prices).[37] Salmond repeated his warning up to the eve of the referendum by which time the share value of firms domiciled in Scotland or with heavy investments there was falling at a time of buoyant stock prices.[38] It was perhaps in order to dampen growing international uncertainty concerning the impact of a Yes vote that on 13 January 2014, the British government announced it would honour all 1.2 trillion pounds ($2.2 trillion) worth of UK government debt regardless of how Scots voted.[39]

Better Together reacted in a low-key way to Salmond's politicisation of debt obligations even though the uncertainty his remarks generated was bound to make it harder for Scotland to borrow on international markets. Business for Scotland, a pro-independence body mainly composed of micro-sized business firms, remained tight-lipped about his intervention. It also refrained from comment after a volley of online attacks from nationalists on the founder, and main shareholder of Barrhead Travel, Scotland's biggest independent travel company, Bill Munro. These occurred after he had written in February 2014 to 697 of the company's staff expressing his misgivings, on economic grounds, about separation.[40]

In his letter, he stated that 'For Barrhead Travel and most, if not all travel companies, it will be a complete disaster, especially with branches in England and Ireland'. Nationalists responded by urging Scots to boycott the firm, which employs more than 800 people, and arguing that Mr Munro's intervention amounted to bullying his staff. He said that he had been determined to set out 'the facts, not the lies being put out by the SNP' after being asked by many of his staff for his views about the ramifications of independence.[41]

A poll of 1,000 Scottish small businesses released just before the Barrhead Travel controversy erupted, found that 48 per cent believed a Yes vote would be a negative step for their company, compared to 37 per cent who said it would be positive.[42] But few business figures were willing to adopt Munro's stance and publicly air misgivings about a separate future. Alistair Darling complained on 1 April that 'In the next six months the eyes of the world will be on Scotland. Frankly, these attacks on business people who have spoken out shames Scotland.'[43]

Two days later when Scottish business chiefs appeared before the Scottish Parliament's committee on economics and tourism, one of their number, Iain McMillan, head of the Confederation of British Industry (CBI) in Scotland, found himself being heckled and talked across by several of the SNP members who comprised a majority.[44] By July 2014 it was being reported in the media that Better Together chiefs were exasperated that 'Scottish businesses are reluctant to speak out publicly in favour of the Union, no matter how vehemently they condemn the idea of separation in private.'[45]

The strong-arm tactics and language of the Yes side did not produce any poll reverses in the spring of 2014. It looked as if its edgy and impetuous approach matched the outlook of many Scots who had crossed over to the independence camp. Voices from civic and intellectual Scotland now began to buttress those of Darling and pro-Union politicians.

Academics Step Back

Professor Ronald McDonald, holder of the chair of political economy at Glasgow University was very visible during the last six months of campaigning. He spoke across the country from Better Together platforms, often teaming up with Adam Tomkins, professor of international law also at Glasgow. His message was a cerebral one which he pitched at a professional audience as when writing in the newly-launched online journal of academic debate, the *Conversation*. There he took issue with one of Salmond's economic advisers, Professor Andrew Hughes-Hallett of George Mason University in the USA who believed that independence was economically viable. McDonald claimed that using the pound without a currency agreement and reneging on debt would 'add 3 to 5% to Scottish interest rates, hence £400-00 per month extra on a Scottish £100k mortgage'. He was convinced that 'the numbers for [the] economy of an independent Scotland look scary'.[46] This was a viewpoint which he enlarged upon in the mass circulation *Daily Record,* just a month before the referendum.[47] He warned that the conditions for maintaining a currency union did not exist and that, if tried, the experiment could eat up an entire year's worth of Scotland's GDP. Overall, if compelled by hostile markets to set up a separate Scottish currency, many years of austerity would be required for it to work.

McDonald was a catch for Better Together since he had advised oil-producing economies across the world to manage their currency as well as advising the central banks of major European countries. But he was challenged by the economist Professor Sir Donald McKay who had advised Conservative Secretaries of State when they ran Scotland up to 1997 and was now a backer of independence. In the same article, McKay contended that a currency union was tenable and that the oil dimension worked in Scotland's favour due to realistic price forecasting by the SNP and the likelihood of more accessible reserves in Scottish waters.[48]

There were relatively few such set piece contests among academics. A pro-Union 'Academics Together' group had been in existence for most of the campaign. It was dominated by academics nearing retirement or who had stood down from major administrative positions. It had certain cards to play. Its chair, Professor Hugh Pennington, a bacteriologist at Aberdeen University, frequently appeared in the media to argue that Scottish academia derived huge benefit from the Union compared with other parts of the country. Scotland obtained over 13 per cent of the UK's competitive funding despite having only 8.4 per cent of its population. The rival Academics for Yes body argued that trans-border cooperation could maintain the strength of higher education. This view was propounded forcefully by the historian Sir Tom Devine who made a dramatic 11th hour conversion to independence accompanied by a round of press interviews and television appearances. He was already a high-profile figure, a 'tele-don' in the mould of the historian AJP Taylor. He was able to pack public halls and his switch to the Yes side was an undoubted coup. With independence, he insisted that the universities could provide the impetus for the knowledge industry in Scotland.[49] But his reluctance to mention how the revenue could be raised for a tax base a fraction of the UK one enabled British-minded academics to challenge the soundness of his vision.[50] Pennington and others had long argued that the austerity likely to accompany independence would ensure a possibly severe contraction in the Scottish universities, especially in the area of research.

Neither camp managed to mobilise large numbers of academics for their cause. Debates were organized, usually by the university authorities, in many of Scotland's fifteen universities. The No side mainly won, though by shrinking majorities as the voting day neared. One of Sir Tom Devine's academic critics, the fellow historian, Professor Christopher Whatley, a vice-principal of Dundee University found himself the centre of controversy after he attended the Dundee launch of the Better Together campaign on 5 November 2013. Shona Robison, one of the city's SNP parliamentarians and a member of Salmond's government, contacted the university's principal to demand an explanation.[51] She was concerned that as he was involved in a state-funded university project examining the referendum, he ought to stay neutral.[52] Whatley protested about being put under unacceptable pressure and he also obtained the backing of Pennington and other senior pro-Union academics. They issued an open letter stating that 'It is unacceptable for a minister to question the integrity of an academic on the basis of his or her political views.... It would be a very dangerous route to go down if the views of academics were required to be in conformity with the government of the day'.[53]

Robison insisted that she had not been seeking to muzzle Whatley but the publicity which this incident obtained may have prompted academics, especially those reliant on state funding or on short-term contracts, to remain on the sidelines of the referendum. This incident prompted Professor Louise Richardson, the head of St Andrews University, to write to all 2,000 staff telling them to defy political intimidation and speak out during the independence debate.[54]

Professor Richardson made headlines in the final stage of the referendum when a London daily newspaper obtained E- Mails, showing that Alex Salmond's office had attempted to have the senior Irish-academic release a statement praising the Scottish government and criticising Westminster over higher education policy. It was also reported that the First Minister had telephoned the Principal of St Andrews University (where he had been a student in the 1970s) demanding that she clarify remarks she made about the consequences of leaving the UK; in a conversation described as 'loud and heated' Richardson refused to comment but Sir David Carter, a former Chief Medical Officer in Scotland and former vice chairman of Cancer Research UK was more forthcoming. In May 2014, he helped draw up a letter signed by 14 clinical professors and biomedical scientists which claimed that Scotland would lose out on millions of pound of UK funding, resulting in severe damage to world-renowned medical research in Scotland. Carter, who chairs the board of academic medicine for the Scottish universities, bringing together the leadership of five medical schools, said that academics had real fears about expressing a position on a vote which had huge implications for their profession. Speaking in May 2014, he claimed that universities did not feel they could speak out against independence for fear of infuriating Alex Salmond's government and jeopardising their funding. He claimed to have contacted senior figures at Edinburgh, Glasgow, St Andrews, Aberdeen and Dundee universities, who privately informed him that they were 'constrained' from speaking out but who offered encouragement. He decried an atmosphere of 'vindictiveness' and said he would not be surprised to ' get a swarm of attacks from Cybernats' (the term coined for aggressive nationalists active online perhaps due to their sheer frequency).[55]

Professor Niall Ferguson of Harvard University, perhaps the most widely-known early 21st century Scottish historian, also found it hard to entice any Scottish-based historians who supported the Union from signing a manifesto opposing Britain's break-up.[56] It must have been frustrating for Alistair Darling and BT that those who were prepared to speak out had their careers mainly behind them or were, as in Ferguson's case, living abroad.[57]

Where's the Passion?

Better Together's 'failure to energise middle-class no voters' had already caused dissension in its senior ranks. A lunch on 27 March 2014 saw two figures, a Liberal Democrat board member and a marketing expert complain about the timidity of Blair McDougall and Labour's electoral strategist Douglas Alexander.[58] Britain's unique selling points were plentiful – three hundred years of calm and continuous governance and successful cooperation between former national rivals being just a few. But it was only occasionally that the theme of a successful partnership in a remarkable political union, one arguably responsibly for more good than ill in the world, was taken up by Better Together stalwarts.

In May 2014, Alistair Carmichael, Secretary of State for Scotland, rhetorically asked in a newspaper article:

'Do we want to go it alone, or do we want – as a nation and as individuals – to be a driving force within the world's sixth-biggest economy, using the size and global reputation of the UK – which, just to labour the point, we helped to build – as a platform for good, for exporting Scottish values and ideas, multiplying our reach and influence by factors unimaginable to and envied by nations who would be of similar size and heft to an independent Scotland?'[59]

In the weekend before the vote, Lord Reid who, as John Reid, held high office between 1997 and 2007, condemned the SNP for popularising the view that: 'If you are involved in something British, you must be diminished in your Scottishness'. He praised the UK for 'honouring the talents of our people, enabling them to go further and higher than they could ever otherwise have done.'[60] Reid had been asked to head the pro-Union campaign in the referendum before turning down the challenge. Alistair Darling, more cerebral and forensic and less pugnacious and emotional, only sporadically alluded to British identity on public occasions. One journalist expressed dismay that in his second televised debate with Alex Salmond, on 25 August 2014, Darling failed to 'mention Britain or Britishness even once'. Alex Massie went on to write: 'It's true that putting the red white and blue centre-stage wouldn't necessarily transform the No campaign. But that misunderstands the point. Britain – and the Union – is the base upon which you build your campaign. Everything else is just tactics. Britain is the grammar; everything that follows is idiom.'[61]

Towards the end of campaigning, the annual Scottish Social Attitudes survey published its annual report. It had long been a benchmark for assessing the national mood on a range of substantial issues. In August 2014, it found that over the last three years a sense of Britishness has been rekindled among Scots. When asked to choose one single national identity, the number of people who answered 'Scottish' fell from 75 per cent in the 2011 survey to 65 per cent in 2014. Those who said they regarded themselves as 'British' increased from 15 per cent to 23 per cent over the same period.

When asked to rank their Scottishness against their Britishness, only 26 per cent said they were 'more Scottish than British', the lowest figure since the survey was first completed in 1992, when it stood at 40 per cent. The most popular answer was 'equally Scottish and British', with 32 per cent saying this description best fitted them.[62]

A Survation poll released in May 2014 and carried out among 1,003 Scots found little sign in the gulf in ethical values between Scotland and the rest of the UK that was one of the Yes side's selling points. Alex Massie wrote: 'a third of Scots wish to leave the European union. Nearly 70 per cent favour sharply restricting immigration. And almost 70 per cent want a 'tougher' line taken on benefit-spending. A benefits cap is favoured by around 80 per cent of Scots and nearly three quarters think the unemployed should be made to work for their giro cheques'.[63] In the *Financial Times* in August, John McDermott wrote:

'Polls show that Scots have similar views to the rest of the UK when it comes to welfare, immigration, benefits, unemployment and public spending. Summarising the data from social attitudes surveys, Lindsay Paterson of Edinburgh University writes: "These differences, though generally placing Scotland to the left of England, are not so huge as to signal a fundamental gulf of social values".[64]

McDermott wondered which English majority was keen on a ruthless dog-eat-dog society after reading the claim of the veteran journalist and convert to independence, Neal Ascherson that 'the Scots, in their majority, do not want to live in permanent job insecurity, in a society of growing inequality, declining real wages, zero-hours contracts, food banks and beggars jostling on the steps of every bank'.[65]

Archie MacPherson, the 78-year-old sports commentator, an instantly recognisable figure to millions of Scots, offered one of the most passionate defences of the British link at a speaking event in Dundee on 27 August. He upstaged Darling and Gordon Brown, the former Prime Minister by invoking past episodes of solidarity, endurance and achievement which had bound Scots together with those in the rest of the UK. In an unscripted speech, he said that he had accepted the invitation out of 'anger' at the 'obfuscation and evasion streaming out of the independence campaign' to the extent that he 'couldn't stand it any longer'. He invoked the end of the Second World War in 1945 and how victory had transformed British society into 'something we must never forget'. 'Our forebears created the welfare state, the education system for which myself and others have hugely benefited'.

He said: 'The television debates are accentuating the feeling that this is, one, a personality contest, and two, that it's a general election in which we are voting for a president. It is nothing of the kind'.

'I am voting for my kids and their kids... it hasn't sunk into people. It is your job to go out and question these people who are thinking about voting Yes'.

'Ask them to provide the evidence, ask them to provide certainty. There is no certainty. It is a gamble, as Alistair said'.

In his conclusion, which drew rapturous applause, Mr Macpherson said: 'The wrong road is the yellow brick road which they are riding at the end of which, as you know from the film (The Wizard of Oz) and the book, ends in deception, deceit and fantasy'.[66]

MacPherson's speech proved a hit on YouTube where it was released with a soundscape of Scottish songs and against a backdrop of scenic and industrial Scotland.[67] But this highly emotive appeal to British solidarity, based on common historical experience, stood out by its sheer rarity in the Better Together repertoire. Perhaps more recent jarring episodes in the British story such as the Northern Ireland conflict or the more controversial features of Margaret Thatcher's premiership, rendered Britishness problematic in the eyes of campaign tacticians.

It was awkward for the heavily-Labour-influenced Better Together to mount a left-wing critique of the SNP in the referendum phase. Outside spectators, noting the degree of vitriol between the two camps, might have been surprised to find that Labour and the SNP agreed on a surprising amount of political matters. Not least there was common ground over: the promotion of the concept of equality through public policy, micro-managing the lives of citizens in pursuit of specific goals, and a willingness to accept high levels of immigration. They differed over who was best qualified to deliver a progressive or paternalistic big state agenda and on whether this objective could be best furthered in, or outside, the Union. A full frontal attack on the SNP's policy record on central issues might only have opened fissures on the Union side which Darling was adept at papering over for the duration of the campaign.

He was most comfortable denouncing the impracticality of the independence goal rather than the harm it could do to identities and relationships forged over centuries. JK Rowling, the author of the Harry Potter novels, had emphasised the impracticality of quitting the Union in the midst of a recession in a 2012 interview. In June 2014, she issued a 1,600 word manifesto in favour of the Union on her personal website.[68] She argued that hazy and un-costed plans for independence meant that too much was in danger of being lost, especially in the health care sector and also the field of medical research. She understood the romantic appeal of Scottish statehood but there were too many unanswered questions and too much reliance on volatile oil revenues.

She warned: 'If we leave, there will be no going back. This separation will not be quick and clean: it will take microsurgery to disentangle three centuries of close interdependence, after which we will have to deal with three bitter neighbours'.[69]

Since 1993, Rowling had lived in Scotland where she had written novels that were turned into successful and much-loved films. They had easily given her global visibility far beyond that of any other Scottish writer. So Better Together could be well pleased that she had produced a manifesto not only emphasising their core concerns but also referring to some of the dangers of future entrenched disagreement and strife which they often preferred to tip-toe around.

Rowling, born in Gloucestershire, emphasised that: 'By residence, marriage, and out of gratitude for what this country has given me, my allegiance is wholly to Scotland and it is in that spirit that I have been listening to the months of arguments and counter-arguments'. She also added that she was bracing herself for abusive attacks from hardline nationalists who questioned her English roots and demonised any critics of independence.[70]

Her wealth and her ability to live beyond the reach of hostile critics spared her some of the problems encountered by other pro-Union champions. To the added pleasure of BT, she was prepared to devote one million pounds of her literary fortune to their cause. This announcement was made 100 days before the referendum at a time when the campaign had received few major donations and was being outspent by the Yes side; the latter was able to rely on the beneficence of an Ayrshire couple, Chris and Colin Weir. In 2011 these SNP supporters had scooped over £161 million in the EuroMillions jackpot. By June 2014, almost 80 per cent of Yes Scotland's total cash income of £4.5 million had been donated by these two supporters. By contrast, Better Together had been relying on mainly smaller contributions until Rowling's donation which was then followed by other large amounts, mainly from business sources.[71]

The online attacks which Rowling was duly subjected to made headlines due to her fame.[72] The military rank of another pro-Union campaigner subjected to 'cybernat' attack had already made headlines in April 2014. General Sir Norman Arthur had been head of the armed forces in Scotland from 1985 to 1988. Now aged 80, his letter writing campaign to raise donations for Better Together had attracted abusive E-Mails which contained expletives. He claimed that such unwelcome attention arose from the decision of Roseanna Cunningham, the minister of community safety, to tweet a photograph of one of Sir Norman's letters, distributing it to her 5,820 followers on her twitter account, despite the image clearly showing his personal contact details. As well as contacting the police, he complained to Sir Peter Housden, the head of the Scottish civil service about her actions.[73]

From Passion to Provocation

In February 2014, the Scottish Secretary Alistair Carmichael, responding in the House of Commons to concerns raised by the shadow Labour spokesperson Margaret Curran, warned that online attacks from cybernats were 'poisoning the well' of public life in Scotland. Both MPs acknowledged other forms of intimidation and he stated that 'incidents she highlights are by no means isolated—we hear them anecdotally all the time'.[74]

By the late summer of 2014 the media had carried frequent reports of pro-Union supporters facing intimidation and vandalism. In the last week of the campaign, Darling accused a minority of Yes campaigners of systematically defacing, or removing, pro-UK placards and billboards in towns such as Inverness, and on major roads throughout Scotland. He talked of 'dark aspects' of the campaign which need to have a light shone on them'.[75] Four months after the referendum, Queen Elizabeth II, in her Christmas broadcast, drew attention to continuing polarisation in Scotland. She referred to the need for reconciliation, acknowledging that 'bridging these differences will take time'.[76] At no stage did Alex Salmond accept the contention of Darling and others that some of his supporters had 'crossed the acceptability line in their conduct and that this needed to be stopped'.[77] He refused to disassociate himself from what were a rolling series of protests against alleged BBC bias.[78] Journalists who asked him hard questions, such as Nick Robinson of the BBC and Faisal Islam of Sky were accused of bias.[79] Shortly afterwards, the Yes campaign head Blair Jenkins conceded that there had been no systematic BBC bias against his side.[80]

Tom Bradby, the political editor of one major British news channel, ITN, found the ill-will to be worse than that he had experienced when working in Ulster in the 1990s: 'the level of abuse and intimidation' was 'highly unusual in the democratic world'.[81] On the day before the vote, Salmond's predecessor as First Minister, Jack (now Lord) McConnell, complained that the recently created centralized police force had shown complacency and a 'shocking' lack of action against intimidation. He said officers from Police Scotland had been 'surprisingly absent' as public meetings were disrupted, people's homes were targeted and threats were made to campaigners'.[82] But the civil authorities in Scotland were unwilling to agree. Sir Peter Housden, much criticized by the opposition for refusing to take seriously concerns over Salmond's alleged politicization of the civil service, was disinclined to intervene over the conduct of the referendum by the government in Edinburgh.[83] Meanwhile, Brian Docherty, chairman of the Scottish Police Federation, complained on the day that McConnell spoke out, of 'exaggerated rhetoric that is being deployed with increased frequency'. He believed that it was 'preposterous' to suggest that normally law-abiding citizens would turn to crime as a result of the independence vote.

Docherty was even prepared to assert: 'One of the many joys of this campaign has been how it has awakened political awareness across almost every single section of society'.[84]

Better Together's chief executive was claiming in May 2014 that it had 30,000 activists on the ground across Scotland – more than the opposing Yes Scotland campaign. They were organised into 250 groups overseen by eight local campaign organisers according to Blair McDougall.[85] But it was difficult to spot these activists and the teams shown on the campaign's web-site were often small in number. The Yes side were able to mobilise activists to canvass commuters at local train stations and shoppers in major urban centres. Far more information was often provided about such initiatives on the online accounts of pro-Indy campaigners than was the case on their opponent's sites.

As 2014 got underway, fears were increasingly expressed in the media that BT's relatively low profile and emphasis on choreographed top-down events was damaging the pro-Union cause. Many Yes events might be evangelical meetings for the already converted but their frequency in localities previously numb to the Yes cause was having a real impact.

Labour Orators Hit the Streets

Several political figures decided it was necessary to mount their own personalised public campaigns. The first to do so was George Galloway MP. This Dundee-born left winger had been chairman of the Scottish Labour party in his twenties and had been Labour MP for a Glasgow seat from 1987 to 2003. After being expelled from the Labour Party for his vociferous opposition to its leader Tony Blair's policy in the Middle East, he had launched his own Respect party, initially in conjunction with the Trotskyite, Socialist Workers Party. This alliance soon foundered but Galloway acquired enough support for his outspoken views about Western intervention in Muslim countries after the 9/11 events, to be elected for two urban English constituencies after 2005. It was as MP for Bradford West in Yorkshire that he launched his 'Just Say Naw' campaign in Glasgow in December 2013. He held 25 mainly evening public meetings in which he explained his opposition to independence.[86] There was also duelling with hecklers which both he and many in the audience often found the highlight of the evening. He sometimes returned on a second occasion to particular venues such as Coatbridge in Lanarkshire. Here, in an area populated by people of Irish Catholic descent, he already had a strong following. This was due to his backing for a united Ireland and outspoken support for Celtic football club, a totemic symbol of diaspora identity. But he was no longer denouncing British misbehaviour beyond the island shores but instead defending Britain as a viable entity where humble folk had managed to obtain social justice. Rather bizarrely he readily conceded that it was Labour, the party which had expelled him, that had been responsible for much of this social progress. But many of those West of Scotland diaspora Irish deserted him because he was no longer endorsing their 'rebel' culture.

Galloway was versatile and uninhibited. He did not disavow his radical pro-Palestinian sympathies or regret his confrontation with US senators over American policy in the Middle East. But he readily defended the Union in right-wing publications and spoke on clearly right-wing platforms as at the debate on independence held in Edinburgh on 24 June 2014 hosted by the *Spectator* magazine. The audience were mainly composed of Edinburgh lawyers, bankers and fund managers who cheered him to the echo on that occasion according to a regular columnist for the weekly.[87] Writing in the *Daily Mail* soon after, he made an old-fashioned appeal to British patriotism (couched in anti-fascist terms) which nearly all Labour MPs would probably have hesitated about delivering. The excerpt below gives a flavour of Galloway's approach:

'Contrary to the claims of the cybernats, Scotland is not an occupied country. Rather, Scotland and England together occupied most of the world. The Scots are not denied self-determination and could have voted at any time in the past century for independence and had it. I was one of the leaders in the movement for Scottish devolution. It was right to set up a Scottish parliament and it is right that it will be given more powers.....

Recently, I spoke at a school in Ruislip in outer London, cheek by jowl to RAF Northolt. I recalled those midsummer days when our RAF came together to save us at a moment of supreme national peril. The Battle of Britain was fought by Brylcreem boys from all classes and every part of our land...'.[88]

Galloway disparaged the SNP's 'pretend' nationalism as here:

'....We've mingled, married, succeeded, failed, occasionally fallen out, made up and got on. As equal partners. So why divorce now?

I know about divorce, believe me. It is never amicable, however reasonable the arrangements seem to be – the division of the record collection, the dog, the car – you can give everything, but the one thing you will never give is the right to continue to use the joint account and credit cards. And that's the nationalists Plan A. They have no Plan B'.[89]

Galloway argued that the redistributive policies which he favoured would be ruled out in a separate state due to the level of austerity that would be needed in conditions of steep economic adversity. The departure of Scotland from the UK would solidify right-wing rule in both parts of the island. Two states would pursue beggar-thy-neighbour policies, resulting in a real international frontier on Hadrians Wall. His oratorical talents and ability to skilfully use demotic language to make his case were assets for a colourless campaign. Social media enabled his pro-British campaign pitch to reach people disinclined to follow Labour stalwarts of the Union .

Galloway made it clear that he was 'not part of the official Scotland Together outfit, whose slogan "No,Thanks" will hardly warm the heather, never mind set it alight'.[90] As the autumn of 2014 approached, he was attracting increasing numbers of former Labour colleagues to his events.

Perhaps inspired by Galloway's success, the Labour MP Jim Murphy also went freelance. In the summer of 2014 he launched a '100 speeches in 100 towns' event. Like Galloway, he was a self-confident politician in a party dominated by colourless office-holders. He had also fallen foul of a Labour leader, Ed Miliband who had demoted him to the lowly job of international development in the shadow cabinet.

The 47-year-old Murphy claimed that the first 70 meetings were 'great' but he drew much fiercer opposition than Galloway had partly because his speeches were held in the open-air, often in the middle of cities and towns where the Yes side had previously appeared to have captured the streets.

On 29 August he announced that he was suspending his one-man speaking campaign due to 'concerted and coordinated' gangs of Yes supporters preventing him speak. He wrote on that day:

'In town after town it's no longer undecided voters going about their shopping that I'm meeting but instead there are Yes crowds occupying the street corners I'm due to speak at. The language of treason is a favourite with them. They're big on Quisling, although I doubt if they know much Norwegian history. Regularly I get called a terrorist and often a paedophile too'.[91]

He claimed that the various Yes sites on Facebook, affiliated to the official Yes Scotland campaign were coordinating the opposition to his street presence. But Alex Salmond defended the public's right to peaceful protest, going on to say: 'My advice to people, and Jim Murphy too, is he should ignore it. If he wants to go and shout at people from a loudhailer in the streets, he should be allowed to do so'. Salmond also alleged that he and others in the Yes campaign had been involved in 'much more serious incidents' without providing details of what they were.[92]

Murphy resumed his campaign a few days later, facing continued opposition but far less intense than before. It is likely that this gritty, resilient political operator had been unfazed by the aggression he had attracted. It enabled him to place the Yes campaign in an uncomfortable light by arguing that ugly street protests were being coordinated by them: 'They have turned this tap on, they can turn it off'.[93] He may have launched his speaking tour fully aware that he was likely to attract high levels of unwelcome attention and that the flagging No campaign would benefit as a result.

Salmond may have been unwise to laugh off the street opposition to Murphy. He appeared, early in 2014, to take a calculated decision to drop the emollient 'social union' message, discarding British continuity and embracing instead a transformed independent Scotland ready to stand up to the rest of the UK so that it could take its rightful place in global affairs. The partisan rhetoric bolstering this message went down well with blue-collar workers, previously mainly Labour supporters according to poll findings. But Salmond's belligerency, as when he laughed off his threat to renege on paying part of the national debt by saying 'what are they going to do – invade?', alarmed many Scots.[94] One poll in July 2014, showed that one in six Scottish voters, approximating to 17 per cent of the population, would consider leaving Scotland if his cause prevailed.[95] Rory Stewart MP for Penrith and the Borders, may have struck a deep chord when he wrote: 'He would force us each to choose an exclusive and separate identity, and in doing so split my family and indeed tens of millions of individuals like myself'

Salmond Troubles the Undecided

When asked in a poll conducted in May 2014 if the thought of Alex Salmond being the first Prime Minister of an independent Scotland made them more likely to vote Yes or No, 36 per cent of Scottish voters said No while only 12 per cent said Yes. This prompted the *Daily Record* to claim that one in three Scots are being put off independence by their dislike of Alex Salmond.[96] The Survation poll of 1003 votes, showed that 36 per cent believed the thought of Salmond running an independent Scotland is pushing them towards a No vote in September's referendum. A YouGov poll, of 1085 adults polled in Scotland between 12 and 15 August, reinforced the trend: 45 per cent believed Salmond, as leader of the independence campaign, was the wrong man for the job, with only 57 per cent of Yes supporters backing him.[97]

Salmond had his own internal critics and one of them, Jim Sillars a very prominent campaigner on the Yes side, branded him a liability.[98] But, arguably, it was largely due to Salmond's self-belief, tactical shrewdness and mastery of communication that the SNP had advanced so far towards its overriding objective.[99] After an indifferent first debating performance against Alistair Darling, the samurai warrior Salmond was on display in the second debate on 25 August. He was aided by a sympathetic audience which the BBC, host of the debate, had commissioned from an independent firm and also by a weak referee who was powerless to prevent Salmond taking over the occasion in a bravura performance in which his opponent was crushed.[100]

Afterwards, poll ratings for Yes surged. Several of these polls suggested that previously undecided voters were prepared to downgrade the risks of independence and instead embrace the challenge. Pro-Indy voices increasingly branded Britain as washed up and obsolete. There was surprisingly little effort by Better Together to counter this assessment.

In the last six months of campaigning Salmond insisted that Scotland was in a healthier condition economically than Britain as a whole and that it was reasonable for it to be ranked as one of the world's successful economies. On 28 May 2014, on the basis of Scottish government data, he argued that Scotland ranked above major economies such as France and Japan in terms of GDP. It was therefore one of the richest countries in the developed world.[101] This assessment was challenged in a study by Glasgow University academics which found it to be a middle-ranking economy with high levels of foreign ownership. According to the study, the level of outside ownership of large parts of the Scottish economy meant that Scotland's actual income was as much as $5,000 (£2,990) less per head than the SNP leader was claiming.[102]

Project Fear

Darling and his team in Better Together had always claimed that full independence was attainable for Scotland but that it got a better deal from remaining in partnership with the rest of the UK. Pollsters may well have advised that to argue Scotland was a nation but that it didn't have what it took to be a successfully independent country, was a certain vote-loser. But it was implicit in the arguments of many on-line campaigners who asserted that the Yes side were offering only a dream and not a coherent plan for the future. 'Hugh_Oxford' writing in the *Daily Telegraph* put it this way:

'You say you want to leave the most successful economic and political union in modern history, one in which your nation has flourished in peace and prosperity for over three hundred years.'

'You want to turn 90% of your domestic market into a foreign market, and shrink your domestic market by 90%'

'You don't know what currency you are going to be using, but it will probably be a foreign currency, and so you won't have any control over monetary policy'

'You don't know what, if any, economic trading unions you will be able to join'.

'And finally, you're promising all your people that they will all receive more money from the state, but be taxed less'.[103]

This was a full-throated rendition of 'Project Fear', a term leaked to the glee of nationalists after having been privately used by Rob Shorthouse, Better Together's communications director.[104] Salmond taunted Darling with it in their 5 August debate but Darling and other pro-Union champions refused to publicly concede that independence in general, and not just the SNP's Panglossian version, would be damaging for Scotland. The No side could have regrouped by claiming that they were patriotic Scots who stood for 'Project Reality'; that the country's economic circumstances made it hard to see how many Scots could be shielded from adversity if not just a political, but an economic and social union, were unpicked.

Instead Better Together relied on major economic institutions and several big economic names to argue that independence just wouldn't work. On 14 September, the *Spectator* summarised a conveniently–leaked report from Deutsche Bank on a post-British Scotland's prospects, written by David Folkerts-Landau, its chief economist which offered evidence that only by greatly reducing the social state and therefore massively increasing inequality, could independence be made to work.[105]

Days earlier, Standard Life, the Edinburgh based financial services company, stated that it could transfer its investments business to England in the event of a 'Yes' vote. In an update on its website, the company said it could also move its pension and long-term savings held by UK customers to England. The company, founded in Edinburgh in 1825, employed 5,000 people in the city and the financial services industry, 200,000 strong, was the largest industry in a largely post-manufacturing country. The letter to shareholders, in which this information was relayed, was seen in parts of the media as an undertaking that Standard Life would relocate its business if Scotland chose independence.[106]

On 20 August Sir Ian Wood, who had been praised by Alex Salmond as the foremost expert in the Scottish oil industry, warned that the First Minister was overestimating the remaining reserves by between 45 per cent and 60 percent. He argued that the industry's looming contraction meant: 'the case is heavily weighted towards Scotland remaining in the UK'. He claimed to be speaking out to ensure young Scots voting in the referendum knew there would be little production by the time they are middle aged. The consequence, he predicted, was a 'real rundown' in Scottish public services and jobs after independence. Pro-Union media organs expected that this intervention from the man who was one of the chief architects of the Scottish oil industry, would significantly weaken the First Minister's claim that only a Yes vote would save the National Health Service in Scotland.[107]

Public admissions came from rueful Better Together figures that the Yes side made headway, particularly in the west of Scotland, by warning that without independence, the NHS was likely to face privatisation from the Conservatives even though the main UK governing party lacked the legal right to interfere in a Scottish-controlled institution. The *Economist* insisted that independence was likely to be a greater hazard to a public service health system since Scotland, with a much smaller tax base, had a population that was older and unhealthier than the rest of Britain's. It believed that 'the nationalist promise to increase NHS spending without also raising taxes or squandering Scotland's dwindling oil revenues is incredible'. But it reflected on 13 September that the 'NH Yes' slogan was 'playing a huge part in the late separatist surge' and, in an article entitled 'How a nation went mad' conceded that 'many Scots have come to believe their [the Yes campaign's]wildest claims'.[108]

In the closing months, Better Together had sufficient revenue to run advertising campaigns meant to demolish the more extravagant claims of its opponents. But few of its billboards or television broadcasts hit home and at least one, focussing on women's issues, was deemed very counter-productive.[109]

Alistair Carmichael, the Scottish Secretary, declared in March 2014 that his side needed to show they were as hungry to win as the nationalists otherwise defeat was a real possibility.[110] However, for most of the time this advice went unheeded. Better Together was the staid advice a weary marriage guidance counsellor might give to a long-married couple contemplating divorce. Its own world-weariness and air of regret about having to go out and fight for the Union were often palpable. A more inspiring slogan such as 'United We Are Strong' could have been far more motivational.[111] *Better Together* failed to frame the debate around a successful partnership that had many concrete achievements and was something special in the world. David Cameron, whose inattention to detail had become notorious on many issues, helped dig a hole for it by agreeing, in negotiations with Salmond, to a question in which Better Together would be campaigning for a negative. A Yes campaign which invested hugely in the most sophisticated techniques of media presentation did not find it hard to depict the 'No' message as a 'no' to Scotland.

Westminster Reacts to Danger Signals

As Prime Minister of the United Kingdom, David Cameron made regular campaign trips to Scotland to persuade it to stay in the Union. In May, prior to one such visit, he was depicted by Salmond as an intruder in 'a country which has never, and will never, elect people like him to govern us'.[112] Salmond took advantage of the widespread anti-political mood, one that was not merely confined to Scotland, to brand his opponents as illegitimate. In February 2014, he had already branded Westminster politicians from the main UK parties as 'thieves' for allegedly stealing Scotland's oil wealth.[113] These parties were already known as 'Lib-Lab-Con' by some disaffected citizens who had flocked to the UKIP party mainly in England and who believed that they were unrepresentative cliques united in defending their own privileges.

Better Together failed to organize any kind of fight-back, defending the performance of British institutions and trying to place them in a favourable light in global terms. Press organs sympathetic to British unity also frequently displayed limp and introspective coverage. The *Spectator* which, under a Scottish editor, devoted ample coverage to the referendum, often sounded bleak about the prospects of the Union's survival. The online reader's forum was largely a preserve of outspoken separatists and Fraser Nelson was reduced to travelling to Scotland to give out free copies of his pre-referendum issue in the streets of central Edinburgh on 11 September 2014.[114]

Industrialists like Sir Ian Wood often made more convincing economic cases for the Union than politicians were able to do. But the business people who spoke with increasing urgency against separation in August and September no longer possessed the credibility they once may have had in Scotland. The banking crash of 2008 and the years of austerity which followed, created a growing anti-capitalist mood in parts of public opinion.[115] The SNP's former deputy leader Jim Sillars in September promised a day of reckoning for companies that had spoken up for the Union, threatening the nationalisation of the oil giant BP if independence was won.[116]

A YouGov poll in September showed that half of Scots polled believed that there were oil finds which the British government were keeping secret and 19 per cent were convinced that MI5, British intelligence, were trying to foil a Yes vote.[117] Sillars and a large part of the yes campaign endorsed these conspiracy claims.[118]

On Wednesday 10 September, normal political business at Westminster was abandoned and the main political leaders headed north to act as persuaders for the Union. They had been panicked by a poll the previous weekend which had put the Yes campaign in the lead for the first time. Salmond proclaimed the arrival of 'Team Westminster' who would be no match for his 'Team Scotland'.[119] On 16 September Labour's Ed Miliband was forced to abandon a walk-about in central Edinburgh after being harangued by Yes supporters who had also attempted to disrupt a No rally in the centre of Glasgow earlier in the week attended by many MPs from the rest of the UK.[120] The BBC even hired a bodyguard for Nick Robinson, the BBC chief's political correspondent due to fears for his safety in Scotland.[121]

Perhaps revealingly, the Scottish comedian Rory Bremner claimed around this time that it's easier to come out as gay than it is to come out as a Unionist. For several decades this accomplished mimic had mercilessly lampooned members of the British political elite but, in an interview with *Scottish Field*, he said: 'If I do impressions of Alex Salmond, people say, "How dare you ridicule him, I voted for Alex Salmond. If you send him up, you're insulting all the people who voted for him".[122] Data supplied by the British electoral Survey in July 2015 found that SNP supporters were twice as likely to take criticism of their party as personal criticism than voters from the other main parties.[123] In such a climate, it's not altogether surprising that numerous Scots, from comics to pub regulars or attendees at sporting events, felt it prudent to keep their opinions to themselves.

Confronted with an ominous poll, on 8 September, Prime Minister Cameron endorsed an impromptu announcement made by his predecessor in that office Gordon Brown of new powers for Scotland.[124] There was amazement among some analysts that a new constitutional settlement was announced in such a contrived way. The 'new union' which Brown talked about was not to be put to people in the rest of the UK but would be hurriedly worked out by a cross-party commission and legislated for before the next general election. In July, the Conservatives had endorsed full-tax-raising powers for Scotland while Labour had hesitated about going as far as this in case it led to independence occurring by default.[125] But it came round to the position of its formerly arch-unionist opponents as the work of the commission on enhanced devolution, headed by Lord Smith of Kelvin, proceeded in the autumn of 2014.[126]

Disagreement exists about the impact the promise of more devolution and the return to prominence of Brown (known to be more popular in Scotland than in England) had on pushing doubters towards the No camp. Alex Salmond would continue to claim that what became known as 'the vow' changed the minds of 10 per cent of voters, around 400,000 people – or the margin by which the Yes campaign lost.[127] But an academic survey of over 4,500 voters, carried out before and after the vote, found that a mere 3.4 per cent of No voters cited the offer of more powers as the main motivation for their decision on 18 September.[128] This academic research also suggested that the 'No' side would have prevailed without the 11th hour pledge to fast-track new powers to Scotland.[129] (Murray Foote, the editor of the *Daily Record* had presented the initiative as the 'vow' after receiving a text written by a senior member of Better Together that had been endorsed by the main British parties).[130]

By the closing weeks, the No Side effectively ceded the streets to their opponents. Only the religiously-orientated Orange Order felt compelled to make a public affirmation for the Union by organizing a march through Edinburgh on 13 September which drew 15,000 people. (Protestants would vote 60.1 per cent in favour of the Union while less than 40 per cent of Catholics would).[131] Previously, a large pro-unity demonstration scheduled for Edinburgh on a weekend in September had been ruled out by Better Together. A 'Hands across the Border' campaign by which British-minded people would join hands across Hadrians Wall was also cancelled abruptly in the summer. At short notice, the TV historian Dan Snow organized a pro-Union rally in London's Trafalgar Square on 16 September which drew 2,000 people. One of the speakers was Bob Geldof who said that 'we're all f***ing fed up of Westminster' but that the United Kingdom was worth saving.[132]

This remark perhaps encapsulated the somewhat dejected tone of the Better Together campaign. Compared with the raucous popular front which had gathered around Alex Salmond and the Yes side, its voice was faltering and its sense of belief hesitant.

The theme of several pre-poll referendum essays was that two Scotlands had emerged with visions of the future totally at odds with each other. Chris Deerin of the *Scottish Daily Mail*, one of the few eloquent champions of the union writing in the Scottish media observed on 8 September:

'There are two distinct conversations going on in Scotland today. One is dreary and fact-based. It is concerned with national debt, currency, interest rates, mortgage costs, pensions, EU membership, the departure of key businesses, the severe austerity that a newly independent Scotland would almost certainly have to implement. It worries about how we can do our bit in a time of great global crisis.

The other is that nationalist fantasy, soundtracked and scripted by middle-class musicians, playwrights and actors, urged along by disenchanted, superannuated newspaper columnists, gleefully led by a pied-piper politician as cynical and self-interested as any of those he castigates at Westminster. Everything will be fine, the detail doesn't matter, we'll cross each bridge as we come to it, it'll be alright on the night. Let's just /get out'.[133]

In the event, it was the un-romantic and under-stated Scots who proved to be in the clear majority when the votes were counted. The No side had beaten Yes by a clear ten per cent on a massive 85 percent turnout. But any victory celebrations organized by Better Together were low-key ones away from the gaze of cameras. Journalists noticed how unwilling still 'No' supporters were to appear on camera. 'Yes' posters remained visible on many windows in big cities long after the vote and the hardcore separatists organized themselves into a '45' movement, seeing their percentage of the vote as a moral victory and only a temporary defeat.

British-Minded Scots after the Referendum

Labour, the mainstay of Better Together, obtained no political lift from its side's victory. The reverse occurred. Previously reliable supporters bolted *en masse* towards the SNP, seduced by the months of intense emotional fervour manufactured by the Yes side. Labour had still been winning many by-elections for council and Holyrood seats up until the first half of 2014 but thereafter it was faced with a haemorrhage of support. Jim Murphy had been almost alone in adopting a combative stance during the referendum; this stance may have secured him his party's Scottish leadership only for both of them to be buried in an electoral landslide for the Nationalists in the May 2015 general election.

David Cameron and his party were the unexpected victors in this British contest. His earlier tactical errors had provided the optimal conditions for an SNP surge. But in the referendum's aftermath, he showed some belated tactical flair. Controversially, he depicted the SNP as a threat to orderly government in the UK and claimed that it would be illegitimate for his Labour foe to work with it in order to attain power. This tactic played well with undecided 'swing' voters in parts of England unnerved by the prospect of a leftward Labour Party taking charge along with an even more militant-sounding SNP.

This Cameron gambit left Unionists disconsolate including many in Scottish Tory ranks. Andy McIver, a former communications director for the Scottish party wrote on 28 April 2015: 'If the SNP could create the Tory campaign, according to my erstwhile colleagues, they would have created the one we have seen for the last week'. In the same article he claimed that 'Downing Street has absolutely no strategy whatsoever when it comes to Scotland. They have tactics; but no strategy. If is for that reason that Downing Street's focus in Scotland is simply about getting over the next hurdle'.[134]

Confronted with 56 SNP MPs who often proved a more combative opposition to the ruling Tories than Labour, Cameron now obtained regular briefings on Scotland from Ruth Davidson. It was the first time in many years that the party had a leader who proved such a morale booster as well as undeniably popular beyond the party's own ranks. The Tories partly buried their reputation for being reactionary by rallying around a leader who was young and also a lesbian. Unless Labour experienced a death-bed recovery, then it even looked possible that the Conservatives could emerge as Scotland's largest pro-Union party. But this would count for little if Davidson and her team were unable to prevent their London colleagues from periodically playing Anglo-Scottish divide-and-rule for seemingly narrow advantage. One breakthrough was her success in persuading the Glasgow University constitutional law professor Adam Tomkins to join the party in August 2015. He was one of the few figures from civil society who had made his mark in the Better Together campaign as a fluent platform speaker and a subtle thinker on constitutional issues. The SNP's conference in Aberdeen in mid-October 2015 coincided with a cover article in the *Spectator* written by Tomkins and entitled 'Centralist, illiberal and authoritarian, the SNP's one-party state'. After an analysis of how the party was micro-managing the lives of individual Scots as well as the universities, he argued that 'it's time for the rebellion to begin'.[135]

Labour had chosen the 34-year-old Kezia Dugdale as leader on 15 August 2015; she would need all of her resilience and poise to keep a grip on a fractious and demoralised party. Her decision the next month to allow Labour candidates to campaign for independence in any future referendum, showed Labour's readiness to retreat to the sidelines on such a major constitutional issue. For some it was a necessary acknowledgement that for a long time, a sizeable portion of Labour voters in Scotland had in fact been pro-independence. But for others, her move allowed certain imponderables to fall into place. One was the bloodless nature of the 2013-14 campaign Labour fought to save the Union and its reluctance to prepare the ground for a passionate grassroots campaign. It suggested to one respected online commentator that the commitment of much of the Labour Party to the Union was in fact tactical and bound up with its own electoral fortunes: achieving a raft of Labour seats and justifying the existence (and salaries) of a party machine was more important than preventing the UK from falling apart.[136] By this stage, the party had a leader, Jeremy Corbyn, in some ways even more opposed to Britain's influence in the world than the SNP and far less coy about making common cause with a range of movements and individuals who it would not be hard to describe as firmly anti-western in their outlook. It was a sign of the desperation in the Scottish party that hopes were raised that this 'real' socialist could deprive the SNP of lots of votes in the forthcoming Holyrood elections. Corbyn whose track-record of militant opposition to moderate or centrist measures suggests that he would have been a Labour convert to the Indy cause if he had been a Scottish-based politician, opportunistically blamed Better Together for most of Labour's Caledonian woes on a visit to Scotland on 1 October.[137] Soon after, at a time when the SNP was beset by scandal, Gordon Brown reinforced that party's insubstantial claim that the 'Vow' was not being implemented.[138] An opinion poll published on 8 October showed Labour a full 35 points behind the SNP and as long as such a senior Labour figure displayed an essentially Nationalist world view in his pronouncements, it was hard to imagine how the party could avoid being buried in the 2016 Holyrood election.[139]

The Liberal Democrats also had a new leader. Tim Farron has paid attention to Scotland making well-aimed attacks at fresh moves by the SNP to impose the grip of the state on previously autonomous institutions. Willie Rennie is an effective Scottish leader, (the vote of whose party fell less dramatically in Scotland than in the rest of the UK but which still performed disastrously). It's only remaining Scottish MP Alistair Carmichael faced a court battle to remain at Westminster in September 2015 after admitting that he was the source of a leak of a note on a meeting between Sturgeon and the French ambassador during the spring 2015 election campaign. A petition to secure his removal as an MP obtained enough votes to trigger a court case under electoral law. It showed how implacable many nationalists were in seeking to whittle down even the tiny number of remaining Scottish MPs opposed to them.[140]

It remains to be seen if the cooperation of the referendum years can be recaptured and augmented by the pro-Union side. It will need to be: on 9 September, the day that Queen Elizabeth II opened the railway linking Edinburgh with the Scottish Borders (and also the day that she became Britain's longest serving monarch), a poll was published which put the SNP on 58 per cent of the vote and revealed that 53 per cent of respondents wished Scotland to be independent. But two weeks later, another showed that 69 per cent of voters in Scotland did not want another referendum in the near future.[141]

As the first anniversary of the independence referendum approached, Blair Jenkins, the media executive who had fronted the 'Yes' campaign would declare on 11 September 2015: 'I do think it's highly likely there will be a second referendum and I think it is highly likely Yes will win'.[142] Nicola Sturgeon, the Scottish Republican who had hosted the Queen on her historic milestone, warned two days later that the party's manifesto for the 2016 Holyrood elections would set out triggers that would cause a second referendum. Under the 1997 devolution legislation, only Westminster has the right to initiate such a binding referendum. But if the hunger for victory is a determining feature of the success of the nationalist cause, thwarting the SNP and its allies will be even harder than it was first time around.

If another referendum looms in the future, the way ahead for British-minded Scots seems to lie in putting together a more passionate and authentic campaign that is not controlled by political parties towards whom much of the population harbour deep reserve. Some of the rhetorical flair and hard intellectual arguments that were in short supply in Better Together emerged online in 2013-14. These campaigners have been augmented by others on twitter, in blog articles, and through online petitions who seek to gradually alter Scottish opinion by showing the downside of SNP rule. They have been aided by some spectacular missteps. On 30 September 2015, the SNP MP Michelle Thomson stood down as the party's business affairs spokeswoman and was automatically suspended from party membership when it emerged that the police were investigating deals involving her property company. They centred on the MP's links with a solicitor who was struck off over 13 potentially fraudulent transactions involving Ms Thomson's company.[143] At the time of writing there is no evidence of any criminal involvement on the part of someone who had been the managing director of Business for Scotland in 2013-14 and who went on to be one of the SNP's most high-profile MPs. Perhaps the main hope for Scots with a British outlook is that, by behaving like a party of the establishment, the SNP will find it increasingly harder to convince lower-income Scots that it can be the architect of a socially just post-British state.

Notes for Chapter 3

1. Private information.
2. Martin H, 'What just Happened', *Politics is Moral Psychology*, 27 May 2015,
   http://politicsismoralpsychology.com/2015/05/27/what-just-happened/

3. Severin Carrell, Nicholas Watt and Patrick Wintour, 'The Real Story of the Scottish Referendum: Britain on the Brink, Part 1, *Guardian,* 15 December 2014. http://www.theguardian.com/politics/2014/dec/15/-sp-britain-on-brink-real-story-scottish-independence

4. Carrell et *al*, 'The Real Story, Part 1'.

5. Angus Robertson, 'Scottish independence will reinforce our social union', *Guardian,* 10 October 2011, http://www.theguardian.com/commentisfree/2011/oct/10/scottish-independence-social-union

6. Simon Johnson, 'Alex Salmond has "bunker mentality" over independence failings', *Daily Telegraph,* 19 September 2013, http://www.telegraph.co.uk/news/uknews/scotland/10321404/Alex-Salmond-has-bunker-mentality-over-independence-failings.html

7. James Maxwell, 'The SNP is paying the price for its botched currency logic'. *New Statesman* 13 August 2014.

8. Andrew Black, 'Scottish independence: Currency debate explained', BBC News, 29 January 2014, http://www.bbc.co.uk/news/uk-scotland-scotland-politics-25913721

9. *Scottish Daily Mail,* 6 May 2015.

10. *Scottish Daily Mail,* 22 August 2014. http://www.dailymail.co.uk/news/article-2731860/Alex-Salmond-s-former-policy-chief-launches-blistering-attack-SNP-s-plan-pound.html

11. Simon Johnson, 'Keeping pound may only be a stop-gap', *Daily Telegraph,* 18 August 2014. http://www.telegraph.co.uk/news/uknews/scottish-independence/11041521/Alex-Salmond-Keeping-pound-may-only-be-a-stopgap.html

12. Calum Ross, 'Leading economist says Scotland should reject pound deal', *Press and Journal,* 25 August 2014. https://www.pressandjournal.co.uk/fp/news/politics/westminster/323539/expert-scots-should-reject-pound-deal/

13. Johnson, 'Keeping pound'.

14. Andrew Black and Aiden James, 'Yes vote means leaving pound says Osborne', BBC news, 13 February 2014. http://www.bbc.co.uk/news/uk-scotland-scotland-politics-26166794

15. Iain Martin, Westminster dynamites Alex Salmond's currency union', *Daily Telegraph,* 13 February 2014. http://blogs.telegraph.co.uk/news/iainmartin1/100259291/westminster-dynamites-alex-salmonds-currency-union-causing-scottish-nationalist-meltdown/

16. Martin Kettle, 'Alex Salmond and co are acting like spoiled children', *Guardian,* 19 February 2014, http://www.theguardian.com/commentisfree/2014/feb/19/alex-sal

mond-acting-spoilt-children

17. Gerry Hassan and James Mitchell, 'George Osborne's High Noon Approach to Scotland will Backfire', *Guardian*, 17 February 2014. http://www.theguardian.com/commentis-free/2014/feb/17/george-osborne-approach-scotland-currency-union

18. Iain MacWhirter, 'The big guns turned their fire on Scotland', *Herald*, 16 February 2014, http://www.heraldscotland.com/comment/columnists/the-big-guns-turned-their-fire-on-scotland-but-courage-can-still-trump-fear.23444291

19. 'Scottish independence: currency union warning 'backfires' on Westminster', *Guardian*, 20 February 2014.

20. Nicholas Watt, 'Independent Scotland "may keep pound" to ensure stability', *Guardian*, 29 March 2014. http://www.theguardian.com/politics/2014/mar/28/independent-scotland-may-keep-pound.

21. See Alan Cochrane, *Alex Salmond: My Part in his Downfall*, London: Biteback Publications, 2014.

22. http://www.telegraph.co.uk/news/politics/11018994/Alex-Salmond-declares-its-our-pound-and-were-keeping-it.html

23. Adam Tomkins, 'The SNP's Currency Nightmare', 16 February 2014, www.notesfromnorthbritain.wordpress.com

24. Scott McNab and Euan McColm, 'Alex Salmond predicts backlash on currency refusal', *Scotland on Sunday*, 16 February 2014

25. Tomkins, 'The SNP's Currency Nightmare'.

26. 'UK-Scotland currency union incompatible with sovereignty', *Reuters*, 9 September 2014, http://www.reuters.com/article/2014/09/09/scotland-independence-carney-idUSL5N0RA2SE20140909

27. Hamish Macdonell, 'Yes campaign launch will cause problems for the independence movement', *Spectator*, 29 May 2015, http://blogs.spectator.co.uk/coffeehouse/2012/05/yes-campaign-launch-will-cause-problems-for-the-independence-movement/

28. Andrew Whitaker, 'Scottish independence – SNP's literary white paper', *Scotsman*, 16 July 2013, http://www.scotsman.com/lifestyle/arts/news/scottish-independence-snp-s-literary-white-paper-1-3001173

29. Ewen MacAskill, 'Glasgow's East End: frontline in the battle for Scotland', *Guardian*, 24 February 2014, http://www.theguardian.com/politics/2014/feb/23 glasgow-east-end-frontline-battle-scotland-independence

30. Simon Johnson, 'Better Together: We're the "Volvo" independence referendum campaign but we're winning', *Daily Telegraph*, 15 May 2014, http://www.telegraph.co.uk/news/politics/10832647/Better-Together-Were-the-Volvo-independence-referendum-campaign-but-were-winning.html

31. Tom Peterkin, 'Scottish independence: EU deals pensions blow', *Scotsman,* 28 March 2014,

32. Simon Johnson, 'Scottish financial services firms "face losing customers if they keep silent about independence"', *Daily Telegraph,* 3 February 2014, http://www.telegraph.co.uk/news/politics/10613121/Scottish-financial-services-firms-face-losing-customers-if-they-keep-silent-about-independence.html

33. Ben Riley-Smith, 'Scottish independence: Who really benefits when big business speaks out?' *Daily Telegraph,* 6 March 2014. http://blogs.telegraph.co.uk/news/benrileysmith/100262416/scottish-indepen-dence-who-really-benefits-when-big-business-speaks-out/

34. Auslan Cramb, 'SNP's 'retribution threat' to pro-UK Scottish firms', *Daily Telegraph,* 6 July 2014, http://www.telegraph.co.uk/news/uknews/scottish-indepen-dence/10950335/SNPs-retribution-threat-to-pro-UK-Scottish-firms.html

35. Magnus Gardham, 'Salmond's threat to ditch debt in sterling struggle', *Herald,* 22 May 2013.

36. Martin Jacomb and Andrew Large, 'Salmond threatens shabby end to beneficial union', *Financial Times,* 24 August 2014., http://www.ft.com/cms/s/0/6f0fb7b6-2a08-11e4-8139-00144feabdc0.html#axzz3P4coCUxA

37. Bill Jamieson, 'How a 'debt dump' would lead straight to austerity', *Think Scotland,* 15 April 2014, /todays-thinking/articles.html?read_full=12592&article=www.thinkscotland.org>

38. Severin Carrell et al, 'Billions of pounds wiped from value of Scottish firms after yes vote leads independence poll', *Guardian,* 8 September 2014, http://www.theguardian.com/politics/2014/sep/08/scottish-independence-compa-nies-billions-of-pounds-value-loss-pro-independence-poll-lead

39. Belinda Goldsmith and William Schomberg, 'Britain promises to honour all state debt as Scottish vote approaches', Reuters, 13 January 2014, http://uk.reuters.com/arti-cle/2014/01/13/uk-britain-scotland-debt-idUKBREA0B0N820140113

40. Simon Johnson, 'Cybernats call for Barrhead Travel boycott over SNP independence 'lies' claim', *Daily Telegraph,* 31 March 2014,http://www.telegraph.co.uk/news/uknews/scotland/10735256/Cybernats-call-for-Barrhead-Travel-boycott-over-SNP-indepen dence-lies-claim.html.

41. Johnson, 'Cybernats call for'.

42. Dean Herbert, 'Independence bad for business, says poll', Daily Express, 31 March 2014, http://www.express.co.uk/news/uk/467801/Independence-bad-for-business-says-poll

43. Ben Riley-Smith, 'Cybernats 'shame Scotland' and must be stopped, Alistair Darling says', *Daily Telegraph,* 1 April 2014, http://www.telegraph.co.uk/news/uknews/scottish-independence/10737197/Cybernats-shame-Scotland-and-must-be-stopped-Alistair-Darling-says.html?mobile=basic

44. Scott MacNab, 'Independence: SNP "bullied" bosses over currency', *Scotsman,* 3 April 2014,

http://www.scotsman.com/news/politics/top-stories/independence-snp-bullied-boss-0 es-over-currency-1-3362675

45. Editorial, 'Speak up for the Union', *Daily Telegraph*,7 July 2014, http://www.telegraph. co.uk/news/uknews/scotland/10950228/Speak-up-for-the-Union.html

46. Ronald MacDonald, 'The numbers for an independent Scottish economy look scary', *The Conversation*, 28 July 2014, http://theconversation.com/the-numbers-for-an-inde pendent-scottish-economy-look-scary-29724

47. David Clegg', 'Top professor warns that a currency union would inevitably fail', *Daily Record*, 14 August 2014. http://www.dailyrecord.co.uk/news/top-professor-warns-currency-union-4051062

48. Clegg', 'Top professor warns'.

49. Tom Devine, 'Why I now say Yes to independence for Scotland', *The Conversation*, 20 August 2014, http://theconversation.com/tom-devine-why-i-now-say-yes-to-inde pendence-for-scotland-30733

50. Chris Whatley, 'Why Tom Devine switch to Yes is confusing and short-sighted', *The Conversation*, 25 August 2014, http://theconversation.com/chris-whatley-why-tom-devine-switch-to-yes-is-confusing-and-short-sighted-3085

51. Paul Gilbride, 'Minister accused of "North Korea" tactics in referendum row with academic', *Daily Express*, 12 November 2013, http://www.express.co.uk/news/uk/442696/Minister-accused-of-North-Korea-tactics-in-referendum-row-with-academic

52. Andrew Argo, 'Shona Robison denies Dispatches claims on independence referendum debate', *Courier*, 8 July 2014, http://www.thecourier.co.uk/news/politics/shona-robi son-denies-dispatches-claims-on-independence-referendum-debate-1.460913

53. Simon Johnson, 'SNP ministers 'waging dangerous campaign to gag university academics', *Daily Telegraph*, 13 November 2013, http://www.telegraph.co.uk/news/politics/10445073/SNP-ministers-waging-danger ous-campaign-to-gag-university-academics.html?mobile=basic

54. Claire Baillie, 'Scottish independence: "Speak out", says uni chief', *Scotsman*, 15 November 2013, http://www.scotsman.com/news/education/scottish-independence-speak-out-says-uni-chief-1-3190278

55. Simon Johnson, 'Scotland's universities "prevented from speaking out against independence"', *Daily Telegraph*, 23 May 2014, http://www.telegraph.co.uk/news/uknews/scotland/10850366/Scotlands-universi ties-prevented-from-speaking-out-against-independence.html

56. Niall Ferguson, 'Scottish referendum: Alone, Scotland will go back to being a failed state', *Daily Telegraph*, 17 September 2014, http://www.telegraph.co.uk/news/uknews/scottish-independence/11102126/Scottish-referendum-Alone-Scotland-will-go-back-to-being-a-failed-state.html

57. Jill Stephenson, 'Be careful what you wish for', *Research Fortnight,* 1 October 2014.

58. Severin Carrell et al, 'The real story of the Scottish referendum: the final days of the fight for independence: part 2', *Guardian,* 16 December 2014, http://www.theguardian.com/news/2014/dec/16/-sp-real-story-scottish-referendum-final-days-fight-for-independence

59. 'Independence essay: Alistair Carmichael on the Union', *Scotsman,* 14 May 2014, http://www.scotsman.com/news/independence-essay-alistair-carmichael-on-the-union-1-3410021

60. Tom Gallagher, 'Salmond's stoking of the Yes mob is reminiscent of the young Ian Paisley', *Daily Telegraph,* 16 September 2014, http://blogs.telegraph.co.uk/news/tomgallagher/100286461/salmonds-stoking-of-the-yes-mob-is-reminiscent-of-the-young-ian-paisley/

61. Alex Massie, 'Come in Britain, your time is up, *Spectator,* 7 September 2014, http://blogs.spectator.co.uk/coffeehouse/2014/09/come-in-britain-your-time-is-up/#disqus_thread>

62. Chris Green, 'Scottish independence', *Independent, 1*2 August 2014.

63. Alex Massie, 'Scotching a myth: Scotland is not as left-wing as you think it is', *Spectator,* 21 May 2014, http://blogs.spectator.co.uk/coffeehouse/2014/05/scotching-a-myth-scotland-is-not-as-left-wing-as-you-think-it-is.

64. John McDermott, 'Scotland and the wish tree', *Financial Times,* 31 August 2014, http://www.ft.com/cms/s/2/b171325c-2f7f-11e4-a79c-00144feabdc0.html

65. Neal Ascherson, 'Scottish Independence – why I'm voting Yes', *Prospect magazine,* 17 July 2014, http://www.prospectmagazine.co.uk/features/independence-referendum-why-im-voting-yes

66. David Clegg, 'Legendary commentator Archie Macpherson stuns politicians and voters with impassioned plea to keep Britain together', *Daily Record,* 27 August 2014, http://www.dailyrecord.co.uk/news/politics/legendary-commentator-archie-macpherson-stuns-4119263

67. Simon Johnson, 'Scottish independence: Archie Macpherson delivers powerful defence of the Union', *Daily Telegraph,* 27 August 2014, http://www.telegraph.co.uk/news/uknews/scottish-independence/11060013/Scottish-independence-Archie-Macpherson-delivers-powerful-defence-of-the-Union.html

68. http://www.jkrowling.com/en_GB/#/news-events

69. Severin Carrell and Libby Brooks, 'Will celebrity endorsement sway yes or no vote in Scotland'? *Guardian*, 11 June 2014, http://www.theguardian.com/uk-news/2014/jun/11/celebrity-endorsement-sway-yes-no-scotland-analysis

70. Carrell and Libby Brooks, 'Will celebrity endorsement'.

71. 'UK Ticket-Holder Wins EuroMillions Jackpot'. *Sky News.* 12 July 2011.

72. Ben Riley-Smith and Simon Johnson, 'JK Rowling subjected to Cybernat abuse after £1m pro-UK donation', *Daily Telegraph,* 11 June 2014, http://www.telegraph.co.uk/news/uknews/scottish-independence/10893567/JK-Rowling-subjected-to-Cybernat-abuse-after-1m-pro-UK-donation.html

73. Simon Johnson, 'General accuses SNP minister of endangering his family after 'Cybernat' attack', *Daily Telegraph,* 6 March 2014, http://www.telegraph.co.uk/news/uknews/scotland/10679203/General-accuses-SNP-minister-of-endangering-his-family-after-Cybernat-attack.html

74. David Maddox, 'Cybernats 'scaring pro-Union voters' – Carmichael', *Scotsman,* 5 February 2014, http://www.scotsman.com/news/politics/top-stories/cybernats-scaring-pro-union-voters-carmichael-1-3295541

75. Severin Carrell and Nicholas Watt, 'Alistair Darling accuses Scottish yes camp of physical and verbal abuse', *Guardian,* 12 September 2014, http://www.theguardian.com/politics/2014/sep/12/alistair-darling-accuses-scottish-yes-camp-physical-verbal-abuse-independence

76. 'Queen urges reconciliation in post-referendum Scotland', *Reuters,* 26 December 2014, http://uk.reuters.com/article/2014/12/26/uk-britain-queen-scotland-idUKKBN0K30LC20141226

77. Carrell and Watt, 'Alistair Darling accuses'.

78. Christopher Hope, 'Alex Salmond in second BBC bias row', *Daily Telegraph,* 15 September 2014, http://www.telegraph.co.uk/news/uknews/scottish-independence/11097713/Alex-Salmond-in-second-BBC-bias-row.html; Alan Cochrane, 'Scotland's escape from the man who thinks he could have saved RBS', *Daily Telegraph,* 17 November 2014, http://www.telegraph.co.uk/news/uknews/scotland/11237142/Scotlands-escape-from-the-man-who-thinks-he-could-have-saved-RBS.html

79. Cochrane, 'Scotland's escape'; Simon Johnson, 'Alex Salmond criticises leading political journalist during heated interview', *Daily Telegraph,* 27 August 2014, http://www.telegraph.co.uk/news/uknews/scottish-independence/11058007/Alex-Salmond-criticises-leading-political-journalist-during-heated-interview.html

80. 'Yes campaign chief says BBC referendum coverage was not biased', STV, 30 September 2014, http://news.stv.tv/scotland-decides/294071-yes-campaign-chief-says-bbc-referendum-coverage-was-not-biased/

81. William Turvill, 'ITN's Tom Bradby says 'abuse and intimidation' from Yes campaign 'highly unusual in the democratic world', *Press Gazette,* 17 September 2014, http://www.pressgazette.co.uk/itns-tom-bradby-says-abuse-and-intimidation-yes-campaign-highly-unusual-democratic-world

82. Dean Herbert, 'Lord McConnell claims police have failed to tackle referendum bullying', *Daily Express,* 18 September 2014, http://www.express.co.uk/news/uk/512151/

Lord-McConnell-claims-police-have-failed-to-tackle-referendum-bullying

83. Claire Newell *et al*, 'Scotland's most senior civil servant "intimidated bosses" over referendum', *Daily Telegraph*, 15 September 2014, http://www.telegraph.co.uk/news/uknews/scottish-independence/11098301/Scotlands-most-senior-civil-servant-intimidated-bosses-over-referendum.html

84. Gemma Hartley, 'Scottish independence: Police deny McConnell claim', *Scotsman*, 17 September 2014, http://www.scotsman.com/news/uk/scottish-independence-police-deny-mcconnell-claim-1-3544523

85. Johnson, 'Better Together: We're the "Volvo". '

86. 'Just Say Naw', www.justsaynaw.net

87. Alex Massie, 'Spectator debate: Independence is the greatest threat to Edinburgh', *Spectator*, 25 June 2014, http://blogs.spectator.co.uk/coffeehouse/2014/06/spectator-debate-independence-is-the-greatest-threat-to-edinburgh

88. *Daily Mail*, 28 June 2014, http://www.dailymail.co.uk/debate/article-2673664/GEORGE-GALLOWAY-This-new-Battle-Britain-nearly-vital-So-I-urge-fellow-Scots-JUST-SAY-NAW.html

89. *Daily Mail*, 28 June 2014.

90. *Daily Mail*, 28 June 2014.

91. Jim Murphy, 'I've been called a paedophile, a terrorist and a Quisling: Jim Murphy on the 'Yes' mob', *Spectator*, 30 August 2014, http://blogs.spectator.co.uk/coffeehouse/2014/08/the-yes-campaign-are-letting-a-mob-mentality-take-over/

92. Tom Peterkin and Scott MacNab, 'Jim Murphy suspends referendum tour after egging', *Scotsman*, 29 August 2014, http://www.scotsman.com/news/politics/top-stories/jim-murphy-suspends-referendum-tour-after-egging-1-3524774

93. Peterkin and MacNab, 'Jim Murphy suspends'.

94. Heather Saul, 'Salmond accused of laughing off national debt with "what are they going to do: invade?" joke', *Independent*, 10 September 2014, http://www.independent.co.uk/news/uk/scottish-independence/salmond-accused-of-laughing-off-national-debt-with-what-are-they-going-to-do--invade-joke-9723997.html

95. 'Scottish independence: 700,000 could leave if Yes', *Scotsman*, 27 July 2014, http://www.scotsman.com/news/politics/top-stories/scottish-independence-700-000-could-leave-if-yes-1-3490006

96. David Clegg, 'Independence Poll: Our bombshell survey shows one in three Scots will vote No due to dislike of Alex Salmond', *Daily Record*, 15 May 2014, http://www.dailyrecord.co.uk/news/politics/independence-poll-bombshell-survey-shows-3544057

97. 'Salmond: I would quit if it meant a Yes vote', *Scotsman*, 20 August 2014, http://www.scotsman.com/news/politics/top-stories/salmond-i-would-quit-if-it-

meant-a-yes-vote-1-3514731

98. David Clegg, 'Alex Salmond has become a liability to the Yes campaign – and could cost them the referendum, says Jim Sillars', *Daily Record,* 13 May 2015, http://www.dailyrecord.co.uk/news/politics/alex-salmond-become-liability-yes-3533466

99. See Gordon Wilson, *Scotland: The Battle for Independence,* Stirling: Scots Independent (newspapers), 2014, p, p. 160-1.

100. Simon Johnson, 'BBC criticised over handling of Scottish independence debate', *Daily Telegraph,* 26 August 2014, www.telegraph.co.uk/news/uknews/scottish-independence/11056540/BBC-criti-cised-over-handling-of-Scottish-independence-debate-between-Salmond-and-Darling.html

101. Severin Carrell *et al,* 'New doubt cast over Alex Salmond's claims of Scottish wealth', *Guardian,* 29 May 2014, http://www.theguardian.com/uk-news/2014/may/29/scotland-wealth-alex-salmond-study

102. 'Scotland's standard of living – full report', http://www.theguardian.com/uk-news/interactive/2014/may/29/scotland-stan-dard-of-living-report

103. Online Letter, See Allan Massie, 'The man who can win the Scottish independence referendum? One Gordon Brown', *Scotsman,* 28 August 2014, http://blogs.telegraph.co.uk/culture/allanmassie/100076040/the-man-who-can-win-the-scottish-independence-referendum-one-gordon-brown/

104. Tom Gordon, ' I admit it: the man who coined Project Fear label', *Herald,* 21 December 2014, http://www.heraldscotland.com/politics/scottish-politics/unveiled-the-man-who-re-vealed-project-fear-label.26133626

105. Fraser Nelson, 'Deutsche Bank: Scottish independence would bring austerity on a scale never seen before', *Spectator,* 13 September 2014, http://blogs.spectator.co.uk/coffeehouse/2014/09/deutsche-banks-devastating-analy-sis-scottish-independence-would-bring-austerity-on-a-scale-never-seen-before/

106. 'As it happened: Scottish independence campaign, 10 September 2014', *Daily Telegraph,*10 September 2014, http://www.telegraph.co.uk/news/uknews/scottish-independence/11088734/As-it-hap-pened-Scottish-independence-campaign-Wednesday-10-September.html

107. Simon Johnson, 'Sir Ian Wood: 15 years of oil left before independent Scotland spending cuts', *Daily Telegraph,* 20 August 2014, http://www.telegraph.co.uk/news/uknews/scottish-independence/11046740/Sir-Ian-Wood-15-years-of-oil-left-before-independent-Scotland-spending-cuts.html

108. Bagehot, 'How a nation went mad', *Economist,* 13 September 2014

109. See Chris Deerin, 'What bright spark thought bullying and patronising us Scots was

the way to win our votes'? *Daily Mail,* 9 September 2014; see also
http://www.forbes.com/sites/marcbabej/2014/09/18/advertising-disasters-scot-
lands-no-campaign/

110. Toby Helm, 'Scottish secretary slams complacency in unionist camp',
The Observer, 30 March 2014

111. Marc E. Babej, 'Scotland's "No" Campaign: An Advertising Disaster', Forbes
Magazine, 18 September 2014, http://www.forbes.com/sites/marcbabej/2014/09/18/
advertising-disasters-scotlands-no-campaign/

112. 'Salmond blast at Cameron ahead of visit', *Evening Times,* 14 May 2014,
http://www.eveningtimes.co.uk/news/salmond-blast-at-pm-cameron-ahead-of-visit-
163395n.24211865

113. Michael Settle, 'Salmond launches attack on oil and gas "thieves"', *Herald,*
24 February 2012, http://www.heraldscotland.com/politics/referendum-news/salmond-
launches-attack-on-oil-and-gas-thieves.23532460

114. Fraser Nelson, Stay Scotland', S*pectator,* 10 September 2014.

115. 'How Unionism lost the plot', *Spectator,* 13 September 2014,
http://www.spectator.co.uk/columnists/politics/9310982/the-unionists-have-been-too-
afraid-to-make-a-proper-case/

116. Oliver Wright *et al,* 'Scottish independence: Nationalist leader Jim Sillars threatens
pro-union companies with 'day of reckoning' after independence', *Independent,*
12 September 2014, http://www.independent.co.uk/news/uk/scottish-independence/
scottish-independence-fear-and-loathing-in-the-battle-for-scotland-9730442.html

117. Jane Bradley and Scott MacNab, 'Half of Scots say oil finds are kept *"secret"',*
Scotsman, 8 September 2014, http://www.scotsman.com/news/politics/top-stories/half-
of-scots-say-oil-finds-are-kept-secret-1-3534186#ixzz3lbotvDRG

118. Mark Wallace, 'When conspiracy theories enter the mainstream, it's time to worry',
Guardian, 25 November 2014, http://www.theguardian.com/commentisfree/2014/
nov/25/conspiracy-theories-secret-oil-fields-north-sea

119. Ben Riley-Smith, 'Alex Salmond dismisses campaign to save the Union as 'Team
Westminster', *Daily Telegraph,* 10 September 2014,
http://www.telegraph.co.uk/news/uknews/scottish-independence/11087314/Alex-Sal-
mond-dismisses-campaign-to-save-the-Union-as-Team-Westminster.html

120. Auslan Cramb, 'Scottish independence: Ed Miliband forced to abandon walkabout in
Edinburgh', *Daily Telegraph,* 16 September 2014,
http://www.telegraph.co.uk/news/uknews/scottish-independence/11100414/Scot-
tish-independence-Ed-Miliband-forced-to-abandon-walkabout-in-Edinburgh.html

121. Andrew Whitaker, 'BBC hired 'indyref bodyguard' for Nick Robinson', *Scotsman,*
12 January 2015,

http://www.scotsman.com/news/politics/top-stories/bbc-hired-indyref-bodyguard-for-nick-robinson-1-3657887.

122. Jenny Hjul , 'Eddie Izzard is campaigning for a No vote. But many Scottish public figures are too scared to defend the Union', *Daily Telegraph*, 4 April 2014,

123. James Dennison, 'The Loser takes all – THE SNP after the referendum', *LSE Election Blog*, 13 April 2015, http://blogs.lse.ac.uk/generalelection/the-level-and-fervency-of-snp-support/

124. Scott MacNab, 'Gordon Brown: Silent majority to secure No victory', *Scotsman*, 13 September 2014, http://www.scotsman.com/news/politics/top-stories/gordon-brown-silent-majority-to-secure-no-victory-1-3540532#ixzz3lcchShgG

125. *Commission on the Future Governance of Scotland, Scottish Conservative Party*, Edinburgh, May 2014, http://www.scottishconservatives.com/wordpress/wp-content/uploads/2014/06/Strathclyde_Commission_14.pdf

126. Torchuil Crichton, 'Labour leadership frontrunner Jim Murphy set to back full income tax-raising powers for Holyrood', *Daily Record*, 25 November 2014, http://www.dailyrecord.co.uk/news/politics/labour-leadership-frontrunner-jim-murphy-4689477

127. Auslan Cramb, 'The 'vow' of more devolution made little difference to outcome of independence referendum', *Daily Telegraph*, 26 March 2015, http://www.telegraph.co.uk/news/uknews/scotland/scottish-politics/11497348The-vow-of-more-devolution-made-little-difference-to-outcome-of-independence-referendum

128. Cramb, 'The 'vow'.

129. Cramb, 'The 'vow'.

130. 'The Vow', *Daily Record*, 16 September 2014, p. 1; see also Roy Greenslade, 'The Vow' and the *Daily Record* - creative journalism or political spin?' Guardian, 31 October 2014

131. Douglas Fraser, 'Study examines referendum demographics', *BBC News*, 18 September 2015, http://www.bbc.co.uk/news/uk-scotland-glasgow-west-34283948

132. 'Scottish Independence: Londoners Rally In Trafalgar Square To Ask Scots To Vote No', *Huffington Post*, 15 September 2014, http://www.huffingtonpost.co.uk/2014/09/15/scottish-independence-trafalgar-square-rally_n_5824342.html

133. *Scottish Daily Mail*, 8 September 2014, https://medium.com/@chrisdeerin/wrestling-with-smoke-7fa728a21318

134. Andy Maciver, 'Conservatives in Scotland are increasingly being hindered by their

association with London', *Conservative Home*, 28 April 2015,
http://www.conservativehome.com

135. Adam Tomkins, 'Centralist, illiberal and authoritarian, the SNP's one-party state', *Spectator*, 17 October 2015.

136. Lily of St Leonards, 'SNP, Lib Dems and Labour out', *Effie Deans Blogspot*, 26 September 2015.

137. David Maddox, 'Better Together to blame for Labour woes – Corbyn', *Scotsman*, 1 October 2015.

138. Liam Kirkaldy, 'Gordon Brown: the Vow is not being delivered', *Holyrood magazine*, 8 October 2015,
https://www.holyrood.com/articles/news/gordon-brown-vow-not-being-delivered

139. Scott MacNab, 'Scottish Parliament poll: Corbyn fails to lift Scottish Labour', *Scotsman*, 8 October 2015.

140. Brian Wilson, 'Court case is a dangerous precedent', Scotsman, 12 September 2015

141. 'Another referendum? 69 per cent of you say No', *Press and Journal*, 25 September 2015.

142. Magnus Gardham, 'Yes chief Blair Jenkins: we will win independence referendum in 2021', *Herald*, 11 September 2015.

143. 'Leader: Michelle Thomson's future hangs in balance', *Scotsman*, 1 October 2015.

CHAPTER 4: A REMARKABLE ELECTION DEEPENS THE SCOTTISH DIVIDE

SNP: Defeat Into Victory

As the British general election of 7 May 2015 approached, the SNP was on a remarkable upward trajectory. There had been a smooth succession. The party was bursting with new committed members. Its poll ratings soared ever higher. By contrast, Labour in Scotland was in total disarray. It had also acquired a new leader Jim Murphy; he was hyper-energetic but he never found a coherent message that even caused defectors from his party to hesitate as they severed their Labour loyalties.

A purposeful Scottish political world, controlled by the SNP was a contrast to the rest of the UK. Here there were listless parties led by figures whose approval ratings in polls were tiny compared with the ones enjoyed by Nicola Sturgeon. Political deadlock seemed unavoidable after 7 May with both Labour and the Tories neck-and-neck in the polls for many weeks. It suggested a dynamic thrusting Scotland in political terms at least compared to an introspective and uncertain England and Wales.

The image of a Scotland poised for greatness was of course one which the SNP's campaign machine was keen to promote. It had mastered campaigning for the digital age, emulating but then far surpassing New Labour by using techniques from the world of advertising to promote its project. Sturgeon used the internet with consummate professionalism. Labour and the SNP's other rivals were nowhere in this vital new electoral arena. Sturgeon used a Facebook Q & A enabling her 'to be completely accessible to people to answer their concerns', according to a senior SNP official. The SNP leader herself claimed that Flip Prior, one of a number of Twitter executives from around the world who were monitoring the UK general election, felt the SNP were social media pioneers:

'I am not misquoting her when I say the SNP are probably the best in the world at using social media in terms of politicians…[Flip] said to me: 'We are here to look at the SNP to learn things for the American presidential election.'[1]

'SNP, Stronger for Scotland' the title of the party's manifesto and its main campaign confirmed the ability of the party and its ability to transmit a message that resonated with Scots who might only be lightly touched by political nationalism. Alex Massie wrote on 25 April: 'While rival parties have produced platitudes, the SNP have an election slogan that is short, sweet and above all memorable, and that is what will win the public vote.'[2]

The SNP's other secret weapon was the thousands of supporters it had assembled who would be a campaigning army the likes of which Scotland had not seen in any previous general election. The *Guardian* was uncertain about what they really stood for: 'There is no disputing that thousands of Scots have embraced the SNP in the hope that it represents a more dynamic and vernacular progressivism than Labour offers. But is this progressivism credible? To what degree is it frustrated separatism in progressive clothing?'[3]

Kevin McKenna, a Labour media stalwart who had noisily gone over to the SNP, was spared such uncertainty. He was in no doubt that it was a progressive miracle in which un-deferential Glaswegians and other Scots were finally taking charge of their own political destiny. Writing in the *Observer* on 5 April, he saluted once scattered and lonely insurgents who have finally rocked to its foundations a Westminster elite long used to patronising Scotland. He had little patience for media colleagues who failed to acknowledge the arrival of a beautiful new dawn: 'In Glasgow's conference centre last weekend, it was curious to witness the extent to which the new nationalist legions have unnerved those privileged few of us who inhabit Scotland's media and political bubble'.

He upbraided one of his 'more sclerotic media chums' for having remarked if Alex Salmond blew his nose the 3,000 SNP supporters in the main auditorium for the party's election campaign conference would cheer him to the rafters. He was dismissive of those inside and outside the media who used the disdainful term 'cult' to describe what they were seeing:
'the implications of such terminology are clear: politics ought only to be conducted and analysed by the professionals – either the politicians and their advisers or we who are paid to scrutinise and report their words and ideas. We become uncomfortable when the franchise is extended to too many people and especially those whom we deem not to be sufficiently sophisticated in their words and thoughts'.[4]

But hours later the art critic and academic Muriel Gray decried the militant fervour that seemed to be sweeping across much of Scotland. 'Politics now like a religion in Scotland' she tweeted. 'Used to be debatable and enthralling. Now? Tribal. Identity politics. For us or against us. Tragic'.[5]

This semi -religious aura may well have stemmed from anger over the referendum defeat. The SNP benefited from that vote being held near to the general election. Many people had plunged into long-term political engagement in order to undo the 18 September result. The journalist James Forsyth observed: 'One of the most striking things about Scotland is how the referendum still dominates politics here. I've seen more Yes posters and stickers than I've seen posters for any political party'.[6]

The occurrence of unsettling incidents which detracted attention from the SNP's main campaign messages, led to contrasting opinions about the impact of people politicised in the referendum on the democratic process. For McKenna, the referendum had been a fantastic event and writing near the conclusion, he had expressed sorrow that it could not be replayed all over again.[7]

The fact that it was felt necessary to provide Nick Robinson, the BBC's chief political reporter, with a bodyguard while he was in Scotland, exposed a troubling facet of nationalism – its intolerance of well-expressed criticism or scepticism. At an SNP rally in Aberdeen at the end of 2014 likely to have been attended by many new activists, Faisal Islam, Robinson's counterpart on SKY TV, tweeted some time afterwards: 'only place in world I [have] been questioned about suitability to report a story on basis of my background, not UKIP, an SNP rally'.[8] The veteran Scottish journalist Kenny Farquharson responded that 'the most shocking thing about the comments made to Faisal Islam is that they come as no surprise. That is just the way Scotland is just now'.[9]

Understandably, there were plenty in the SNP who while deploring any behavioural excesses saw a genuine revolution in full flow. One of them was Roger Mullin, an educational writer, standing in Kirkcaldy, a seat being vacated by Gordon Brown. He was destined to overturn a Labour majority of 23,000 votes and convert it into a majority of nearly 10,000 votes on a 35 per cent swing on a 69.3 per cent turnout.

He told the *Daily Telegraph*'s Dan Hodges: 'When I ask him for his take on the dramatic upswing in his party's fortunes he trots out all the usual stuff about Labour arrogance and post referendum betrayal. But then he pauses. "Something is happening here at a deeper level. People are asking for something more. For their communities. For their culture. What we're seeing here is the birth of a different sort of movement. Something more akin to the sort of political movements you see on the continent"'.[10]

Mullin is not the only scholarly low-key activist in the SNP but his type were easily overshadowed by other candidates like the combative Mhairi Black, a 20-year-old politics student at Glasgow University. She had gained admiration for her dedication and militancy in the referendum campaign. Valour in this epic struggle became a qualification for political advancement. The new-look SNP desired white knights who, in the words of Alex Salmond would 'rumble up' Westminster. Business, academic, community or other professional qualifications were helpful. But they no longer possessed the automatic prestige that they had in an era of more genteel politics. Bold activists were needed who were ready to take the struggle for Scottish rights to the very floor of the Commons itself.[11]

With politics now dominated by radicalised voters and activists, there was little interest in scrutinising the SNP's past record. At one level this was very strange. After all, the party had been in office for longer than Cameron's Tories. Controversial decisions were taken (especially after the acquisition of an overall majority in 2011). The party's attitude to personal liberties, the decentralisation of power and the release of information to the public hardly suggested that it was a citadel of progressivism. Nor was this even the case in the economic field where the party had successfully promoted itself as more just and caring than Labour in key respects.

An Issueless Election

But there were figures from bodies regarded as firmly impartial, at least in the rest of the UK, such as the Institute for Fiscal Studies (IFS) which suggested that a different interpretation was possible. Between 2010 and 2015, figures from the IFS showed that spending on health in England was forecast to have increased 6 per cent in real terms over the same period, compared with 1 per cent in Scotland. Spending on schools in Scotland actually fell by 5 per cent in real terms from 2010 to 2013, according to the Scottish official body, Audit Scotland.[12]

Remarkably, SNP decisions, such as severe cut-backs in further education, failed to concern many voters in 2015. In a controversial decision, the SNP had slashed the number of students in further education – sixth-form colleges, vocational training and the like – by more than a third after 2011. The number of these colleges actually fell from 37 in 2011 to 20 in 2014-15.[13] Maintenance grants for poorer university students were also being cut at this time. The savings made enabled Salmond's government to maintain its policy of free university tuition fees.[14]

But, despite favourable comparisons being made with England, there was rather less to the flagship policy of free tuition fees than met the eye. The access of poor Scots to university continued to lag behind the rest of the UK. The financial help directed in England towards poorer students has also been absent in Scotland. In a letter to the *Times* on 23 April 2015, the Liberal Democrat peer Shirley Williams pointed out that graduates in Scotland have to start repaying loans as soon as their incomes reach £16,500 while the figure in England is a more generous £21,000.[15]

Nicola Sturgeon would struggle to find an example of an SNP policy that actually redistributed income towards poorer Scots and therefore justified her party's claim to be an unrivalled champion of equality. 'Free tuition in Scotland is the perfect middle-class, feel good policy', contended Lucy Hunter Blackburn, an educationalist and author of a recent report for the Centre for Research in Education Inclusion. She argued that: 'It's superficially universal, but in fact it benefits the better-off most, and is funded by pushing the poorest students further and further into debt'.[16] The council tax freeze is another policy which has greatly benefited the wealthiest but left councils deeply in debt and required to cut services, ones upon which poorer Scots often depend.[17]

But mainly lower-income voters flocking to the SNP in 2015, appeared supremely unmindful that the policy choices made by the party were often geared more towards strengthening middle-class welfarism than tackling inequality across the boundaries of social class.[18] Many were willing to believe that Edinburgh was still bossed about by London when in fact the Scottish government had absolute control over health, education and most other domestic policy, except welfare. It had no need to follow the departmental spending choices made south of the border and it didn't. Since 2010, the annual block grant from Whitehall had been cut by around four percentage points less in Scotland than in England, having been interpreted (under the Barnett formula) to ensure that Scotland obtained £1,200 per head more in spending than the rest of the UK.[19]

It is true that funding increases did occur with this extra revenue. Free care for the elderly was one area where this happened. Culture, transport, and economic development were others, some being areas where the SNP had particular ideological goals.[20]

The former Labour MP Brian Wilson wrote in March 2015:

'Ask supporters of the Scottish Government to name a single measure of the past eight years which redistributed wealth from the better to less well off and you can expect one of two responses. The first is silence followed by a rapid change of subject. The second is a list of measures which actually, whether they understand it or not, moved scarce resources in precisely the opposite direction such as tuition fees and the council tax freeze'.[21]

But the SNP had no trouble in placing itself in a virtuous light before numerous voters who it was expected would give it a commanding endorsement. They soaked up the rhetoric from Sturgeon and others that the SNP's objective was to keep a future Labour government honest and minimise the spread and impact of austerity. One rueful Labour canvasser observed to the journalist, Alan Cochrane:

'The nationalists have managed to create two boxes in this campaign.
The first marked "Policies"' is where we, the Tories and Lib Dems try to argue out where we stand on different issues. But the SNP doesn't bother with this.
They have created a second box, marked "Scotland", and that's where they stay – saying that only they represent this country and that only they have solutions to Scotland's problems. It's rubbish but it is very difficult for the rest of us to get into that box'.[22]

Nor was Sturgeon's SNP under any pressure from voters to map out a costed policy agenda and show how it might impact on the lives of everyday citizens. Perhaps even to the surprise of some leading officials, the party was able to easily fend off the claim that implementation of the SNP manifesto would deepen austerity and also ensure that Scotland would probably be the last part of the UK to emerge from it.[23]

The main challenge to Sturgeon's claim that her 'number one priority' was ending austerity came from the Institute for Fiscal Studies, a think-tank respected at least in Westminster and in the London-based media for being politically unaffiliated. It examined the impact of the pledges made in the SNP, Tory, Labour and Liberal Democrat manifestos and on releasing its findings, it reported that if the SNP honoured its promise to protect UK spending on the NHS and foreign aid, this would mean £6 billion of cuts to other departments or else a sharp increase in taxes. The IFS told the *Guardian* that key SNP pledges, such as freezing the state retirement age, increasing universal credit payments, scrapping the bedroom tax and retaining child benefit, were not accounted for in the First Minister's proposal to raise public spending across the UK by 0.5% a year The SNP was the only party to take issue with the IFS's evaluation of its spending plans. Sturgeon's response was that it had made a series of incorrect assumptions in its calculations. In a supposedly new questioning climate where Scots were urged to no longer to be deferential to British institutions however impeccable their credentials, the SNP was unscathed in the eyes of public opinion. According to the journalist Alex Massie, the campaign revealed that the party now possessed the ability to create its own reality and for voters to lap it up.[24]

As long ago as 1929, José Ortega y Gasset, in his book the *Revolt of the Masses,* had predicted the rise of a self-referential society. Changes in culture and education which produced a levelling down effect in which doubt was increasingly cast on any 'expert' judgment, helped prepare the way. Many people chose to be guided by their instincts and emotions even on big questions of economic importance upon which their livelihoods might depend. The Spanish philosopher was writing long before the rise of cultural relativism and post-modernism had created an even more favourable environment for populists who wished to simplify complex issues in order to cement their hold over the masses. Increasingly, in universities such as the 15 which Scotland had by the dawn of the 21st century, objective truth and a hierarchy of values were being dismissed as bourgeois, reactionary and Western impositions.[25]

Suddenly Oil is Irrelevant

The reluctance of many voters to allow sobering economic news to restrain their messianic fervour was amply shown by the collapse in the price of North Sea oil. It had fallen from a price of $130 a barrel when the SNP released its blueprint for independence in November 2013 to around $60 a barrel early in 2015. Tax revenues from oil exports would be a substantial proportion of a fully independent Scotland's income. So budgets would be very sensitive to oil price fluctuations.

In March 2015, the IFS calculated that, in the next financial year, there would be a £7.6 billion budget shortfall due to plummeting oil prices. Of course in the Union state that Scotland was part of, oil price variations were financially absorbed across the UK, so Scotland did not feel their full impact.[26] But, in the light of the revolution in shale gas in North America, the glum outlook for the commodity which many in the SNP had long argued made independence a viable proposition, seemed to deal a heavy blow to the economics of separation. However, it was hard to find many people in the electoral season who worried about the economic viability of going it alone. According to a pre-electoral YouGov poll, 56 percent of SNP supporters believed collapsing oil prices were neither good nor bad for Scotland. In other words, they were of scant importance as crucial changes to Scotland's territorial status were being eagerly awaited by many.[27] The fact that in the 2013 White paper, the SNP had inflated the amount of revenue to be derived from oil by thirteen times, failed to cause an electoral ripple. The Office for Budget Responsibility's (OBR) March 2013 report found that instead of earnings of nearly £8 billion from oil, the figure would only be £600 million in the next financial year due to the steep fall in price.[28] But the Scottish government was prepared to leave nothing to chance. In April it refused to release its own figures in all likelihood because they hardly varied from the ones released by the OBR.[29] This proved to be the case and the OBR itself has been challenged for looking at long term-funding projections for North Sea oil through 'rose-tinted spectacles'. Between 2011 and 2015, it radically scaled down its forecasts for likely oil revenue in the *two decades* from 2020 from £130 billion to £36 billion to £2.1 billion ('equivalent to a single year's revenue in a bad year now').[30]

The SNP's invincibility in the face of any economic news which hindered its case, was assisted not only by the prevalence of 'groupthink' in a large swathe of the Scottish population but by a friendly attitude from media organs which had savaged the party in other election years. In particular, it was a beneficiary of the decision of one of the biggest-selling tabloids the *Sun* to pursue an aggressively anti-Labour stance in the election campaign. In pursuing this objective, it had two separate narratives. Outside Scotland, Nicola Sturgeon featured on the front page on 10 March, clad in a tartan bikini, swinging from a chain attached to a large steel ball. In a double-page spread on the same day, the English readership was warned that she intended to 'swing her wrecking-ball of extreme policies in their direction'. To avoid the ugly consequences, the only recourse was to swallow all doubts and swing behind the Tories.[31]

But in Scotland, the *Sun* backed the SNP on the basis of the competence displayed by its leader. On the Thursday before voting, under the front page headline 'STUR

WARS, A NEW HOPE, May the 7th be With You: Why It's Time to Vote SNP" it de-voted much of that day's edition to portraying her as a providential figure compara-ble to one of the heroes of the Star Wars film. 'She's a straight-talking working-class woman from a council estate' readers were told. 'The *Scottish Sun* is always about aspiration and bettering yourself...'[32]

Some reserve was expressed about the left-leaning big state agenda of the SNP without readers being told that Sturgeon had been one of its main drivers since 2007. Rupert Murdoch's Scottish flagship had no appetite for fiscal autonomy or more constitutional warfare. For the online commentator on Scottish politics, Emeritus Professor Jill Stephenson of Edinburgh University's History department it was a crass intervention: 'Scottish Sun editor - we don't want FFA or a second ref, but we urge you to support the SNP. How naive can people get? Utter stupidity'.[33]

The Queen of Scotland Campaigns

In making light of bad economic news and unfurling a manifesto which was vague in key places, Nicola Sturgeon was perhaps the SNP's greatest asset in 2015. Her elevation and central role in the British general election seemed like a new start for a party already eight years in office. On 2 April, in the only debate involving all the main party leaders, she was widely felt to have stolen the show. A headline with 'Sturgeon steals the show' was actually the page one lead in the *Times* the next day.[34] It wrote: 'Her style… was deliberately calm, natural and direct – qualities that are rare in politicians in this age of spin and slipperiness'. According to Google, the most searched-for phrase halfway through the debate was 'Nicola Sturgeon'. By the end, "can I vote for the SNP?" was also trending.[35]

If it had been Salmond who had been duelling with Cameron and Miliband, then it might have been harder for him to rise above his role as a noisy regional player. His bombastic personality made it hard for him to be seen as the leader of a dis-advantaged country who nevertheless could empathise with other British citizens under the heel of an arrogant Westminster elite. Certainly, his swashbuckling man-ner often appealed to men usually on the left nursing memories of the Thatcher era but this was as far as his reach extended beyond Scotland. Sturgeon, by contrast, managed to reach out to a far wider swathe of the British public and it was easier to imagine her in the typical left-wing role of standing up for an oppressed group. According to Matthew Engel of the *Financial Times,* she was the 'only one of the seven contestants who succeeded in both shoring up the base and impressing them-selves on the rest of the country. The great skill of the Sturgeon performance came in the way she married the sectional interest with the hint of statesmanlike stature … On this form, the SNP ought to consider running candidates in Kensington and Tunbridge Wells'.[36]

But she was very much given a free ride by the Westminster leaders who concentrated on undermining the credibility of each other. According to Engel, 'No one actually said it, but Thursday's party leaders debate was the We Agree With Nicola show. Or to put it another way: "Agree with Nicola — or else"'.

She had already demonstrated her appeal in a speech at University College London in February where she set out her alternative plans for public spending and cutting the deficit more slowly. According to the *Guardian*, these 'won widespread interest and plaudits' and she came over to an educated audience as a more appealing advocate of high spending than Ed Miliband.[37] After her 2 April success, she turned up the next day in the affluent Edinburgh suburb of Corstorphine which is on the way to the city's airport. It was a well-managed campaign event and from the crowd there were shouts of 'Nicola Queen of Scotland'.[38] Back in 2010, the SNP was in a hopeless fourth place with a mere 13.17 per cent of the vote in Edinburgh West. But a month later Michelle Thomson, a property landlord, captured the seat for the SNP with a 25.8 per cent swing.

Voters Sleep Through Fiscal Autonomy Flip-Flop

In between, Sturgeon had revealed her fallibility by stumbling in Scottish debates over full fiscal autonomy (FFA), the issue which probably enjoyed most campaign prominence in Scotland. If implemented it meant that Scotland would be removed from the UK spending system and that its spending would be dependent on the income that it could raise in the absence of any input from the rest of Britain.

Alex Salmond in January 2015 had declared that the price of SNP support for Labour was FFA.[39] He may have still been relying on the 2013-14 campaign rhetoric which insisted that Scotland was sending more to Westminster than it got back and that (in his own words) oil was just 'a bonus', not a commodity whose continuing availability was crucial for the well-being of an independent Scotland.[40]

An embattled Labour party might have hoped that (the by now) ex-leader of the SNP, had thrown it a lifeline by saddling the party with an objective as fraught with difficulties as the currency union had been in the referendum. The Labour politician Brian Wilson wrote in March that 'this was a rare example... of a political leader demanding the right of his people to be substantially worse off than they are at present'.[41]

General Expenditure and Revenue figures for Scotland (GERS) released on 11 March had shown that per capita spending in Scotland was £1200 higher than in the UK as a whole (due in part to the cost of services in far-flung and lightly-populated areas far from the main cities). It costs more, per capita, to provide health, education, transport and other services in less densely populated areas.[42] Per capita revenues from Scotland were higher than per capita revenues for the UK as a whole (due in large measure to income from oil). Against the background of an oil price collapse, there would, according to the IFS in March, be a likely financial shortfall of £7.6 billion if Scotland opted to go-it-alone financially.

Initially Sturgeon and the rest of the party had weighed in behind Salmond's call for fiscal autonomy. Her fullest public backing for the proposal came in the second leaders debate on 8 April. Under questioning from BBC Scotland's James Cook, she said: 'I don't think it is any secret that I want Scotland to have as many powers over our own economy and our own fiscal position as soon as possible'.

'As Scotland's voice in the next House of Commons if the SNP [is] there in numbers we will be arguing for as many powers to come to Scotland as quickly as possible'.

When asked by Cook directly when she wanted full fiscal autonomy, she said: 'I would like to get it as quickly as the other parties agree to give it'.

She was then challenged by the Scottish Labour leader, Jim Murphy, who asked: 'Would your MPs vote for it [full fiscal autonomy] next year?'

Sturgeon replied: 'Yes I would vote for it. Would you support it?'[43]

But fiscal autonomy was placed in an obscure part of the election manifesto released in April.[44] On 9 April, Derek Mackay, the chief whip in the Scottish government, speaking on BBC Radio 4's Today programme had accepted the IFS forecast of a £7.6bn black hole. He stated that: 'I'm not challenging the work that the IFS has done' while going on to claim that fiscal independence would allow the Scottish economy to expand rapidly and close the gap.[45]

Debating with Sturgeon on 13 April, Labour's Jim Murphy argued that: 'To make this £7.6 billion up, Scotland would have to grow at twice the rate of the rest of entire advanced world, so how would you do that Nicola? What's the magic policy you have that the rest of the world doesn't have on this issue?'[46]

The SNP quickly began to back-track from the demand of financial independence after media scrutiny revealed the pitfalls. On 12 April, in a BBC interview, Sturgeon pointed out that fiscal autonomy would take several years to implement. This brought reminders from opponents that the SNP had frequently asserted that independence could be achieved in 18 months. On 16 April she stated that any new tax powers 'could take years' and that '…for as long as Scotland's funding is still determined by Westminster then the Barnett formula should stay in place'.[47]

After the election, the economic journalist George Kerevan, by now SNP MP for East Lothian, pulled even further away from fiscal autonomy. He argued that 'inbuilt UK-wide fiscal balancing' would be required for Scotland.[48] Kevin Hague, an East Lothian-based entrepreneur (employing more than 200 people as chief executive of the M8 group) and one of the most incisive followers of the SNP's shifting economic outlook, wondered why Kerevan did not just say 'subsidy' or 'pooling and sharing'.[49]

Hague, an opponent of separation, reflected on Kerevan's admission that full fiscal autonomy would be 'economic suicide' because of our reliance on 'UK wide fiscal balancing' to fund our higher spending.[50] He contrasted Kerevan's sober post-electoral assessment with the assertions of colleagues at the height of the campaign that the IFS's financial 'black-hole' was just another variation of 'project fear'. A gung-ho Sturgeon had herself claimed on 22 April that 'the referendum "Project Fear'" campaign has been reborn before our eyes.[51] Her remarks very much bore the imprint of Wings over Scotland which had proclaimed on 10 April that 'Project Fear 2' was being unveiled.[52]

In more normal times, the SNP would probably have been heavily punished for its erratic policies on the future financing of Scotland. The release of the detailed IFS report in the spring, which suggested that a massive deficit was unavoidable, produced rebuttals but then an admission that the IFS figures were soundly based. In the face of opposition attacks, the SNP occasionally reverted to its core view that Scotland could stand on its own two feet economically. But there were increasing assertions too that financial aid from the rest of the UK would be necessary even as Scotland headed for complete self-government.

But these unsteady pirouettes about how the country could pay its bills in the future, made no difference at all to its standing in the polls. Nor did contradictions in other areas: few voters appear to have been struck by the irony that a party implacably opposed to long-distance control from London, had been busy, since at least 2011, establishing a rigid form of Edinburgh centralism. 'The first thing that comes to mind when thinking about the SNP government is centralisation', said Alison Payne, research director at the Reform Scotland think-tank when interviewed in 2015.[53]

'Indeed, the SNP in power has resembled nothing as much as New Labour in its pomp, combining the worst reflexes of authoritarian statism and market liberalism with a superior, "we know best" attitude that brooks no opposition.[54] Only opposition to Trident sets it apart; hardly an act of principle given that an independent Scotland wouldn't be able to afford nuclear weapons.

Uncivic Electioneering

According to the commentator David Clark: 'at a time when Britain is crying out for a politics of the common good, the SNP stands for a militant politics of sectional advantage. It is rapidly acquiring the characteristics of a political religion, a faith-based movement'.[55]

The journalist Andrew Gilligan also saw strong elements of millenarianism in the SNP's current appeal:

'As political scientists will tell you, voting anywhere is seldom a wholly rational choice, but is governed by people's emotions and feelings. In Scotland this spring, national emotion appears to be sweeping all before it, and the SNP has been able to create an impregnable parallel reality. Enormous chunks of what was once a sceptical, questioning country are about to take part in mainland Britain's first faith-based election.[56]

He went on to observe:

'Educated and serious people believe that the referendum was stolen. Nationalist canvassers are blitzing council estates like payday loan companies, promising goodies up front but forgetting to mention the years of repayments. Doe-eyed members of the Scottish chattering classes embrace the SNP as progressive. True and relevant facts to the contrary are automatically dismissed as the lies of the Westminster elite'. [57]

Such a mood of militant zeal was already being displayed by party officials before the election campaign properly got underway. In Paisley, a trio of SNP councillors publicly burnt the Smith report on 3 December 2014 even though it had been endorsed by the SNP government. They were later suspended by the party for several months. A spokeswoman said: 'These kinds of acts do not have a part to play in moving the debate forward.' This has been made perfectly clear to those involved, who realise their error and removed the video once this was raised with them'.[58]

A video, placed on YouTube, had shown the councillors standing outside Renfrewshire Council's headquarters with copies of the report. One of them, holding a lighter to his copy of the document above a bucket, looked directly at the camera and said: 'The Smith Commission report - this is exactly what we think about it'.

' No real powers for Scotland yet again from Westminster.'

'We've been lied to again. There you go, Gordon Brown.'[59]

Arguably in the whole pre-election period, it was unruly SNP members and supporters, not the opposition, which gave the new SNP leader by far her biggest headaches. A series of incidents showed that managing the new and greatly expanded movement would be no simple undertaking. On 21 April 2015, at the launch of the SNP's election manifesto, Sturgeon felt the need to tell SNP activists in the hall to treat journalists 'respectfully' and that they should be allowed to 'scrutinise our manifesto'.[60]

SNP member Pat Anderson had already published a book (briskly selling on Amazon in the first months of 2015) which argued that it had been systematic defamation from a desperately pro-Union media that had prevented the SNP from securing endorsement for independence in 2014.[61] By April 2015, the BBC political correspondent James Cook, exasperated at warding off accusations of bias from SNP supporters, was ready to tweet: 'What do you want? Five minutes on how fabulous and popular the SNP are and nothing else? Is that what journalism is for?'[62]

In an atmosphere often tipping over into self-righteousness, the composer James MacMillan retweeted the observation from Muriel Gray ('ArtyBagger') that 'sceptical parodic comedies targeting the Scot Gov [Government] don't exist, and perhaps couldn't exist here just now'. 'If there was a Scottish version of *Spitting Image* made just now the writers would have to go live on the moon' was a view from the same original source.[63]

On 28 April an interview with Sturgeon herself on the popular BBC radio 'Call Kaye' programme fronted by Kaye Adams, provoked much anger among her supporters. The SNP leader's mother Joan Sturgeon even tweeted: 'no point in an interview if folk are not allowed to hear answers to questions... this lady comes across as very biased'. Minutes beforehand, an SNP member had tweeted: 'Kaye needs to remember the public pay her wages & the Scottish public are pro-snp at the mo[ment]'.[64]

Duncan Hothersall, a prominent member of the Labour Party in Edinburgh, observed on Twitter on 1 May: 'Barely see any SNP canvassers out, but always see protesters at Labour events. Weird way to campaign. And always with flags'.[65] Indeed, not only un-deferential media voices but the very presence of opposing forces on the streets turned out to be unacceptable for some in the SNP.

In February 2015, it was reported that the Edinburgh West SNP branch had asked supporters to photograph Labour activists who canvassed their homes and to then place the pictures on the internet. According to Labour MP Anne McGuire, this was 'an absolutely outrageous attempt to intimidate Scottish Labour activists into silence. People should not feel threatened for canvassing voters or expressing their own political opinions, and the idea of photographing someone against their will is incredibly sinister. The SNP need to get their members in line, this form of politics should be nowhere near the general election in May'.[66] The SNP eventually issued a statement that declared: 'We absolutely do not condone this and we have told the branch that'.[67]

But the rules of electioneering proceeded to be broken in a far more absolute way in the Glasgow East constituency where a fierce struggle was being waged between the Labour incumbent and the SNP which had held the seat after a 2008 by-election until 2010. According to the journalist Andrew Gilligan, the treatment meted out to Margaret Curran, the shadow Secretary of State for Scotland amounted to the 'delegitimising and dehumanising' of an opponent, so that the rival was denied the very right to present a case to members of the public.[68]

As she canvassed constituents in early April 2015, Curran found herself in the unusual situation of being followed by two SNP activists, Piers Doughty-Brown and Helen Tennant. They filmed her and also heckled. Gilligan describes how, as a woman voter opened her front door, the pair 'are standing at the garden gate, shouting at them both:

"Will you be telling her the truth, Mrs Curran?" yells Piers Doughty-Brown.
"The bedroom tax! Why did you abstain from the bedroom tax!" screams Helen Tennant. "We've already leafleted these doors!"'

A video of the scenes was posted on the Facebook page of Doughty-Brown where he wrote: long day hunting with Helen Tennant, but it paid off in the end when we cornered Margaret Curran".[69]

On this occasion, the party adopted a 'hands-off' approach although within weeks it would be compelled to suspend Doughty-Brown's membership for a more serious incident that made world headlines. The SNP candidate in the seat, Natalie McGarrie, issued 'a low-key rebuke' while adding the significant rider that Mrs Curran was a 'fair target for community justice'.[70]

Frank McAveetie, a veteran local Labour politician and former minister of culture, observed: 'People getting filmed is a regular feature... There's been incidents where our street stalls have been filmed by two people simultaneously – one on foot, one in a car. We've had women canvassers intimidated by groups of men. They get shouted at – things like "you're finished in this town", like it was the Wild West or something. It's targeted disruption, a very fevered atmosphere'.[71]

Highly personalised attacks on Curran appeared in a recently-launched pro-SNP newspaper that was part of the group which produced the *Herald,* a major daily paper of west-central Scotland. The *National,* edited by Richard Walker, gave a regular column to Mark Cavanagh who, using the pseudonym, 'Wee Ginger Dug' specialised in hard-hitting attacks on particular politicians. Due, perhaps, to the nature of his polemics, the paper hesitated about carrying his byline and only relented when a petition was launched for him to appear. By the close of the general election, several articles a week from Cavanagh were being published. One devoted to Curran contained this passage:

'Margrit [Margaret Curran] is about to give her name to a foodstuff, like peach Melba or Pavlova pudding,... Margrit's toast is dry, stale, mouldy, and spread with invisible Labour jam. It's difficult to swallow, and even harder to keep down. Her career is about to be regurgitated by the electorate of the East End, and a bit like Linda Blair in *The Exorcist* doing her revolving head thing, projected forcefully into far distant corners'.[72]

How fevered the campaign atmosphere would become was shown in the treatment received by Dawn Rodger. She was an undecided first-time voter in the audience for the Scottish party leaders' television debate on 7 April who said on air that she'd been won over by Labour's Jim Murphy.[73] The fevered nature of Scottish politics was well illustrated when both an SNP MSP and MP retweeted a picture suggesting, inaccurately, that Ms Rodger was a Labour plant.[74]

These tweets were later removed by the parliamentarians. After several days, Ms Rodger stated: 'I've deactivated my Facebook because I just can't take any more abuse, I haven't eaten and I haven't slept.' She was left in peace after she told the media: 'I'm a massive fan of everything [SNP leader] Nicola Sturgeon says. I stupidly said I'd back up Labour for reasons beyond me'.[75]

The degree to which the pro-SNP online cybernats were officially encouraged, or organized from within the party, is unclear. But Alex Salmond, in his referendum diary made clear that the online battleground was a crucial one for the SNP if it hoped to secure its key goals.

Certainly Salmond's delight in mixing it with his Westminster foes made him genuinely respected among many nationalists on the far-left who might not have liked his mainstream outlook on economics. The quote from his memoirs suggests that, like a wartime leader, he was ready to rely on fringe forces to lend a hand if this helped to ensure victory for the independence cause.

More cerebral figures on the nationalist side found online enthusiasts to be an obstacle to the cause. A staffer in 'Yes for Scotland' told the journalist Aidan Kerr that he had spent a lot of time in the referendum campaign, keeping Nick Durie, a party activist in the Maryhill and Springburn constituency, away from the world's media. According to Gilligan, Durie believed that 'the UK – sorry, the "British empire" – is "one of the most vile polities in history"'.[76] After pro-government demonstrations outside the BBC's Glasgow offices in the autumn of 2014, Durie wrote: 'While nobody should insult or smear individual state broadcaster employees, it clearly is a sign of success for the democracy movement that the state broadcaster is having to take special measures to prevent its staff from being held to account. Long may that venal Unionist institution's slow decline accelerate'.[77]

The degree of acrimony evident in the campaign led the author Allan Massie to conclude with three weeks yet to run, that 'Scotland is more divided – and, I would say, bitterly divided – than it has been for a very long time. Perhaps even since the 17th century, the most bitter and horrible in our history'.[78] Massie, a longstanding Conservative supporter, was normally an optimist despite the dreadful results obtained by his party since the mid-1990s. Perhaps the online treatment received by the able young leader of the Scottish Conservatives Ruth Davidson, one month previously, had contributed to his mordant outlook.

On 18 March, Marc Hughes, a member of the SNP, placed posts on social media full of expletives attacking Ms Davidson's sexuality. They were posted on the Twitter profile Laird O'Callaghan, under the username @SparkyBhoyHH. Speaking at Holyrood the next day, Nicola Sturgeon told MSPs that she wanted to take the opportunity to 'condemn unreservedly the vile homophobic abuse that was being directed at Ruth Davidson on Twitter last night and this morning'. Upon being identified Hughes apologised to Davidson who decided not to make a complaint after the police contacted her about the incident. Sturgeon announced his suspension from the party and the initiation of disciplinary procedures against him.[79]

There were media claims that in the words of Andrew Gilligan, the SNP leadership was 'starting to realise how awful all this looks'. Sturgeon was far less keen on berating the BBC than her predecessor had been and she swung to the defence of prominent journalists subjected to pressure from SNP activists. But there was little sign that bully-boy tactics from supporters of the ruling party was prompting many Scots to think twice about endorsing the SNP (many for the first time).

Nevertheless, perhaps anticipating tense times ahead when it might be difficult to contain grassroots passions, the First Minister intervened after Sky News' Political Editor Faisal Islam claimed that an independence supporter had questioned his suitability for reporting on a rally in Aberdeen because he was not Scottish. Sturgeon had been the main speaker and through her spokesperson, she declared: 'The First Minister thinks Faisal is a fantastic journalist – tough but fair – [*****ditto James Cook] and as she has made clear on a number of occasions denigration of people has absolutely no place in democratic political debate'.

The incident belatedly came to light when Islam tweeted: 'Only place in the world I have been questioned about suitability to report a story on basis of nationality – not UKIP, an SNP rally.'

He related his experiences shortly after it had been reported that Conservative and Labour offices in Aberdeen had been attacked by vandals. Police reported that a swastika and the word 'scum' had been spray-painted on the Tory office. Both of them had the letter 'Q' painted on them – presumed to stand for 'quisling' – a reference to the Norwegian wartime collaborator Vidkun Quisling.[80]

Niall Paterson, a colleague of Islam's on Sky News had revealed that he had been called a 'quisling p****' while reporting a Scottish dinner of the Confederation of British industry (CBI) which had drawn a large crowd of pro-independence protesters. For Margaret Curran MP it was yet more evidence of the march of intolerance to the heart of Scottish public life:

'No one – whether senior politician or a grassroots activist – should engage in the online abuse of journalists, who are simply doing their job…. when a mob uses these tools to try and silence journalists we need to ask serious questions about the state of Scotland's political culture'.[81]

But there was a radically different explanation provided by Craig Murray. The former British ambassador had joined the SNP after becoming a fierce opponent of the UK establishment ever since he had quit the diplomatic service due in part to his disagreement with the foreign policy of the Blair government. On his blog, he claimed that 'there is something delightfully old fashioned about MI5. Is spraying Q for Quisling not rather an obscure reference to today's generation?' Rather than SNP hotheads lashing out, he believed that 'a coordinated security service plan was in progress'. He wrote:

'A sweeping SNP victory on May 7 is considered enough of a threat to the United Kingdom for the security services to use up some assets. Long term sleepers within the SNP will now be activated. Security service agents within the SNP will be trying to initiate… impressionable members to vandalism or violence. Be very, very wary of such people and do not be tempted' was his appeal to the party which had declined to place him on its accredited candidates list the previous December.

Any incident involving injuries is more likely due to the machinations of MI5 than to the militant fervour of local activists: 'The worry is of course that some manufactured incident will go wrong and somebody will get hurt. The still bigger worry is that, as the security services get increasingly desperate as polling day approaches, they will manufacture a false flag incident in which people deliberately get hurt'. The aim, he believed, would be to bounce lukewarm supports of the SNP back into the pro-unionist camp and therefore dent the scale of the SNP's victory on 7 May.[82]

Labour Dies on the Election Trail

The SNP hardly lost an opportunity to paint Labour as 'anti-Scottish' for aligning with the Conservatives in the referendum. The party of Miliband and Murphy was one of 'Red Tories' even though the SNP had closely collaborated with the Scottish Tories at Holyrood before winning an outright majority in 2011. At other times Sturgeon offered to give Labour the 'backbone' which seemed to be lacking in order to lead an effective left-wing British administration.[83]

There was plenty of campaign rhetoric about preferring a Labour government but only as long as it was heavily Scottish-orientated in its policy preferences. Stewart Hosie, the deputy leader, told the BBC on 19 April that if a minority Labour government fails to reach an agreement with the SNP then it will vote against 'any bit of spending' that it didn't agree with, such as the Trident nuclear deterrent. According to the *Daily Telegraph*, this meant that the SNP was 'prepared to paralyse Britain's armed forces and shut down government departments, raising concerns his party will force a US-style government shutdown'.[84]

Labour found itself in increasing disarray as it confronted a party whose popularity increased perhaps even in part due to its militant stance on this and other issues. Miliband's campaign proved increasingly hapless. It was based around mobilising a core vote sympathetic to left-leaning policies, perhaps no more than one-third of those in Britain likely to vote. The party's hitherto solid Scottish support, had always been a key ingredient for Labour. Now it was fast receding which meant that the strategy of spurning the middle-ground would be meaningless. Early in the campaign, Ian Murray, Labour MP for Edinburgh South, admitted Ed Miliband would not become Prime Minister if he did not win Scotland.[85]

But even if the dire polls were proven wrong and Labour preserved a portion of its Scottish base, nearly all of them suggested that the chances of it being the largest party and forming a stable government appeared meagre. However, right up until the eve of voting, Miliband avoided spelling out what his approach would be to the SNP in the event of a 'hung parliament'. He had the chance in the Leader's debate of 2 April. But, along with Cameron, he declined to take on Sturgeon even though her prowess in the campaign already showed that she was capable of launching a new territorial offensive against the Union.

Miliband also spurned unambiguous political advice from the Labour Party in Scotland to steer clear of the SNP. In early March 2015, Rob Marchant, a moderate Labour commentator, blogged that a pact-minded Labour Party would be telling undecided Scots (as many as 29 per cent in some polls at this point) that 'the SNP will likely form part of our government anyway but, hey, please "vote for us not them"'. The likelihood is that forming a shaky alliance with a party many Labour voters told pollsters was standing up for Scotland, would speed defections towards the SNP away from the ill-led Labour Party.[86]

David Clark, a former adviser to the senior Scottish Labour politician, the late Robin Cook, warned:

'When Nicola Sturgeon says that she wants to help the Labour Party, she does so in the same spirit that Lenin once advised his British followers to support the Labour Party of Arthur Henderson: "as the rope supports a hanged man"'.[87]

In mid-April, the commentator Brian Wilson, who had served in the Blair government, deplored Miliband's reluctance to eliminate the progress of the 'grotesque hybrid' of a Labour-SNP pact.[88] It was high time to call out the SNP for promoting an insincere proposition that only served to reinforce its pro-independence constitutional agenda at the expense of Labour and (Wilson argued) ordinary Scottish voters.

On 17 April, when asked on four occasions whether he would do a deal with the SNP, Miliband refused to give a clearcut answer.[89]

Finally, on 1 May, on a BBC programme where the three Westminster leaders were questioned separately by the audience, Miliband declared:

'I am not going to have a Labour government if it means deals or coalitions with the Scottish National Party.' He also ruled out a so-called confidence and supply arrangement which would involve the SNP backing specific Labour measures.

'It's not going to happen. I couldn't be clearer with you,' he pointed out upon being pressed further: 'If the price of having a Labour government was coalition or a deal with the Scottish National Party, it's not going to happen.'[90]

Labour had prepared no emphatic rejoinder for Sturgeon's anticipated reaction that Miliband would never be forgiven if he let the Tories retain power rather than work with her party. It might have been argued that a deal was simply unworkable because the SNP, with a bogus anti-austerity outlook, was in reality just not interested in stable UK government. Labour's incoherence and delay in seeking to contain the SNP enabled a dangerously capable foe to control the narrative.

The point could also have been driven home, but wasn't, that the SNP had no interest in boosting the chances of the political left across the UK. It had called for a vote for the poorly-performing Greens in England even though the party was hostile to the oil industry, one of Scotland's biggest employers on environmental grounds.[91] The claim of wishing to foil the return of a Conservative-only government was hard to credit given the alacrity with which the SNP campaign machine affixed the 'Red Tory' label to Labour in Scotland. On 3 March 2015, Sturgeon had allegedly confided to the French ambassador Sylvie Bermann, who was on a visit to Scotland, that her preference was for Cameron to beat Miliband. This view was conveyed in a briefing which French diplomats delivered to Whitehall about this protocol event. The Scottish Office leaked the claims which the *Daily Telegraph* broke as a sensational news story on 4 April 2015.[92]

The key part of the Scottish Office memo read:

'The Ambassador also had a truncated meeting with the FM (FM running late after a busy Thursday...). Discussion appears to have focused mainly on the political situation, with the FM stating that she wouldn't want a formal coalition with Labour; that the SNP would almost certainly have a large number of seats; that she had no idea "what kind of mischief" Alex Salmond would get up to; and confessed that she'd rather see David Cameron remain as PM (and didn't see Ed Miliband as PM material). I have to admit that I'm not sure that the FM's tongue would be quite so loose on that kind of thing in a meeting like that, so it might well be a case of something being lost in translation.'

But even though it was a Friday night, the SNP's media machine swung into action to refute what was becoming known as the Frenchgate affair. The story had been dismissed by Sturgeon as 'categorically 100 per cent untrue' on Twitter even before the paper had gone on sale. She said that the *Telegraph* leak suggested 'a Whitehall system out of control - a place where political dirty tricks are manufactured and leaked'.[93] Within two hours, the SNP managed to set out a detailed rebuttal, called 'Storify' and subtitled 'A lesson in how not to report the general election'. It gave ammunition to the numerous supporters who defended whatever was the party's case of the moment. The story occupied a lot of media space in subsequent days. But the ascendancy of the SNP in the media battle was shown by the manner in which the story was turned on its head. It soon centred on the hunt for a mole in the Scottish Office who had leaked claims, the most damaging of which would be denied by the French embassy.[94]

Sturgeon proved a dream candidate for her astute media handlers. She was poised, natural, patient and empathetic in crowd scenes, and quick-witted and usually combative in debate. By contrast, there were occasions when Miliband had proven maladroit in public, his seeming inability to consume a bacon sandwich, leading to merciless jibes from the media. His awkward public persona and hesitant and mechanical speaking style prevented him establishing a positive image that could be exploited by Labour-supporting parts of the media. He showed passion and energy in April when his campaign acquired some momentum but there was no recovery in the polls, nearly all of which showed Labour remaining static in England and heading for a crushing defeat in Scotland.

Jim Murphy's Doomed Fight Back

An insipid campaign from an upper-middle-class London socialist who struggled to offer economic measures that could protect family incomes and seemed most relaxed at preaching a revived form of class warfare, immensely benefited the SNP's task of acquiring electoral supremacy on its home turf. Sturgeon proclaimed herself to be the most capable and progressive contender on the left of British politics. This played well with voters still lukewarm about the SNP but drifting away from Labour. Jim Murphy, who had only been appointed leader of Scottish Labour in December 2014, proved quite unable to persuade undecided voters to stay loyal to Labour and, in the end, even Murphy would lose his own middle-class seat of Renfrewshire East.

In early 2015, he had criticised Labour for failing to prevent the technical defeat suffered by the SNP in the 2014 referendum from becoming a huge political success as its numbers surged and it insisted that Scotland was still on course for independence. During the referendum campaign, he had been rather more visible than his predecessor as leader, Johann Lamont. Later as leader, and in daunting circumstances, he would be articulate, energetic and unafraid to mount offensives in a bid to halt the relentless SNP juggernaut. He gave a forty-minute speech, without notes, at his party's Scottish conference on 14 March in which he set out a detailed programme of social justice measures. It was directed in particular at Scots without educational qualifications and who were ill-prepared for the challenges of work. He promised funding that would enable them to acquire qualifications, skills and attributes, such as a driving licence, that would enable them to make their way in life rather than to become socio-economic casualties.

But this conference was perhaps most notable for the endorsement of a new constitution for Scottish Labour that pledges its members to work "for the patriotic interest" of the people of Scotland. In January Murphy had signalled the change when Scottish Labour was unveiled as a distinctive entity which would work 'in coalition' with Labour and no longer be seen as a branch office of London. Nor would the party be defined by its pro-Union stance that had been a special necessity in the conditions of 2014.[95]

Murphy hoped to change the weather by re-emphasising social justice and Labour's ability to protect the vulnerable and the needy. He even denied being a unionist himself due to hailing from a minority, Scotland's Irish heritage Catholics where an anti-British outlook in fact resonated for longer than it had with most other Scots. For this he was criticised for suddenly being 'more nationalist than the nationalists': ' Disappointingly, Murphy has already presented his claim by invoking his Irish, Catholic, immigrant, (and by extension Republican) credentials as he distances himself from the concept of the Union when it comes with the suffix ist'.[96]

Labour, he asserted, would be open to Yes voters. There would be less emphasis on being an anti-SNP force. 190,000 Yes voters had been Labour supporters: their endorsement of Yes was seen as springing from the belief that this was the best way to oust the Tories.

Universal services would be protected. 'The Labour party has to be a party that supports people who have never been able to afford to pay in – the genuinely vulnerable', Murphy avowed. But he also pointed out that it couldn't be 'at the expense of those who have paid in.' Speaking to the David Hume Institute in Edinburgh in February 2015, he boldly declared: 'I want working-class parents to have the chance to have middle-class kids.'

This was a challenge to the orthodox view on the British Left that upward mobility meant a betrayal of class heritage and that people should remain in their allotted station, looked after of course by a responsive British state. It won him some media backing but the idea that bright working-class children should avail of opportunities to make their mark in life was seen as 'Daily Mailish' by intellectuals who set cultural norms in Scottish life.[97]

Such modernising heresy may also have removed any inhibitions on the part of Len McCluskey, the boss of the powerful Unite union, about praising Nicola Sturgeon. He was reported as doing so on 27 April and for saying that Labour should be prepared to work with the SNP. The fact that, more than anyone else (thanks to his union's voting bloc), he was responsible for ensuring that Ed had defeated his more moderate brother David Miliband in the 2010 Labour leadership election, may have helped to show the absolute incoherence at the heart of Labour's 2015 campaign.[98]

When the election campaign was over, Tony Blair would declare that 'Labour must be the party of ambition as well as compassion'.[99] The ex-Prime Minister's own political career showed no sign of revival even as Miliband, the archetypal state socialist, crashed in flames. Foreign policy failures and years of offering consultancy services to somewhat unappealing governments from the Balkans to Central Asia, had shattered Blair's image as a potent electoral force.[100]

Jim Murphy's loyalty to Blair until the end of his 1997-2007 premiership would constantly be thrown in his face. But it was his own active role in allegedly positioning Labour as an arch-Unionist force during the referendum which proved a daunting obstacle to overcome. He was accused of collusion with the Tories even though his controversial Scotland tour in the summer of 2014 had been pursued quite separately from them. Accusations of being 'treacherous' and 'unpatriotic', counted in an atmosphere often laced with emotional fervour. The election revealed that a huge number of Labour supporters no longer made their electoral choice primarily guided by economic issues. Owing to the post-referendum mood, numerous Scots were being drawn into the orbit of existential nationalism; so, it was Sturgeon's message and not Murphy's which counted for them.

Labour's malaise in its former Glasgow heartland was conveyed in a revealing report from the Glasgow South constituency. The SNP's membership in the seat had risen from 400 to over 2,000 in less than a year. The Irish journalist Mark Hennessy found little sign on the ground of an active Labour campaign. Stewart McDonald, a former tour guide and holiday representative in Spain had joined the party in 2006 when his branch had only a handful of activists. But on 7 May, he would sweep to victory as the SNP's voting percentage soared from 20.15 (in 2010) to 54.89 per cent.[101]

For months Murphy had found himself on the receiving end of a torrent of abuse. He had happened to be on the scene on 29 November 2014 when a police helicopter ploughed into the Clutha Bar on the north bank of the river Clyde, killing ten people. Despite helping the emergency services, Murphy, according to Euan McColm, a Glasgow-based press columnist, was accused of benefiting from the tragedy. He tweeted on 14 February, 'revolting lies being spread by yes campaigners that jim murphy took money from the clutha fund. How do these people look at themselves?'.[102]

On 17 May 2015, the day of his resignation, Malcolm Robertson tweeted, 'The nature of the abuse that has followed Jim Murphy should be a national embarrassment. An advertisement for avoiding public service.'[103]

Perhaps the fury directed against him eclipsed even that which descended on Thatcher in Scotland during the 1980s. Columnists like Mark Cavanagh and Michael Gray on the *National* flayed Murphy day after day and demanded his head in the period after the SNP's election triumph. The tone of online sites, notably, Cavanagh's own vehicle 'Wee Ginger Dug' was even rawer.[104]

Murphy went from being a popular constituency MP who, in the past, had increased his majority in a largely middle-class seat even when Labour was faring badly across the UK, to being a pariah.[105] One constituent was prepared to tell a journalist in April: 'I pass him every day. I park my car outside his house. He's always so cheerful, saying, "Hello," and I just want to kick him in the kneecaps.'[106] Yet despite turning into an ogre thanks to being showcased by his opponents in the SNP and across the online media, he still jogged for up to 16 miles most nights around the south of the city which was poised to decisively reject Labour.

Glasgow's St Enoch's Square: Monday 4 May 2015

The defiance and visibility of the Labour leader may have revealed the territorial mindset of fervent nationalists in a city where in the past disputes over turf had exacerbated religious rivalry and provoked gang warfare. On 4 May, in Glasgow's St Enoch's Square, while attempting to hold a public rally along with the comedian Eddie Izzard, he was assailed by SNP supporters who turned up with loudhailers, loud amplified music, and proceeded to chant and drown out any speeches, pushing placards into his face.

James Cook the BBC journalist on the scene, tweeted: 'Absolute chaos on the streets of Glasgow as Jim Murphy and Eddie Izzard try to be heard over protestors'.[107] The online response from the veteran folk singer Eddi Reader, on friendly terms with prominent SNPers such as the former culture minister Linda Fabiani, may have given some clue to the strongly territorial outlook:

'@BBCJamesCook 'walking into a YES city and trying to create chaos and aggro.. Jim Murphy is a trouble maker'.[108] It prompted Neil Lovett, a prominent online critic of the SNP to ask her: 'are you saying Glasgow is a No Go area for those that oppose independence? Am I required to move out'?[109]

Magnus Gardham, the political editor of the *Herald*, tweeted that he was 'Surprised so many people who were not there seem so keen to defend what was, by any standards, an unpleasant and intimidating protest'.[110] Alex Thomson, a senior reporter for Channel 4 News who, in the past, had reported sympathetically on the SNP's challenge to the UK political order, witnessed the incident and wrote: 'Because free speech was unquestionably denied on Buchanan Street today. It was ugly and it was perpetrated by people who say they will vote SNP'.[111]

Alan Roden, the political editor of the Scottish *Daily Mail* reported: 'I asked all the main organisers of today's ugly protest if they thought scenes like this helped the nationalist cause. They all said yes'.[112]

Yet on the very same day, one of Scotland's best-known actors Brian Cox had claimed: 'unlike anywhere else in the so-called United Kingdom, Scotland has a unity and Nicola is greatly responsible for that'.[113] Alex Salmond, writing in the *National* also on 4 May was asserting: "Our appeal should be for national unity in seizing this extraordinary moment'.

Yet Denise Mina, one of Scotland's best-known crime writers had a different slant. She tweeted, with the St Enoch's Square incident still very fresh: 'Yes, if your face isn't painted yellow [the colours of the SNP], it's quite shit here'.[114]

But Kevin McKenna, a prominent media convert to nationalism, whom the *Times* gave a platform to during the election campaign as 'Glasgow Man', made light of the incident, cynically tweeting: 'Outrageous behaviour. Poor Jim and Eddie. I shall light candles for them at Mass tonight; perhaps send a card. Are they okay?'[115]

But footage of the incident had been shown on CNN and it made the front page of the *Financial Times*.[116] In the face of an outcry, several days later the SNP suspended two figures thought to be instigators of the incident (at which no arrests were made), Piers Doughty-Brown and James Scott.[117]

Murphy would resign on 16 May a week after the party had lost 39 of its 40 Scottish seats. On the day of his announcement, he attacked Len McCluskey for orchestrating a campaign against him. The union boss's contention that UK Labour had lost the election because of Scottish Labour's disastrous performance was a 'grotesque insult' to the party's membership and activists.[118] At least ever since Scotland's only oil refinery, at Grangemouth, had been threatened with permanent closure in 2013 due to the anger of the company about the union's alleged militancy, Unite had been a source of strife in a debilitated Scottish Labour party.[119] Murphy said in May: 'Sometimes people see it as a badge of honour to have Mr McCluskey's support. I kind of see it as a kiss of death to be supported by that type of politics'.[120]

But, on the personal level it was not a meddling trade-union boss that was the source of the Scottish party's woes but Ed Miliband himself. He proved to be a 'useless leader' with an unelectable package of incoherent policies.[121]

The rule still applied even in the Scotland of 2015 that the calibre and campaigning prowess of the main leader was absolutely crucial in contributing to the electoral performance of the party. Instead of being derided, Alex Salmond was widely believed when he boasted in April that 'I'll be writing Labour's budget!'[122]

In January 2015, one poll had found that in decidedly anti-Tory Glasgow, David Cameron was more popular among voters than Miliband was.[123] The absolute nadir for the party was probably Miliband's main campaign rally in Scotland on 1 May. Held at a sports centre in a working-class area of Glasgow, the audience which included children, had to rush past protesters who screamed 'scum', 'quisling', 'Red Tories out', 'No more Union' at them.[124] A leader with more authority than Miliband would not have been easy game for such an intimidatory crowd and in an anodyne speech he failed to make a rallying appeal for democracy against street-level aggression.

Mutinous Scotland and the Conservative Comeback

In its Machiavellian approach to Labour, the SNP at that time was calling for cooperation with Miliband's party in order to foil a Tory victory. But many in the SNP viewed Labour as an extension of the UK governing party despite a radical electoral programme which for plenty of others was reminiscent of Labour back in the early

1980s. Labour faced a pincer movement in Scotland not only from the SNP but also from the Conservatives. David Cameron and his advisers emphasised the danger to English voters if a minority Labour government found itself at the mercy of demands from a militant SNP.

As early as 3 April, the journalist Iain Martin anxiously observed:

'What should be plain now is that the Conservatives are working unashamedly for an SNP victory in Scotland. They actively want the Nationalists to wipe out Scottish Labour because that way lies the road to Tory victory in the rest of the UK. In pure electoral arithmetic they are right, although it involves taking huge risks with the future of the UK'.[125]

Similarly, the BBC's James Cook reported that in conversations with Nationalist politicians several had volunteered that a Tory electoral outcome was the best outcome for the SNP. In March a poster of a giant Alex Salmond, with Labour leader Ed Miliband a tiny figure in his top pocket, had gone up in seats which were thought to be crucial for Tory fortunes. The journalist Michael Deacon wryly observed: 'When I was growing up in Scotland I never guessed that one day I'd see Salmond's face on billboards all over Essex'.[126]

The Tories fought a lacklustre campaign. Its strategists were alarmed to find that contrary to expectations UKIP's support was not disappearing into single figures and that it enjoyed a polling average of around 15 per cent well into April 2015. Cameron's poll ratings also remained unimpressive. He had alienated traditionalist Labour and Conservative supporters alike with his neglect of Britain's defences at a time of rising international tension and his championing of measures such as same-sex marriage that primarily appealed to metropolitan liberal opinion. On 21 April the influential BBC journalist Andrew Neil tweeted: 'Spoke to major Tory donor tonight. "Tory campaign useless. Cameron's heart not in it. Not looking good"'.[127] The next day, David Cameron claimed to be shocked by a recent boast from Alex Salmond. 'This footage will shock you' he tweeted. 'Alex Salmond laughs & boasts he'll write Labour's budget. Vote Conservative to stop it'.[128]

Numerous other campaign players portrayed the surging regional party as a menace to the interests especially of English voters. John Major, Prime Minister from 1990 to 1997, had already, in March, appealed to Ed Miliband to rule out coalition with the SNP in order to save the UK.[129] Typically, the most uninhibited warning of the dangers stemming from the SNP wielding power came from Boris Johnson, the Conservative who was mayor of London and standing for a seat at Westminster. His flair for public relations meant that he was a popular Conservative whose pronouncements often generated headlines.

Writing on 19 April he declared:

CHAPTER 4: A REMARKABLE ELECTION DEEPENS THE SCOTTISH DIVIDE

'You wouldn't get Herod to run a baby farm, would you?...' 'So can someone tell me why in the name of all that is holy there are some apparently rational people who are even contemplating the elevation of the Scottish Nationalist Party to a position of effective dominance in the government of the United Kingdom – an entity that they are sworn to destroy?

They want to end Britain, to decapitate Britannia, to cause a constitutional upheaval that would gravely weaken this country, a rupture that has provoked horror in Britain's friends around the world – and a silent chuckle among those who do not wish us quite so well.

And yet it is now clear that it is only with the help of the SNP – a party that is literally anti-British – that Ed Miliband can have any hope of governing this country. [...]. Yes, he will be sitting in the driving seat, pretending to be steering the car – but all the time he will have clever Nicola next to him, whispering in his ear, and perpetually yanking the steering wheel to the Left. Eventually there will be another terrible crash, just as there was in 2008/9'.[130]

The SNP was unlikely to be discomfited at being 'othered' by a quintessential southern English toff like 'Boris'. It could only result in its electoral windfall in Scotland being greater still. But concern reigned among many Scottish Tories. Few of them were likely to have been cheered by the May Day stunt of the Scottish-born Chief Whip Michael Gove. He accompanied around 50 party workers in central London who were dressed as Nicola Sturgeon. He even claimed that his party would end up with more seats in Scotland than the Labour Party which was at variance with the mood in Scotland where Tory MSPs were very guarded in their predictions.[131]

Ruth Davidson, the Scottish Conservative leader, who had grown into a genuinely popular politician, dismissed as 'hyperbole' the warning by the Home Secretary Theresa May that the SNP would cause the greatest constitutional crisis since the Abdication of 1936 if the party acquired a major say in the government at Westminster. Davidson observed that the Second World War and the independence referendum of 2014 last year had posed a greater constitutional threat than the SNP's chances of wielding central influence after 7 May.[132]

Michael Forsyth, a former Scottish Secretary in the Major government, told the *Guardian* on 20 April that his own party was putting electoral tactics above a historic commitment to the defence of the UK union. Mr Cameron's implicit support for the advance of the SNP into Labour's Scottish strongholds threatened 'the integrity of the UK'.[133]

Magnus Linklater, a Tory sympathiser in the media writing in the *Times,* a paper which he had once edited, under the title 'SNP is feeding off Tory scare tactics', was impressed by the irony of what was happening. He was left in no doubt that 'a Conservative party, dedicated to saving the union, is stirring up anti-Union sentiments among the Scots'.[134] Philip Stephens, a columnist on the *Financial Times,* pointed out that Tory fears about separatists rampaging at the very heart of power, were probably groundless. The SNP could only dominate a minority Labour government if the Tories chose to let it. Without the Conservatives entering the voting lobby at Westminster alongside the SNP, the latter's hopes of blocking the renewal of Britain's nuclear deterrent were going nowhere. The SNP could only play a really obstructive role at Westminster if the Tories, in a determined bid to shorten the life of a Labour government, actively colluded with them.[135] He warned that the SNP were likely to be the main beneficiaries of a Tory campaign operation that helped turn Scotland into an even more unsettled place politically. Anti-Union sentiment would have been further stoked in the process.

One wonders if Tory strategists, desperate for victory, looked beyond the electoral period. If the Tory gambit worked and Cameron returned to government, his second administration might well be required to devote time, patience, and probably resources to the Scottish Question, a burden most had shown scant interest in bearing hitherto.

Stephens is perhaps worth quoting here:

'...by seeking to delegitimise the SNP they are reinforcing the Scottish Nationalist narrative of victimhood – that the English will always seek to do it down. A party fit to govern Scotland, the Tories are saying, cannot have any say in the governance of the UK. In those circumstances, what point the union?

There is nothing to welcome in the SNP's advance in Scotland. Ms Sturgeon's demands for home rule – combining fiscal autonomy with a blank cheque from the Westminster government – belong to the realm of the absurd. The answer from unionist parties should be a simple "No".

Instead Mr Cameron, and now Sir John [Major], have decided to put party before country and join with the SNP in playing the nationalist game. This can only be bad for the future of the union'. [136]

Oli Waghorn, a former special adviser to Liam Fox, once a major rival to Cameron for the Tory leadership, believed that the danger of an SNP-Labour coalition was 'a failed message' as 'most people don't care'.

'Their latest ploy sounds like a Monty Python sketch, or an amateur pantomime, with an Englishman manning the barricades shouting at the Scots as they advance: "Watch out! That man is wearing a skirt".[137] But 48 hours after this dismissive claim, polling evidence suggested that the Tory strategy of 'bigging up' the SNP was having a definite impact. A poll commissioned from Survation, and published in the *Mail on Sunday* on 26 April, asked the question 'if 'Ed Miliband ruled the UK with Nicola

Sturgeon, who would have the upper hand?' 51 per cent of UK respondents believed it would be the SNP leader while only 28 per cent thought that it would be Miliband. In answer to a further question, 'Would you vote Tory to stop Ed Miliband ruling the UK with Ms Sturgeon (and directed at UKIP voters only), 37 per cent said they would as against 51 per cent who stated that it would make no difference.[138]

Sturgeon's effective performance in the leader's debate, held on 2 April, showcased her as a formidable politician, one capable of tilting a far more prosaic Labour leader in a radical left direction if the electoral cards fell in his favour and there was a hung parliament. In terms of party advantage, it made sense for Cameron to overlook her in the debate and for his chief ally in government, George Osborne to have praised her performance immediately afterwards.[139]

In the final stretch of the 2015 election campaign, there is hardly any evidence that the SNP tried to foil Tory tactics of building the party up as a force that could threaten the well-being of English voters fearful that the mildly benign economic times could be abruptly swept away. Instead, in early May the SNP made fresh demands which it couched in aggressive terms.

Speaking at a rally in Dumfries on 4 May, Sturgeon warned Ed Miliband that he would not receive a 'free pass' to be in Downing Street, declaring that the price for any SNP support was billions of pounds of extra spending.[140] She repeated an assertion, made in a speech one week earlier, that votes cast in Paisley and Kirkcaldy in Scotland 'must have equal weight' to those in Carlisle and Oxfordshire in England. She claimed that the 'test of legitimacy' for the victor in Thursday's general election is that it 'cannot simply be that it is the largest party in England'.[141]

Scotland, having one-twelfth of the population of the UK, therefore in SNP eyes deserved compensation and perhaps even a right to shape particular UK policies affecting it (such as ones in the defence field). There was no pause for thought that compensation might be at the expense of areas of the UK such as the north of England which received rather less per head in state spending than Scotland did and, in large parts of which, hardly any Tory MPs had been returned for many years.

Divided Unionists

Alarm about what was seen as the SNP's barely concealed efforts to try and permanently break-up the UK, had spawned non-party initiatives to halt its electoral juggernaut. The best-known one was Scotland in Union (SiU) which had the long-term aim of seeking to unite people around a positive view of Scotland in the UK.[142] Its online site published articles making the case for tactical voting; it was pointed out that the division of the pro-Union camp into at least three separate parties meant that the NO side, winners of the 2014 referendum were in danger of having very little representation. This meant that the independence issue could surface again with a vengeance. To counteract the effects of the British electoral system, which disproportionately rewarded cohesive parties with support concentrated in geographical areas, SiU, in April, published a guide to tactical voting.[143] In 59 Scottish seats, it identified which party was best placed to halt the SNP and urged that opponents of separatism rally behind that party. In no less than 45 seats the majority of cases it was Labour, but surveys had shown that still-loyal Labour voters were less inclined to vote tactically than were Tories or Liberal Democrats. Senior UK Tories, Malcolm Rifkind and Lord Tebbit had urged Scottish Conservatives to vote tactically.[144] In the seat of Perth and Perthshire North, Unite Against Separation was a local initiative hoping to unseat the SNP MP Pete Wishart.

The other main target seat was Gordon in Aberdeenshire. Alex Salmond had chosen it as his launch-pad for a Westminster come-back. It had been Liberal Democrat for many years and he faced an energetic candidate for that party in the journalist Christine Jardine. The day before the vote the *Scottish Daily Mail* published a 2-page guide to voting entitled 'How your tactical vote will impact'.[145] On the basis of a YouGov poll it had commissioned, SiU contended that 1 in 7 Scottish voters would be voting tactically.[146] But the SNP landslide suggested that this united front had been a feeble affair, though not everywhere. Wishart increased his majority in his Perthshire seat from just under five thousand to nearly ten thousand votes. But the swing to the SNP of 10.91 per cent was easily the lowest in the country. The Liberal Democrat vote fell by three-quarters and Labour's was halved but the Tory vote went up. Meanwhile, Gordon was won by Salmond on a 25.46 per cent swing; the swing against the Liberal Democrats of 3.31 per cent was the second smallest in Scotland.

Where tactical voting did appear to deprive the SNP of victory was in Edinburgh South. In 2010 Labour only had a majority of 316 votes. But there was actually a swing to the party of 4.41 per cent and Ian Murray increased his small majority to 2,637 votes. Working-class ex-Labourites turning to the SNP were compensated for by many Lib Dems, and perhaps even some Conservatives, switching to Labour possibly angered by controversial remarks that had been made by the SNP candidate Neil Hay about elderly pro-Union citizens.[147]

Paradoxically, a lot of tactical voting against the SNP seems to have occurred in places where the party wasn't standing. Its existence had been revealed in Tory election billboards and by some effective media performances from Sturgeon. In the final leg of the campaign, Tory voters who had decided to defect to UKIP returned to the fold, especially in parts of southern England. Nigel Farage, who was the clear favourite to capture Thanet South, instead lost by nearly 3,000 votes (though it became the first council anywhere in Britain won by UKIP).

Once all the votes had been counted, it emerged that the Conservatives had won an overall majority of 12 seats on 36.9 per cent of the UK vote. David Cameron was one of only a few European government leaders in recent times to have won re-election with an increased majority.

The SNP triumphed with almost 50 per cent of the vote on a 71.1 per cent turn-out, 5 per cent higher than in the UK as a whole. It won all but 3 of Scotland's 59 seats, enjoying swings unknown in modern electoral history. The SNP had fought a campaign centred around its new leader and her ability to be of service to Scotland. It was a stunning endorsement for Nicola Sturgeon and, five months after becoming leader, she found herself the chief with the strongest legitimacy in the 76-year history of her party.

She remarked correctly that the tectonic plates of Scottish politics have shifted: there was need to go beyond the enhanced devolution of the Smith commission. At UK level there was a readiness to explore ways to accommodate the sharply diverging voting patterns across the 4-country union. The responses from senior political figures were varied ones though. Some insisted that Sturgeon should use her existing range of powers to improve Scotland rather than constantly asking for more. Others accepted the desirability of asymmetrical devolution across the UK, while others, such as Sir Malcolm Rifkind, a former Scottish Secretary, accepted the need for an all-encompassing constitutional settlement for Britain.[148] But there were outspoken voices in the SNP who seemed happy to reignite the constitutional question, conveniently forgetting that their leader had made it clear it was not an electoral issue. Alex Salmond, unlike her, now an SNP MP at Westminster, described the result as 'a staging post on the way to independence'.

He added: 'I think the main thing we can say is that we're not now the same country we were a year ago. I think the biggest factor behind the massive, overwhelming mandate for the SNP last Thursday is that this is a changed nation. It's a changed nation having gone through the referendum process; a changed nation and a better one.'[149]

Pressed by the media, Sturgeon dampened down such rhetoric: 'I said that repeatedly, I said it consistently and I said expressly to people in Scotland that if they voted SNP, and half of the Scottish population did, I would not take that as an endorsement of independence'. SNP MPs had been elected in such numbers to ensure that Scotland's voice was heard louder than ever.[150] Perhaps years of electoral defeats made her cautious. But trans-generational rejection had given way to runaway success on a scale that nearly every other party in the democratic world was finding elusive. It was a remarkable turnaround. Sturgeon was adept at signalling not only competence but virtue. A highly personal campaign saw her not only packaged but also regarded by countless Scots as a kind of 'mother of the nation'. 'Stronger for Scotland' was the SNP's campaign slogan. But what purpose would that added strength be put to? The SNP never even offered a manifesto as comprehensive as that of the despised Labour Party in Scotland. Voters perhaps looking for a sacrificial object upon which to direct their anger and frustration fixed upon Jim Murphy, hitherto a very effective vote-gatherer. Few, if any, showed any sign of wishing to discover what the SNP would do with an imposing mandate in policy terms. It was enough to clamber onto a turbo-charged political vehicle that enabled many of them to express their Scottishness.

Obviously, Scottish politics was set apart from politics as practised in the rest of the UK. But it was also very different from politics in perhaps nearly every other competitive democracy where scarcity and insecurity meant that voters often scrutinised rival offerings very carefully indeed. In 2015, many Scots appeared to find fulfilment in minimising the differences between them and instead rallying around a chief and her cause offering vague presentiments of change. Populism reigned supreme and there were other countries where a personalised form of politics was making headway. But nowhere in modern times has the switch from politics usually involving uncharismatic leaders and competing programmes given way to a brand of identity politics in such a complete way as is happening in Scotland in our own times.

Notes, Chapter 4

1.Mike Wade, 'Everything clicked in the selfie campaign', *Times*, 9 May 2015
   http://www.thetimes.co.uk/tto/news/uk/scotland/article4435591.ece
2. Alex Massie 'Message that matters most', *Spectator*, 25 April 2015
3. Editorial, 'The *Guardian* view on the election in Scotland: when the slogans hit the facts', *Guardian*, 10 April 2015
4. Kevin McKenna, 'Scotland's SNP revolution terrifies the main parties', *Observer*, 5 April 2015,
   </commentisfree/2015/apr/05/scotland-snp-revolution-terrifies-main-parties#img-1>
5. Muriel Gray @ArtyBagger on Twitter 7 April 2015 (accessed 7 April 2015).
6. James_Forsyth, 'The referendum is still defining Scottish politics', *Spectator*, 8 April 2015.
7. Kevin McKenna, 'The referendum campaign's not toxic but intoxicating', *Observer*, 15 June 2014, http://www.theguardian.com/commentisfree/2014/jun/14/better-together-mistakes-scottish-independence
8. Faisal Islam on Twitter, 10 April 2015. (accessed 30 August 2015).
9. Kenny Farquharson on Twitter, 11 April 2015. (accessed 30 August 2015).

10. Dan Hodges, 'What does the SNP surge look like up close?', *Daily Telegraph,* 5 May 2015, http://www.telegraph.co.uk/news/general-election-2015/politics-blog/11581766/What-does-the-SNP-surge-look-like-up-close.html#disqus_thread>

11. 'They want White knights in Westminster', *Between the Hammer and the Anvil,* http://www.flyingrodent.blogspot.co.uk/ 19 April 2015.

12. John McDermott, 'The SNP's record in power: less radical than you might think', *Financial Times,* 2 May 2015; Audit Scotland http://www.audit-scotland.gov.uk/docs/local/2014/nr_140619_school_education.pdf

13. McDermott, 'The SNP's record'.

14. Andrew Gilligan, 'The SNP's very Scottish conspiracy', *Daily Telegraph,* 19 April 2015.

15. *Times,* 23 April 2015; see also Euan McColm, 'Students worse off with free tuition', *Scotland on Sunday,* 30 August 2015.

16. 'The SNP's very Scottish'.

17. Editorial, *Guardian,* 10 April 2015, Editorial</commentisfree/2015/apr/10/guardian-view-on-election-scotland-slogan-hit-facts#img-1>

18. David Clark, 'If you think the SNP are a left-wing force, think again', *New Statesman,* 30 April, 2015, http://www.newstatesman.com/politics/2015/04/if-you-think-snp-are-left-wing-force-think-again>

19. McDermott, 'The SNP's record'.

20. John McDermott, 'The SNP's record'.

21. Brian Wilson, 'SNP faces a question of competence', *Scotsman,* 3 April 2015.

22. Alan Cochrane, 'Nicola Sturgeon's policies backed "no matter what"', *Daily Telegraph,* 2 April 2015.

23. Simon Johnson, 'IFS, longer austerity under SNP plans', *Daily Telegraph,* 23 April 2015, http://www.telegraph.co.uk/news/politics/nicola-sturgeon/11559430/IFS-SNP-spending-plans-mean-longest-austerity.html#disqus_thread

24. Alex Massie, 'The SNP create their own reality – and voters lap it up, *Spectator,* 21 April 2014.

25. Tom Gallagher, 'Why charlatans and demagogues are flourishing', *Commentator,* 12 February 2015, http://www.thecommentator.com/article/5605/why_charlatans_and_demagogues_are_flourishing

26. Frances Coppola, 'Smith, Barnett and the wily Salmond', *Coppola Comment,* 16 April 2016.

27. Gilligan, 'The SNP's very Scottish'.

28. Simon Johnson, 'The SNP's oil figures, 13 times higher than reality', *Daily Telegraph,* 18 March 2014.

29. Daniel Sanderson, 'SNP accused of deception after government refuses to release oil revenue forecast', *Herald,* 27 April 2014.

30. David Smith, 'The Great Escape: how Scotland Dodged a Bullet', *EconomicsUK.Com*, 12 September 2015, http://www.economicsuk.com/blog/002120.html

31. See Brian Wilson, 'Labour must rule out deal with SNP', *Scotsman*, 14 March 2015.

32. The *Sun* (Scottish edition), 30 April 2015.

33. Jill Stephenson @Historywoman, 30 April 2015.

34. *Times*, 3 April 2015.

35. "Nicola Sturgeon, Calling the tune', *Economist*, 11 April 2015.

36. Matthew Engel, 'TV debate that was the "we agree with Nicola"' show', Financial Times, 3 April 2015.

37. Severin Carrell, *Guardian*, 9 April 2015

38. *Daily Mail*, 4 April 2015. http://www.dailymail.co.uk/news/article-3024345/Surging-Sturgeon-Nightmare-Miliband-Tory-Labour-MPs-admit-SNP-chief-triumphed-historic-TV-debate.html

39. Simon Johnson, 'Alex Salmond to demand tax autonomy despite oil price', *Daily Telegraph*, 8 January 2015.

40. 'Oil just a bonus Salmond says', *Sunday Times*, 21 July 2013., http://www.thesundaytimes.co.uk/sto/news/uk_news/scotland/article1290543.ece

41. Brian Wilson, 'Labour must rule out deal with SNP', *Scotsman*, 14 March 2015

42. Alex Massie, 'Why the latest economic statistics are a disaster for the SNP but that doesn't matter' *Spectator*, 11 March 2015.

43. http://www.scotsman.com/news/uk/snp-postpones-ffa-push-in-battle-for-smith-plus-1-3788372

44. *Financial Times*, 21 April 2015.

45. Severin Carrell, 'Promises would require cuts or tax raises', *Guardian*, 9 April 2015.

46. Sturgeon grilled over fiscal policy, as she accuses other parties of reviving Project Fear', *Scotsman*, 13 April 2015.

47. *Scotsman*, 16 April 2015.

48. George Kerevan, 'Federalism or Bust', The *National*, 9 May 2015, http://www.thenational.scot/news/george-kerevan-federalism-or-bust-snp-mandate-now-goes-far-beyond-smith-powers.2

49. Kevin Hague, 'George Kerevan, my new SNP MP', *Chokka Blog*, 10 May 2015. http://chokkablog.blogspot.co.uk/2015/05/george-kerevan-my-new-snp-mp.html?m=1

50. For some background information on Hague, see Euan McColm, 'Toe the Line in Nicola's State or the Trolls Will Get you', *Sunday Times*, 24 May 2015.

51. *BBC news* 22 April 2015, http://www.bbc.co.uk/news/election-2015-32408329

52. 'Tilting at Windmills', Wings over Scotland, 10 April 2015, http://wingsoverscotland.com/tilting-at-windmills/

53. McDermott, 'The SNP's record'.

54. Clark, 'If you think the SNP are a left-wing force'.

55. Clark, 'If you think the SNP are a left-wing force'.

56. Gilligan, 'The SNP's very Scottish'.

57. Ibid.

58. Gerry Braiden, 'SNP councillors under fire for burning copy of Smith commission report', *Herald*, 2 December 2014.

59. Information about this incident and its aftermath was obtained from Brian Swanson, 'Outrage as SNP trio burn Smith report', *Daily Express*, 3 December 3, 2014

60. Tom Gallagher, 'Nicola Sturgeon shallow empress of North Britain', *Commentator*, 22 April 2015.

61. *Fear and Smear: The Campaign Against Scottish Independence*, Scotland: Createspace, 2015.

62. James Cook on Twitter, 25 April 2015. (accessed 30 August 2015).

63. Arty Bagger, (Muriel Gray) on Twitter, 27 April 2015, accessed 30 August 2015. [Spitting Image a hit television programme of the 1980s featuring sharply mocking political satire.]

64. Simon Johnson, 'Nicola Sturgeon, 'I would vote for twitter troll candidate', *Daily Telegraph*, 28 April 2015.

65. Duncan Hothersall on Twitter, 1 May 2015 (accessed 30 August 2015).

66. David Clegg, 'SNP accused of using "Intimidation" tactics', *Daily Record*, 18 February 2015.

67. Clegg, 'SNP accused'.

68. Andrew Gilligan, 'The bullying behind the SNP's smiles', *Sunday Telegraph*, 11 April 2015.

69. Gilligan, 'The bullying behind the SNP's smiles'.

70. Gilligan, 'The bullying behind the SNP's smiles'.

71. Gilligan, 'The bullying behind the SNP's smiles'.

72. *National*, 5 April 2015, http://newsnet.scot/2015/04/election-special-the-dug-explains-why-magrit-is-toast-in-the-east-end/

73. 'Labour calls for public apology after senior SNP politicians encourage "abuse" of TV debate youngster', *Herald*, 9 April 2015. http://www.heraldscotland.com/politics/scottish-politics/labour-calls-for-public-apology-after-senior-snp-politicians-encourage-ab.122836546

74. Gilligan, 'The bullying behind the SNP's smiles'.

75. Gilligan, 'The bullying behind the SNP's smiles'.

76. Gilligan, 'The bullying behind the SNP's smiles'.

77. Gilligan, 'The bullying behind the SNP's smiles'.

78. Allan Massie, 'Patriotism applies to all parties', *Scotsman*, 15 April 2015.

79. Scott MacNab, 'SNP suspends member over Ruth Davidson abuse', *Scotsman*, 20 March 2015.

80. Tom Peterkin, 'Journalists "abused over nationality" at SNP rally', *Scotsman*, 12 April 2015.

81. Peterkin, 'Journalists "abused"'.

82. Craig Murray, 'False Flag is Starting', 11 April 2015
    <https://www.craigmurray.org.uk/archives/2015/04/false-flag-is-starting/

83. Peter Jones, 'Say no to hypocrisy and No to SNP', *Scotsman*, 5 May 2015.

84. Steven Swinford, 'Election 2015: SNP prepared to paralyse Armed Forces unless Trident is Scrapped,' *Daily Telegraph*, 19 Apr 2015.

85. Marta Cooper and Rosa Prince, 'Major tells Miliband to rule out coalition with SNP to save UK', *Daily Telegraph*, 6 March 2015.

86. Rob Marchant, 'Six reasons why Labour should rule out an SNP deal', *Labour Uncut*, 10 March 2015, http://labour-uncut.co.uk/2015/03/10/enjoy-your-daily-paper-during-the-campaign-it-might-not-be-there-next-time-round/

87. Clark, 'If you think the SNP are a left-wing force'.

88. Brian Wilson, 'Tories were real winners of debate', *Scotsman*, 18 April 2014.

89. Steven Swinford, 'Ed Miliband refuses to rule out SNP deal', *Daily Telegraph*, 17 April 2015.

90. 'I won't be PM with SNP deal, says Miliband', *BBC News*, 1 May 2015.

91. Brian Monteith, 'SNP only cared about their voice', *Scotsman*, 11 May 2015.

92. Simon Johnson and Peter Dominiczak, 'Revealed: Full text of Nicola Sturgeon memo', 4 April 2015.

93. Jack Sommers, 'BBC's James Cook Condemns Cybernats' 'Vicious Abuse' After Nicola Sturgeon Interview', *Huffington Post UK*, 5 April 2015.

94. Wade, 'Everything clicked in the selfie campaign'.

95. Tom Peterkin, 'Jim Murphy: Labour party 'open to Yes voters', *Scotsman*, 11 January 2015.

96. Lily of St Leonards, 'Goodbye to all that', *Effie Deans Blogspot*, 24 January 2015.

97. Kenny Farquharson, 'Murphy is right about class', *Scotsman*, 19 February 2015.

98. http://www.theguardian.com/politics/2015/apr/27/len-mccluskey-says-prime-minister-ed-miliband-would-work-with-snp

99. Tony Blair, 'Labour must be the party of ambition as well as compassion', *Guardian*, 10 May 2015.

100. Danny Hakim, 'Tony Blair Has Used His Connections to Change the World, and to Get Rich', *New York Times*, 5 August 2014.; http://www.dailymail.co.uk/news/article-2674476/Serbia-hire-Mandelson-adviser-help-country-join-EU-Blair-costs-much.html

101. Mark Hennessy, 'SNP a major threat in Labour Glasgow stronghold', *Irish Times*, 2 May 2015.

102. Euan McColm on Twitter, 14 February 2015 (accessed 31 August 2015).

103. Malcolm Robertson on Twitter, 17 May 2015 (accessed 31 August 2015).

104. http://weegingerdug.wordpress.com/2014/11/02/jim-murphys-bogof/;
    https://weegingerdug.wordpress.com/2015/04/01/by-the-power-of-numbskull

105. Tom Gallagher, 'Scotland's Catholic Pariah', *Catholic Herald*, 22 May 2015.

106. 'Interview: Jim Murphy Laments Labour complacency', *Scotsman*, 2 May 2015.

http://www.scotsman.com/news/politics/top-stories/interview-jim-murphy-laments-labour-complacency-1-3761161

107. James Cook on Twitter, 4 May 2015 (accessed 31 August 2015).

108. Edi Reader on Twitter, 4 May 2015 (accessed 31 August 2015).

109. Neil Lovett on Twitter, 4 May 2015 (accessed 31 August 2015).

110. Marcus Gardham on Twitter, 4 May 2015 (accessed 31 August 2015).

111. Alex Thomson, 'Jim Murphy confronts the ugly face of nationalism', 4 May 2015. http://blogs.channel4.com/alex-thomsons-view/scotland-labour-jim-murphy-eddie-izzard-scottish-national-party/9501

112. Alan Roden on Twitter, 4 May 2015 (accessed 31 August 2015).

113. 'SNP Welcome Brian Cox Support for Nicola Sturgeon, SNP statement, 4 May 2015, http://www.snp.org/media-centre/news/2015/may/snp-welcome-brian-cox-support-nicola-sturgeon

114. Denise Mina on Twitter, 4 May 2015 (accessed 31 August 2015).

115. Kevin McKenna on Twitter, 4 May 2015 (accessed 31 August 2015).

116. Stephen Collinson, 'CNN Scottish campaign turns nasty at Labour Party rally', 4 May 2015.

117. 'SNP suspends members over Glasgow protest', *Scotsman*, 5 May 2015.

118. Severin Carrell, 'Jim Murphy's resignation throws Scottish Labour into turmoil', *Guardian*, 16 May 2015.

119. Michael Kelly, 'Salmond lost, but Labour hasn't won', *Scotsman*, 30 October 2013.

120. Carrell, 'Jim Murphy's resignation'.

121. Nick Cohen, 'Labour must understand that Unite is its enemy', *Spectator*, 18 May 2015, <http://blogs.spectator.co.uk/coffeehouse/2015/05/labour-must-understand-that-unite-is-its-enemy/#disqus_thread

122. Tom McTague, *Daily Mail*, 22 April 2015, </news/article-3050631/I-ll-writing-Labour-s-budget-Salmond-caught-camera-laughing-boasting-call-shots-election.html#comments

123. http://www.dailymail.co.uk/news/article-2959855/Labour-woes-Scotland-deepen-poll-reveals-Miliband-popular-Cameron-SNP-course-landslide.html

124. Alan Roden, James Chapman and Jason Groves, 'Ed's Big Lie on SNP Deal', *Scottish Daily Mail*, 2 May 2015, https://twitter.com/bbcjamescook/status/594183236479221762

125. Iain Martin, 'The Tories are working for an SNP victory', *CapX*, 3 April 2015.

126. Michael Deacon on Twitter, 15 April 2015 (accessed 31 August 2015).

127. Andrew Neil on Twitter, 21 April 2015 (accessed 31 August 2015).

128. David Cameron on Twitter, 22 April 2015 (accessed 31 August 2015).

129. Marta Cooper and Rosa Prince, 2015 'Major tells Miliband to rule out coalition with SNP to save UK', *Daily Telegraph*, 6 March 2015.

130. Boris Johnson, 'If Ed Miliband's in the driving seat, Nicola Sturgeon will be steering

him to the Left', *Daily Telegraph*, 19 April 2015.

131. Steerpike, 'Michael Gove claims Tories will win more seats in Scotland than Labour', *Spectator*, 1 May 2015, http://blogs.spectator.co.uk/steerpike/2015/05/michael-gove-claims-tories-will-win-more-seats-in-scotland-than-labour/#disqus_thread>

132. Hamish Macdonell, 'Davidson and may at odds as anti-SNP line exposes Tory split', *Times*, 27 April 2015.

133. http://www.theguardian.com/uk-news/2015/apr/20/tories-playing-dangerous-game-scotland-lord-forsyth

134. *Times*, 28 April 2015.

135. Philip Stephens, 'Why the Scottish nationalists cannot call the shots', *Financial Times*, 21 April 2015.

136. Stephens, 'Why the Scottish nationalists'

137. 'The Tory campaign to date. A failed message and polling   stagnation', *Daily Telegraph*, 25 April 2015.

138. Simon Walters, 'Tories lead in third poll in a row as Ed's voters turn to Ukip', *Mail on Sunday*, 26 April 2015.

139. Iain Martin, 'The Tories are working for an SNP victory', *Cap X*, 3 April 2015.

140. Simon Johnson, 'Nicola Sturgeon: UK Government 'illegitimate' without Scottish support', *Daily Telegraph*, 4 May 2015.

141. Simon Johnson, 'Nicola Sturgeon: UK Government 'illegitimate' without Scottish support', *Daily Telegraph*, 4 May 2014, http://www.telegraph.co.uk/news/politics/nicola-sturgeon/11582077/Nicola-Sturgeon-UK-Government-illegitimate-without-Scottish-support.html#disqus_thread

142. http://www.scotlandinunion.co.uk/

143. Simon Johnson, 'Guide to tactical voting against the SNP published', *Daily Telegraph*, 14 May 2015, http://www.telegraph.co.uk/news/general-election-2015/11533602/Guide-to-tactical-voting-against-the-SNP-published.html

144. Nicholas Watt, 'Tories should vote Labour in Scotland to keep SNP out, Lord Tebbit suggests', *Guardian*, 21 April 2015, http://www.theguardian.com/politics/2015/apr/21/lord-tebbit-conservative-supporters-vote-labour-scotland-keep-out-snp

145. *Scottish Daily Mail*, 6 May 2015.

146. http://www.scotlandinunion.co.uk/http www scotsman com news politics top stories one in seven to vote tactically to stop snp 1 3756167

147. David Maddox, 'Nicola Sturgeon won't sack 'cybernat' SNP candidate', *Scotsman*, 23 April 2015.

148. Sir Malcolm Rifkind, 'Our differences can help to keep us together', *Times*, 12 May 2015.

149. Scott MacNab, *Scotsman*, 10 May 2015.

150. Euan McColm, 'Nicola Sturgeon must rein in Alex Salmond', *Scotland on Sunday*, 10 May 2015.

CHAPTER 5: NATIONALIST PEOPLE

CHAPTER 5: NATIONALIST PEOPLE

Nationalism is a highly emotive political creed. Considerable power and prestige can be accumulated by leaders who can harness this pool of emotional intensity and channel its energy towards realising the territorial goals of the movement.

The appeal of nationalism for ambitious, idealistic and sometimes unscrupulous and unbalanced figures is obvious. It gives them a hold over people's emotions and sometimes disables their critical faculties so that followers acquiesce in decisions which they would shrink from in more contemplative moments. At best, nationalism is capable of promoting striking altruism as people sacrifice their own interests and well-being for a wider common good. At worst, it enables lots of people to endorse foolish or selfish actions springing from neurotic fears or greed for territory and power. Personalities often count for more in the politics of nationalism than in other movements where the primary focus may be on carrying out policies rather than altering the status of territories.

This chapter profiles the gallery of political figures who have attempted to surf this emotional wave in Scotland during differing peaks of intensity. They are presented here in reverse chronological order. This is because success for Scottish nationalism has come late, making it a neophyte in the world of political nationalism.

Nicola Sturgeon

The near clean-sweep of seats in 2015 understandably is viewed in many quarters as the SNP's greatest triumph. But this may be to overlook an internal party matter: the leadership hand-over from Alex Salmond to Nicola Sturgeon in the aftermath of the referendum. Political successions often go awry even in well-ordered parties. It is necessary to look no further than the Liberal and Labour parties, the two alternating forces of reform in post-19th century British politics. Arguably they came unstuck, after 1914 and after 2000 respectively due to corrosive rivalries at the top.

Nationalist parties often tend to be refuges for people with strong egos, figures who sometimes believe that they are the ones uniquely gifted to look into the heart of the nation and shape its future. Sturgeon, the current leader, is no collegiate first among equals. At times, in what was a slow and difficult rise to the top of Scottish politics, she showed ruthlessness in elbowing aside colleagues. During his longer political career, Salmond struggled to subsume his own ego, which means that he fell out, sometimes quite badly, with several of his colleagues.

But there was an apparently seamless succession at least until the actual handover on 14 November 2014. Salmond's announcement of his retirement after the party's referendum failure transferred attention from the defeat to his apparently selfless sacrifice and the emergence of a new leader from a different generation. Sturgeon had been a loyal adjutant since 2004 when she abandoned her bid for the vacant party leadership and agreed to a joint ticket with Alex Salmond, then returning for a second go as leader. They energised a previously becalmed party and worked together, apparently smoothly in government from 2007.

Perhaps their contrasting styles provided an effective symmetry at the top of the party. Sturgeon was deliberate and strategic, drawn to planning for the long-term, whereas Salmond could be tactical and impulsive able to launch *coup de theatres* which could wrong-foot his opponents but also quite capable of launching gambits such as the currency union which proved damaging for the SNP just when its core independence goal was never closer. She is more of a team player, prepared to admit failings as when she confessed her error to the Scottish Parliament in 2009 over pleading in writing with a judge not to send a constituent who was a fraudster to prison.[1] The risk-taking and combative Salmond is arguably more in tune with the assertive and militant-sounding party, one awash with new members, which emerged with astonishing rapidity after the referendum. Party management is likely to be more of a headache for Sturgeon than it ever was for Salmond.

Both are instinctive centralisers. They see Scotland's 15 universities not as allies to cooperate with in disseminating knowledge at home and clinching the reputation of successful research-orientated institutions abroad but as a rival estate of corporate power whose autonomy needs to be cut back. At the time of writing the Higher Education Governance Bill, being discussed by the Scottish Parliament, is intended to give ministers the power to use secondary legislation to impose unspecified conditions on universities without consultation.[2] Alarmed university chiefs fear that divested of their autonomy, the Office of National Statistics will be required to reclassify universities as 'public' rather than independent entities. The removal of their charitable status will then be unavoidable leading to a huge income loss.[3] Heriot-Watt university may already have been acting like a body in the orbit of a party-state when in 2013 it agreed to host a one-tonne sculpture with words from Alex Salmond proclaiming: 'The rocks will melt with the sun before I allow tuition fees to be imposed on Scottish students'.[4] In reality, many working-class young Scots have been victims of SNP higher education policies which have resulted in a huge decline in the size of the college sector.

Talking left but acting the managerial conservative appears to be a standard Salmond technique that Sturgeon is content to keep recycling. A large proportion of the career conscious figures who they have enlisted to champion or implement their ideas turn out to be figures who lack strong Scottish roots and may have been born in Australia, France, Central Europe, Kent, Liverpool or Ireland, North or South. The quasi-revolutionaries who flourished in the England of Henry VIII, during the French revolution, or in Russia after 1917 were also often outsiders. They were unwilling to be mere cogs in boring professions and thrilled at the opportunities provided by ruthless political leaders to imprint their will on different parts of society. There may not be enough really talented egotists in Scotland itself to accomplish a change in the historical direction of the country as significant as the one desired by the SNP. But its leaders are quite prepared to recruit adventurers and ideologues from much further afield who will help to ensure that there is no going back to quieter times.

Perhaps buoyed up by the remarkable polling lead for the party in early 2015, Salmond attempted to fly solo. By late March 2015, he was 'portraying himself as kingmaker in a hung parliament'.[5] He talked about writing Ed Miliband's budget for him but suggested, in another interview, that his terms for installing, and keeping in office, a minority Labour government would be less stringent than hers; he made no mention of scrapping the Trident nuclear programme which was one of the SNP's conditions for cooperation.[6]

After five days of being forced to respond to questions about Salmond's reading of the future, Sturgeon stated in an interview: 'I'm the leader of the SNP, I will lead negotiations, I will lead my party...' She saw Salmond's role as being 'a member of the Westminster Parliament'.[7]

Some of the SNP parliamentarians at Westminster were even more exasperated with Salmond. Stewart Hosie, who had succeeded Sturgeon as deputy leader, contradicted him by saying the party would want Ed Miliband to clear his Queen's speech with them in advance if he wanted SNP backing for a Labour minority government, even on a vote-by-vote basis.[8] Hosie is married to Sturgeon's closest friend among elected SNPers, Shona Robison. As if to leave no further room for doubt, he bluntly stated:

'Nicola Sturgeon is leader of the Scottish National Party, I am the deputy leader of the Scottish National Party and Angus Robertson is leader of the Westminster group'.

'While we all very much hope and expect Alex Salmond to be returned to Westminster, Nicola Sturgeon leads the party'.[9]

Pat Kane, an indefatigable nationalist from the cultural sphere, had remarked just beforehand: 'I will defend AS against most detractors. But his weekend media did seem like an older era of politics. Sturgeon sets new (& winning) tone'.[10]

On 3 April, in the only televised debate involving all the UK's party leaders, the main UK ones barely noticed her. It was forgotten by her opponents in what looked more than ever like the Westminster Bubble that 'her primary ideological and political objective is Scottish Independence. Everything else is sublimated to this objective'.[11] After watching the debate, the veteran commentator Bruce Anderson was convinced of the inevitability of a constitutional crisis in North Britain and that 'we will be arguing about Scottish independence for the foreseeable future'.[12]

Sturgeon actually possessed the most experience of governing of any of the seven politicians taking part in that TV debate. The fact is that she dominated her party and increasingly her country 'in a way that David Cameron or Ed Miliband can only dream of', probably reinforced her confidence on that occasion.[13] She was a figure from the British periphery who displayed the authority which many felt had been lacking at the centre of politics for a long time. Her background was in total contrast to the wealth and connections enjoyed both by Cameron and Miliband whose fathers had been respectively a successful financier and a high-flying intellectual who came to own an expensive property in one of the most affluent parts of north London.

Sturgeon grew up in a working-class family in Irvine, Ayrshire. Her father was an electrician, her mother a dental nurse. They were not strongly political in outlook although today her mother is an SNP councillor.[14]

She told the *Guardian*'s Simon Hattenstone on the eve of her 2015 general election triumph that, from the age of seven, she wanted to be a lawyer: 'Nobody in my family had been to university, let alone been a lawyer. I'm not sure what gave me that ambition. I didn't even know what it really meant. In my head it was about fighting for justice and the underdog'. In reality, after graduating from Glasgow University with a solid law degree, she had spent a very small amount of time practising law. She became a full-time politician in her twenties which means that she is very much a creature of her time, someone who has mixed professionally and socially with other aspirants for office and power and therefore whose contacts with the ordinary public are somewhat constrained.

Reasonably enough, her political handlers wished to portray someone who possessed a real hinterland but it was difficult to construct a compelling back story for Nicola Sturgeon. She possessed no hobbies other than reading non-fiction works geared towards politics. She didn't drive, she had not extensively travelled, she was not anchored in any civic or religious institution. She was an ascetic figure who had devoted almost 30 of her 45 years to politics. Quite unlike Salmond with his passion for golf and horse-racing, she was a self-disciplined figure.

Yet among very few members of the general public in Scotland could suspicions be found that she was a classic apparatchik assembled in the laboratory of nationalist politics. Clearly from the election result (and her reception on the campaign trail) she had convinced many people that she was to be trusted (and indeed was *one of them*). Politicians do evolve and she came over in the spring of 2015 as someone who had a sense of humour and showed patience and fortitude on the campaign trail. She was good with children, less good with dogs, and appeared happy to pose for 'selfies' with innumerable fans. An unconvinced Scot on twitter remarked afterwards that at the rate at which these were taken, by 2020, every Scot would have had the chance to enjoy a selfie with Nicola Sturgeon.

Her opponent Alistair Darling appeared almost relieved by her elevation while having no illusions about what it meant: 'She is an astute politician and very different from Alex Salmond, who antagonises large numbers of people...but the message is still the same...'[15] Salmond had been a polarising figure. He had suggested to Scots who would be won over by Sturgeon that Scottish nationalism was an outlet for his turbulent personality. His successor raised fewer doubts about why she was in politics and what she would do with the power. But the *Telegraph*'s Janet Daley who often referred to her own background in radical politics, was far less convinced. Writing shortly before the election, she complained that a politician with banal and hazardous economic views had hi-jacked a credulous Scottish electorate:

'The rise of Nicola Sturgeon is a lesson in the magical effectiveness of impassioned belief. Ms Sturgeon offers a combination of economically unjustified claptrap and CND rhetoric, but she does it with a degree of emotive conviction that excites people who don't have a clue what she is talking about.'[16]

Her personal appeal, quite unique for a politician in Scotland, at least until then, is well-conveyed in this vignette about her appearance in the heart of Glasgow:

'A crowd gathers around Glasgow's Buchanan Street steps...The crowd quietens, and then there is a mighty roar as Scottish comic Elaine C introduces "the fabulous Nicola Sturgeon". This isn't politics, it's rock'n'roll. And what's astonishing is that the star is Sturgeon, known to the crowd as "wee Nicola", a woman who struggled for years to win any kind of election, who was derided in the past as dull. Now here she is, revered. Sturgeon, the only party leader with a positive personal rating, has become the story of this election – and she's not even standing for Westminster.

Sturgeon is an old-fashioned orator. Her speech is impassioned, fluent and toughened by the grit in her voice..."On May 7th, we have the opportunity to make Scotland's voice at Westminster be more loudly heard than it ever has been before." The crowd roars. "The SNP stands within touching distance of doing something we have never done in our history, winning a Westminster election in Scotland." Another roar. "It will not be a victory for the SNP, it will be a victory for Scotland'".[17]

A few days later, in Kirkcaldy, the seat which the SNP's Roger Mullin was aiming to capture from Labour after Gordon Brown had stood down, the journalist Dan Hodges described her magnetic appeal:

'The SNP faithful are gathering for a rally in the Old Kirk. Well over a hundred people are in attendance. They hear a band, a speech from Winnie Ewing's daughter and an appeal from a Buddhist monk on behalf of the Nepal relief fund.

Then Roger Mullin takes to the stage. He has an important announcement, he says. But before he makes it, he needs a promise that no one in the room will tweet what he has to say. People nod expectantly.

"I've just had a phone conversation". He counts a beat. "Nicola is coming to visit us again tomorrow". A burst of electricity surges through the audience. She is coming. The Khaleesi of Scottish nationalism ...

[Next day]

To be a truly great politician, you have to have it. That ability – and it is a natural ability, it cannot be taught or coached – to transmit to the person in front of you the feeling that for that brief moment of interaction they are the only person on your planet. Blair had the thing. Clinton patented the thing.

Nicola Sturgeon has the thing. The eyes lock. The body leans in. The free hand reaches over in the classic "double clasp".

So off she goes, doing the thing. Her thing. Children are swept up (she really is very good with children). Supporters are hugged. Selfie after selfie after selfie is snapped'.[18]

One of the most perceptive pro-Union bloggers, 'Effie Deans' often refers to early years spent in Russia to make sense of the Scottish mood in 2015 and to her the Nicola craze was reminiscent of the adulation shown by humble folk when the Tsarist royal family briefly moved among them: 'Peasants used to weep at the sight of the Tsar, now they weep at the sight of Nicola. They listen to the words and accept her blessing with gratitude'.[19]

From 2009, she has been married to the longstanding chief executive of the SNP Peter Murrell. Some inevitably view this as an excessive personalisation of political power but in practice Murrell may be a curb on any tendency in Sturgeon to become greater than her party. The couple were seen at cultural events in the pre-election period. The artist and playwright John Byrne is far from being a dedicated Nationalist but he was impressed when she turned up for the rehearsals of *the Slab Boys* when it was being revived at the Citizens Theatre in Glasgow. Later, Murrell and Sturgeon sat among hundreds of theatre-goers at his play's opening night, something bound to do her image absolutely no harm.[20]

Even before the 3 April leaders debate, a YouGov poll had shown Nicola Sturgeon to be more popular across the UK than any of the Westminster party leaders. In England alone, she was the only party leader who has a positive approval rating.[21] 'It was hardly surprising that by now her popularity was reaching stratospheric levels in Scotland. Before she even became leader, a Panelbase study (commissioned by the SNP) found 54 per cent of people believed Sturgeon would stand up for Scotland's interests compared to 33 per cent who felt she wouldn't.[22]

While her predecessor's occasional demagogy may have made some Scots flinch from espousing nationalism, Sturgeon was appearing to have the opposite effect by the spring of 2015. Her well-rounded public persona, and the care with which she used language, seemed to remove inhibitions about indulging in displays of nationalist enthusiasm. Her calm and authoritative style made people relaxed about letting go and using national colours for political purposes whereas the more outwardly partisan Salmond only had this effect for Scots who were already nationalist 'true believers'. So, there was no let up in the extraordinary display of nationalist symbols between the referendum and the general election. Flag poles in gardens, posters and stickers in domestic windows and in cars made an appearance everywhere. There were fewer to be seen in downscale areas but they were prominent in middle-class areas of cities like Glasgow and Edinburgh. An unsuspecting visitor might have assumed that Scotland had just been liberated from onerous foreign occupation or was facing a threat from some external menace. West of the rivers Elbe or Danube, it is difficult to think of any other European country where national symbols have figured so overtly in a European election campaign in the modern democratic era.

The new SNP leadership may well have benefited from Ed Miliband and Labour's failure to form a government after 7 May. It would have been a challenge for any new leader based in Edinburgh to head negotiations in London in which her principal cohorts where 50 new and inexperienced SNP MPs many of whom would have been total strangers to her. Whatever concessions she might have wrung from a minority government relying on SNP votes would have been seen as inadequate for many new SNPers absorbed not with governing but with securing independence quickly. The columnist Joyce McMillan, an admirer, had pointed out the possible pitfalls in February 2015:

'What she should be asking herself, though, is how far she can go down this road of involvement in Westminster politics, and of possible deals with the Labour Party, without at least unsettling, and perhaps finally disgusting and disappointing, the hundreds of thousands who now support the SNP precisely because it is not part of that metropolitan system.'[23]

For a while she basked in the glow of a spectacular electoral victory. But the honeymoon had worn off as inadequacies were displayed on various policy fronts during the summer of 2015. The wisdom of creating a centralized police force continued to be widely criticised as any savings in amalgamating separate forces appeared to be undone by police demoralisation and lethal inefficiency. A former SNP leader, Gordon Wilson alleged that 'Police Scotland suffered from delusions of grandeur. It saw itself as the equivalent of the Met and responsible to no one. Community policing got small shrift. It also became arrogant at top levels. The views of the public came second'. He went on to pointedly ask: 'Why was the head of the largest police force, Strathclyde, given the job of chief constable when it was known that he was an authoritarian likely to impose controversial Strathclyde policing policies on other parts of the country?'[24]

The chief of Police Scotland, Sir Stephen House clung to his post due, it seemed, only to his iron will and the top-level government backing that was forthcoming. He issued an apology in July after officers failed to attend a fatal car crash which killed a man and left a woman seriously injured for three days. House admitted that an experienced official failed to log the call from the member of the public on 5 July before the couple were found on the M9 road near Bannockburn three days later.[25]

The SNP was understandably vocal about proposed changes to the law that would enable the British intelligence services to eavesdrop on parliamentarians, including MSPs. The Scottish Government demanded answers but, along with its supporters, it was reticent when it emerged that Police Scotland had used covert monitoring to try and uncover a journalist's confidential sources.[26]

Sturgeon's government was also under pressure on the health front. This is a sensitive topic not least because she had been in charge of this policy area for nearly all of the SNP's time in government. In 2014, after comparing the performance of the NHS in the four nations of the UK, two independent think-tanks, the Health Foundation and the Nuffield Trust claimed that health provision was falling behind in Scotland. According to the journalist John McDermott: 'They found that all countries' "amenable mortality" (deaths that could have been prevented through better care) halved between 1990 and 2010, but the rate remained 20 per cent higher in Scotland than in England. The report also found that the northeast of England—which has demographics akin to those north of the border—had improved faster than Scotland. In 1990, mortality rates were similar. But by 2012/13, after high spending growth in Scotland but even greater increases in the north east, mortality rates in Scotland were up to 19 per cent higher'.[27]

In July 2015, it was disclosed that Scotland was facing acute difficulties in the recruitment of medical general practitioners (GPs) that threatened to push the NHS into crisis. Kevin McKenna, one of the most high-profile media backers of independence tartly observed that 'the SNP has had eight years to get the NHS right. Only when it finally does should it start thinking about independence once more'. He highlighted two embarrassing failures in the delivery of services. During the final quarter of 2014, the NHS failed to meet a legal obligation for treatment to start within 12 weeks of its being agreed by a specialist. The Scottish government had also pledged that 95 per cent of patients would be treated within four hours in accident and emergency. An exasperated McKenna pointed out: 'They've been missing that target every week for the last six years or so....'[28]

The new minister, Shona Robison was appointed in a drive to create a gender-balanced Cabinet. She was joined as education minister by Angela Constance who soon struggled to articulate a coherent approach to an under-performing education service. In May 2015, she found herself mocked across the media for a press release on improving standards of English which was packed with jargon: 'It was supposed to be a frank admission that standards of reading and writing in schools were not good enough'.[29]

The Scottish edition of the *Times* summed up much deeper problems with education in an editorial on 19 August 2015:

'When it was first elected, in 2007, the SNP administration set itself demanding targets: among them, smaller classes, a 50 per cent expansion of nursery education, and the firm aim of putting science, languages and technology at the heart of the curriculum. Eight years on it would be hard to claim that any of these had been achieved, even harder to assert that they have succeeded in the ultimate objective of raising standards. The statistics are grim. Earlier this year, a report from Scotland's chief statistician showed that the performance of [pupils] in primary four, primary seven year and second year had actually dropped between 2012 and 2014, with both literacy and numeracy attainments going in the wrong direction'.[30]

Scotland, once known globally for allowing able youngsters from poor backgrounds to reach university, now had the lowest number of deprived pupils going to university in the UK (England 17 per cent, Wales 15.5 per cent but in Scotland only 9.7 per cent).[31] Maintenance support for these students has been cut back in order to fund the SNP's totemic policy of abolishing university tuition fees, levied at up to £9,000 in the rest of the UK. As the *Financial Times* noted, 'such a policy ends up supporting all students, including the affluent'. This populist approach to education is affecting standards.[32] One SNP councillor in Dundee conceded: 'there are a substantial numbers of people who come out of school and cannot cope with anything but the most basic written information'.[33]

It was very hard to blame Westminster for failings in Scottish education. The new leader of the Scottish Labour Party Kezia Dugdale (the 6th in 8 years) had made it clear on taking over that education would be her key priority. Dugdale had called for standardised testing in primary schools. The SNP had previously resisted such a move. But Sturgeon made a dramatic intervention on 18 August, announcing that she would put her own 'neck on the line' to improve education especially in Scotland's most deprived areas. One of these was Glasgow Govan in an area where she had been the MSP since 2007. The performance of the school Govan High was lamentable compared with Jordanhill in Glasgow's prosperous West End. Govan High was one of a number of schools to score zero or close to zero for pupils leaving with five Higher qualifications or more whereas at Jordanhill, such a result was attained by 75 per cent of its pupils. Overall, only 3.9 per cent of pupils in Scotland's most deprived communities managed to get three A grades in their Higher exams compared to 24.2 per cent in the wealthiest places.[34]

Legislation had already been drawn up by the civil service but it was slammed by Lindsay Paterson, professor of education at Edinburgh University because of the absence of any proposals for enabling local authorities to tackle an 'extremely difficult' long-term problem. He told the media that creating a legal obligation for the worst schools to improve would make no difference as teachers are already doing 'the best they can' for their children.[35]

The SNP treats local government as a vassal which is expected to obey instructions from a centralised high command both within the party and the Edinburgh-based government machine. The idea of partnership is anathema for a party with a rigidly managerial outlook. In several of Scotland's leading councils, it keeps close watch on elected SNP councillors by texting and E-Mailing instructions on a regular basis about which issues need to be promoted so that local councillors keep fully in step with the central organization.[36]

Scotland has witnessed none of the structural reforms which have led to an improvement in educational performance particularly in London schools. Sturgeon did concede that Scotland could learn from London's success. This will mean regular assessment of standards.[37]

Carole Ford, the former head teacher at Kilmarnock Academy argued that in Scotland, 'the most significant barrier to excellence is the complete absence of a formal primary school curriculum and the total absence of expected standards or of assessment of pupil progress'. She pointed out that 'for the first seven crucial years of a child's education there is no monitoring of the work of teachers or the schools in the state sector. To her this was not only 'in direct contradiction to professional advice' but also, 'in some cases, in direct contradiction to common sense'.[38]

It is quite possible that a busy (indeed over-extended) First Minister, instinctively drawn to top-down statist approaches to major policy challenges, will simply tinker at the margins and swiftly be diverted to other issues. If so, policy will continue to be shaped by influential educationalists who view Scotland's schools as a laboratory for their own crusading ideological instincts. One 'heroic' initiative has been the policy of restorative justice. It means, in practice, that teachers are no longer able to punish their pupils. A staff member in an underperforming school attended by the journalist discussing this issue in the *Spectator,* summed up the problem with the approach:

'We can't send a disruptive child out of the class anymore, because it's seen as punitive. The theory is that sending the problem away doesn't make it go away. The whole class has to deal with it together, but it doesn't leave much time for education.'[39]

A landslide Holyrood victory for the SNP in May 2016 was predicted in August 2015 as support for it increased to 62 per cent in a TNS opinion poll. However, the survey also found only modest levels of satisfaction with the SNP's performance in government, with no more than a third of voters believing the Nationalists had done well in four key policy areas.[40] The SNP appeared 100 per cent sure to win the next Scottish election no matter what it did in the time ahead, a remarkable occurrence in what used to be a 4-party political system. Voters appeared to view the party mainly as a repository through which they could proclaim their Scottishness by voting for it.

Troubling examples of state incompetence regularly surface, such as the announcement on 21 August 2015 that the European Commission was withholding £45 million from the European Social Fund. It was meant for Scotland's poorest but the Scottish Government had been unable to demonstrate that it would be spent properly. There was something not right with the EU's timing since the problem had been highlighted in December 2014 just as the party was focussing on its first love, electoral campaigning and deadlock ensued despite 'extensive dialogue'.[41]

This is an indulgent electorate which any competitive party can only dream of. It means that the emphasis will be on rituals and stage-managed events pitting Scotland's ruling party against Westminster. But a drag on the SNP's future success is likely to be the lack of a vibrant internal party life; so professional and alert in different respects, the party lacks think-tanks and opportunities for free-wheeling discussions from which good quality ideas for public policy can emerge. There is no sign that under Nicola Sturgeon the party might veer towards becoming if not a factory, at least a workshop, for ideas. The party is very much fixated with campaigning, media management and removing the opposition as any kind of threat to its ascendancy. Internal criticism has already been stifled by the decision, approved by the SNP conference in April, that elected members are forbidden from publicly questioning or criticising the conduct of their colleagues. This bid to create a monolithic force is likely to break down at the edges and perhaps even pave the way for a small number of defections. Meanwhile, the imposition of orthodoxy makes it easier for coterie politics to prevail, involving decisions on the allocation of public money to be made sometimes on a rather informal basis.

Sturgeon had made clear her unhappiness about tactics by party members which escalated into harassment and intimidation of opponents. She must have known that the mob scenes which occasionally marred the SNP's triumphant 2015 electoral campaign were hardly necessary for its success and threatened to tarnish its image.

It emerged after the death, on 25 May 2015, of the former leader of the Liberal Democrats Charles Kennedy that he had been systematically hounded by opponents in the SNP who wrested his seat of Skye, Inverness and Lochaber from him. Brian Wilson, the journalist and former Labour MP who had been in touch with him, wrote of the activities of Brian Smith, an ex-policeman on the Isle of Skye and ally of Kennedy's successor as MP, Ian Blackford:

'Day after day, he bombarded Charles Kennedy's Twitter and Facebook sites with allegations, abuse and innuendoes. On 27th January, replying to a tweet from Peter Wishart MP, he referred to Mr Kennedy as "our own arch-Quisling".

Mr Smith sent at least 115 offensive tweets to Charles Kennedy between January and May as well as countless Facebook messages. He was not alone. A member of Charles's constituency staff worked full-time on deleting abuse from his own social media sites.'[42]

At times, according to one of Scotland's most senior Lib Dem officials, the behaviour of SNP loyalists, seeking to defeat Kennedy, strayed close to harassment. 'I have never known aggression like it in 30 years of politics,' said the official, speaking on condition of anonymity for fear (according to the *Daily Mail*) of SNP reprisals. 'He and his staff were shouted at on doorsteps, and had leaflets thrown in their face. But the worst of it happened online, where he was just monstered...'.[43]

Early on May 8, a few hours after losing the Parliamentary seat which he had held for 32 years, Kennedy drove to his home only to discover his bins upturned and the contents everywhere'. Later in the month, a few minutes after news of Charles Kennedy's death had broken, one SNP supporter posted a very instructive final message to the late MP on Twitter: "Oh dear,' it read. 'Now I'm supposed to feel guilty or something. Well f**k you. I'm not'.[44]

To the consternation of some SNP supporters who regarded the *Daily Mail* as one of their most implacable Unionist foes, Nicola Sturgeon wrote an article in that newspaper on 25 June which repeated party policy on behaviour but went on to say:

'But when tweets or postings from SNP members that cross the line are brought to our attention, we will act - as we have done before.

That is why I am making clear today that the SNP will take steps to warn those whose behaviour falls short of the standards we expect - we will tell them to raise their standard of debate, to stick to issues not personalities, and to ensure robust and passionate debate takes precedence over abuse and intemperate language. And I am also making clear that, where appropriate, we will take disciplinary action'.[45]

But almost exactly one month later David Mundell, the only Tory MP returned to Westminster from Scotland was forced to flee from an angry mob after he had been invited to open a foodbank in Dumfries, the nearest town to his rural constituency. Remarkably for some, a local branch of the SNP posted a video of the scenes on its online site. It prompted concerns over a branch of the governing party displaying nonchalance or even sympathy towards a mob of people intimidating an elected representative.[46]

In Galloway, the same part of Scotland, Yen-Hongmei-Jin, the SNP's only councillor from an ethnic Chinese background, quit the party in August 2015 after claiming that senior party staff had taken no action against discrimination she faced from within the local party.[47] With the opposition seemingly crushed, it is not totally surprising that aggression may have been directed inwards by some of the more bellicose members who had attached themselves to the SNP. The season for nominating candidates for the 59 constituency seats at Holyrood was beginning and in several areas, adoption meetings spilled over into fierce acrimony. Nationalists unhappy at the SNP's apparent foot-dragging over independence also provoked the wrath of members when they announced, via social media, their intention to form a new Scottish Independence Party. It proved a 24-hour wonder, one of the founders explaining why they were backing off: 'The page received such a torrent of abuse from SNP members including physical abuse that you should all be ashamed'.[48]

In the approach to the 2016 Holyrood elections it is unlikely that the party will be basing its credentials around policies and programmes. Independence was sidelined at the October 2015 SNP conference as the 2013 referendum prediction that more revenue from oil and expanded production would fund an exit from Britain was, within months, revealed to be fantasy economics. The party is likely to try and harness energy from an emotional tide of Scottishness. In populist parties that often works best by showcasing a leader. Touring Scotland in the spring of 2015, using a helicopter emblazoned with her image, this worked well for Nicola Sturgeon. In Edinburgh South, the only Scottish urban seat not to fall to the SNP, the local Yes cafe has spray-painted an image on an adjacent wall which is a blend of Che Guevara and Sturgeon complete with revolutionary beret. But this is the same Sturgeon who, along with her husband, occupied the royal box for the 2015 Wimbledon tennis final. She has also discarded functional power suits for stylish and expensive costumes. This was noticed even before she became leader: 'While in 2001 Nicola Sturgeon was a dead ringer for Angela Merkel – all elephantine linen trouser suits, death row haircut and M&S shoes – today she is as sleek as an otter'.[49]

Understandably, for many being Scotland's First Minister absolutely justifies her looking good. But there have been complaints online from those who prefer an ascetic leader along the lines of: 'Too busy swaggering around in clothes that cost more a month than the idiots who voted can spend on food in a year'.

She has also made two foreign trips to the United States in June 2015, the principle purpose of which appears to have been to take part in the *Daily Show* on Comedy Central. She emerged unscathed in jousts with the show's combative host Jon Stewart, displaying a gift for quick repartee. She told him: 'You billed me on your website as a comedian, so you've raised all these expectations that I'm going to be funny.[50] And I'm a politician, and as you know, politicians are rarely very funny'. But she also had a brief encounter with Tony Blinken, the US Deputy Secretary of State, America's second most senior diplomat.[51]

A 5-day trade mission to China followed in July heavy with protocol. It is unclear what her hosts thought of her republicanism but it is an asset rather than a liability at home especially for former Labour voters. But it remains to be seen for how long she can convincingly play the role of the rebel princess who is somehow also the centre of power. For a while Margaret Thatcher got away with acting like an opposition insurgent leader while actually governing Britain. Heavy-handed decisions, above all the poll tax, eventually revealed her to be an out-of-touch autocrat.

Under Sturgeon, the SNP may also be revealing a tendency to impose arbitrary controls without offering any serious justification. There were headlines beyond Scotland when it was announced in August 2015 that genetically-modified crops were to be banned without the scientific basis for this decision being published. There was little support for the decision from the scientific community in Scotland and much dismay. Such a move had probably much less to do with protecting the consumer from any unexplained danger than with reaching out to the Scottish Green party as more elections approach.

But a ruling party, restrained by few checks and balances and unwilling to listen to independent advice, is in danger of over-reaching itself if a backlash is provoked as happened with Thatcher over the poll tax (but the discontent then was mainly in England and not Scotland despite the legend).

If she favoured consensus over partisanship, Sturgeon would be displaying the kind of self-awareness not always to be found among nationalist leaders who may be convinced that destiny has elevated them to the ruling heights. One obvious place to start is with patronage. Several decisions in 2015 showed the ability of SNP supporters with political connections to enjoy sway over the allocation of public money for private projects. No criminal wrong-doing was detected but it was enough for one former leader to issue a stern rebuke to Sturgeon for exercising lax controls over expenditure. It remains to be seen if Sturgeon has the wisdom and presence of mind to confront some of the unedifying features of her own party which might (if left unchecked) turn it into one of the biggest obstacles to realising Scottish independence. The alternative is to retreat to the political comfort zone and play the role of 'mother of the nation'. It is one that the pro-SNP media is already keen to bestow upon her: on 28 August one of the main stories in the *National* was the fact that she had agreed to deliver a proposal of marriage from a graphic designer to his male partner. When a leader gets to play cupid in front of an admiring nation, then she has amassed tremendous political capital and may even stand apart from her own party in terms of influence.

There was a return to reality on the first anniversary of the referendum when Sturgeon delivered a subtle speech. Her insistence that the United Kingdom was 'living on borrowed time' tilted towards hardline members. But she also made it clear that a second referendum was unlikely to happen in the near future and that, until it did, the concerns of Scottish voters would need to be addressed, 'patiently, carefully and comprehensively'.[52]

This pragmatic message was taken further by the MEP Alyn Smith. As a member of the national executive committee of the SNP, he had been required to adjudicate in a disputed selection contest in an area near Glasgow where membership had surged. This may have impressed on him the perils of radicalism without limits. In a detailed press interview on 20 September he stated his view that a referendum was off the agenda for the 'foreseeable future'. 'I don't think there's an appetite for it', he said, 'beyond the 30 per cent of the population that really wants to see this happen. They'll always want to see this happen and that is great, that's my team, but in terms of the others I just don't think we would be thanked for bringing it forward'. These 'others', the No voters instead of being dismissed as dupes of the SNP's enemies would need to be won over by the SNP being effective in government: 'I don't think we lost the argument, but we assuredly lost the vote. We need to be a bit sanguine about that and just get on with the day-to-day job the people of Scotland have sent us to do'.[53]

There's no doubt that Sturgeon will throw red meat to the party faithful at future conferences but it looks as if the epic scenes at Glasgow's main concert venue on 22 November 2014 when she addressed 12,000 adoring followers, will be shelved at least for now. Sturgeon has more than one register. She is able to combine the stateswoman with the agitator, the community representative with the conviction politician. It is what makes her probably the most formidable exponent of self-determination that Scotland has produced in modern times. But due to putting independence into cold storage, she will face dissent from within a party swelled by new recruits for whom rapidly acquiring independence is an obsession. She is busy centralising control of the state but rendering these ultras harmless might be less easy and could destabilise the SNP.

Alex Salmond

Alex Salmond has been in front-rank politics for over 25 years, yet remarkably a sympathetic political biography of him has yet to be written. Nationalists everywhere have a weakness for hagiography and this is a strange omission. Salmond has rattled the British elite. He even seriously considered arresting Tony Blair, (an architect of Scottish devolution) if he showed up on Scottish soil after 2007.[54]

He has energised but also polarised perhaps millions of Scots. And here may lie the root of the problem. It may be simply too hard to base a sympathetic narrative around such a formidable but divisive personality. During the referendum, he claimed Scotland for his party and its supposedly neutral national symbols were co-opted by the Yes campaign. But opinion polls showed that he was unpopular among key groups of voters vital if the Yes side was to be victorious on 18 September 2014.

Afterwards, he claimed (erroneously as it turned out) that the result lacked credibility because No votes were concentrated in one particular age group, the over 55s: the elderly should 'wonder if we...have actually impeded progress for the next generation...'.[55] He was suggesting no less that a generation which, arguably, had been more responsible for defending and building up Scotland in the war years and those of post-war recovery, had somehow delegitimized the result.

It is difficult to take the measure of such a protean figure who enabled a fringe cause to go spectacularly mainstream but released a lot of negativity in the process. If a tolerably united people is a necessary prerequisite for the difficult transition to independence for a country lacking resources and with numerous social problems, then even some cerebral nationalists might shake their heads and ask just what has Salmond really accomplished.

Divided Scotland has two irreconcilable views about him. Those who would buy an admiring Salmond biography, and perhaps even treat it as a family heirloom, admire him for restoring faith in Scotland as a country with a viable political future.

He has shattered the mystique that an undivided Britain is part of the natural and unchanging order of world politics. He is a charismatic figure in an era of colourless and uninspiring politicians. He has motivated tens of thousands to become involved in politics at a time of plunging political activity by citizens in most other democratic states. He has dragged Scotland from obscurity and made it a country whose battle to shape its own future absorbs the rest of the world at least intermittently. He is a swashbuckling operator admired for his skill in political machinations, always reputedly done for a higher cause. His at times cavalier attitude to the truth, readiness to go back on undertakings made over any early re-staging of the referendum, and occasional low blows against opponents, are hailed as political artistry, entirely necessary tactics given the perfidious nature of the British foe in London.

He has allowed many thousands of Scots to live out fantasies of being engaged in epic political deeds that could transform the face of the nation forever. Their leader is self-confident, shrewd, articulate, a master tactician who has out-witted some of the leading political figures at the heart of the British state. For many, he has restored national self-belief, banishing the feeling that the Scots are doomed to be perennial subalterns. His commitment to social justice means that Scotland can be an exemplary voice in a world of harsh capitalist exploitation, a symbol of virtue as well as visionary thinking.

But for his numerous detractors, Salmond is viewed as a cunning and dangerous opportunist. He is seen as being prepared to wreck a country, as well as the economic livelihood of many of its inhabitants, in pursuit of his own personal glory. He is disliked and feared for his ability to polarise a country not previously known for its sharp political divisions. He has failed to condemn raucous public rallies, the mobbing of opposition speakers, and protest rallies outside BBC television headquarters due to perceptions of bias. Salmond's detractors and champions have fought it out for several years on social media, making Scottish personal and campaigning online sites some of the most militant and uninhibited to be found anywhere in the English-speaking world.

To his critics, he is a figure of Machiavellian cunning who has swept Scotland from the path of common sense and reason. Conspiracies have been made respectable in an atmosphere at times spilling over into cult-like hysteria. Indeed, he seems to have hypnotised numerous citizens into ardently desiring objectives which are likely to be personally injurious to them. His ruthlessness, and ability to grow in popularity even as economic events apparently shred the case for independence, cause despair and foreboding among the numerous Scots who are still firmly un-revolutionary in outlook.

Fears have grown that the rules of politics were being re-written during the ascendancy of Alex Salmond, so that outcomes like the referendum defeat on 18 September 2014 which impede nationalist ambitions, are simply ignored. One poll towards the end of the referendum campaign indicated that no less than 17 percent of Scots were ready to emigrate if Salmond's plans came to fruition. Opponents fear that his populism will lead to national decay, internal strife, a new epoch of rivalry with, and estrangement from, England, and unwise international alignments. A state-led model of rule which the SNP's supporters regard as progressive, humane and inclusive is viewed by many others as restrictive and impractical, and perhaps only capable of being fully implemented by means that are alien to Britain's democratic traditions. But the doubters look on almost helplessly as his energy and ability to motivate huge numbers of Scots men and women to rally around his political cause, appear to make his bandwagon unstoppable. He handed over the leadership of his party in November to a successor, Nicola Sturgeon who may find it hard to abandon his populist approach to politics even if she wants to. He continues to take initiatives and define particular aspects of the nationalist strategy. Some compare him with the Irish nationalist Charles Stewart Parnell. In the 1880s, he combined parliamentary disruption with agitation in Ireland. His 'third force' prised numerous concessions from Liberal and Tory governments and, some argue, paved the way for Irish independence. One thing is clear: a form of highly personal and assertive leadership has been developed by Salmond which could well become a trademark of Scottish politics as disagreement about the future direction of the country harden.

During and after the referendum, it is not detractors who Alex Salmond has encountered but many thousands of grateful, sometimes even delirious, supporters. The tour for his book, *The Dream Shall Never Die* in early 2015 saw him regularly bathed 'in a warm glow of love'.[56] Alex Perry, a reporter from *Newsweek* described the mood of adulation at the launch in Glasgow on 4 March 2015:

"Alex," says a middle-aged woman at the front, trying not to cry, "you took the nation into your hands. You helped us go forward. When we lost, I went up to your house and sat there for an hour and a half, crying my eyes out..."

"Oh, Alex," says a neatly suited man in a trembling voice, "September 19th was such a day of heartbreak. How did you find the strength and resources to come back?"

He tells the Glasgow audience how, as a helicopter took him and his wife Moira home to the small northern Scottish town of Strichen, Robert Burns's reworking of an old Jacobite song, *Bonnie Dundee* came into his head as they passed over Dundee:

'Then awa' to the hills, to the lea, to the rocks,
E'er I own a usurper, I'll couch wi' the fox!
Then tremble, false Whigs, in the midst o' your glee,
Ye ha' no seen the last o' my bonnets and me'.

The reporter describes the scene well, a politician who is a talented actor manager adept at casting a mesmeric spell over his audience:

'Salmond reads the poem quietly. The audience cranes in to hear. As he speaks the last, defiant line, they erupt in a swell of clapping, stomping and yelling that lasts a full minute. When the applause finally dies, Salmond tells them how Dundee gave him the seminal moment of his political life. He is canvassing in the city when he comes across a queue of hundreds of people registering to vote. Many are doing so for the first time in their lives. "This is the first time there has been anything worth voting for," a man tells Salmond.

He wipes away a tear. "The country which started the referendum campaign is not the same Scotland we are living in now," he says. "The people who emerged are different from those who embarked on this journey. They are more energised, more mobilised. That's why they are likely to take the first opportunity to move this country forward."

Salmond stares out at the audience, then looks up.

"And it's coming soon!" he roars.[57]

But what grounds did he have to feel this way. He lost by a convincing 10 per cent margin overall, in 28 of the 32 referendum constituencies. Post-referendum Scotland was divided with people in two camps having their backs firmly turned to each other.

'The people have awakened! They have become knights!' Salmond proclaimed within earshot of *Newsweek*'s Alex Perry. Such quasi-martial rhetoric is music to the ears of folk who wish to be part of the elect. He and some of his allies have long indicated that their affection and concern was reserved for 'our people' not 'the people'.

Salmond in 2015 felt unconstrained about speaking to the Scottish public in the demotic style he reserved for party conference addresses. Exactly twenty years earlier, at the SNP's 1995 conference, he concluded his speech by invoking the medieval Scottish hero William Wallace: 'with Wallace – head and heart – the one word that encapsulated all our hopes – *freedom, freedom, freedom*'.[58] The film Braveheart, very loosely based on the Wallace story, had just appeared. It was destined to win five Oscars and according to Salmond 'the film had a profound effect...'.[59]

In 2015, a year which has seen a drive to commemorate the date when the prototype of *Braveheart*, William Wallace was executed in London on 23 August 1305, Salmond has restored a sense of adolescent rebellion in at least some older Scots. They can throw the furniture around and berate those whom they dislike without adverse consequences. After all conditions are fundamentally secure for most people despite the rhetoric about grinding hardship and poverty. In office for over seven years, Salmond saw no need to carry out any measure of redistribution to reduce the social inequality which he and his party so often railed against.

I was in central Edinburgh on Wednesday 25 March, when Salmond was launching his book and I encountered a knot of well-attired folk who looked as if they had left the city's comfortable suburbs, to come up to town for the event, gleefully mentioning 'Alex' as they stood near the venue, the George Hotel.

These were probably people who instead of cringing with embarrassment when he held aloft a large Saltire behind David Cameron's head after Andy Murray defeated Novak Djokovic in the 2013 Wimbledon tennis final, might well have egged him on to even more daring bravado.

Derek Bateman who hailed Salmond as 'a Great Scot, the best politician of his era' was nevertheless left somewhat troubled by the emotions Salmond unleashed at this Edinburgh book event which he chaired:

'I was ...taken aback by the thunderous reception he received. (His quiet aside that it was actually for me didn't wash...) [He is] the man who used every skill to bring us to the very edge of independence. He deserves our gratitude. And I like him. But I can't for the life of me forget that the Alex Salmond I know is a politician.

That means representative, advocate, lawmaker etc but on Thesaurus.com the associated sections are Bureaucrat, Demagogue and Sycophant. I'm delighted the membership has surged and the enthusiasm is infectious but I have an inbuilt alarm when support veers into adoration. The best politics occurs through engagement, not devotion. Politicians perform best when the route to achievement is marked by checks and balances.'[60]

It is a mixed blessing for a nationalist movement emphasising sacrifice for a higher cause to have been led by someone whose own tireless projection of self conveys the impression at times that Scotland may actually revolve around him.

In 2014 he told the *Sun* that if he had not left his job as one of the RBS bank's oil economists to pursue a political career, 'I hope and believe we could have avoided the international banking crisis'. He went on to add: 'I'm not like Gordon Brown thinking I could save the world but I might have been able to save the Royal Bank from the company into which it fell.' This is the same man who wrote to the disgraced former RBS head Fred Goodwin in 2007, urging him to press ahead with the disastrous takeover of the Dutch bank ABN Amro which sunk RBS: 'It is in Scottish interests for RBS to be successful and I would like to offer any assistance my office can provide. Good luck with the bid'. In the same year Salmond had called for lighter regulation of the banking and financial services sectors, criticising the UK's procedures as 'gold plated'.[61]

In his very last speech as leader, to the SNP's conference in November 2014, he defiantly proclaimed:

CHAPTER 5: NATIONALIST PEOPLE

'After the referendum, those very opponents believed that Scotland had been quietened, that we'd had our day in the sun and we should be politely put back in our box'.

'They thought it was all over… well it isn't now because in truth, delegates, everything in Scotland is now different. All has changed and changed utterly'.[62]

The latter sentence is a quote from a Yeats poem titled *Easter, 1916*, describing Ireland's Easter Rising against British rule. This is stirring stuff for a huge number of Scots, but an even bigger segment are left apprehensive or even repelled.

Shortly before the referendum one of them spoke out. It was the daughter of the rector of Linlithgow Academy, John Ferguson who had taught the young Salmond maths. She publicly requested that he stop invoking her late father's memory, and accused him of creating divisions across Scotland.

Fiona Scott claimed that her father would have been appalled by the intimidation, violence and vandalism caused by the referendum. She described him as a fair and compassionate man who hated 'bullying', and said her family was unhappy that the First Minister had, over the years, referred to his teaching and beliefs.

In a letter to the *Herald* newspaper, she added: 'Freedom of speech is under threat. Relationships between neighbours are now threatened if you indicate which way you are voting'.

'For these reasons and many others, on behalf of my family I respectfully request that Mr Salmond never mentions my father in public again as, were he alive, he would be appalled at what is happening across our country'.[63]

I had written a lot about Alex Salmond during his year at the top of Scottish politics. I saw him as a supreme manipulator of the emotions of everyday folk and more than once wrote about him in light of Thomas Mann's *Mario and the Magician*. This novel describes how the minds of normally-level headed people in an Italian town in the 1920s are captured by a travelling magician who gets them to debase themselves until one among them wakes up and slays their tormentor.[64]

For a long time, I thought of Salmond as a Svengali or as an instigator of mischief like the Norse god Loki. He had dredged up atavistic passions which had largely lain dormant for one-third of a millennium. Many restraints on what is acceptable behaviour in Scotland had been swept away and at times he appeared to revel in this. But, increasingly, I have wondered if he is in fact more victim than perpetrator. He has helped to create what increasingly appears to be an edgy, emotion-laden but essentially superficial country, one that is ill-equipped to undertake the hazardous and demanding journey towards a viable form of independence.

During the referendum, people were encouraged to give vent to their frustrations and hatreds without pausing for much thought. They could be boorish and threatening but still feel good in themselves because their cause was a supremely virtuous one. Within Yes ranks, there was no lack of dedicated people wishing it to triumph by regular means. But it is hardly surprising that it attracted very different Scots - people who fled from any kind of discipline in their own lives and who looked the other way when their own children aped their standards by being disruptive-flocked to the Yes cause and areas with social problems swung from indifference to Scottish Nationalism to overwhelming adherence to the cause.

Salmond rarely showed any qualms about the coarsening of Scottish politics after 2012. He and his supporters often reduced the menacing scenes filmed on television when opposition figures faced aggression merely for appearing in the public square to one egg thrown at Jim Murphy in August 2014. After eight years in power, when questioned in March 2015 about intimidation, he said that 'those who accuse the SNP of prejudice and sowing division "are often in leadership positions who want to keep things as they are. They like the idea of divide and rule because they're ruling".

"Who are the people just now who are feeling uncomfortable?" he asks. "Who are downtrodden? Whose families are being divided?" Those queuing up at foodbanks. Those trying to have their welfare claims assessed. Sons and daughters forced to leave town to find work. "Families divided?" he asks. "We've got 90 million Scots across this planet and five and a quarter million in Scotland. Families divided? Yeah, we've had a lot o' that."'

In the same interview, he said the time for healing is after Scotland wins its freedom. 'In victory, magnanimity; in defeat, resolution,' he says. 'We're not in the victory yet'.[65] But during the campaigning period, he offered no convincing economic perspective about the future that under independence foodbanks and real hardship could be banished from the new Scotland. Food banks were of course an affliction of the Unionist era, the result of deep-seated injustice that could only be defeated by separating from the rest of the UK. No influential figure in the SNP was ever heard to argue that it was quite possible there were numerous Scottish households where poor parenting had led to family crises, forcing people to resort to them.

Irresponsible and self-harming inhabitants of Scotland just don't exist for Salmond. To acknowledge the existence of Scots who figure in published statistics on poor parenting, drug addiction and other forms of self-harm, would be to instantly raise doubts about the feasibility of independence. The people have to be mounted on a pedestal but their true spiritual condition is ignored by Salmond in ways that suggest that deep down, he is not terribly interested in them and they may hardly be central to his future plans about how Scotland will unfold.

It is difficult to avoid the conclusion that this dominating and driven individual is responsible for profoundly dividing Scotland in a way that might cause successful but more measured nation-builders elsewhere pause for thought. His own appetite for confrontation helped to make numerous Scots, perhaps for the first time, feel at ease about forcefully expressing their feelings in elections without much trace of guilt. Why? Because their feelings were politically correct and eminently patriotic ones.

On the other hand, there were cowed Scots who found their views delegitimized as the Yes campaign set the tone for Scotland in 2014 and indeed beyond. They were apprehensive about displaying their British allegiances in public either through having posters in their homes or cars or saying what they thought in the social places where they normally gathered.

Salmond, astonishingly, frequently compared the illiberal atmosphere culminating in the Scottish referendum with the first free elections in South Africa 20 years previously. It was an insult to the millions of black voters who were denied the franchise; also to Nelson Mandela who went out of his way to avoid creating an atmosphere of grievance and resentment which Salmond promoted especially in the second half of the referendum campaign.[66]

If he had riled a section of English opinion into behaving in a surly and threatening manner, it would have suited his objectives. But most people in the rest of the UK were largely bewildered and concerned witnesses of what became a raucous intra-Scottish faction fight. He either failed to realise or else simply didn't care that he was breaking a spirit of trust and consensus which allows most countries with a liberal past to debate their differences but not push them to outright division.

Scots are now divided into two perhaps nearly equal camps. There are realists who are aware of the benefits which the country derives from the Union and who fear that these could vanish in an impetuous and poorly planned rush for statehood based on emotion and what many see as one supremely talented politician's will to power.

These Scots are not confined to any one class, but they are more likely to be middle-class than working-class, they often are religious, they rely on the state for a limited number of needs, and may have obtained a solid education which has given them a long-term perspective. They fit the global stereotype of the Scots which existed for several hundreds of years until the eruption of Alex Salmond on the north British scene.

By contrast, there are new Scots who are the children of the post-industrial, consumer-orientated and increasingly secular Scotland. They are unlikely to be involved in civic initiatives and receive much of their information from the social media where the Yes side has shown impressive flair. They often look to celebrities from the entertainment world (overwhelmingly pro-independence) for a lead even on political issues. Rather than recoil from increasingly overt bids by Salmond to equate his cause with that of the entire nation, they admire his chutzpah.

A lot of these present-orientated, often lightly educated and sometimes economically underactive Scots have a sense of entitlement which they believe a populist movement like the SNP is likelier to satisfy than the conventional parties. Many, particularly on Clydeside are steeped in a grievance culture which has class and ethnic targets: the Conservative Party and the English who back the Tories far more than the Scots as a whole.

Salmond's new followers have mainly transferred from the Labour Party. Many are determinedly parochial. They refuse to concede the risks of living in a tough and unequal globalised world in which Scottish welfarism is an exotic anomaly. The fate of millions of unemployed Greeks, Spaniards and Italians who got ensnared in the wrong currency union, appears to be of no relevance to them. In reflective moments, some will concede that in following Salmond they are behaving recklessly. But the culture of risk that has been fashionable in a hedonistic Scottish society for several decades indicates that it is the cool thing to do.

After the referendum, he separated patriotic Scots from cowardly ones. According to one reviewer of his referendum diary, Salmond put 'a predictable populist, faux revolutionary spin on the situation by claiming: "The accepted order has been smashed – and it is the people who have achieved it"'.[67]

Perhaps a shrinking number of journalists covering the referendum were convinced by the SNP's insistence that it was a civic nationalist force. They could see the nature of the campaign and it was not unreasonable for reporters with experience of international trouble-spots to conclude that all was far from well when only one side was really free to express its opinions in pubs and on the campaign stump.

Ironically, his own family background would have offered much useful lessons about how to transcend political differences. He was born on 31 December 1954 in the town of Linlithgow, a centre of light industry. Winston Churchill was still Britain's Prime Minister. His son remembered that his father thought Winston Churchill was 'too good for hanging' due to his firm handling of industrial disputes. He admitted that in contrast his late mother thought Churchill was 'the greatest man who ever lived'. While still a teenager, she had enlisted in the Women's Royal Naval Service – popularly known as the Wrens – in the Second World War, and had worked in London during the Blitz and then in Plymouth. She was a Conservative supporter and died aged 81 while walking near Glenmore in the Highlands in 2003. His father still lives, a former Labour supporter and civil servant who was nicknamed Uncle Joe when he served in the Royal Navy because of his radical left-wing sympathies.

CHAPTER 5: NATIONALIST PEOPLE

'Underlying my mother's belief and politics was the very strong British identity and underlying my father's attitude was a developing, vigorous Scottish identity', Salmond reflected in August 2014.[68]

Yet the Salmonds had shelved their very real differences in political outlook to provide a stable and affectionate home background for their children. Such mutual restraint and underlying solidarity were absent from the brawling collective family that Scotland had become by 2014 and arguably their son had played no small role in masterminding the creation of a very dysfunctional national household.

Alex Perry, the journalist who profiled Salmond for *Newsweek* got a whiff of the widespread ill-feeling when he had his haircut in Inverurie, a town north-west of Aberdeen where Salmond stood for Westminster in 2015. The women in the salon would not talk about the referendum. But the hairdresser spoke out: It 'tore families apart, tore this place apart. People still aren't speaking'.[69]

The young Salmond went to St Andrews University where he studied medieval Scottish history and economics. This seat of learning may well have been the place where he acquired some of his contempt for toffs and Old Etonians. In March 2015, while on his book tour, he stated that David Cameron, 'like most posh boys, given half-a-chance will run away from a fight'.[70]

The 20th century war record of Old Etonians would show this to be a baseless slur.[71] His fellow students would inevitably have included some upper middle-class young people, often from southern England, whose sense of entitlement was not always matched by intellectual gifts. David Cameron was not one of them. He had obtained a first class degree from Oxford University (compared to Salmond's own lower second). On page 2 of his memoir, Salmond reveals his contempt for the UK Prime Minister when he insisted on 19 September 2014 that further decentralisation for Scotland must be 'in tandem' with similar moves in England. He recalls thinking then, 'You silly arrogant man... no one realises the door that Cameron has just opened'.[72] Earlier, on 24 February 2015, Salmond had regarded Cameron's decision to hold a cabinet meeting near Aberdeen as a territorial incursion and he staged one of his own a few miles away, issuing a statement complaining about Westminster 'thieves', an epithet he had used previously to blacken the name of the UK parties represented there.[73]

When Salmond announced he was quitting as First Minister, Cameron displayed magnanimity. He said on 19 September: 'Alex is a politician of huge talent and passion. He has been an effective First Minister and always fights his corner'.

'While we disagree profoundly about his goal of a separated Scotland, and many other things, I respect and admire his huge contribution to politics and public life'.[74]

This was one of those occasions when Salmond was too hastily written off by politicians from English elite backgrounds who were not as shrewd or battle-hardened as the SNP's insurgent leader. It is clear from Cameron's remarks that he assumed (erroneously) Salmond was quitting politics when in fact he was making a well-timed political manoeuvre with an eye on future battles. By the following spring, he was sitting down with Jason Cowley, editor of the *New Statesman* to tuck into fish, chips and mushy peas, washed down by pink champagne which according to Salmond was an appropriate gesture 'to toast my book'.[75] He was gleeful about the prospect of the SNP finally being strong enough to bring down any Tory minority government and play a significant role in the next UK government. As Cameron appeared destined to be only a one-term Prime Minister, he confidently predicted that 'It's not a question of if, but when', there's a second referendum.

It is perhaps not altogether far-fetched to compare Salmond with a highly talented but personally wayward musical performer; he is definitely box-office due to his artistry but also volatile and at times undisciplined. He has people skills which range from the sublime to the awful. On the campaign trail, he is good at remembering faces and names but he also remembers slights and broods over some of them. It is hardly surprising that he needs to be surrounded by handlers to avoid getting into mischief and end up discrediting a lucrative brand.

Salmond himself appears to be regularly locked in battle between the avuncular, droll and charming persona and the aggressive, tribal and at times even menacing *doppelgänger*. Much of the time, he recognises the need to keep his elemental instincts in check for the good of the higher cause. Self-discipline is exercised, whether it be battling against his weight or acting as an encouraging rather than bullying general towards his foot-soldiers which he did for most of his time as First Minister. Well-chosen adjutants such as Bruce Crawford, his empathetic party manager at Holyrood from 2007 to 2011 or Kevin Pringle, who choreographed his dealings with the media over a much longer period, were invaluable. Without advisers who can direct his energies in constructive directions, he becomes a loose cannon sometimes raining down fire on his own side. But as an MP back in Westminster without anyone to keep him in hand, the bully has at times triumphed over the mature nationalist. His re-igniting of the quarrel with Nick Robinson is an emblematic example. One of the first things Nicola Sturgeon did as leader was to extend peace feelers to the then BBC political editor after Salmond had reacted angrily to his questioning at a Glasgow press conference about the possible relocation of the RBS bank. Robinson later publicly expressed regret for wording a news report badly to suggest that Salmond hadn't answered a question when in fact 'he'd tried to avoid answering it to focus on something he preferred to talk about'.[76] It was a single incident in a heated election campaign and outside the Yes fold many assumed that the attempt to engineer a row and personalise it was designed to draw attention away from Salmond's much disputed claims about Scotland's future currency.

A mass protest quickly followed outside the BBC offices in Glasgow on 14 September 2014. Prominently displayed was a giant banner with Robinson's face on it denouncing him as a liar and calling for his dismissal. Salmond though had no qualms about describing the event as 'peaceful and joyous...'.[77]

Sturgeon's decision to lunch with Robinson towards the end of 2014 appeared prescient since, soon after, a battle with cancer made him the object of much public sympathy. But the row flared up again following a talk which Robinson gave in Edinburgh, in August 2015, to promote a new book on recent political events which he had covered. In his talk, he compared protests against his coverage of the Scottish independence referendum to something out of Vladimir Putin's Russia. He hit out at the 'intimidation and bullying' of himself and other journalists.[78] Instead of letting the matter go, Salmond, referring to 'Auld Nick', wrote that Robinson should be 'embarrassed and ashamed' of his coverage of the Scottish independence referendum which was a 'disgrace'.[79]

In his own referendum book, he had lambasted BBC Scotland for its handling of the referendum but the BBC overall played very safe. The second referendum debate of 25 August 2014, which it was responsible for staging, was hopelessly mismanaged.[80] The audience was strongly pro-nationalist in sympathy and little effort was made by the journalist chairing it, Glen Campbell, to prevent Alex Salmond from turning it into a virtual Yes rally. This is perhaps the one moment in the BBC's coverage of the referendum that is most clearly etched in the minds of many. Yet there was no demonstration by pro-Union supporters outside the BBC's offices despite the widespread dismay felt about its performance.

In its overall referendum coverage, the BBC focused disproportionately on constitutional matters. This suited the SNP since it was far more interested in process than in practical outcomes flowing from independence. The BBC rarely, if ever, explored the consequences for local communities dependent on British state jobs of a partition of the island and how the architects of independence could replicate them. Neither did the BBC draw on the experience of other countries which had opted for independence in challenging economic conditions. Pro-independence figures such as Lesley Riddoch enjoyed regular platforms on the channel and it is difficult to identify combative or incisive journalists on the No side who were given similar amounts of exposure.

It is hard to avoid surmising that Salmond continues to seek an alibi (namely an allegedly biased BBC) for a referendum defeat made worse by his own failure to present a feasible economic case for independence and indeed the failure of his colleagues to realise how damaging his currency union claim was for Yes hopes. A Yes sympathiser, G.A. Ponsonby, has even written a book which he entitled *London Calling: How the BBC Stole the Referendum*.

At the start of the referendum campaign, the BBC was one of the British institutions which Scots had a high degree of respect for; around 60 per cent wished it to continue broadcasting in Scotland after independence.[81] Accordingly, given what has emerged about the ruthlessness at times displayed by the Yes campaign, it would have been perfectly in character for its planners to find grounds to discredit the BBC, however flimsy their basis might be.[82]

No senior colleague reiterated Salmond's charges against the BBC which in some quarters had been viewed as a diversion in 2014 as he struggled to make a persuasive economic case for independence. But he was backed up by numerous bloggers who cater for the militant outlook of many of those who had flocked to join the party in 2014-15.[83] One of them, Derek Bateman, formerly a presenter of the BBC Radio Scotland's morning news programme, had earlier helpfully indicated the deference that a nationalist politician running Scotland in the future might expect: 'One day the clowns in the media will have to learn to treat a Scottish leader with the respect they do one from Ireland, Iceland or Denmark. It's because we remain a region that the metropolitan elite treat us and our First Minister as upstart regional types who should know their place. Well I think we are learning, just not the lesson they think...'[84]

Salmond himself tried to 'patronise his way out of his difficulties' especially when pinpointed about his implausible currency plans. On 27 August 2014, upon being pressed by Faisal Islam, Sky News political editor, about this issue, he accused the senior reporter of trying to impersonate Alistair Darling, sarcastically telling him to 'get with the debate, man'.[85]

He was gratuitously offensive to Ben Riley-Smith, the *Daily Telegraph's* Scottish Political Reporter: twice at a press conference on 2 September 2014 he pressed a packet of sweets on the 27-year-old journalist reporter who had been asking him if the accountancy firm Goldman Sachs was right to issue a series of warnings about Salmond's currency plans and a run on the Scottish banks. It was a deliberate attempt to 'patronise Riley-Smith and thus devalue his ability in front of other journalists and, of course, the SNP leader's ever-obsequious aides' according to the journalist's senior colleague on the paper Alan Cochrane.[86] As the countdown to the vote approached, there were increasingly forceful complaints from Salmond about the 'metropolitan media'. He barred three newspapers regarded as hostile to the SNP from his resignation press conference, with another, the *Guardian* refusing to take part out of solidarity with those colleagues.[87]

CHAPTER 5: NATIONALIST PEOPLE

On the day his tactical withdrawal from frontline Scottish politics was announced, Iain Martin wrote that Scotland had narrowly avoided a brush with disaster. He seemed in little doubt that:

'If Yes had prevailed, Scotland would not have been a free society. Dissent would have been squashed, journalists would have been intimidated and Salmond, with his majority in the referendum and a majority at Holyrood, would have been rampant as he constructed a constitution and led negotiations with London'.[88]

Martin's article was entitled 'Alex Salmond was a giant of his age'. But his self-indulgence at times damaged the cause that he had come to personify. Thus early in the referendum battle, he insisted to the interviewer Andrew Neil that he had sought advice from Scottish Government law officers to justify his claim that an independent Scotland would not need to re-apply for membership of the European Union. He then presided over a costly attempt to keep any details of this secret until a statement to the Scottish Parliament from Nicola Sturgeon revealed that no such legal advice had ever existed. For the journalist Euan McColm, it highlighted the fact that Salmond was both a formidable asset and the greatest challenge to the Yes cause.[89]

However adept at popularising ideas in chunky sound-bites, Salmond often struggled to explain and defend complex and detailed matters. He would make assertions about economic issues which he could not easily stand over. Thus for years, he promised (if given the chance) to set Scotland's corporate tax threshold at 3 per cent below that of the United Kingdom's –which stood at 23 per cent in 2014. He insisted that thousands of jobs would be created by inward investment. But he failed to produce any reliable evidence to back up what a prominent media supporter of the SNP described as 'the SNP's corporation-tax folly'.[90]

Joyce McMillan, another prominent independence backer, had lost patience with Salmond by May 2014, writing that 'the First Minister has this week been giving a pyrotechnic display of his many imperfections'.[91] She was particularly exercised by 'Alex Salmond's flirtations with the wealthy and powerful'. It demonstrated how '21st-century politicians in office come under huge pressure to align themselves with the world's elites, against the interests of the people as a whole'. In an open letter to Salmond written earlier, Gerry Hassan, an even better-known Scottish political analyst, had pleaded with the SNP leader: 'Don't become the voice of Scotland's establishment, whether it is the quangocracy, civic society or wider institutional elites. In that lies the blunting of your political edge and intelligence'.[92]

One of Salmond's abilities was the knack of talking in emancipatory left-wing style while pursuing firmly centrist economic policies and striking up relations with capitalists who could be as hard-driving in their business activities as he was in politics. The relationship that preoccupied the anti-British Scottish Left the most was that with the media mogul Rupert Murdoch. The head of News Corp is an unabashed admirer of the man who relishes the chance to rock the British state to its foundations. He admires his human qualities - chutzpah, tenacity, and presentational gifts of a high order - more than the big state socialist philosophy of his party in which bureaucrats micro-manage the lives of Scots.

In 2014, both men had the same enemies: David Cameron and his court who had appeared to stand idly by as the metropolitan left sought to topple some of his newspapers and make illegal his intrusive journalistic methods.

Murdoch tweeted during the final stages of the 2014 referendum campaign: 'Alex Salmond clearly most brilliant politician in U.K. Gave Cameron back of his hand this week. Loved by Scots... Scots better people than to be dependants of London'.[93]

Murdoch was in Glasgow during the tumultuous final days of the campaign. At least through his tweets, he made common cause with the demonstrators who, like him, hoped that Salmond might ignite a national revolution which would sweep away a tired old order. It was a fascinating if ill-matched tryst. He was making common cause with shouty, resentful Scots (many, economically under-active middle-aged men). Each party had had enough of being patronised by a distant elite. They felt themselves victims of a conspiracy to do them down. Any problems were the fault of others.

The magnetism of Alex Salmond means that the elderly but still combative Australian tycoon of Scottish lineage and less competitive Clydeside malcontents, were reading off the same page. But he could not bring himself to throw his papers behind the Yes side due to the influence of the far-left in its ranks. However, his best-selling Scottish title enthusiastically backed the SNP in the 2015 election.

Without Salmond's self-belief would his movement have accomplished the journey from the political wilderness to the centre of power? There is no clearcut answer. But it is easy to exaggerate Salmond's prowess as a vote-winner. The SNP's constituency vote only rose by 4.16 percentage points between the 1999 and 2007 Scottish Parliament elections when it narrowly overtook Labour as the largest party. A bigger swing to the SNP might have been expected after a slick campaign and 8 years of somewhat drab Labour-Liberal Democrat government. In 2010, the Labour Party obtained one of its best-ever Scottish results in a British general elections winning 41 seats against the SNP's six. One month later, in an outburst of candour, Salmond admitted: 'The centre of gravity in Scottish politics currently is clearly not independence. You must campaign for what is good for Scotland as well as campaigning for independence'.[94] Of course, there was the surge in SNP support in 2011, delivering it an overall majority at Holyrood. But the arrival of SNP electoral domination perhaps had more to do with the crass electoral campaign fought by Labour and, even more so the suicidal Lib-Dem decision to go into coalition with the Tories in London than with Salmond's general-ship (effective though that undoubtedly was). As late as June 2014, with just a few months to go before the referendum, the SNP could only manage 29.0 per cent of the vote in the European elections (slightly less than its total in 2009).

Salmond liked to project himself as a national 'educator' capable of instilling confidence in his countrymen. He did help persuade lots of ordinary folk to obsess about constitutional issues that previously had only concerned several tens of thousands of party activists. But he did put a lot of Scots off with his glibness about oil booms and currency unions when it was clear that the reality simply did not fit his breezy prospectus.

Jim Sillars had declared in May 2014: 'At almost every meeting I have spoken at, it has been necessary to emphasise that the vote on September 18 is not about Alex Salmond and the SNP'. 'When it becomes necessary to repeat that over and over, it means he in his First Minister role has become a liability'.[95]

At least Salmond made an inspired exit on 19 September 2014 that greatly assisted his party's post-referendum standing and the prospects of his successor. But as the months elapsed it became clear that he was going to spurn an elder statesman role and be an occasional thorn in the side for Nicola Sturgeon who grasped (correctly) that the moment had arrived for more conciliatory leadership. In August 2015, he had unwisely chosen to re-ignite the quarrel with Nick Robinson following the appearance of a book in which he reflected on the large demonstration in Glasgow against him almost a year earlier. But no longer it seemed was the SNP politician's occasionally idiosyncratic outlook, and sometimes intense dislikes, to be regarded by his colleagues as an acceptable part of the Salmond persona. In the week this row re-ignited, a private dinner took place at the official residence of the First Minister, Bute House, in Edinburgh. It was hosted by Sturgeon and her husband and the only guests were Nick Robinson, his wife and their two children. According to the *Times*, it was a 'white glove dinner served by footmen', one that managed to be 'friendly and informal' despite the main topic being Scottish politics.[96] On the anniversary of the referendum itself, Sturgeon gave a much-quoted speech while Salmond was in a Glasgow shopping centre; at 1.05pm he rather plaintively tweeted: I'll be signing copies of my book in the St Enoch's centre in Glasgow until 14:30. 1st floor, next to BHS. Come along'.[97] He was quoted as saying by the journalist Michael Gray, 'The guardian of progress... are the new activists who will not retreat into the shadows'.[98] But the next day Alyn Smith MEP stated: 'The more we talk about not accepting the result of the Scottish people, 'we wuz robbed, the BBC was against us' etc – I just don't see that it helps'.[99]

Salmond needs to avoid becoming the Scot with a perennial grievance. Unless he can turn into the elder statesman of nationalism, the danger is that he will end up as a disruptive regional figure, a Caledonian version of the professional Yorkshireman with pronounced views on most things but slightly ridiculous due to the vehemence with which they are put across. It may even be necessary for him to retire from the fray if the cause of Scottish nationalism is to continue to make decisive advances and not be bogged down in disputes over tactics or personal ranking. On 20 August 2015 the National Front in France expelled from its ranks Jean-Marie Le Pen who had founded the ultra-nationalist force which his daughter Marine now leads.[100] It was a sign that not even a 20th century giant of the French far-right was sacrosanct in the eyes of his successor. Alex Salmond did immense service for his party but it is no longer one dependent on a few individuals for success. It remains to be seen if he realises that Scottish Nationalism may, in fact, have largely outgrown him.

The Professions

Scotland's legal system is perhaps the key pillar of the country's institutional distinctiveness. Lawyers have been prominent in the SNP but they are far from being an influential professional segment perhaps due to the fact that they are satisfied with the freedom they have long enjoyed to regulate their own corporate affairs. Indeed, the only recent challenge to the distinctiveness of Scots law emanated from SNP after the acquisition of its parliamentary majority. There were frequent clashes between the justice minister Kenny MacAskill, (a doctrinaire lawyer who attended the same school in Linlithgow as Alex Salmond) and different parts of the profession, most notably over his plan to abolish the rule of corroboration in Scots law. It requires two different independent sources of evidence to be in support of each crucial fact before a defendant can be convicted of a crime. The police and certain advocacy groups supported its abolition but most of the Scottish legal world was opposed, fearing that miscarriages of justice would became far likelier. Not only over this measure but over the arming of a centralized police force and the introduction of heavy-handed measures to outlaw 'sectarian' singing at football matches, MacAskill could seem as deaf to the views of much of the profession, the public and the parliamentary opposition as any long-distance London power-broker. There was barely disguised relief in legal circles when he was removed by Nicola Sturgeon at the end of 2014 to be replaced as justice minister by an occupational therapist Michael Matheson; the arrival of someone from outside the legal world who had shown himself to be a competent minister was viewed as the onset of more normal times when dialogue could resume between members of the legal and political worlds.

But MacAskill's doctrinaire mindset is quite likely to prevail in his party. In May

2015, he candidly admitted that the Scottish government's policy is subject to one overriding test: whether it advances the independence cause. Introducing voting rights for prisoners, a just and overdue step according to Macaskill, had recently been shelved by his government because it would harm the prospects of success in the 2014 referendum [*Herald*, 27 May 2015]. Nicola Sturgeon would say, not long afterwards, that the main condition for having a second independence referendum was whether her side could command enough popular support to prevail. Current economic conditions or the implications of independence for Scots on meagre incomes who were vulnerable to sudden political shocks did not count as decisive factors. As Kevin Hague has written: 'to introduce those concepts would be to admit that there may be logically sound economic reasons for staying in the UK, reasons that best serve the interests of the Scottish people' [Kevin Hague, 'The Fabulously Absolute SNP', *Chokka* Blog, 22 October 2015.].

Figures associated with the Glasgow legal world have played pivotal roles in the story of Scottish Nationalism. The solicitor John McCormick played a crucial role in the formation of the SNP in the 1930s, enabling it to reach out beyond idealists and ideologues. Energetic and eloquent, he was unable to prevent centrifugal tendencies detonating the party's one serious split, in 1942. Along with gradualists committed to Scottish Home Rule within a looser British territorial arrangement, he left, drew close to the Liberal party, and threw his energies behind a Scottish Covenant. Much of Scotland's then extensive civic associations endorsed this petition for Home Rule and two million signatures were obtained. But McCormick's bid to erect a trans-party home rule consensus that would force Westminster to concede autonomy, was unlucky in its timing. The 1940s were one of the high-points of British unity. In the year of his death, 1955, the Scottish Conservatives, known then in Scotland as the Unionists, obtained an outright majority of votes. McCormick probably suffered professionally because of his pioneering outlook on how best Scottish interests could be represented in the political sphere. But his isolation showed the absence of an effective nationalist sub-culture in Scottish public life at least in the mid-20th century.

Barely a dozen years later, another Glasgow lawyer, Winnie (as she preferred to be known) Ewing broke the mould of Scottish politics with a sensational by-election victory in the Labour stronghold of Hamilton on 21 November 1967. The elimination of a 20,000 Labour majority on a 37 per cent swing convulsed Scottish politics. For the first time Scottish nationalism emerged as an outlet for Scottish discontent about the direction of public affairs. Ewing failed to hold the seat and never really played a decisive role in the affairs of the party. But she was a figure of influence. From 1979 to 1999 she represented the North-East-of Scotland in the European

Parliament and played a crucial long-term role in orientating the SNP towards the cause of European integration. Generally, she was more outward-looking than many big names who preceded or followed her. She enjoyed good relations with Irish and Welsh constitutional nationalists and ensured that the SNP was seen as mainstream rather than cranky in the European Parliament.

An incident revealing that perhaps many nationalists may be unduly preoccupied about how they are portrayed in the media occurred in 1969 while she was in Dublin, appearing on the enormously popular *Late, Late Show*. She had threatened to walk out because the programme appeared to be a caricature of stateless European nationalisms. Ireland's venerable nationalist patriarch, Eamon de Valera by now his country's President, phoned her as she was leaving for home to say that he had complained to the state broadcasting corporation about its treatment of her. Already a hero of hers, de Valera's death in 1975 led her to hire a small plane at her own expense so that she could attend the funeral. The British political representation was poor but she was proud that her small aircraft 'stood at Dublin airport alongside the US presidential plane and the one that had brought Princess Grace of Monaco'.[101]

It was the unenviable task of the lawyer Gordon Wilson, from a west of Scotland background (born in Glasgow in 1938) but with a professional and political base in the east of Scotland (specifically Dundee) to steer the party through the downbeat 1980s. He had been one of only two SNP MPs to survive the electoral rout of 1979 that followed the collapse of modest devolution proposals for Scotland. The 1980s were a dispiriting time for the party marked by serious dissension in 1982 which saw some of its brighter stars of the future (such as Alex Salmond) briefly suspended from the party due to their membership of the left-wing '79 group'. More alarming was the emergence of Siol nan Gaidheal (Seed of the Gael) which struck a belligerent and ethnocentric tone in its pronouncements. Its manifesto (in 2015) read:

'The Siol nan Gaidheal organisation supports the revival of the Folkic traditions of Scotland and the Gaelic and Scots languages. The land of Scotland from which we as a people and our culture spring, is central to our vision. Sustainable land use is vital for the future of our country. Land must be reclaimed for the benefit of our people. Siol nan Gaidheal seeks to liberate the Scottish people from the worst excesses of English/British Cultural Imperialism and believes that English people resident in Scotland will integrate into and make a full contribution to the community of Scotland. SnG will dedicate itself to fulfilling our commitments to our country and people, we will thus not stand idly by and watch our country being used, abused or betrayed by enemies both internal and external. We are content to leave party political action to the Scottish National Party and the forth-coming Scottish Parliament. SnG exists to promote, safeguard and stimulate a third Scottish Renaissance which will use the best past traditions of Scotland to forge a new Nation which will be an example to the world.'[102]

Gordon Wilson has stated that Siol nan Gaidheal 'recruited largely from SNP members living in working-class housing areas'. He observed ruefully that an early unsuccessful attempt to ban membership of the SNG, moved by Prof Neil McCormick at the SNP's December 1980 conference, was defeated by an overwhelming majority. It was noticeable, he wrote in 2014 that 'the left-wing 79 Group gave support to the SNG which many SNP members regarded as proto-fascist'.[103] Soon after the SNP decided to ditch the SNG but the early 1980s was an inglorious period for the SNP. Wilson even told the political analyst Gerry Hassan in 2008 that 'Nobody in their right senses should have voted SNP in 1981-82'.[104]

Later on, there were divergences over whether to endorse the plans for a devolved Scottish parliament supported by the Labour Party and by various civic forces. Wilson was dour and deliberate but he showed grit and indefatigability in steering the party through some of its lowest moments. He was on the moderate left while Mrs Ewing was one of the last figures on the moderate right of politics to wield influence in the SNP. He was sceptical about quick-fixes that might release the SNP from the doldrums. He was cautious about embracing the EU with its supra-nationalist agenda already clear by the 1980s. He was far less enthusiastic than his successor Alex Salmond in wanting to make devolution work for the party in case it transform it into a force interested in governing primarily for its own sake. He lost his parliamentary seat in 1987 and his influence waned after he stepped down as leader in 1990.

The memory of Willie McRae, a gifted but volatile Glasgow lawyer who only narrowly avoided being elected MP for Ross and Cromarty during the party's first major electoral surge in 1974, appeared to burn brighter than the cerebral Wilson's among romantic nationalists. McRae was found shot in his car in a remote corner of the Highlands in 1985 and controversy has periodically flared up about whether he had taken his own life or been violently disposed of by some dastardly wing of the British state. Wilson himself was in no doubt that the intelligence services, including those of the USA, were prepared to impede the SNP's independence hopes.[105] But his conclusion that the evidence did not amount to a conspiracy in the case of McRae did not prevent poems and plays later being written and performed about this turbulent patriot.

In his seventies, Wilson himself has become a historian of the party with two volumes written about its long struggle to shape Scotland's future. He has also discomfited party officialdom by warning about falling prey to the arrogance of power. In August 2015, he published a paper setting out the need for a regional police force to be established in Scotland along federal lines. The creation of a centralized force, Police Scotland, in 2013 had been the most ambitious undertaking in public policy undertaken by the SNP. But the move had been unpopular both inside and outside police ranks and Wilson was expressing a widespread view when he claimed that Scottish policing was broken and that there was the need for 'root and branch' reform following a succession of crises. He argued that the problem lay not so much with an unpopular police chief but with 'parliament, ministers and civil servants'. The solution, as he saw it, was the re-establishment of regional police forces, each with a chief constable who would be overseen by local authorities. He was careful not to be seen as a stalking horse for the SNP's opponents, accusing them of 'shallow political posturing' in their response to the crisis in policing.[106] But in the Salmond era and beyond, the SNP preferred to pursue a centralised approach to public policy and the quest for sound administration of public bodies which citizens could have confidence in was not an issue that excited the rank-and-file.

Wilson struck much closer to home early in Sturgeon's leadership tenure when he criticised an ex-party adviser over her involvement in helping to secure £150,000 for the T in the Park rock festival, held each summer. Jennifer Dempsie, previously a special adviser for former First Minister Alex Salmond and the partner of Angus Robertson, the SNP's Westminster leader, helped broker a meeting, in May, with festival organisers DF Concerts Ltd prior to the injection of 'state aid' on 2 July 2015. Wilson alleged that both she and the Scottish Government had lost 'credibility' over the issue. He argued that 'the SNP should toughen up on relationships of Ministers, MSPs, MPs and MEPs with all lobbyists, regardless of their affiliations. This is all the more important given the new prominence of the Party at Holyrood and Westminster and its access to patronage.[107] Absolutely no criminal impropriety has been alleged but the incident raised questions about whether a party now enjoying dominance in Scottish politics unparalleled for many years, has become too arrogant in its conduct of public affairs. (SNP MPs cannot speak out under recent rules). The Scottish parliament lacks a second chamber with oversight over the decision of the main elected body. So perhaps the existence of figures like Gordon Wilson prepared to play the role of Cicero, the guardian of public ethics in the final days of the Roman Republic, is to be commended rather than deplored (especially by SNP members themselves).

Lawyers are likely to play a significant role in the SNP in the future if only due to its exponential growth and the various interests that will need to be reconciled. They manage conflict, negotiate, and (at least occasionally sometimes) seek common ground. These skills are not always visible in other professions and the business sector which have provided notable SNP figures. Lawyers can also be controlling and manipulative, expanding regulations in order to reinforce their influence. But these are traits hardly confined to one profession alone.

Members of the liberal professions have not made their mark in the contemporary SNP. In the 1940s they loomed larger. Douglas Young, the poet and later Professor of Greek, actually led it for a time in the 1940s. William Power, the journalist was also a leading light in the early SNP. Later George Reid, the television journalist was one of 10 SNP members returned to Westminster in 1974. He later worked in demanding international roles for the Red Cross and as an intermediary in ethnically-riven Moldova. Perhaps such challenges enabled him to see political nationalism in a starker light since he did not rejoin the SNP after he stood down as presiding officer of the Scottish Parliament in 2007.

The SNP, under Alex Salmond, has successfully courted the media from a titan like Rupert Murdoch to commentators who were formerly Labour backers such as Joyce McMillan and Ruth Wishart. Joan McAlpine, formerly of the *Herald* and the *Sunday Times,* has at times eclipsed Salmond as an intransigent nationalist. She reached Holyrood in 2011 and from 2015, the more cerebral journalist, George Kerevan has been the SNP MP at Westminster for East Lothian.

It is perhaps understandable that medical doctors are not conspicuous in the upper reaches of the SNP. Their status, earning capacity, and often busy professional life might make a backbench existence appear a startling demotion. Yet it was a medic, Dr Robert McIntyre who had the distinction of being the first SNP member returned to the House of Commons. He won Motherwell in April 1945 but his tenure was cut short by the general election three months later. As a consultant chest physician at Stirling Royal Infirmary over many years, McIntyre played a distinguished role in combating tuberculosis. Highly respected locally, he stood at every election in Stirling for the SNP without success from 1950 to 1974. He led the party from 1947 to 1956, taking a firm line against the party's 'wilder forces'. In retirement, he told a journalist much later that it was only the existence of the SNP as an organized political force which had prevented the wider Nationalist movement from descending into sporadic violence.[108]

Political fortune was more benign towards Dr Philippa Whitford, a consultant breast cancer surgeon in Ayrshire. She was elected MP for Central Ayrshire in 2015, just months after entering the party, whose vote in this seat went up from 19.05 to 53.17 per cent. Born in Northern Ireland, where she lived until the age of ten, she was a strong advocate of Palestinian nationalism having spent a year working as a volunteer in Gaza early in her medical career.[109] She made headlines after delivering a speech for the Yes side at Strathaven on 1 May 2014. In it she made claims about the dangers to gullet cancer surgery in Gateshead, in the North-East-of England. The head of NHS hospitals in the region, Sir Leonard Fenwick described them as completely baseless.[110] However, her presentation was viewed more than 68,000 times on YouTube with many Yes websites linking to it. At frequent public meetings, she warned Scots that the NHS would wither away within a decade without a Yes vote, becoming one of the best-known faces of the Yes campaign. In its final stages, the YES camp made headway with the claim that privatisation of the NHS was on its way in England and that it would lead to a reduction of the funds available for health spending in Scotland. Fenwick pointed out that one of the leaders of the pro-independence lobby group 'Business for Scotland', is Tony Banks, whose business is running private care homes, and that the Co-founder of 'NHS for Yes', Willie Wilson, owns a chain of private community pharmacies.[111]

Sir Harry Burns who retired as Chief Medical Officer for Scotland in 2014 kept a lower profile but he helped popularise the Yes campaign's assertion that inequality is at the root of poor health in Scotland in various public addresses that were extensively reported in the media.[112] By 2015, he was a member of the Scottish government's Council of Economic advisers.

Polls showed that medicine was one of the professional sectors where the No side enjoyed very high support and Dr Anna Gregor, awarded a CBE after leading a successful anti-cancer strategy in Scotland expressed the unhappiness of perhaps many colleagues when she declared that some were 'using our highly privileged position of trust with the patient population and the community to politically scaremonger'. Dr Gregor claimed that 'unreasonable distress and panic' was being spread among patients on absolutely no basis because 'we have had complete freedom about how we run the NHS in Scotland'.[113]

From Margo to Mhairi

Scottish Nationalism, through its periods of influence and success, has often been understood beyond Scotland through the activities of its women politicians. Winnie Ewing has already been mentioned. Perhaps it is appropriate to discuss Margo MacDonald ((1944-2014) and Mhairi Black (1994-) in the same breath. Certainly there are outward similarities. Both reached Westminster at an early age. MacDonald captured the seat of Glasgow Govan in 1973 aged 30. Mhairi Black won her seat aged only 20. She obtained far more publicity for this feat because she was part of a huge wave of nationalist MPs who had crushed the parties which had won 53 Scottish seats in 2010. She grabbed headlines on 14 July 2015 with an eloquent and passionate maiden speech that was quickly viewed ten million times on various social media.[114] In it she displayed the oratorical prowess which had made her such a formidable asset to the Yes side in the referendum campaign of 2013-14. The *Times* and the *Financial Times* beat a path to her door for lengthy interviews in which she was asked about her anger and her background but not about what she wished to do with the power and influence that she had acquired at such a precocious age.

Black did not contradict the portrait of herself as someone who had grown up surrounded by poverty and deprivation. Jeremy Paxman wrote:

'When at home in her constituency she still lives with her parents, surrounded by "schemes" (council housing estates), the indications of deprivation — unemployment, a wrecked town centre, substance abuse — all too easy to find'.[115]

It required another journalist, Iain Martin who came from Paisley the same town as the new MP to point out that the claim that she was a silver-tongued proletarian, perhaps like Aneurin Bevan, was 'nonsense':

'As I understand it, according to her crowdfunder appeal, Black lives with her parents in thoroughly-middle class Ralston, near the golf course. Anyone who knows Paisley will identify owner-occupied Ralston as one of a perhaps surprising number of attractive residential areas that ring the town. I'm from another such affluent area on the other side of Paisley. The tough "schemes" that exist, and they do exist, are not in Ralston or even particularly near it'.[116]

Black describes the Scottish working-class as blameless victims of an unjust system which has its epicentre in Scotland's traditional overlord and sometime oppressor England. It is not unreasonable to see her as having a partly ethnocentric message: in her speech, she referred to the minor nobleman William Wallace who resisted the English under King Edward I 700 years earlier as a powerful influence and in August 2015, she commemorated the day of his execution in 1305. She is probably one of the most convincing exponents of the nationalist grievance culture yet to appear at the forefront of Scottish politics.

Admittedly, due to being older at the time of her parliamentary debut, MacDonald had seen more of life. But while being firmly on the side of the poor and disadvantaged, she did not paint ordinary Scots in such elegiac terms. One of the few advantages deriving from her inability to hold onto her Glasgow Govan seat for only 3 months in 1974 and subsequent failure to make it back to Westminster, was that she was required to take jobs which gave her insights and experience even mature parliamentarians simply never acquire. Working for the housing charity Shelter after failing to win the seat of Hamilton in a 1978 by-election, she recalled afterwards shocking her colleagues :

'We were discussing whether there was any such thing as anti-social tenants. To me that didn't need any discussion. Of course there are anti-social tenants. There are folk you don't want to live next door to, because they don't look after the place properly, they don't take their turn on the stairs. My colleagues were quite disgusted with me, I think. But when I asked around the table who'd ever lived in a council house, I was the only one'.[117]

MacDonald did not pursue a university education, obtaining qualifications for a career as a physical education teacher and she was already married with two children by the time she arrived at Westminster. By contrast, Mhairi Black was sitting her final exams in politics and public policy at Glasgow University when returned by the voters of Paisley and Renfrewshire West. She obtained first class honours but it is unlikely if that, or tweets on social media about her personal life, influenced her supporters view of her. She was a symbolic icon of revolt, a La Pasionaria of the lower Clyde, who reflected the mutinous outlook of perhaps thousands of her constituents.[118] Irrespective of their age, many of the working-class Scots who had flocked to the Yes banner had felt misunderstood, patronised and put upon by distant rulers. Much of the Scottish electorate in 2015 may in fact have felt the frustration and restlessness of the teenager that Mhairi Black had only recently ceased to be. There were no questions put to her in 2015 about how a Scotland with plunging oil revenues could easily support these people. If they had been, the answers are unlikely to have been more substantial than the ones contained in the SNP's 2013 Independence White paper which looked even more utopian in 2015 than it had been when it first appeared.

She had called her defeated opponent Douglas Alexander 'a careerist politician' but that is what she has become herself.[119] Soon she was complaining about her conditions of work at Westminster, the deafening sound of Big Ben's chimes, the high temperatures, the fact that 'I just have to wear a suit all the time. It's such a pain'.[120] In a less soft Scottish age, Black would have been called out (and not just by the media) for such self-indulgence. At least she made a valid point about the strange refusal of the Westminster Parliament to embrace electronic voting. Yet, hardly having settled in, she was prepared to complain about the costs of refurbishing Westminster. This led one *Financial Times* reader, Malcolm Tucker, to observe: 'Ah, to be lectured by a Scot on the costs associated with parliamentary buildings. The SNP continues to hammer the nails into the coffin of satire'.[121]

The futuristic Scottish Parliament building, originally due to cost £40 million, ended up costing ten times that amount. One of Margo MacDonald's greatest contributions as a parliamentarian was to leak the classified report in 2004 which catalogued how its construction had been mismanaged particularly by senior civil-servants. She was at Holyrood from the Scottish parliament's inception in 1999 until her death in April 2014. Her readiness to articulate the concerns of ordinary voters and also champion unpopular causes, ensured that she was re-elected three times as an independent after the hierarchy of her party tried to silence her by giving her a low ranking on the party's list. It's unlikely that she would regard her job as 'bizarre', Mhairi Black's own description of her parliamentary job.

MacDonald also got on well with political opponents if she was convinced they were people of principle. She admired the arch-Labour Unionist Tam Dalyell because he resembled her husband (and political soulmate) Jim Sillars in one key respect: 'I only know he's one of the most honest men I've ever met. He has a quality that is absolutely priceless in a politician – he doesn't care what people say or think about him'.[122] He returned the compliment by voting for her in 2011.

She even confessed in an interview only published after her death, that she had 'a lot of time for Michael Forsyth', the archetypal Scottish Thatcherite politician.

When her interlocutor said: 'That's a pretty odd choice', she replied: 'Well, I admire him for sticking to his guns. We need ideologues like him. Without them, the benevolent compromisers wouldn't have touchstones, would they?'[123]

The most fulfilling part of MacDonald's political career was probably as a non-aligned politician at Holyrood, still committed to full Scottish independence and able to articulate the goal often more eloquently than colleagues on the SNP benches. Her reputation for shrewd and effective interventions on a wide range of policy matters made her one of the most listened to MSPs even after she became physically incapacitated by a virulent form of Parkinson's disease. She earned respect from colleagues even though, in more than one intervention at Holyrood, she made plain her scepticism about the degree of talent, vision and energy in political ranks necessary to alter the country's fortunes. Belonging firmly on the left she did not automatically assume that the source of Scotland's ills was external nor offer simplistic remedies for banishing them. Fiercely critical at times of many of the practices of modern capitalism especially in the corporate sphere, she was careful not to brand private enterprise in general as an enemy of Scottish progress. On 25 April 2014, her memorial service took place in Edinburgh and was broadcast live on BBC Radio Scotland. It drew people from across the Scottish political spectrum and, indeed, it may have been the last occasion when an already badly-divided country displayed significant common ground about any political matter.

Mhairi Black took a tartan scarf belonging to Margo MacDonald with her to Westminster and regards her as a heroine. But in her maiden speech it was William Wallace and Tony Benn whom she singled out as exemplars. At first glance they might not seem to have very much in common, but the Renfrewshire laird of Norman origin and the upper middle-class British socialist are not that far apart. They were bold, egotistical and stubborn characters able to sway lesser folk around them. But they do not quite fit the image of liberators 700 years apart. The male tenants on Wallace's estate had little alternative but to go and fight for him whether or not they believed in the practicality of his cause. Benn firmly believed in equality and the need for the wealthy to release large parts of what they owned for the greater good of society. But he ensured that very little of the estate worth £5m that he left to his children upon his death in 2011 went to the state. He left nothing to charity, not even to the Labour Party, the only organization which he worked for upon completing military service.[124]

There are individuals whose example Mhairi Black might hopefully draw upon in future speeches who arguably made a greater contribution to the well-being of humankind. Three who are Scots spring to mind but are rarely if ever mentioned by leading nationalists in public. They are the scientist John Boyd Orr (1880-1971), awarded a Nobel Prize in 1949. Regrettably, his pioneering work on nutrition appears to have been forgotten in some working-class areas of Scotland where poor diet contributes to premature death and where young mothers sometimes start families lacking the domestic skills that can contribute to a well-run household. But a long time may elapse before any SNP figures call on Scots to revive these skills. It is perhaps simply content that many cast aside their apathy to vote so that in a seat like Mhairi Black's the turnout leapt from 65.36 per cent in 2010 to 75.4 per cent in 2015.

A figure the SNP has always been remarkably silent about is the industrialist and philanthropist Andrew Carnegie (1836-1919). In some eyes, his career was blighted by the ruthless way he confronted strikers in his steel plant. But he spent a large part of his life divesting himself of a vast fortune to promote educational and humanitarian endeavours across the world. He opposed British imperialism and America acquiring colonies and he strove in vain to avoid the eruption of the First World War through years of campaigning for peace and disarmament. If Scotland ever becomes independent, it is highly unlikely that any political leader will ever contribute as much to human progress and the overall standing of Scots in the world as Carnegie did. He believed strongly in British-American cooperation which may account for his neglect: his Scottish residence, Skibo Castle, overlooking the Dornoch Firth, 'flew the imaginary flag of his projected racial union, the stars and stripes and the Union flag sewn together'.[125]

The SNP's two First Ministers have both made high-profile visits to China but neither Salmond nor Sturgeon seem ever to have referred to the Scotsman who helped transform the face of Hong Kong as its governor from 1970 to 1982. Murray Maclehose (1917-2000) (later knighted and appointed a life peer) presided over changes every bit as transformative as those associated with the 1945-51 British Labour government. During his governorship from 1971 to 1982, the colony acquired modern housing, health and educational systems that made it a beacon of efficiency for much of East Asia. Major engineering projects, in which Scots often played a prominent role, equipped the territory with a transport system that was the envy of much of the world. Corruption was uprooted and he skilfully prepared the way for

Hong Kong's return to Chinese sovereignty while still enjoying major autonomy. Hong Kong was invigorated and it became the first part of the Chinese world to experience significant levels of democracy.[126] The Beijing authorities were reluctant to sweep away the achievements that substantially occurred in the Maclehose years, but he is barely known in Scotland to which he returned upon retiring from public life and (as mentioned) completely overlooked by the SNP.

The SNP's leaders on their China trips are likely never to have referred publicly to the contribution of several generations of Scottish missionaries to health care and educational work in the country. It might be felt to discomfit their hosts in the ruling Chinese Communist Party. Yet the seeds of this endeavour can be found in the remarkable revival of Christianity in 21st century China just as it is fading in Scotland. It is hardly remarkable that Margo MacDonald died a professed Christian even though a tenacious advocate of assisted dying. Her mother gave her a grounding in Christian ethics so that she could say: 'I'm not a church attender, but I am a Christian. I believe in Christ the saviour, I believe in God, I believe in the teachings of Christ.'[127]

By contrast, it is hardly surprising to learn that despite her mother having a background in Catholic good works, Mhairi Black is an atheist. For many nationalists who have an evangelical faith in their ability to transform the status of a territory and the condition of its people, there may simply not be enough room left for another one.

Business

It was a businessman, William Wolfe, who led the SNP from 1969 to 1979, the time of its first real breakthrough. He was an accountant in a family manufacturing business in West Lothian. This was a time when the voluntary sector still absorbed the social energies of numerous Scots; being county head of the scouting movement was just one of the responsibilities of this energetic and idealistic pillar of local civil society. Business figures used to be prominent in local politics, especially in a city like Edinburgh which the Labour party only acquired municipal control of in the 1980s. But they have retreated from the political scene. Jim Mather, minister for enterprise in the 2007-11 government at Holyrood had a background in computing and, through his online blog talked up the SNP's supposedly innovative approach to economics. But, by the time of Wolfe's death in 2009, the vigour had largely gone from Scottish civil society and it was rare to spot a troupe of scouts or guides in Scotland. There was nobody in the SNP to champion 'the small is beautiful concept' for organizing society. The party's own George Kerevan (MP for East Lothian from 2015) had candidly admitted several years before that the SNP had become addicted to the centralisation of power; he wrote:

'We now have a single police force and single fire service for Scotland. The SNP government has set its face against charter schools or decentralisation (as opposed to marketisation) of the NHS. Michael Russell has ordered the wholesale merger of further education colleges and mandated social composition of university places. John Swinney has nationalised adjudication of major planning applications'.[128]

'This represents a dramatic rupture in SNP thinking', he wrote and he feared the outcome might be a form of 'bureaucratic conservatism, inhibiting all experiment and reform'. He seemed to guess that his call for ' the SNP collectively... to take stock of how it has governed the nation' was likely to fall on deaf ears at the impending 2013 conference of the party. A sign of how power had swung in Scotland away from people with economic wealth to those who enjoyed media capital in the world of online agitation was provided six months later. Bill Munro, the kind of successful entrepreneur who previously would have been seen as essential for an economically viable self-governing Scotland, found himself treated as a pariah overnight with no Scottish government figures coming to his defence. The founder, and main shareholder of Barrhead Travel, Scotland's biggest independent travel company, had written in February to 697 staff expressing his misgivings, on economic grounds, over independence. When the news leaked out, scores of online Nationalist backers took to the Internet to castigate Munro, many calling for his company to be boycotted.

By now, it was becoming obvious that the SNP desired a politically obedient business sector that would see itself as a cog in a largely state-driven economy. This was despite the party's awareness that in the Scottish business world, there was little appetite for a battery of controls and regulations which even the late Tony Benn might have hesitated about imposing.

But an organization called Business for Scotland did spring up which appeared to share the SNP's view of the state performing an intrusive and paternalistic role guiding the business sector. BfS was a campaigning vehicle designed to give the Independence case a veneer of business credibility. It positioned itself as politically neutral, but key luminaries had been SNP candidates and two made it to Westminster in 2015.

Kevin Hague, a businessman who has published appraisals of the SNP's approach to economic issues that were increasingly noticed in the media from 2014 onwards, researched the background of Business for Scotland members. He found a core of 30 affiliated members who could be described as 'business professionals'. 28 of them were 'people who have Small Company directorships; businesses with no declared turnover or employee figures. These are predominantly consultancies, property companies and service companies; there were another 6 members who had larger scale business experience'. But remarkably, he could identify nobody who was involved in cross-border trade, valued at £47.6 billion by the Scottish Government in 2012.[129]

BfS was absolutely miniscule compared to the Scottish wing of the Confederation of British Industry which encompassed a huge range of business activity. Yet its luminaries appeared constantly on the media, BBC Scotland in particular, often confidently expounding on issues ranging from the currency union to the ability of an independent Scotland to weather the slump in the oil price.[130] They used statistics which appeared euphemistic or out-of-date to their critics but ones about which they were rarely tackled by the BBC. The principal failing of the BBC during the referendum campaign, and for that matter other parts of the broadcast and print media, was not asking nationalists hard questions often enough about their proposals.

And the Future....is it John Swinney?

John Swinney has occupied the relatively undemanding role of minister of finance from 2007 onwards, perhaps the person with the longest tenure in such a post in any western democracy. This has been a time of financial shocks nearly everywhere but Scotland has enjoyed a block grant under the 1999 devolution settlement which means that the level of financial pain has been relatively slight. Swinney's previous financial experience was obtained working in a strategic capacity for an Edinburgh insurance firm in the mid-1990s. He graduated in politics from Edinburgh University and had already been in the SNP for 5 years when this occurred. He led the SNP when in his late thirties from 2000 to 2004, not a period many in the party care to dwell on since it was marked by factionalism and poor electoral results. Still only 51 he is already seen in the party as its main elder statesman, a dedicated nationalist but less ferocious in his instincts than some of his contemporaries.

Despite his low-key image, Swinney doesn't deserve to be forgotten. He could even go down in history as a path-breaker, an example of a new political class in the making. Swinney has been followed by dozens of others elected for the SNP for whom politics has been their life from university onwards. MPs and MSPs are emerging who have done nothing else but be campaign coordinators, media strategists for the party, and assistants to Holyrood members. An emblematic example of the committed party apparatchik is Derek Mackay, the current minister of transport. His biography on Wikipedia mentions that he joined the SNP aged 16 and dropped out of university to concentrate on local politics, becoming an elected councillor at just 21 years old. Upon being elected to Holyrood in 2011, he quickly became business convenor, forcefully using the SNP's overall majority to consolidate the party's grip on parliament, but he soon moved on to be minister of local government before assuming his present job in 2014 aged only 37.[131]

Another meteoric rise which made headlines because of the manner in which it was accomplished, belongs to Toni Giugliano. He was selected as the SNP's candidate for Edinburgh West in August 2015. In the ballot, he defeated the sitting SNP member Colin Keir, a former Edinburgh municipal councillor for whom he had acted as parliamentary assistant. A university graduate in politics and French, he had played a prominent role in the Yes campaign and also worked as a liaison figure between the central SNP machine and the SNP group on Edinburgh council.[132]

It is hard not to draw comparisons with the Labour Party where many people rose quickly without any experience of a job, career or voluntary activity which could bring them into contact with large numbers of ordinary people. Their rise was slightly different from the young political operators of the SNP, left-leaning quangos and politicised NGOs were likelier to be stepping stones to being an MP than media roles. Nevertheless, the SNP has turned into a party dominated increasingly by individuals whose background and full-time career is politics and nothing else. They are likelier to enjoy a much longer track-record of success because Scotland lacks the alternative spheres of influence to be found in the rest of the UK in academia, the media and business. The SNP makes no secret of its intention to tighten its grip on academia by appointing people to influence the governance of universities.[133] The party enjoys much greater control over the civil service in Scotland than the rival parties in the rest of the UK do there. A political class is fast emerging in Scotland untrammelled by any of the checks and balances to be found in most other Western democracies. The referendum showed that the civil service is amenable to act as an informal campaign agency for the SNP. There is no revising chamber in the Scottish Parliament to check the often highly conformist SNP majority.

It may be going too far to suggest that the democratic process is on the verge of being captured by a cohesive group which is unembarrassed about having a monolithic grip on power. In other Western democracies that have evolved into being dominant party systems, the outcome has sometimes been laws that grant a permanent rent from state funds for members of the political class and ancillary groups. There is no evidence that any of the individuals mentioned in this section have been linked with such developments. But New Labour managed to establish much greater access to state patronage than its predecessors in office had done and it politicised hitherto neutral semi-state and civic bodies from charities to quangos. This happened when it enjoyed only a fraction of the power that the SNP currently enjoys in Scotland. So the omens for Scotland, the competitive nature of its politics, the quality of its public services, and ultimately even for the SNP itself, are not particularly bright when there are so few restrictions on the powers of the political class. Societies have rarely become more prosperous, more free, or more efficiently governed under the supervision of such a directory of highly-motivated but sometimes also highly fallible people.

Notes for Chapter 5

1. David Torrance, *Nicola Sturgeon: A Political Life*, Edinburgh: Birlinn, 2015, p.p. 144-5.

2. Nick Cohen, 'What Scottish professors have to fear from Nicola Sturgeon's power grab', *Spectator,* 17 October 2015.

3. Severin Carrell, 'Scottish universities warn over new measures by Sturgeon government', *Guardian,* 10 September 2015.

4. Cohen, 'What Scottish professors'.

5. Simon Johnson, 'Alex Salmond defies Nicola Sturgeon's attempts to sideline him', *Daily Telegraph,* 29 March 2015.

6. Simon Johnson, 'Nicola Sturgeon: I will lead Labour talks while Alex Salmond does "day-to-day" work', *Daily Telegraph,* 28 March 2015, http://www.telegraph.co.uk/news/politics/SNP/11501429/Nicola-Sturgeon-I-will-lead-Labour-talks-while-Alex-Salmond-does-day-to-day-work.html#disqus_thread

7. Johnson, 'Nicola Sturgeon: I will lead'.

8. Johnson, 'Alex Salmond defies'.

9. Johnson, 'Nicola Sturgeon: I will lead'.

10. Pat Kane on Twitter, 23 March 2015 (accessed 23 March 2015).

11. Luke Akehurst, 'We don't need leaked memos to understand what Sturgeon wants'. *Labour List,* 7 April 2015, http://labourlist.org/2015/04/we-dont-need-leaked-memos-to-understand-what-sturgeon-wants

12. Bruce Anderson, 'Never has Scotland been quite this deluded', *Sunday Telegraph,* 6 April 2015. http://www.telegraph.co.uk/news/uknews/scotland/11515597/Never-before-has-Scotland-been-quite-this-deluded.html#disqus_thread

13. Chris Deerin, 'Nicola Sturgeon holds all the aces in the general election', *Daily Mail,* 3 April 2015.

14. Simon Hattenstone, 'Nicola Sturgeon: 'I just want to shake things up a wee bit', *Guardian,* 2 May 2015.

15. Magnus Linklater, 'I wonder if the scars in this country will ever be healed', *Times,* 2 May 2015

16. Janet Daley, 'A Labour-SNP pact would be an outrage to democracy', *Sunday Telegraph,* 25 April 2015.

17. Hattenstone, 'Nicola Sturgeon'.

18. Dan Hodges, 'What does the SNP surge look like up close?', *Daily Telegraph,* 5 May 2015.

19. Lily of St. Leonards, 'We no longer even share truth in Scotland', http://effiedeans.blogspot.co.uk/, 25 April 2015.

20. Private information.

21. 'Poll shows Sturgeon most popular leader across UK', SNP 25 March 2013.
22. http://www.scotsman.com/news/politics/top-stories/nicola-sturgeon-tops-politician-trust-rating-poll-1-3562244
23. Joyce McMillan, 'Perils of playing Westminster game', *Scotsman,* 12 February 2015.
24. Tom Peterkin, 'Ex-SNP leader calls for break up of Police Scotland', *Scotsman,* 20 August 2015.
25. Police sorry over fatal car crash and admit officer failed to log call', *STV,* 10 July 2015, http://news.stv.tv/scotland/1324484-sir-stephen-house-admits-police-scotland-mistakes-in-m9-crash-delay/
26. http://www.theguardian.com/media/greenslade/2015/aug/04/political-row-in-scotland-over-police-snooping-on-journalist
27. John McDermott, 'A veneer of competence', *Prospect,* July 2015.
28. Kevin McKenna , 'Does the SNP have a cure for our health crisis'? *Observer,* 19 July 2015.
29. Matt Chorley, *Daily Mail,* 20 May 2015,</news/article-3089297/Minister-gobbledegook-SNP-minister-ridiculed-jargon-guff-press-release-improving-standards-English.html#comments>
30. Editorial, 'Must try harder', *Times,* 19 August 2015.
31. http://www.scottishconservatives.com/2015/08/report-shows-scotland-by-far-the-worst-in-uk-at-getting-poorest-pupils-to-university/.
32. Editorial, 'The SNP's incompetence as a party of government', *Financial Times,* 1 September 2015.
33. http://www.thecourier.co.uk/news/local/dundee/skills-failings-could-mean-locals-miss-out-on-dundee-waterfront-jobs-1.895519
34. Simon Johnson,'Gulf between schools in rich and poor Scotland revealed', *Daily Telegraph,* 5 November 2014. http://www.telegraph.co.uk/news/politics/11209035/Gulf-between-schools-in-rich-and-poor-Scotland-revealed.html
35. 'Expert attacks futile SNP law to improve state schools', *Daily Telegraph,* 25 March 2015, http://www.telegraph.co.uk/news/uknews/scotland/11493090/Expert-attacks-futile-SNP-law-to-improve-state-schools.html#disqus_thread
36. Private information.
37. McDermott, 'A veneer of competence'.
38. Carole Ford, 'What is the SNP doing to Scottish education'? *Scotland in Union,* 6 August 2015, http://www.scotlandinunion.co.uk/what_is_the_snp_doing_to_scottish_education
39. Daniel Jackson, 'The Stalinist logic behind the SNP's approach to education', *Spectator,* 28 May 2015, http://blogs.spectator.co.uk/coffeehouse/2015/05/the-stalinist-logic-behind-the-snps-approach-to-education/#disqus_thread

40. Magnus Gardham, *Herald,* 10 August 2015
41. David Clegg, 'SNP accounting blunder loses £45million for Scotland's poorest as European Commission refuses to pay out', *Daily Record,* 22 August 2015.
42. Brian Wilson, 'It is time SNP called online tormentors to account', *Scotsman,* 11 June 2015
43. Guy Adams, 'Hounded by SNP hate mobs', *Daily Mail,* 6 June 2015, news/article-3112992/ Hounded-SNP-hate-mob-weeks-lonely-death-Charles-Kennedy-endured-vile-campaign-bullying-abuse-separatist-fanatics-deeply-wounded-vulnerable-man.html#comments>
44. Adams, 'Hounded by SNP'.
45. Nicola Sturgeon, 'Let us all aim for higher', *Daily Mail,* 25 June 2015.
46. David Taylor, 'Watch as angry protesters chase Scotland's only Tory MP out of town after he turned up to open a FOOD BANK', *Daily Record,* 24 July 2015, http://www.dailyrecord.co.uk/news/politics/watch-angry-protesters-chase-scot-lands-6130021
47. http://www.scotsman.com/news/politics/top-stories/chinese-snp-councillor-quits-amid-racism-claims-1-3852813
48. Jamie Ross on Twitter, 11 August 2015 (accessed 11 August 2015).
49. http://www.dailymail.co.uk/femail/article-2795023/liz-jones-goodbye-death-row-hair-hello-super-sleek-soon-minister-nicola.html#ixzz3jWZrw0sq
50. http://www.theguardian.com/politics/2015/jun/09/jon-stewart-daily-show-nicola-stur-geon-snp-success
51. *Daily Telegraph,* 19 September 2015.
52. Simon Johnson, 'Nicola Sturgeon warns SNP – no second referendum soon', *Daily Telegraph,* 18 September 2015
53. Tom Peterkin, 'SNP has 'no early independence referendum plans', *Scotland on Sunday,* 20 September 2015.
54. Alex Perry, 'Behind the scenes with Alex Salmond, the man who would break up the United Kingdom', *Newsweek,* 1 May 2015.
55. Jack Sommers, 'Scottish Independence Vote Was NOT Swayed By Elderly People, Despite Conspiracy Theories', Huffington Post, 24 September 2015, http://www.huffing-tonpost.co.uk/2014/09/24/scottish-independence-vote-elderly-young_n_5872036.html
56. Alex Salmond, *The Dream Shall Never Die,* London: William Collins, 2015.
57. Perry, 'Behind the scenes'.
58. Hugo Rifkind and Kenny Farquharson, 'Braveheart battle cry is now but a whisper', *Times,* 24 July 2005.
59. Quoted in Colin McArthur, Braveheart, *Brigadoon and Scotland,* London: IB Tauris, 2003, p. 18.
60. Derek Bateman, 'Hail The Sun God', 29 March 2015, http://derekbateman.co.uk/2015/03/29/hail-the-sun-god/aten/>

61. Alan Cochrane, 'Scotland's escape from the man who thinks he could have saved RBS', *Daily Telegraph,* 17 November 2014; Simon Johnson, 'Alex Salmond: I could have saved RBS from meltdown', *Daily Telegraph,* 17 November 2014.

62. Simon Johnson 'Alex Salmond warns independence fight 'not over' as he steps down as SNP leader', *Daily Telegraph* 14 November 2014.

63. Letter to the Editor, *Herald,* 13 September 2015.

64. Tom Gallagher, 'The Scottish Piazza Echoes to the Liberation Beat', *Harry's Place,* 26 September 2009, http://hurryupharry.org/2009/09/26/the-scottish-piazza-echoes-to-the-liberation-beat/

65. Perry, 'Behind the scenes'.

66. Editorial, 'Alex Salmond's stance will drag Scotland down', *Daily Telegraph,* 11 September 2014.

67. Gerald Warner, 'How Alex Salmond manipulated the Unionists into destroying the Union', *CapX,* 21 March 2015.

68. Simon Johnson 'Alex Salmond links referendum with father's Churchill dislike', *Daily Telegraph,* 11 August 2014.

69. Perry, 'Behind the scenes'.

70. Daniel Sanderson, 'Alex Salmond wades into debate row', *Herald,* 11 March 2015, http://www.heraldscotland.com/news/13205280.Alex_Salmond_wades_into_debate_row___like_most_posh_boys__David_Cameron_will_run_away_from_a_fight_/

71. Fraser Nelson, 'If Alex Salmond thinks posh boys are cowards, he should visit Eton's war memorial'. *Spectator,* 12 March 2015, http://blogs.spectator.co.uk/coffeehouse/2015/03/if-alex-salmond-thinks-posh-boys-are-cowards-he-should-visit-etons-war-memorial/

72. Salmond, *Dream,* p. 2.

73. Mark McLaughlin, 'Scottish First Minister Alex Salmond calls Westminster MPs 'thieves' over North Sea oil and gas reserves', *Independent,* 24 February 2014, http://www.independent.co.uk/news/uk/politics/scottish-first-minister-alex-salmond-calls-westminster-mps-thieves-over-north-sea-oil-and-gas-reserves-9149680.html

74. 'Senior politicians and business leaders pay tribute to Alex Salmond after he announces resignation', *Daily Record,* 19 September 2014, http://www.dailyrecord.co.uk/news/scottish-news/senior-politicians-business-leaders-pay-4289896

75. Jason Cowley, 'Alex Salmond: I would bring down any Tory minority government', *New Statesman,* 24 March 2015, Jason Cowley =http://www.newstatesman.com/politics/2015/03/alex-salmond-i-would-bring-down-any-tory-minority-government

76. Nick Robinson, 'The BBC must resist Alex Salmond's attempt to control its coverage', *Guardian,* 24 August 2015.

77. Severin Carrell, 'Alex Salmond backs protests against 'bias' shown by BBC's Nick Robinson', *Guardian,* 15 September 2014, *http://www.theguardian.com/politics/2014/*

sep/15/alex-salmond-bbc-protest-nick-robinson
78. 'Nick Robinson condemns Putin-like protests against referendum coverage', *Press Association,* 21 August 2015.
79. Dave Lord, 'Exclusive: "Insulting, Embarrassing and Shameful"', the *Courier,* 23 August 2015.
    http://www.thecourier.co.uk/news/politics/exclusive-insulting-embarrassing-and-shameful-alex-salmond-lashes-out-over-bbc-coverage-of-the-independence-referendum-1.896091
80. http://www.telegraph.co.uk/news/uknews/scottish-independence/11056540/BBC-criticised-over-handling-of-Scottish-independence-debate-between-Salmond-and-Darling.html#disqus_thread
81. *If Scotland became independent what would be your preference for public broadcasting (currently the BBC) in Scotland?* Economic and Social Research Council, no date or place of publication, http://whatscotlandthinks.org/questions/if-scotland-became-independent-what-would-be-your-preference-for-public-broadc-3
82. Kevin Hague, 'BBC Bias and the Referendum Campaign', 30 November 2014, http://chokkablog.blogspot.co.uk/2014/11/bbc-bias-and-independence-referendum.html
83. See Wee Ginger Dug (Paul Cavanagh), 'The Nick Robinson Show', 21 August 2015, https://weegingerdug.wordpress.com/2015/08/21/the-nick-robinson-show/
84. Derek Bateman, 'Britain's Pravda', *Derek Bateman Blog,* 28 April 2014, http://derekbateman.co.uk/2014/04/28/britains-pravda/
85. http://www.telegraph.co.uk/news/uknews/scottish-independence/11058007/Alex-Salmond-criticises-leading-political-journalist-during-heated-interview.html
86. Alan Cochrane, 'Alex Salmond: Meet the bully behind the mask', *Daily Telegraph,* 3 September 2014.
87. William Turvill, 20 September 201, 4 http://www.pressgazette.co.uk/telegraph-mail-and-express-journalists-barred-alex-salmonds-resignation-press-conference
88. Iain Martin, 'Alex Salmond was a giant of his age', *Daily Telegraph,* 19 September 2014, http://blogs.telegraph.co.uk/news/iainmartin1/100287066/alex-salmond-was-a-giant-of-his-age/#disqus_thread>
89. Euan McColm, 'Salmond both a formidable asset and the greatest challenge to Yes cause', *Scotland on Sunday,* 28 October 2012.
90. James Maxwell, 'The SNP's corporation-tax folly', *New Statesman,* 26 June 2014.
91. Joyce McMillan, 'When fair play is posted missing', *Scotsman,* 2 May 2014.
92. Gerry Hassan, 'Note to Salmond', *Scotsman,* 13 October 2012.
93. Martin Robertson, 'Get tae, Rupert! Murdoch stokes fury', *Daily Mail,* 10 September 2014, http://www.dailymail.co.uk/news/article-2750835/Get-tae-Rupert-Murdoch-stokes-fury-dropping-biggest-hint-maybe-papers-battle-Scottish-Yes-vote-citing-Scottish- ancestors-reason-meddle.html#ixzz3Up9V9B7b>:

94. *Times,* (Scottish edition), 25 June 2010.

95. David Clegg, 'Independence Poll: Our bombshell survey shows one in three Scots will vote No due to dislike of Alex Salmond', *Daily Record,* 15 May 2014.

96. Magnus Linklater, 'Look who's coming to dinner: Salmond won't be pleased'. *Times,* 25 August 2015.

97. Alex Salmond on twitter, 18 September 2015, accessed 19 September 2015.

98. Michael Gray (Gray in Glasgow) on Twitter, 19 September 2015 accessed 21 September 2015.

99. Peterkin, 'SNP has 'no early independence'.

100. BBC News, 20 August 2015.

101. Winnie Ewing, *Stop the World: the Autobiography of Winnie Ewing,* Edinburgh: Birlinn, 2004, p.p. 95-96, 156.

102. Siol nan Gaidheal, 'History of our Movement', http://www.siol-nan-gaidheal.org/hstoom.htm (accessed 27 August 2015).

103. Gordon Wilson, *the SNP, The Turbulent Years 1960-1990,* Stirling: Scots Independent, 2014, p. 205.

104. Gerry Hassan, *The Modern SNP: From Protest to Power,* Edinburgh: Edinburgh University Press, 2009, p. 172.

105. Wilson, *The SNP, The Turbulent Years,* p.p. 88-90.

106. Tom Peterkin, 'Ex-SNP leader calls for break up of Police Scotland', *Scotsman,* 20 August 2015.

107. The above information was obtained from the article by Paul Hutcheon, 'Former Salmond adviser faces fresh claims over T in the Park role', *Herald,* 13 August 2015.

108. Brian Taylor, *The Scottish Parliament: the Road to Devolution,* Edinburgh: Polygon, 1999, p. 166.

109. 'Philippa Whitford', *Wikipedia,* https://en.wikipedia.org/wiki/Philippa_Whitford, accessed 28 August 2015.

110. Lynsey Bews, 'Scottish independence: NHS claim "codswallop"', *Scotsman,* 26 August 2014.

111. 'The NHS and Scottish Independence', Scottish Research Society, 8 September 2014, http://scottishresearchsociety.com/nhs-scottish-independence; 'Scottish independence: Healthcare staff form NHS for Yes', *BBC news,* 24 May 2014.

112. 'Health inequality is Scotland's biggest issue, chief medical officer warns', BBC News, 19 December 2012, http://www.bbc.co.uk/news/uk-scotland-scotland-politics-20783744

113. Helen Puttick, 'Leading clinician: some of my colleagues are lying about NHS's future in Indy debate', *Herald,* 21 August 2014.

114. 'Mhairi Black's maiden speech tops 10m online views', *BBC News,* 19 July 2015, http://www.bbc.co.uk/news/uk-scotland-scotland-politics-33585087

115. 'Lunch with the FT: Mhairi Black', *Financial Times,* 31 July 2015,
    http://www.ft.com/cms/s/2/9af5a680-2fb4-11e5-8873-775ba7c2ea3d.html

116. http://www.capx.co/jeremy-paxman-gets-mhairi-blacks-paisley-dead-wrong/

117. Kenneth Roy, 'The strange background of Margo MacDonald', *Scottish Review,*
    9 April 2014.

118. La Pasionaria, the pseudonym, of the internationally famous Spanish Communist
    politician, Dolores Ibarruri (1895-1989).

119. Peter Geoghegan, 'The People's Election: Part 8, Paisley and Renfrewshire South',
    7 May 2015, http://www.petergeoghegan.com/2015/05/07/the-peoples-election-part-8-
    paisley-and-renfrewshire-south/

120. Janice Turner, 'some of these Westminster traditions are ridiculous', *Times,* 25 July 2015.

121. Online letter, 'Lunch with the FT: Mhairi Black'.

122. Roy, 'The strange background'.

123. Roy, 'The strange background'

124. Richard Dyson, 'Tony Benn's inheritance tax dodge: how it works (and how you can
    use it too)', *Daily Telegraph,* 27 October 2014.

125. Colin Kidd, 'Race, Empire and the Limits of 19th century Scottish Nationhood',
    Historical Journal, Vol. 46, No 4, 2003, p. 889.

126. Roger Buckley, *Hong Kong: the Road to 1997,* Cambridge: Cambridge University
    Press, 1997), p.p, 84-103.

127. Roy, 'The strange background'.

128. George Kerevan, 'Small no longer beautiful for the SNP', *Scotsman,* 17 October 2013.

129. Kevin Hague, 'Who Do "Business for Scotland" Represent?' *Chokkablog,* 17 June 2014,
    http://chokkablog.blogspot.co.uk/2014/06/who-do-business-for-scotland-represent.html

130. Kevin Hague, 'Business for Scotland and the SNP', Chokkablog,30 December 2014.
    http://chokkablog.blogspot.co.uk/2014/12/business-for-scotland-and-snp.html
    Anonymous said...

131. *https://en.wikipedia.org/wiki/Derek_Mackay,* accessed 30 August 2015.

132. See 'Second SNP MSP ditched by own supporters ahead of Holyrood election',
    STV News, 14 August 2015; also 'Toni Giugliano', Wikipedia,
    https://en.wikipedia.org/wiki/Toni_Giugliano, accessed 30 August 2015

133. Cohen, 'What Scottish professors'.

CHAPTER 6: THE CULTURAL WORLD AND NATIONALISM
Scotland Becomes Central For Creatives

Exactly a year after the 2014 referendum, the National Library of Scotland hosted a 1-day event on culture and what had been (by most reckonings) a phenomenal occurrence in Scottish politics. Efforts were made by the organizers, two postgraduate students of literature, to ensure balance and representation. But nearly all the 12 speakers were backers of independence. It was also launched with introductions from three prominent supporters of Scottish independence linked to the arts, Professor Robert Crawford, a distinguished academic and prolific literary historian and poet, the author Scott Hames, and the minister of culture herself Fiona Hyslop.

In a blog accompanying the event, the no-show by those from the arts, literature and music fields not part of the Indy wave was discussed.[1] The point was made that it may confirm the impression that 'there appear to be more supporters of Scottish independence in the arts community than supporters of the Union'. Individuals from a liberal arts background were certainly at times very vocal and engaged. But they were largely engaging in a political act rather than opening up a new front for cultural experimentation. In many cases, probably little time was available for pursuing the cultural work that Indy intellectuals had previously been involved in.

The part of the conference which I attended did not suggest that any major new and overtly Scottish work had appeared in the shadow of the referendum (except perhaps for a new Irvine Welsh novel). Where there had been innovation had been in the realm of online communications. At least one blog had appeared, Wings over Scotland, the brainchild of the previously unknown (Reverend) Stuart Campbell which reached and kept a mass audience and had a consciousness-raising role. Its polemics in favour of Scottish independence perhaps made it online propaganda art of a high order. But it was also extremely aggressive and it contributed to shaping an atmosphere of intense partisanship. The jury has long been out on how conducive such a fevered atmosphere is for cultural endeavour. But intellectuals, artists and performers whose work did not imply, or lead to, engagement with Scottish independence felt very uncomfortable during this period. With few exceptions, they hung back due to lack of sympathy or apprehension. Creative figures from the arts uninspired by politics or at least nationalist politics may or, may not, be a minority of the total to be found in early 21st century Scotland. But the fact that not one would appear at a retrospective event on the arts and the referendum suggests that a sizeable cleavage now exists in the Scottish cultural world. It sets apart those who see identifying with the nationalist cause as perhaps a core part of their artistic being and others who find it hard to understand or approve of such a stance. So the intellectual world may be little different from post-referendum Scotland in general through having become a fractured landscape. This chapter argues that it is one where the risk is real that creativity will be sacrificed before political expediency and that nationalism may in fact succeed in shrivelling the cultural distinctiveness of Scotland.

Inevitably, in a rare period when Scottish politics has become a subject of mass interest, intellectuals who cultivate a political role enjoy not only visibility but influence in defining the broader cultural mood. The words of several of them suggest that they see themselves as guardians with a responsibility for uplifting the people, perhaps even revealing to them hitherto unimagined ways Scotland can be transformed. '[T]here is a terrible passivity...deeply ingrained in many folk...' complained the artist Alexander Moffat when in conversation with the poet Alan Riach in 2014.[2] Their book *Arts of Independence* published in 2014 makes it clear that the people deserve to be brought closer to the arts by an interventionist state.

Pat Kane, a veteran rock performer, who also doubles as a promoter of avant-garde ideas, also sees the cultural sphere as one of the keys for accomplishing a triumph of a progressive Scottish model that might even come to be deserving of world attention. He emphasises the potential that an online community of creative and technologically skilled people has of being this vanguard of liberation. Kane claimed in 2014 that Scotland was already the world's most highly-educated country but he lamented about: 'the existential self-wounding that a No vote would be. If the turnout is as high as predicted, a No vote will have been a spectacle of a national citizenry refusing to move to the next level of its development.
We will have held the power tools of nation-state sovereignty in our hands. And we will have decided to – quietly, quickly – put them back in their box.'[3]

The novelist Alan Warner also warned of the consequences if Scotland's voters turned their backs on recommendations from politically-active figures from the world of arts and letters by spurning independence. He claimed a Yes vote would 'free us as Scottish writers from a hidden war that rages inside our minds; it would grant us the light wings of a new responsibility'. A No vote, on the other hand, would have 'sinister and depressing implications': 'These would 'create a profound and strange schism between the voters of Scotland and its literature; a new convulsion.'[4]

Creativity minus a vanguard: Scotland 1707-2007

Writers acting as a cultural vanguard for a political cause or a creed have not been unusual in the modern age. From Poland to Peru many nationalist movements would receive that vital spark from intellectual endeavour which enshrined and popularised the national idea. But until near our own time, Scotland had not witnessed such an overt literary mobilisation in favour of a political cause. This political disengagement was not necessarily due to intellectual backwardness or state restrictions on the dissemination of new ideas. Far from it. In 1789, at the dawn of the age of European nationalism, Scotland had, for a century, already been the most literate society in Europe. It had double the number of universities England possessed and the curriculum was much broader than that of Oxford and Cambridge. In the middle of the 18th century, a country with a population of just over one-and-a-quarter million, had spawned an intellectual culture whose relevance to the modern world still ensures its influence in the realm of ideas three centuries later.

The Scottish Enlightenment was crucial in shaping or revitalising academic disciplines, from anthropology, ethnography, sociology and psychology to history and economics, enabling the modern world to be understood and its energies harnessed for constructive purposes. Thinkers like Adam Smith, David Hume, Adam Ferguson, Lord Kames and Francis Hutcheson were forward-looking individuals who believed in gradual progress, leading to the cumulative ascent of man. They could be contrasted with the thinkers of the French Enlightenment, the most influential of whom were drawn to utopian blueprints for re-organizing society. Edinburgh's pioneers of political economy and representative government were generally pragmatic figures. They believed in moderate, incremental change rather than sudden ruptures hopefully preceding an age of virtue.[5]

Britain and its growing empire provided an outlet for these intellectual pragmatists and the successive generations reared on their ideas. Scotland's 18th century thinkers were united in the belief that the broadening of the mind and spirit through education was vital for creating a responsible population who could make wise decisions in their own lives and strengthen the civic character of society. Adam Smith, whose fame has been most enduring, perhaps due to his book *The Wealth of Nations,* worried that industrialisation might dash such hopes. He feared the growth of an army of wage slaves, alienated and subject to 'mental mutilation' who could be a disruptive force in the future.[6]

It wasn't industrialising Britain with its limited democracy and constitutional monarchy that spawned revolution but autocratic France. The experiment in republican rule, one that acquired its legitimacy from the doctrine of equality, collapsed into terror and a fresh bout of French imperialism within less than a decade after 1789. Nearly all of the British intellectuals who had seen the dramatic French events as marking the birth of progress were repelled by the grisly turn of events. The preservation of morality, laws and traditions which had grown up over long centuries came to be seen as essential for the maintenance of civilized human conduct. There were few if any Scottish intellectuals ready to promote the doctrine of nationalism, increasingly fashionable in continental Europe and the Americas. Scotland, having renounced its independence for a compact with England a century before, appeared to be flourishing through the economic and professional opportunities that had resulted. Freedom fighters struggling against continental overlordship were welcomed by the 19th century Scottish liberal middle-classes. But few of its members believed they were groaning under any English yoke.

Sir Walter Scott was by far the most prominent writer to have emerged during this long era of Scottish improvement and rising expectations. He combined an overt commitment for orderly change with a nostalgia for the vanishing age of epic struggles over religion, land and territorial allegiance. The blending of the modern with the heroic past was the sub-plot for a string of best-selling novels which turned him into a literary giant translated into innumerable languages.

Following his death in 1832, literature failed to influence the story of Scotland for at least a century. The country was absorbed with economic issues and how to produce some fitful social progress from the often brutal reality of headlong industrialisation. A philistine business class failed to offer the patronage which would have enabled an architect and designer of the genius of Charles Rennie Mackintosh to flourish. The prospects of many people were blocked at home due to rank injustice and blinkered decision-making. Intellectuals might have occasionally expressed their unease and dissatisfaction. This was certainly happening in other countries with far steeper class boundaries and unjust practices than in Scotland. But emigration provided an outlet for economically unfulfilled Scots. Intellectuals were drawn to London where generations of Scottish journalists, and others with talent and skills in disseminating information and ideas from the knowledge industries, found an outlet for their energies over at least three centuries. Innovative or staid British culture, from the highbrow to the profane, was shaped and directed by many Scots drawn to London.

It was hardly surprising that a reaction to the British sway over Scottish life occurred in the aftermath of the First World War. Scotland had suffered enormous military casualties. The industries which had placed it in the first rank of global manufacturing began an inexorable decline which, by the end of the 20th century, left Scotland in some respects a post-industrial country. Scotland's unemployment rate was 28 percent by 1933 compared with 16 per cent in England and Wales.[7] There was huge anger and despair but it was not channelled in a nationalist direction.

Intellectuals were prominent, however, in the early stirrings of an overtly Scottish Nationalist movement in the 1920s. The poet Hugh MacDiarmid was undoubtedly the most energetic as well as the most controversial. According to a sympathetic study, the most important literary figure of twentieth century Scotland believed that the Scottish culture of his day was making the nation satisfied with its subordinate status within the UK. Such a fate was demeaning to the volatile poet which is why he strove for a self-reliant and independent European nation.[8] His poem *A Drunk Man Looks at the Thistle* revealed, according to MacDiarmid himself 'that a Scot could contribute to international literature by writing in Scots'.[9]

The first candidate standing on a clearcut Scottish National platform was another poet Lewis Spence. He contested Midlothian and Peebles in 1929, obtaining a derisory vote. John McCormick put it down to his appearance: 'he habitually wore spats and a bowler hat, distracting greatly from his literary reputation'.[10] Spence was better known as a pioneer in the field of writing which speculated about lost civilizations such as Atlantis and the mysteries of ancient Britain. Like his political cause, his literary field appeared exotic and irrelevant in a Scotland confronting steep economic adversity. But in today's far more imaginative and escapist age, interest in some of his numerous books has revived in tandem with the fortunes of his party. No less than seven of his books were re-issued in the first quarter of 2015 alone.

Sir Patrick Dollan, Scotland's most influential left-wing politician in the 1930s, described the nationalist movement NPS as 'a mutual admiration society for struggling poets and novelists, of no use to the working-class'.[11] The sharp-eyed poet Edwin Muir may have disapproved of the qualified socialism of this Clydeside machine politician. But he failed to detect any coherent nationalist programme that could improve the distressed and downbeat condition of inter-war Scotland. Nor did the radical educationalist A.S. Neill (born and raised in Forfar). He wrote in 1934: 'Home Rule would [not] make a scrap of difference to Scotland; the rulers (finance, monopoly capital, vested interests etc) would simply make Edinburgh their headquarters instead of Westminster. In political matters, Scotland is a nowhere. It accepts British rule with due servility...'.[12]

In his 1938 book *Scott And Scotland: the Predicament of the Scottish Writer,* Muir deeply angered MacDiarmid by contending that the Scots language was incapable of expressing modern consciousness. He stated that MacDiarmid had left 'Scottish verse very much where it was before. MacDiarmid took this as a personal slight and 'bitter public debates regarding the appropriate linguistic medium for Scottish writers ensued'.[13]

CHAPTER 6: THE CULTURAL WORLD AND NATIONALISM

Nevertheless, Scottish letters were in better health than they had been for several generations. But London, not Edinburgh nor Glasgow, remained the urban platform which provided Scottish novelists, poets and playwrights with publishers, audiences and earnings. Arthur Conan Doyle was one of the most successful novelists of the 1920s in terms of sales; in the 1930s, J.M.Barrie's plays dominated the London stage, John Buchan's novels sold well and were favourably reviewed. These were authors who did not revert to being English writers. They gravitated towards the metropolis of the British world where they had the patronage and opportunities often denied to them in Scotland. In the words of Edwin Muir: 'we are neither quite Scottish…nor are we quite delivered from our Scottishness'.[14]

Scottish commitment to the British war effort between 1939 and 1945 was impressive. But there was intellectual dissent as shown by Hugh MacDiarmid's poem, 'On the Imminent destruction of London, June 1940':

'Now when London is threatened
With devastation from the air
I realise. Horror atrophying me,
That I hardly care. [...]
For London is the centre of all reaction.
To progress and prosperity in human existence
Set against all that is good in the spirit of man,
As Earth's greatest stumbling block and rock of offence'.[15]

In several letters, Douglas Young, the poet and classicist, offered the impression that the rise of Nazism, rather than being an elemental danger to civilization as a whole, offered an opportunity for patriotic Scots to release the grip of 'the London imperialist Boss Class'. A leaflet with such views, stating that it was 'high time for another Bannockburn', was released in 1943 by which time he was a senior figure in the SNP. Young and others in the party, without being fascist in sympathy, were unimpressed by the need to put aside peacetime objectives and back the fight against Hitler's movement. He was questioned by the police for his anti-war activities and Arthur Donaldson, leader of the SNP in the 1960s, spent six weeks in prison in 1941 for his anti-war activities.[16]

British politics settled down into an era of consensus after 1945. Periods of near full employment, a relatively smooth process of decolonisation and the creation of the welfare state maintained the legitimacy of the British state. Class conflict diminished and economic and social progress arguably contained whatever discontent there was with the Union in wider society. It was a quiescent period for the arts and genuine talents as well as heretics tended to be drawn towards England or else abroad. Scotland remained culturally placid even during the 1960s, a decade which gave rise to a counter-cultural movement challenging a range of established norms. But this occurred within a British context and the explosion of pop culture in which Scots bands fully participated had few nationalist connotations.

When Scottish Nationalism emerged from the electoral wilderness in the mid-1970s, it lacked a cultural dimension. Soon the narrowness and inexperience of the SNP upsurge enabled it to be easily contained and Scotland failed to obtain an elected assembly. An amendment to the devolution bill successfully introduced by the Scot George Cunningham, representing Islington at Westminster, required limited Home Rule to not only win a majority of the votes cast but forty per cent of those eligible to vote. According to the literary historian Robert Crawford, this ploy 'ignited literary resistance… not least through poems in Douglas Dunn's *St Kilda's parliament* (1981), Edwin Morgan's *Sonnets from Scotland* (1984) and the present writer's *A Scottish Assembly* (1990); in fiction landmark works included Alasdair Gray's *Lanark* (1981)… as well as the novels of James Kelman, then, later Irvine Walsh and others…'.[17]

Scotland endured 18 years of rule by the Conservatives, a party whose legitimacy slumped in a country where, as recently as 1955, it had acquired over 50 per cent of the votes. Its perceived anti-manufacturing bias and absorption with the priorities of the South East of England, led to political agitation against Tory policies like the poll tax and, more fitfully, in a campaign for home rule. The non-Tory parties were initially hesitant about using pro-autonomy nationalism as a means of challenging externally-imposed Conservative policies. The SNP never became reconciled with a Campaign for a Scottish Assembly even though its 1989 Constitutional convention declared that sovereignty belonged not to Westminster but to the Scottish people. Besides, its goal fell short of outright independence.

This was a movement in which the Labour party, local government and the trade-unions largely held sway. But civic Scotland, the churches, universities and various professional and local bodies were also active and may have been decisive in getting a renewed drive for home rule off the ground in the sombre atmosphere after the 1979 referendum defeat. This was a time when members of the cultural world were still largely absorbed in their own artistic pursuits. But it was a rising novelist, William McIlvanney who at particular moments provided an eloquent indictment of unwieldy long-distance-rule and the need for a better Scottish alternative. He remained free of party attachments but gave a lecture to the 1987 SNP conference, entitled 'Stands Scotland Where it Did' in which he delivered a searing indictment of the impact of Thatcherism on Scotland. Later, in 1992, at a 'Democracy Demonstration' in Edinburgh, coinciding with a European summit in the city and just after the Conservatives' fourth successive British electoral victory, McIlvanney spoke to over 25,000 people, invoking a Scottish sense of pluralism which he felt was imperilled by dogmatic London rule.[18] He considered standing as an Independent when a Scottish parliament was finally established in 1999 after Labour's 1997 electoral victory, but opted to remain a radical, firmly Scottish-orientated voice above the political fray.[19]

The arts are an area of policy devolved to the new Edinburgh parliament at Holyrood. But culture was not heavily politicised, certainly in any nationalist direction. Catherine Lockerbie of the Edinburgh International Book festival even reflected: 'Now devolution has been achieved, people don't have to prove they are Scottish writers anymore…'.[20]

The beginning of Arts Politicisation

After 1999, with the retreat of the churches due to accelerating secularism and the decline of local identities, cultural figures began to fill the space once occupied by religious and local elites. Sponsorship from the Scottish government made them more visible and influential. James Robertson, the author of the much-praised and overtly nationalist novel *And The Land Lay Still,* became writer-in-residence at the Scottish Parliament while Labour still headed the government. But the devolutionist Scottish left was at a loss about how to make effective use of culture in order to maintain its contested ascendancy. It was just one of many missed opportunities which showed that Labour was unable to devise a social democratic formula for Scottish self-government. After the SNP took charge, Alex Salmond showed that for him the arts were not an esoteric theme remote from power. In 2009, he wrote: 'Culture is the beating heart of the nation, it is very much part of the way we understand and project ourselves…'.[21] Irvine Welsh revealed in 2015 that 'Alex Salmond asked me to join the SNP'.[22] Probably, other cultural figures had been similarly wooed by him.

This highly-motivated public figure wooed the cultural world and made its members feel valued and significant especially if they showed any readiness to dance to a nationalist tune. As First Minister, he regularly burnished his 'literary credentials, quoting from Robert Burns and Alasdair Gray in his speeches, interviewing Ian McEwan onstage at the Edinburgh international book festival, flagging up James Robertson's [nationalist] novel …as his summer reading'.[23]

The civil service had proven to be the key early ally of the SNP in government. Ambitious bureaucrats may have sensed that, unlike the irresolute Labour Party, the SNP was comfortable with power and was likely to be at or near the top for a long time to come. As was already the tradition in corporatist Scotland, senior civil servants took charge of major universities as Principals; soon, nationalist academics in disciplines like English literature became more prominent than they had ever been, holding down prestigious chairs. The cultural atmosphere became more receptive for cultural interpretations of Scotland's past which emphasised some of the themes articulated by MacDiarmid about Scottish identity being distorted and damaged by a stifling association with a 'monolithic' England.

Labour itself had arguably stirred cultural nationalism into life in Scotland by downplaying an over-arching British identity and promoting instead ethnic and religious identities, across the UK, under the guise of multiculturalism. Britain's status was impaired after 2003 when Prime Minister Tony Blair manoeuvred parliament into supporting ill-prepared military interventions in several Muslim countries along with the United States. Opposition was particularly pronounced in Scotland with intellectuals vocally condemning the greatest foreign policy miscalculation since the Suez crisis of 1956. In 2004, Irvine Welsh joined Edwin Morgan, Alasdair Gray, Iain Banks and other Scottish writers in supporting 'the Declaration of Calton Hill' (an initiative of the Scottish Socialist Party) in calling for an independent Scottish republic.

Understandably, a radical Scottish future in which the country's intellectuals acquired a platform previously lacking when British arrangements prevailed, was alluring for plenty of them. A decade began when Scotland was increasingly romanticised as a land of progressive thought and action deserving of greater world attention. But this 'dreamtime' vision of Scotland was challenged by one of the country's established novelists who believed that it was escapism which ignored some awkward and unattractive realities of national life.

In an extended review of Neal Ascherson's book, *Stone Voices: The Search* for Scotland shortly after its 2002 publication, Andrew O'Hagan revealed the existence of an emerging fault-line in Scottish culture. Ascherson, a journalist who had acquired a reputation similar to McIlvanney's as someone able to articulate a distinctive Scottish voice and vision of the future, would become, by 2014, an outspoken backer of Scottish independence. Living in London, he used his access to parts of the highbrow London media to argue that the British state was a pointless, and sometimes dangerous, anachronism and that it was now overdue for Scotland to shape its own destiny.

In 2002, Ascherson was still a devolutionist and member of the Liberal Democrat Party. He portrays a dramatic, beautiful and sometimes torn landscape that evokes powerful emotions and memories. He is convinced Scotland is a land of powerful solidarities, a chain of small collective loyalties, providing the fellowship that will enable Scotland to find its own way in a big and turbulent world. But O'Hagan is having none of this. He made his reputation with realistic and sometimes grim novels in which economic hardship, social divisions and their effects on individuals and communities often provided the chief backcloth. He doubted Ascherson's insight when he invoked the generosity of spirit of an often conflicted people and believed that the critical faculties of this journalist (displayed in reportage from different upheavals in mainland Europe), had deserted him on his own native soil:

'I begin to worry that the great explicator of velvet revolutions has dithered too long in the purple heather, and has forgotten to ask what life is actually like over in Greenock, Buckie, Cumnock and Cowdenbeath. A chain of collective loyalties? A nation at home? You must be joking.'[...]'

Inter-cultural strife on religious or quasi-religious grounds, mainly working-class in character, is just one of the 'sociopathic elements' that Ascherson swerves away from discussing, according to O'Hagan. The novelist argued that too often there was an embargo on candid discussions about the Scottish condition due to deep-seated collective anxieties:

'The deep geological fault running underneath national self-confidence is still there . . . and from time to time it makes itself felt.[...]

'Free-falling anxiety about Scottishness has a tendency, among Scots, not only to turn into hatred of others, but into hating bad news about the country itself, and seeing critics as traitors. There are few European nations in which intellectuals are so willing to serve as soft-pedalling merchants of "national character"....[...]

O'Hagan chastised Ascherson for being too bound up with 'the stones' in the title of his book and being unwilling to take the measure of the people comprising the country. He strongly implied that genuine political progress was bound to be elusive unless thought patterns and discourse were encouraged that made a genuine new departure possible rather than a superficial changing of external symbols:

'Scotland is a place where good men and women busy themselves shaking the dead hand of the past, but the naming of a tradition is not the same as the forging of a nation, and modern Scotland, now more than ever, needs a new way of thinking, a new kind of relation to the old, a way to live, a way to make itself better than the badness that's been and the badness to come. The question of what the past amounted to can lie about the grass.'[24]

O'Hagan's review was described by Pat Kane, already long an ardent nationalist as a 'bilious' example of 'sociopathic abuse' about a Scotland far removed from the progressive and even sophisticated features of the nation which it was not hard to encounter. The novelist would mainly keep out of the referendum debate but he continued to be the subject of occasional acerbic remarks from cultural nationalists.[25]

Troubadours for Nationalism: The National Collective

Events moved quickly after the SNP's victory in the 2011 Holyrood elections. In early 2012, Prime Minister David Cameron signalled an impending referendum on Scotland and the Union. By May of that year the Yes campaign was ready for its launch. It was held in an Edinburgh cinema and would be a slightly amateurish version of a formula which would become far more professional as the campaign evolved. There was patriotic music and film clips of quintessential Scottish land-scapes. Liz Lochhead, Scotland's Makar or official national poet read from her play, *Mary Queen of Scotland Got Her Head Chopped Off.* The actor Brian Cox spoke about the injustices in the story of London overlordship, culminating in denuncia-tions of Margaret Thatcher, Tony Blair, and the Iraq War. Right-wing supporters of independence, such as the historian Michael Fry and the businessman Peter de Vink were among the invited guests but they were kept in the background. According to the journalist Hamish Macdonell this was because they might be treated unkindly by the left-leaning audience.[26]

Actors, musicians, poets and songwriters dominated the occasion. Fifteen months later, Kenneth Roy, veteran of journalism and editor of the *Scottish Review* was scep-tical about the emphasis on these self-styled 'creatives' in the Yes campaign. The date of the referendum was still almost a year away and the 'No' side showed no sign of losing its poll lead. The literati and others of an artistic temperament had usually been a bane not a boon for Scottish nationalism in times past. He reflected: 'The Scots are not naturally lyrical as the Irish are lyrical. They prefer to listen to char-tered accountants' was his dry conclusion. The support for independence from the Scottish liberal establishment' was 'relatively narrow'.[27]

But a low-key arts establishment was having to jostle for attention with appar-ently radical voices who wished their art to reflect an awakened nation. They were harnessing the power of the social media to create an alternative public space from which to influence politics. In a post-industrial society where traditional elites were in retreat and the rules for social behaviour were becoming fluid, cultural agitators and dreamers had more leverage than in the past.

Scots, many of whom would become absorbed in the Yes campaign, looked more positively at risk and experimentation. The writer Alan Bissett, who emerged as one of the emblematic figures in the Yes campaign, argued that 'the creative heavy-lift-ing most Scottish artists had already been doing in their work' meant that they were predisposed to be independence-minded.[28] He was one of a number of creatives who polarised opinion with self-indulgent and uninhibited behaviour. He per-formed naked on stage and a number of his tweets were designed to overthrow the conventions of restraint which governed Scottish public taste.[29] He discussed what to wear in television appearances and once tweeted, 'fucking hell, the young Winston Churchill was a hottie'.[30] Although the extent of his talent soon became a subject of debate, he can perhaps be viewed as a belated Scottish response to the Bloomsbury scene of post-1920 southern England or to unconventional poets such as the Sitwells. Their prominence stemmed not so much from their artistic output but from their ability to persuade others that they were original and fascinating people with distinctive tastes. Bissett was a regular draw at SNP conferences and his lengthy and combative poem 'Vote Britain' rounded off a well-attended pro-independence rally held in Edinburgh on 21 September 2012.

The journalist Kevin McKenna was another uninhibited convert to the nationalist cause. His Labour sympathies had regularly caused his Scottish column in the *Observer* newspaper to be mocked and derided. But when he pronounced the Union to be obsolete and socially unjust, his ratings soared and television appearances and contributions across the media field increased. The revival of a career which appeared to be stalled before the referendum was a potent illustration of the professional benefits that could be derived from embracing nationalism and it is unlikely to have been lost on others who wondered about what position to adopt in a Scotland that was becoming very politicised.

The National Collective would be the forum for politically-minded 'creatives' who wished to play their part in the struggle for independence. McKenna described it as 'a significant challenge to Scotland's old media order'.[31] He noted that the number of followers it claimed to have on Twitter and Facebook (30,000 and 47,000 respectively) compared well to Scotland's older media (the *Herald* newspaper had just 32,400 Twitter followers). The playwright Andrew Greig would describe it as 'the inspiration of the independence debate so far'. Andrew Eaton-Lewis of the *Scotsman* noted that 'they signed up 3,000 members' and, according to an admirer, organised hugely popular public 'sessions', a blend of polemic, music and poetry, which evolved into a nationwide tour called Yestival.[32]

Others were sceptical. The name 'collective' smacked of left-wing agitprop masquerading as cultural originality according to a publisher who, over several decades, had promoted the cream of Scottish literary talent.[33] The journalist Alex Massie thought that 'the National Collective's definition of "artist" was so broad as to be almost meaningless'. It included 'folk styled as "fashion blogger", "organiser and creative", "English teacher" and "comedian"'.[34]

He would not be alone in believing that this was a self-promoting group composed of enthusiasts with talents that were sometimes hard to define. But Mairi McFadyen of the NC brushed aside accusations of boosterism and also one claim from a disappointed member that it had allowed itself to be a political arm of the SNP. She wrote in 2015:

'....National Collective was never a huge organisation or institution with a full or even part-time staff. The truth is that we are a small group of people who have become friends, desperately trying to make things work. Between us we are passionate artists, stewards and facilitators who work with other artists to try and make the world a better place. Some of us are freelancers, some of us students, some of us teachers. Some of us are members of political parties. Many of us are not....

Our big success was as a platform for a huge range of people during the referendum campaign – online, in dozens of events, in a book we published and a zine. We wanted to create spaces for alternative voices to be heard and amplified'.[35]

In previous decades, the SNP had been unable to interact with and harness Scottish culture. This cultural front demonstrated that there was rather more to the Yes side than the SNP and it probably punctured the philistine image that had often clung to the party. According to the National Collective's Robin Weaver, the [referendum] campaign provided Scots with 'a collective identity shaping experience'.[36] The journalist Iain MacWhirter even believed that the Yes movement's combination of culture, social media and public events allowed its participants to live 'as if Scotland was already independent'.[37]

For his part Alan Bissett dared to make a comparison with West Coast America and London in the 1960s:

'The finest minds of our generation, to borrow from Allen Ginsberg's Howl, are poised to re-imagine Scotland from top to bottom: politically, economically, socially and culturally. The summer of 2014 – dare we call it the Summer of Independence? – could be to Scotland what 1967 was to London and San Francisco, its artists and radicals conjuring songs, essays, poems, speeches and plays which offer fresh vistas and challenge a hideously conservative status quo'.[38]

But perhaps a more apt one was with earlier phases of European history when certain countries witnessed the rise of cultural movements seeking to challenge blocked systems of political power, ones in which younger figures often predominated. Given the importance of intellectuals in national life, it is not surprising that France had periodically witnessed such phenomena. Ireland after the disgrace and fall of the nationalist leader Parnell in 1891 is another.

The example offered by Spain in the earliest years of the 20th century indicates the exalted view of intellectual regenerators and their self-role as missionaries seeking to revitalise the people. The influential philosopher Jose Ortega y Gasset (1882-1955) was one such figure as a young man. He wrote:

'...we must go to the villages not just to ask for votes, but so that our propaganda will be creative of culture, of technology, of social cooperation – in short, of human life in every sense. The league for Spanish Political education would therefore side with society against the state. ...'

Ortega believed that the enthusiasm of mainly city intellectuals could have a catalytic effect on a torpid society:

'We are going to flood with our curiosity and enthusiasm the most remote corners of Spain: we are going to get to know Spain and sow it with our love and indignation. We are going to travel the fields like crusading apostles, to live in the villages, to listen to the desperate complaints...we are going to begin by being the friends of those whom we shall later lead. We are going to create among them strong bonds of sociability – cooperatives, circles of mutual education; centers of observation and protest...We are going to make these fraternal spirits, lost in provincial inertia, understand that they have in us allies and defenders...'[39]

These words (to me) faithfully re-enact the mood among at least some pro-Indy 'creatives' in Scotland a century later. By early 2015 when an inquest was taking place over the impact of the NC and the nature of its links with the SNP, Mairi McFadyen conceded that the overtly political often squeezed out its cultural dimension:

'We were fighting a political campaign with an explicit goal. Part of this meant that National Collective was also a giant PR exercise full of campaign rhetoric. As we gained more visibility, we deliberately projected a movement larger than life. ....of course there were contradictions – the foremost of these between the need for a directed campaign and the desire to be an open artists' collective'.[40]

Alex Massie saw a movement in which too often the ego was given free rein. He mockingly referred to a 'National Collective [that] was keen on promoting selfies in which citizens posed with placards proclaiming "I am National Collective'. In 2015, 'Judy' an adult literacy teacher, after reading an article in which Alan Bissett claimed that theatre innovators in Scotland had boosted the Yes vote, protested. She complained about the inflated claims of allegedly 'radical...artsy types in a small clique' who were 'utterly removed from most people'.[41]

The Silences of the Creatives

The composer James MacMillan alleged that an opportunist attempt was being made to create a new cultural establishment on the basis of very flimsy artistic achievements and he was stung by some of the claims made by Pat Kane. This cultural theorist had long argued that 'culture, values and ideology', were capable of transforming the landscape of politics. 'We have the soft power', he wrote in February 2014: 'Scotland holds a positive image in the world through the strength of its culture and values'.[42]

But to MacMillan and others talk of the 'national brand' and its cultural impact globally was utterly pretentious. In 2011, prior to the referendum turmoil, he had revealed in an article that it had been the seemingly proprietorial attitude of Pat Kane towards the national cause which had led him to sever any remaining affinities with political nationalism: 'The last time I saw him was at a post-devolution party at the National Museum of Scotland; the kind of lavish event where the Scottish liberal elites gather to exult in one of their regular self-congratulatory orgies of entitlement and privilege. He looked at me, with tears in his eyes and said falteringly "Look at all this James; we are now the new modern Scottish establishment." Something snapped in me that night...'[43]

The versatile writer, Allan Massie (father of the journalist Alex), author of historical novels, crime thrillers and works of non-fiction, many about Scotland, also found it hard to rein in his impatience with Kane. After the cultural activist had written in the summer of 2014 that if Scotland voted No, 'it will be a depressed place', Massie retorted that 'deep down he has a contempt for democracy' since a majority of Scots in that situation were bound to be relieved rather than downcast. He also branded Kane as an essentially traditional figure behind the radical veneer:

'He is playing an old tune, familiar to anyone with a knowledge of Scottish history. It's the Calvinist tune. On the one hand you have the Elect, the Chosen People, among whom Mr Kane is a distinguished member. On the other hand you have the Damned, rejected by the Almighty because they are...lukewarm...'[44]

But a qualified defence of Kane and other politicised artists can perhaps be made. They were overtly wooed by the SNP and made to feel like key players in the referendum drama, so the urge to dramatise their own role, (never far below the surface in some cases) may have simply been too overpowering. The *White Paper,* launched in November 2013 with much fanfare to show that independence could be viable, was earlier billed as having a section in which 'creatives' could be lyrical about the impending separate future for the country. Salmond announced that a special role was being preserved for 'creatives' in this document. Alan Bissett responded with delight:

'I must admit that I was surprised to learn that Alex Salmond is to enlist Scotland's finest writers to help pen the SNP's much-anticipated white paper on Scottish independence.[45] The "yes" campaign has successfully galvanised the artistic community as part of the cultural drive in advance of next year's referendum..... This is a sign that Salmond's engagement with the arts goes beyond superficial courting, and that he genuinely wishes to place imagination at the heart of the new Scotland'.[46]

But in the event writers like McIlvanney, who had spoken and written powerfully about Scottish identity in the past, were absent from the pages of the White Paper.

Arguably, epic prose, bound up with the cause of Scottish freedom, failed to arise at any other point in an extended political drive lasting over thirty months. Creatives may have become simply too wrapped up in campaigning and the unromantic tasks associated with it. The novelist Denise Mina observed:

'Quite a number of the creatives I knew became so involved in the Yes campaign that it would have been impossible to put aside other time to work. I grew concerned for some of them because they were unlikely to be earning much money.

Ultimately creating art, and literature is not something that emerges on its own volition. It mainly involves graft and there were a lot of people who abandoned their calling and found themselves doing exciting but also fairly routine things, such as making the tea, so as to make Yes events to happen.'[47]

The journalist Alex Massie feared that such misguided priorities meant that 'no art of any consequence' was likely to emerge from the many months of agitation and ferment. He believed that the National Collective's emphasis on having a 'wish tree' at Yes events, comprised of scraps of paper upon which participants write what they wanted to see in an independent Scotland was a sign of a cultural movement, with vaulting ambitions, gone badly astray:

'Whatever this may be, it's not art....

And that's the real problem with National Collective. For all the wishing trees and student union agitprop, and for all the concerns about the organisation's supposed lack of "transparency", "accountability" and "democracy", their greatest shortcoming was their lack of actual art.'[48]

Some writers who clearly desired a Yes vote were keen to differentiate themselves from the main driver of political separation, the SNP. As it was riding high in the opinion polls two months before the 2015 general election, William McIlvanney publicly stated that the party remained unconvincing for him.[49]

The novelist James Kelman made it clear that he was inspired by 'self-determination' and not nationalism. He was unhappy with the SNP's approach to the monarchy and its 'servitude to the ruling elite'.[50] For Kathleen Jamie, the poet, it was 'collectivism and not nationalism that drew her to the Yes cause.[51] For the poet Janice Galloway, it was 'close and accessible government'.[52]

Kelman looked ahead to a time when a radical Scotland might outgrow the gradualism of the SNP. But few Yes writers were willing to criticise the 7-year governing record of the SNP where it impinged on cultural matters. The preference of the SNP for centralised government from Edinburgh was well-known by 2014 and it vested enhanced power in bureaucrats whose approach to decisions affecting 'creatives' often produced alienation. The Scottish publishing industry had long been disappointed by the government's failure to support Scottish cultural material through its purchasing policy. Independent booksellers have obtained little backing from the government and a behemoth like Amazon is actually subsidised by it, leading to job losses in Scottish publishing according to one of its pillars.[53]

The decision of the Scottish government in 2012 to devote well over one-third of its overseas budget to back an animated cartoon film *Brave,* promoting a kitsch image of Scotland, led to protests from voices in the Scottish film industry such as producer Gillian Berry. First Minister Salmond intervened in the supposedly hands-off process of arts funding right up until he stood down and he was in attendance at the Hollywood premiere of *Brave* held one month after the start of the 2012-14 campaign.[54]

But the absence of any discernable government strategy to strengthen Scottish publishing or boost its struggling film industry never became issues which creatives felt emboldened to raise in the referendum period. This suggests that Alan Bissett's characterisation, here, of Indy creatives as people who speak truth to power is rather wide of the mark:

'Salmond should be careful of what he wishes for, however. The poets whom he courts will be the same ones asking serious questions of the SNP after independence. Writers of the calibre involved are not guns for hire, and they will know when they are being fooled'.[55]

Nor did any figures express concern about the attacks on the pro-Union 'No' campaign, stretching from concerted attacks on campaign material like placards and posters, even when displayed on private property, to attempts to howl down speakers in public. This may help to explain the unwillingness of some British-minded Scottish intellectuals to debate with them at the first anniversary conference discussed at the start of this chapter.

This silence rather places in doubt the self-proclaimed view that in a politically volatile Scotland, the Indy-minded intellectuals would be critical and outspoken, fully engaged as agents for meaningful change. Even cross moves like Salmond's decision to unfurl a large Saltire at the 2013 Wimbledon tennis final and wave it close to David Cameron, sitting in a nearby seat, raised no public misgivings among creatives keen to imagine a different future for their country. A century previously, such a gesture might well have been seen as gauche even in those insecure Balkan countries seeking to escape from external rule.

The veteran journalist Neal Ascherson wrote about the descent into intolerant nationalism of some of the countries in the Balkans as a columnist in the *Observer* at the end of the Cold War. But as a recent convert to outright independence, he found little to criticise in the behaviour of the nationalist movement. Writing from London, he saw Scots who were fascinated by their country while powerful people in England were annoyed because now they were being overlooked.[56]

Yet the degree to which Scotland witnessed cultural effervescence leading to large numbers exploring their identity is questionable. As the 18 September voting day approached, campaigning became increasingly raucous and there were plenty of media reports and video footage of rowdy scenes, especially when high profile No supporters from across the Border appeared in public. But for top-selling crime novelist Val McDermid, 'it was an overwhelmingly civil debate about a kind of civic nationalism. It's been about an inclusive Scotland, not a narrow-minded, bigoted, hate-filled breakaway. We want our country to be better, not just more of the same'.[57] She was writing on 22 August 2014, the day on which Jim Murphy, a high profile No campaigner decided to suspend his open air speaking campaign. He claimed that organized intimidation of a kind which was very unusual in a British election campaign, made it pointless to continue (though he later resumed his tour).

McDermid could not spot any 'jingoistic Braveheart nationalism' at play but at an early stage of the campaign, in December 2012, the novelist Alasdair Gray had caused a stir by attacking the appointment of English "colonists" to influential and powerful positions in Scotland. He singled out Vicky Featherstone, who had been artistic director of the National Theatre of Scotland since 2006, as well as Andrew Dixon, who had resigned his post as head of the state culture body, Creative Scotland shortly before the appearance of the essay.

Featherstone had been influenced by the work of the radical 7:84 theatre company and she put on Gregory Burke's *Black Watch*. It was fiercely critical of Tony Blair's intervention in Iraq and it dramatised the feelings of ordinary Scottish soldiers without pushing an overt message on the constitutional issue.[58] After she admitted to having been unnerved by anti-English sniping, she received backing from John Byrne, the veteran playwright and artist. He expressed disappointment at Gray's comments and stated that it was 'healthy' to have English and Scottish arts administrators crossing the border. Posts in the arts field should simply go to the best candidate for the job.[59]

Much of the polemic about Scotland's future was being waged on Twitter and, in the same month, the poet Kevin Williamson tweeted: 'Time has come for a social audit of institutional Scotland. Who are these people? Who do they speak for? What class, demographic, ethos?' There was a media outcry but censure from fellow creatives was conspicuous by its absence.

In other countries facing polarisation due to ethnic strains, such a non-reaction might have seemed unusual. In countries lacking Scotland's tradition of stability, it had sometimes fallen to intellectuals to promote civility and moderation during times of volatility. Perhaps such traditions will need to be learned, or else copied, from Latin American or South European countries if Scotland renounces stability for an extended period.

To his great credit, Williamson later posted: 'Reading back ... the words 'social audit' do sound bit fascistic, even if not meant that way. Ah well. Live & learn'.[60]

Deborah Orr, Scottish-born and raised and a columnist on the *Guardian* wrote that it was 'appalling' John Byrne had to speak out about inappropriate remarks by a fellow arts professional. She was one of many Scots who had found success in the London media, publishing and arts world. Such people were not organized into any pressure group comparable to the National Collective perhaps due to the fact they were too busy pursuing separate careers. But a Scotland separating itself from the rest of the UK was bound to have implications for some of them and for many more Scots of the future who might wish to embark on the centuries old road south, towards professional success; a parochial attitude is not a one-way process and it could be replicated in England if a messy divorce marked the departure of Scotland from the Union.

Growing up in Motherwell Deborah Orr recalled that:

'As the child of a Scottish father and an English mother, I learned from an early age that my English blood made me an outsider. Resentment against the English was strong. At the age of five or six, I was told my mother was taking the houses and jobs that should by rights have been going to locals. At that time, my mum didn't even have a job, or a house. She was a mother and housewife, living in a council flat with her family of three Scots.

But just by breathing Scottish air, she was, apparently, stealing something that wasn't hers, playing her own small part in a process of pillage that had been going on for centuries, making England rich and powerful while Scotland stayed small and puny'.[61]

During 2014, such examples of everyday ethnic suspicion and resentment were described many times over in the online forums of the Scottish media. At least concerning his own remarks, Alasdair Gray retreated somewhat at the Edinburgh International Book Festival of that year. He stated that his main concern was that too many cultural jobs were being handed to 'bankers and businessmen' and he expressed his doubt that artists had any more right to be heard than labourers or trades people'.[62] Such views were at variance with the postures being adopted by many of the writer's own colleagues who, by means of interviews, statements and platform appearances sometimes acted as if they were guardians of a national cause.

'Yes' views and publicity material filled Scottish public spaces in the lead-up to the referendum, suggesting to many people the distinct likelihood of independence being chosen. Similar sentiments dominated the Scottish cultural world. But on 18 September 'Yes' was clearly rejected. The extent of pro-British sentiments had not been picked up and perhaps in the world of arts and letters appearances were equally deceptive.

On 13 June 2014 the cultural polymath John Byrne wrote in the *Scotsman* 'I think most artists in Scotland are terrified to speak out. They are cowardly in the Scottish arts scene. They're all keeping their noses clear for fear that people will dislike them and will not buy their stuff, and that they will not get any funding from Creative Scotland'.[63]

Unconscripted Intellectuals

The composer James MacMillan echoed and expanded upon these views. On 5 June 2014, he mentioned on Twitter that he was in no doubt that artists were unwilling to speak up for fear of the consequences: 'Major Scottish artist to me this morning: "I am afraid to speak. I do not want to get my head kicked in"'.[64] Elsewhere he was reported as saying that the artist was 'one of many who've said more or less the same thing'.[65] The music critic Barry Gordon said No supporters whom he encountered told him of their fear of being ostracised, losing work, losing out on funding, of being categorised, or even of being bullied. The Radio Scotland disk jockey Tom Morton received 'relentless' online abuse when he wrote in favour of Better Together. Afterwards, he remarked: 'There seems to me a kneejerk, politically naïve response from strident voices within the arts community but a number of people on that scene have told me they fear going public on their No stance because of the potential repercussions'.[66]

However, it was the musical world which saw a tenacious mobilisation to prevent the imposition of a political frontier across Britain, one that was seen as calamitous for different branches of the musical industry.[67] Eddie McGuire, the composer, and flautist with the folk group, the Whistlebinkies, was particularly energetic. He straddled the worlds of classical and folk music. From July 2013, he was active in Better Together and he wrote a 'Concert' for Unity that was performed for another group, 'Vote No Borders' on 5 September 2014. This piece of music 'embraced the characteristics of folk music from all the parts of Britain'.[68] He believed strongly in a common musical culture. Thanks to having a strong left-wing and trade-union background, he was able to reach out across the industry to performers, composers, arts organisers and others who earned their livelihood from music in Scotland. A range of prominent figures signed letters, took part in public concerts and debates, and were active in their own professional spheres.

The folk music world appeared to be unsympathetic to this message, however. One of the undoubted pillars of cultural nationalism in Scotland had been the poet and folk musicologist Hamish Henderson (1919-2002). 'Trad for Yes' was launched by the National Collective in 2013 and drew several hundred adherents from the world of Scottish traditional music. But McGuire states that plenty of people from this world discreetly remained apart from the nationalist clamour. Indeed, the most prominent musician who figured in online publicity material for 'Trad for Yes' was the eclectic Essex-born performer Billy Bragg whose work was shaped around not only folk music but punk rock. He saw Scottish Nationalism as progressive and invoked a comparison with the English Roundheads who triumphed in the civil war of the 1640s.[69] Others from England (some living in Scotland) have also viewed the SNP as a much needed counterweight to English/British nationalism and a few with such an outlook have held elected office for the party.

While some endorsed the view of Alex Salmond that his movement could promote radical change elsewhere in Britain, others thought such a perspective was unrealistic. The leading Scottish crime writer Denise Mina was of this view. She was one of a very small number of writers prepared to go on the record to set out their reservations about the case for Yes. She argued that in a globalised world, genuine independence, or even meaningful autonomy, was beyond the reach of those who sought it: 'We would not be autonomous. We would be disadvantaged. Factionalizing can only benefit stateless corporations as we vie to give them the best deal. [...] 'And, in a rapidly warming world, forming a small country, reliant on continued oil production, is in no one's interests, not even our own'.

She was also wary of the evangelical faith of the Yes side and the reluctance to take a cool and clinical look at what was possible for Scotland: '...the consequences of a Yes vote are shrouded in mystery. Attempts to anticipate any negatives are dismissed as scaremongering'.

'A whole Yes belief system has built up around this: consistent signals from the EU that our membership would not be automatic - don't believe it'.

'The rest of the UK tell us they don't want a currency union - don't believe it. Belief is not a plan. Belief is a refusal to discuss'.[70]

In a conversation with Denise Mina, she admitted that her No affiliation did not result in any adverse consequences for her work. But she put this down to being commercially independent, as a polymath whose range covered comic writing, writing plays, television work and her best known emanation as a crime writer. She believed that she was 'much freer to speak out than people who rely on grants or contract work. It was tough for such people to get engaged'. She was struck to find that, nearly six months after the vote, people still thank me for speaking up, some of them clutching my arm as they do so'.[71]

Her apostasy on the Independence issue was also well regarded by acquaintances on the Yes side. Several wrote to say: 'I fully support your wish to have a contrary opinion...but don't tell anyone'. It was interesting that such 'a fear of breaking ranks' existed. To Mina, it denoted a Yes cultural world where orthodoxy reigned rather than a desire to have a freewheeling debate: 'There was competition to see who was most dedicated. Were you badgy enough? Were you converting people?'[72]

She also found it astonishing that (to the best of her knowledge) the impact of Union break-up on neighbouring Northern Ireland was never discussed. She believed that it was certain to pose huge challenges for a still fragile peace process there.[73]

The playwright and film-maker Ewan Morrison was also someone who felt that so important were the issues surrounding Scotland's future, a cutting edge debate among intellectuals eager for change was absolutely essential. In 2014, *Bella Caledonia,* the main online platform for pro-Independence argument, hailed the arrival on the Yes side of 'one of the most celebrated and innovative of novelists to emerge in post-Devolution Scotland'.[74]

Once inside the Yes camp Morrison 'attempted to find the revolutionary and inclusive debate that I'd heard was happening. But as soon as I was "in" I was being asked to sign petitions, to help with recruitment, to take part in Yes groups, to come out publicly in the media, to spread the word and add the blue circle Yes logo to my social media photograph – even to come along and sing a "Scottish song" at a Yes event'.

He declined to sing but tried to participate in other ways only to come up against 'an ethos of "Shh".:

'I noticed that whenever someone raised a pragmatic question about governance, economics or future projections for oil revenue or the balance of payments in iScotland, they were quickly silenced by comments such as "We'll sort that out after the referendum, this is not the place or the time for those kinds of questions". Or the people who asked such questions were indirectly accused of "being negative" or talking the language of the enemy. There was an ethos of "Shh", if you start asking questions like that we'll all end up arguing (and that'll be negative) so in the interests of unity (and positivity) keep your mouth shut'.[75]

A perusal of Morrison's Twitter account reveals an unconventional thinker still very much in tune with ideas, debates and challenges that are occurring far beyond Scotland. So his expectations of what he would find in the Indy camp may have been inflated. But he was crestfallen to find that there was 'Zero debate', and that 'the focus was instead on attacking the enemy'. As a former member of the Trotskyite, Socialist Workers Party, he found discouraging parallels:

'The Yes camp had turned itself into a recruitment machine which had to silence dissent and differences between the many clashing interest groups under its banner. This was what YES had started to mean – it meant YES to everything – everything is possible – so don't question anything. You couldn't talk about what would happen after the referendum because then all the conflicts between all the different desires and factions would emerge.[76]

Morrison concluded that he had stumbled into a movement that acted more like a cult whose 'campaign has had to be emptied of almost all actual political content. It has had to become a form of faith'. The domination of this group-think approach prompted him to cross over to the No camp. It was not due to a revelation that after all 'I like the UK or think the status quo works well as it is. No. I think things are as complicated and compromised as they always are and that we live in trying times. The Yes camp understand that and so have created an illusion of a free space in which everything you've ever wanted can come to pass – overnight'.[77]

Upon joining the Yes camp, Morrison never concealed views that were somewhat sympathetic to innovative and socially responsible forms of capitalism. These were mentioned in an article which he published in the emphatically left-leaning *Bella Caledonia* without any critical reaction from readers.[78] It may have been an unconscious acknowledgment that the goal of independence itself, rather than the social system coming afterwards, was the primary inspiration for even many self-styled radicals on the Yes side.

Certainly this fixation with territorial separation was what made one of Britain's major historical novelists, Edinburgh-born C.J. Sansom, deeply distrustful of the SNP. On the eve of the referendum, he reinforced earlier claims he had made that the SNP was a populist movement which had swithered blindly in its social and economic policies because it lacked any coherent vision for the future.[79] He believed that its stance on what currency a supposedly independent Scotland should have, confirmed his misgivings. With a separate Scottish currency impractical the SNP's leader Alex Salmond was promoting a currency union or else a unilateral link with sterling. For the socialist-minded Sansom:

'this is an economic policy which, abandoning any state control over monetary policy and interest rates, is far to the right of anything Thatcher considered at her wildest.

(...) any of the yes side's economic options will bring serious economic trouble. As always, it is the poorest who will suffer most. Is that really a price worth paying for the ability to "run our own affairs" – as though any country can do that alone in the modern world'?

He feared that those 'who disrupted Jim Murphy's talks with screams of "traitor"' might prove to be the successors of those who had harnessed 'the dangerous power of populist nationalism, which ruined Europe between 1900 and 1945 and is rising again all over the continent, turning neighbours into "others" and blaming them for all domestic ills'.[80]

CHAPTER 6: THE CULTURAL WORLD AND NATIONALISM

Rather unusually, Sansom had devoted part of a postscript in his 2012 novel *Dominion* to warning about Scottish Nationalism's allegedly authoritarian tendencies and the preparedness of high-profile nationalists, in the past, to consort with Britain's enemies.[81] He wrote about finding it 'heartbreaking – literally heartbreaking – that my own country Britain, which was less prone to domestic nationalist extremism between the wars than most, is increasingly falling victim to the ideology of nationalist parties...'

[the most] 'dangerous, is the threat to all of Britain posed by the Scottish National Party...'[82]

In the spring of 2014, he donated more than quarter of a million pounds to Better Together. This gesture coincided with an article in the *Daily Record* going much further in his criticisms of nationalism. In it he criticised left-wingers who had converted to the Yes cause as naive because they were making common cause with an un-progressive force which would use and then discard them as soon as it was convenient to do so.[83]

Scottish Nationalism was described as obsessed with one big idea for which a sprawling bureaucratic state would be erected devoid of any real social or practical economic vision. He did not see why 'millions like me who are British Anglo-Scots and wish to be allowed to remain so...' should become collateral victims of its triumph.[84]

Rather similar sentiments were attributed to Angus Deaton, the Scots-born Princeton University professor who was awarded the Nobel Prize for Economics in 2015. He was reported to have said that the break-up of Britain would have made him feel 'personally dismembered'.[85]

The voices of such people were not often heard in the referendum campaign. Up to 800,000 Scots-born citizens resided in England and were denied a vote in the referendum under the terms of the Edinburgh agreement. They would very likely have been required to choose between a British and new Scottish citizenship if the territorial division of Britain had ensued. Perhaps in invoking the dangers of Europe before 1945, Sansom had in mind those cosmopolitan people who because of mixed race, their Jewishness, or sudden boundary changes found themselves odd-people-out in the new nationalist order.

Michael Russell, the SNP's minister, first of culture and then of education from 2009 to 2014, rejected Sansom's characterisation of his party and assumed that he had never in the past even met a party member. Russell assumes that he could vouch for all the members as broadly civic in outlook. He implies that the novelist has led a hopelessly sheltered life, at least where contemporary Scotland was concerned. Yet thanks to social media and the internet, the 2012-14 years presented to the world thousands of Scots who might have emerged from the vociferous era of hyper-nationalism in the post-1918 Europe of insecure small states.

Scotland's fifteen universities, recipients of disproportionately high levels of UK funding due to the prowess of several in different research fields were a powerful symbol of the benefits that inter-cultural cooperation brought this part of the United Kingdom. But neither Russell nor Yes-minded academics could convincingly show how equivalent funding levels could be preserved when in the post-British context, the tax-base funding state spending fell by 90 percent. Nor could Fiona Hyslop, make any serious case that the BBC Scottish Symphony Orchestra (SSO) could continue without ready access to British funding and recording assignments provided by the BBC. Yet writing in the *Classical Music Magazine* in August 2014, this is what she attempted to do. To the incredulity of the music journalist Ken Walton, she argued that the SSO had good prospects of continuing in what was already an era of cuts in the British arts sector through future contracts with the BBC even though it would have become a foreign orchestra after a Yes vote. He urged the 76 members of the orchestra to be brushing up on their cvs: 'The simple truth is this: there's a good chance that the BBC SSO could become collateral damage in the creation of an independent Scotland. No amount of political spin can change that. So why not just admit it?'[86]

Forms of cultural expression that do not always endear themselves to political nationalism usually have to fend for themselves. It might have been a different story if Scottish classical music had produced a composer whose output had patriotic overtones such as Chopin or Dvorak or musical prodigies like Wagner or Verdi who, in various ways, threw themselves into the national struggles of Germany and Italy respectively. But there were no such figures in a branch of culture which, as a matter of course hired conductors, managers and musicians on the basis of talent not national origins.

Scotland did have a world-renowned composer James MacMillan. But he was numb to the SNP's cause and publicly dismissive of various adherents of separatism particularly in the media and the cultural world. He was a Roman Catholic and his music was often influenced by religious motifs. The community which he belonged to, dominated by the descendants of Irish immigrants, had been seen as a problematic element in national life until well into modern times. In 1999, he had received little support from any political quarter when, in a keynote address at the Edinburgh Festival, he offered an unsettling portrait of ongoing anti-Catholic attitudes by no means confined to marginal quarters of society.[87]

During the era of political nationalism, he found himself out on a limb due to his frequent acerbic comments in press articles or on social media about the harm being done to culture as a result of 'some Scottish artists' having become obsessed with the 'constitutional question to the detriment of their work as artists'. Too often, he believed cultural forays into politics were contrived and even self-seeking: 'It's just not interesting in any artistic context, as evinced by the universal ennui which the rest of the world shows when local cultural figures get up on their bar room stools and chunter on about it. The sound of yawns everywhere else is deafening.'[88]

Some figures from the world of Scottish publishing and literary criticism have claimed that writers, actively nationalist in their sympathies, are using the ideology for professional reasons. They are not always especially good at their craft and they rationalise rejection, especially from beyond Scotland (and notably from London), not as a verdict on their artistic merit but as a gesture of hostility towards Scottish culture. Some of these figures wish to reduce the British cultural space to a narrowly Scottish one. 'If the dimensions of the pool shrink, it means they will be bigger fish' as the journalist and literary critic Stuart Kelly put it.[89]

MacMillan, for his part, believes that highly politicised cultural figures have a vested interest in promoting a Scottish *kleinstadt,* a claustrophobic intellectual atmosphere in which writers are judged by their contribution to various nationalist shibboleths and not according to any canon of critical merit. He was unsparing about this cultural trend in 2015:

'There are some in the separatist movement who see a fast chance - of becoming big fish in a small pond. Some have even advanced this as a reason why they should support independence. It is pathetic. And it shows the depressing absence of vision, aspiration and transcendence among nationalist artists. They have jumped on the bandwagon of a divisive and poisonous campaign as a form of self-promotion. They have contributed to a cultural diminishing of Scotland in spite of their boasting bravado and infantile political posturing. Tame commentators and critics have colluded with them. They have nothing to say on bigger, more serious cultural questions, and the next generation of artists would do themselves a favour by rejecting their petty provincialism.'[90]

MacMillan's discordant voice is awkward for the nationalist establishment which is spreading from the political world into the media and academia. If his was an intellectual voice with limited reach, then he could easily be dismissed as a crank, as a kind of Unionist Hugh MacDiarmid. But he is a prolific and successful composer, increasingly viewed as the most important Scottish one to have emerged in modern times, perhaps ever. The response of the SNP-influenced establishment is to treat him as a wayward talent. He appears in the Scottish media far less often than figures with a much weaker cultural footprint but with an inclination to express political views which are clearly fashionable.

In the event of independence, it is unlikely that intellectuals who clearly challenge the official political orthodoxy will be treated any differently and they could find themselves far worse off than MacMillan. He receives regular invitations to perform his own work abroad and his concertos, operas and sacred works have often been highly praised by critics. Arguably, he acquired his breakthroughs as a result of his talent finding an outlet in the institutional world of British music. But if this sphere is effectively Balkanised, then any Scottish prodigies of the future might find the road to recognition and professional success blocked off, unless that is they bow to political expediency and redirect their work to suit political requirements.

Festival Anxieties in Edinburgh

Since 1947, the city of Edinburgh has played host to an arts festival which has grown into the world's biggest. High art increasingly shares a space with avant-garde productions as well as comedy which dominates a parallel event, the Edinburgh Festival Fringe. In 2014, the six week festival and fringe coincided with the last frenetic burst of campaigning in the referendum. It might have been expected that there would have been a pronounced Scottish theme in areas like comedy, but it was markedly absent.

Brian Ferguson, an arts journalist, reported that 'the "bitter" tone of the Scottish independence debate and the prospect of performers suffering abuse is to blame for the dearth of Edinburgh Festival Fringe shows tackling the referendum issue this year, promoters and performers have claimed'.[91] The reticence of the well-known comic impersonator Rory Bremner has already been discussed in chapter 3. As early as 2013, the critic Clyn Gallagher had observed that 'satire is essential for democracy' but it was at a premium in Scotland due to the huge volume of unwelcome attention comedians were likely to receive online.

The 2013 experience of one figure, Susan Calman had proved dissuasive perhaps for others. The Glasgow comedienne (the daughter of a medical professor who had chaired a commission on furthering Scottish devolution) made fairly mild remarks on a BBC radio comedy show which almost immediately sparked off a torrent of online abuse. She wrote afterwards about the 'humour failure that many believe has characterised online discussion of the Scottish political scene':

'Being honest, I think the whole process surrounding Scottish independence is funny. There's more propaganda, from both sides, than North Korea produces in a decade … I've talked about a lot of things in my comedy career – my sexuality, capital punishment, depression, cats'.

'But nothing, and I mean nothing, has ever created such a sh*t storm of aggression than when I've talked about Scottish Politics'.

She observed that she had been accused of 'betraying my country, of being racist towards my own people'.

Her conclusion was: 'We are over a year away from the vote. If we don't start laughing soon it's going to go horribly wrong. The idea that because I'm Scottish I should, in some way, protect my nation by not criticising it is appalling'.[92] Bremner expressed similar alarm: 'it's almost deliberate, this intimidation, and I find that very sinister and unpleasant. Just because people think the interests of Scotland are better served in a union doesn't make them less patriotic'.[93]

Beforehand, Alan Bissett had claimed there was huge expectancy around the 2014 Edinburgh Fringe: 'Everyone drew up their battle plans for the summer of 2014 with the intention of creating such a carnival of noise, colour, ideas and stories around the Edinburgh Fringe that we'd make independence seem like the Greatest Show on Earth. Minds, we were determined, would be changed. Lives would changed'. But during or after the 6 week event it was hard to find reports that such claims had been realised.

A reader 'Lit Grrrl' complained, after reading the article containing this claim from him about an exclusive arts brethren: 'Scottish arts in danger of becoming "a closed shop" for a select few, irrespective of, and certainly not because of talent, but more dependent on their politics and who they know and which badge they wore. It's also very west of Scotland centric'.[94]

Unheeded Warnings

Chris Deerin, whose thoughtful essays on Scotland's identity within the wider British context often proved to be one of the rare pleasures in Scottish media coverage of the referendum period, abandoned his restraint when it came to assessing the role of the cultural world. He openly expressed the baleful view that 'Scottish culture has destroyed its worth for a generation, even if the fuds don't realise'. Initially, he had thought it 'reasonable to expect' that Scotland might see 'the appearance of a Vaclav Havel at such a crucial period', a playwright capturing a pivotal moment of change. Instead, there were lesser talents who were 'cliched and mediocre', exploiting a pivotal moment for self-promotion.[95]

The veteran actor Bill Paterson, performing in a production of *Waiting for Godot* in Edinburgh a year after the referendum, told the journalist Magnus Linklater that the country 'had never felt so Scottish'.[96] But what was his yardstick for such a claim? The Edinburgh Festival and Fringe, the nation's main cultural platforms, had found few, if any notable Scottish-themed works to perform during the years of political ferment. There was of course clamorous state-sponsored nationalism which reached street level. And which, arguably, was quiet *alien* to recent Scottish traditions.

The National Collective, was the platform in which artists, writers and performers attempted to express and interpreted the national spirit. According to the culture minister, Fiona Hyslop, the National Collective 'changed Scotland', though, according to Alex Massie 'the manner in which this "change" can be seen or substantiated remains puzzlingly elusive.[97] It wasn't a force that reached beyond the petit-bourgeois and avant-garde fringes of Scotland's cities. The critic Stuart Kelly noted that it didn't have an impact in the wider Scotland: 'the main working-class areas that swung from British parties towards nationalism in 2014 were largely untouched by the missionary efforts of these cultural warriors.'[98]

Much of the referendum noise in 2013-14 consisted of an interior dialogue. Free-wheeling discussions rarely materialised, certainly in places like pubs and social clubs where numerous Scots regularly socialised. Debates in universities and colleges, where young Scots reputedly would have their preconceived ideas tested and subjected to other viewpoints, were infrequent occurrences. The cultural world failed to break these glass partitions and may have built higher ones of its own. It is notable that there were never any public encounters between those swayed by the rhetoric of Scottish liberation and others who felt that their work benefited from the strength and elasticity of the British cultural dimension.

In 2002, a year of political calm when some hoped that devolution would enable a multi-level culture to emerge, one not fixated with political grievances, the novelist Andrew O'Hagan had issued a warning about the long-term obstacles blocking the release of a plural cultural spirit in Scotland. He warned about a continuing and 'chronic mistrust of the public dimension. The invitation to "participate", especially to offer critical comment in public, touches a nerve of anxiety. This derives partly from the instinct that to disagree with another person before witnesses is to open a serious personal confrontation; the English or American assumption that "free, open discussion" is non-lethal and even healthy is not widespread in Scotland.'[99]

At a post-referendum private gathering which I attended, a pro-Union Scottish historian confessed that to express these views in public felt as if he was covering himself with dirt. With great reluctance, he was deserting the academic tower of studied neutrality because so much was at stake. The London-born British historian Simon Schama was appalled at the timidity of his fellow intellectuals in the face of Scottish developments: 'The liberal chattering classes are so nervous, and shuffling around in coils of political correctness that they're badly equipped to cope with the monster of the revival of tribalism.'[100]

He had become an outspoken critic of the SNP's separatist ambitions, warning in 2014 that: 'If nation states are devolving into the Scots and the English, the Flemish and Walloons, that's an awful, surprising return to the most visceral, romantic ethnicity left over from the 19th century, and it's got to be a dangerous reaction against globalisation and the pulverisation of our distinctiveness, our identities.'[101]

He observed that 'in dreadful places' '...the same forces behind calls for Scottish independence were causing ethnic and tribal wars, immense massacres'.[102]

In the Scotland of 2014, there was no scholar with Schama's wide hinterland of cultural and historical knowledge prepared to place the possible break up of Britain in such a broad framework. Scotland's most prominent historian, Sir Tom Devine came out in favour of independence on the eve of the referendum. He claimed that the 307-year-old union had now become a 'destabilising' influence across 'the archipelago' of the British isles.[103] South Britain beckons, a rump state far less important for Scotland's economic well-being than the European Union, Devine contended.[104] Ironically, Devine had been content to play along with one of the most contested features of the British state, its heraldic honours system, by accepting a knighthood just weeks before he declared that the union was no longer fit for purpose.

In the face of warnings from figures as contrasting as the novelist Alexander McCall Smith, George Galloway MP, and the economics journalist Alf Young that separation might well be bitter and traumatic, Devine confidently asserted that it would be possible for a sovereign Scotland to 'develop a truly amicable relationship with our great southern neighbour'.[105] In several high-profile media interventions, he failed to map out how this could be possible especially if Scotland faced economic adversity and was locked in fierce negotiations with the rest of the UK about dividing the economic assets accumulated in a 307-year partnership.

Non-separatist voices from the cultural world saw an inclusive United Kingdom not as a drag, but as an affirmation of their Scottishness. Among some of them, there was fear about the kind of cultural landscape that would exist in a country where nationalism was loudly affirmed perhaps to compensate for poor economic conditions. It was noted in several quarters that there had been a deliberate attempt to expropriate the symbols of the country by a movement which is far from containing a monopoly of patriotic spirit. I observed that much of the pro-Indy cultural scene had assumed that the Saltire (a flag whose St Andrew's cross is actually a religious symbol) was a nationalist emblem rather than a symbol above politics.

In an atmosphere that at times tipped over into nationalist fervour, cultural folk unenthused by nationalism may have felt it was best to keep a low profile until the political storm passed over. As a result, even in newspapers like the *Scotsman* with a pro-Union editorial line, it was often cultural voices firmly optimistic about the future which predominated. Billy Kay, the enthusiast for the restoration of the Scots language expressed, perhaps in a particularly vivid way, the belief that a Yes vote would be seen as an important progressive breakthrough in a global sense:

'I will vote Yes on 18 September because I am a Scot and want my wonderful multi-ethnic, multilingual mongrel nation to draw on its rampant egalitarian traditions and create a country which the world will regard as a model for progressive social, environmental and political ideals of inclusion, fairness and justice'.[106]

In the eyes of pro-Indy creatives, Britain had become an archaic, mock imperialist country with its nuclear arsenal and pretentions of great power status - one that it was imperative to cut free from. But in much of the rest of the world, Britain was often seen in rather more positive terms, indeed as a country which many would have preferred to have as a neighbour or a partner, to the ones they already had.

The prominent Canadian scholar and broadcaster Michael Ignatieff was in no doubt that 'Where peoples have lived in peace, secession is the worst sin in politics'. Of part-Scottish descent, he stated in June 2014 that his 'visceral opposition to Scottish, Catalan, Quebec and other projects of independence is not to nationalism, but to secession – to the breaking apart of political systems that, without violence, have enabled peoples to live together. For the breaking apart does not merely shatter a political union, it forces apart the shared identities that people like me carry in their souls'.[107]

It is rare for arresting literature or art to follow. Sometimes the best is bound up with dissecting the shattered relationship. If art imitates politics, this is likely to be the case. All the signs are that England would remain the chief reference point for nationalists of the independence era, perhaps to a morbid degree.

In post-1918 Ireland and East-Central Europe some of the best non-fiction writing was indeed bound up with a recently vanished past. Britain is arguably the equivalent of the central European cultural space which Austro-Hungary oversaw in the last forty years of its existence. But cross-fertilisation soon shrivelled up; the Hungarian capital, Budapest which, at a stretch, Edinburgh might be compared to in the British context, turned inwards. Its culture became parochial and wedded to the requirements of political nationalists. Life became constricted, and eventually very uncomfortable, for writers and artist with a plural and cosmopolitan identity, most notably, but not only, Jewish ones. Their counterparts would be Anglo-Scottish writers or artistic directors, publishing editors or cultural administrators who had previously flitted between two worlds.

Some think this cross-fertilisation is still possible and that it could even extend to Ireland. Irvine Welsh, the author of *Trainspotting,* became a vocal supporter of Scottish independence. He saw Britain as an imperialist, class-based state, believing symbols of Britishness to be just Englishness writ large. But he believed there was a chance (writing early in 2014) that an inter-island cultural unity could be established with the political partition of Britain.[108]

When assessing the examples of state break-up in messy and financially arduous circumstances, it is hard to see how such a benign cultural Commonwealth could easily evolve. It is more likely that in the condition of heightened nationalism, not a few writers would spring up who would effectively trade in nationalism, building careers by defining the literary personality of a newly free nation. Wole Soyinka, writing in the early years of post-colonial Africa glimpsed what was likely to be the fate of many writers; they would have to set aside independence of spirit and trade in the ideas that were fashionable in the new political order. He wrote in 1967: 'in the modern African state especially, the position of the writer has been such that he is in fact the very prop of state machinery...the writer must, for the moment at least (he persuades himself) postpone that unique reflection on experience and events which is what makes a writer...and constitute himself into a part of that machinery that will actually shape events....'[109]

The British-orientated musician, Eddie McGuire has composed and performed works containing Scottish themes all over the world. He believes, however, that undue emphasis on nationhood and identity in Scottish literature is in danger of stifling creativity and perhaps encouraging a new parochialism. He believed that 'profound questions about life, love and the wider world' were responsible for some of the most enduring writing and that literature functioning in close partnership with a national project has usually produced nothing comparable.[110]

Britain, for all its shortcomings, has managed, at times, to promote a genuinely liberal spirit in which some of this creativity flowed without intrusive political oversight. A country which for several hundreds of years had a major international role was simply too big for cultural uniformity to be attempted or maintained for long. But in smaller political jurisdictions, the prospects for cultural pluralism are far more uncertain. Independent Ireland censored the novels of perhaps most of its writers during the first forty years of independence. Such crude interference may not be on the horizon in Scotland but active management of the arts cannot be ruled out. Alex Salmond is very much in the style of the African 'Big Men' such as Jomo Kenyatta and Leopold Senghor who offered a form of autocratic rule in the post-colonial era. He has displayed the paternalist approach to the arts which he displays towards other branches of Scottish life in his revealing 2015 book *The Dream Shall Never Die*.

Nationally-minded literary experts have hailed the model of France, a country which has long used cultural policy as a conscious arm of promoting the prestige of the French state as one Scotland should not overlook. France clearly inspires the authors of *Arts of Independence* Alex Moffat and Alan Riach. Andre Malraux and Jack Lang, intellectuals who were at the helm of cultural policy as cabinet ministers in both rightist and leftist governments are saluted for what they achieved. But this is the very same France where a form of cultural imperialism was used after 1789 to impose a uniform culture on a previously very diverse country, especially in linguistic terms. In a review of the their work I wrote: 'If the French realm had included a few islands inhabited by Scottish Gallic speakers, I suspect they might have fared even worse than they did at the hands of London overlords or land hungry Scottish fortune-hunters'.[111]

In 2012-14 much dedicated energy was invested into combining different branches of the arts with a national programme. Some branches of Scottish culture were more receptive to nationally-minded expressions of culture in their spheres than others. Literature and folk music stand out. It remains to be seen if a new nationalist strand of writing and performing will become a dominant feature of the arts and letters scene in Scotland. I am doubtful that this will easily happen despite a politically-compliant civil service now having control over the direction of much arts funding. This is an ominous departure; if other places are any guide, then the state-sponsored cultural field will be largely confined to those who fit in thanks to agreeing with the agenda of the ruling party.

Despite the noise generated, the numbers active in the pro-Indy cultural front were not particularly large as Mairi McFadyen of the National Collective admitted after the referendum. A small number of cultural pundits and experimental writers and performers became dominating figures. These self-confident extroverts advanced their eclectic visions for the arts in an independent Scotland with much gusto. They tended to sometimes too readily dismiss others from the arts world who either wore their national identity lightly or else believed that whatever degree of Scottish patriotism they possessed could be absorbed in an over-arching British identity. In gathering material for this chapter, I wrote to one of the prominent cultural personalities on the Yes side requesting an interview. I was told in no uncertain terms that mine was 'a divisive' voice and that an interview was out of the question since I lacked any kind of serious integrity. I fear that the assumption of intransigent postures like this was far from uncommon in the Scottish arts world and that the divisions have been far-reaching, (in particular splitting people who would view themselves as belonging to the political left, into hostile camps). Instead of being a time of originality and effervescence, the new cultural departure initiated by the referendum might be seen as presaging an era of conformity and orthodoxy when a great silence may in fact start to fall over Scotland.

In his 2015 novel, Irvine Welsh has a character declare: 'Scots, once again are realising that they are back at the centre of the world'.[112] If this occurs through promoting writing that extols nationhood and identity, then this may be the surface impression. However, it is likely to be a brittle and ultimately provincial world where absorption with Scottishness fails to be the formula to create literature that travels well. Quality Scottish work is likely to emerge more easily outside the hothouse conditions of state-sponsored cultural nationalism. The National Collective episode ought to have demonstrated that intellectual absorption with political nationalism produces burn-out among many cultural folk as well as the political expropriation of culture. Works of critical merit may well be in short supply until writers especially cease to rely on nourishment from demonstrably Scottish sources alone.

Notes for Chapter 6

1. 'Blog', Poetic Politics Conference, 23 September 2015,
    https://poeticpoliticsconference.wordpress.com/category/blog/, accessed 24 September 2015.
2. Alexander Moffat and Alan Riach, *Arts of Independence,* Edinburgh: Luath
    Press, 2014, p. 46.
3. Pat Kane, 'No vote would stifle Scotland', *Scotsman,* 16 June 2014,
    http://www.scotsman.com/news/pat-kane-independence-vote-yes-or-no-1-3445064
4. David Torrance, 'Curious case of creatives who support independence', *Herald,*
    28 July 2014.
5. See Arthur Herman, *The Scottish Enlightenment: The Scots Invention of the Modern
    World,* London: 4th Estate, 2001, especially chapters 3, 4 and 8.
6. Herman, *The Scottish Enlightenment,* p.p. 209-10.
7. Edwin Muir, *Scottish Journey,* Edinburgh Mainstream Press, 1979, p. 244.
8. See Bob Purdie, *Hugh MacDiarmid, Black, Green, Red and Tartan,* Cardiff: Welsh
    Academic Press, 2012.
9. See Susan R. Wilson (ed.), T*he Correspondence Between Hugh MacDiarmid and
    Sorley MacLean,* Edinburgh University Press 2010, p. 32.
10. Andrew Marr, *The Battle for Scotland,* London: Penguin, 1992, p.66.
11. Richard Finlay, *Independent and Free,* Edinburgh: John Donald, 1994, p.91.
12. A.S. Neill, *Is Scotland Educated?,* Edinburgh and London: The Edinburgh Press,
    1936, p.p. 16-17.
13. Wilson, *The Correspondence,* p. 33.
14. Aileen Christiansen, 'Edwin Muir', *Oxford Dictionary of National Biography, Vol. 39,*
    Oxford: Oxford University Press,2004, p. 660.
15. Gavin Bowd, *Fascist Scotland: Caledonia and the Far-Right,* Edinburgh: Birlinn 2013, p. 160.
16. Bowd, *Fascist Scotland,* p.p. 170-2.
17. Robert Crawford, *Bannockburns: Scottish Independence and Literary Imagination,*
    Edinburgh University Press 2013, p.p. 184-5.
18. Gerry Hassan, *Caledonian Dreaming: The Quest for a Different Scotland,*

Edinburgh: Luath Press, 2014, p. 134.

19. *Scotsman*, 15 August 2010.

20. Stuart Kelly, *Headshock*, London: Hachette, 2009, p. 4.

21. Alex Salmond, foreword., Kelly, Headshock, p. viii.

22. David Whitehouse, Shortlist.com [2015], http://www.shortlist.com/entertainment/books/irvine-welsh-alex-salmond-asked-me-to-join-the-snp

23. Alan Bissett, 'The writers Alex Salmond is courting now will hold him to account', *Guardian*, 14 July 2013.

24. Andrew O'Hagan, 'Beast of a Nation', *London Review of Books*, vol 24, nr 21, 31 October 2002, p.p. 11-12.

25. 'Letter', *London Review of Books*, vol 24, nr 21, 31 October 2002.

26. Hamish Macdonell 'Yes campaign launch will cause problems — for the independence movement', *Spectator*, 25 May 2012; David Torrance, 'Amateur hour at Yes campaign launch', Scotsman, 26 May 2012.

27. Kenneth Roy, 'I agree. I agree entirely. I couldn't agree more', *Scottish Review*, 27 August 2013.

28. Pat Kane, 'Imagining a new nation', BBC Arts, 6 January 2015.

29. Daniel Jackson, 'How the sight of a podgy, naked Alan Bissett convinced me there's no hope for an independent Scotland', *Daily Telegraph*, 24 April 2014,.http://blogs.telegraph.co.uk/news/danieljackson/10028763/how-the-sight-of-a-podgy-naked-alan-bissett-convinced-me-theres-no-hope-for-an-independent-scotland

30. Alan Bissett on Twitter', 4 February 2015

31. Kevin McKenna, 'More power to Glasgow's online journalists', *Observer*, 30 March 2014.

32. Andrew Eaton-Lewis, 'Trust vs democracy', https://andreweatonlewis.wordpress.com/2015/03/11/trust-vs-democracy/> accessed 20 April 2015).

33. Interview 24 March 2015.

34. Alex Massie: 'Where's the art, National Collective?', *Spectator*, 14 March 2015.

35. Mairi McFadyen, 'Reflections', National Collective, 14 March 2014, http://nationalcollective.com/author/mairimcfadyen/ 14 March 2015.

36. Massie: 'Where's the art'.

37. Kane, 'Imagining a new nation'.

38. Alan Bissett, 'Who Carries The Carriers?', National Collective, 6 June 2013, http://nationalcollective.com/2013/06/06/alan-bissett-who-carries-the-carriers/

39. Robert Wohl, *The Generation of 1914*, Cambridge,Mass., Harvard University Press, 1979, p.p. 132, 133.

40. McFadyen, 'Reflections'.

41. Alan Bissett, 'How Scottish Theatre Predicted the Referendum', *Bella Caledonia*,

2 April 2015, reply from . 'Judy', 3 April 2015,
http://bellacaledonia.org.uk/2015/04/02/how-scottish-theatre-predicted-the-referendum/

42. Pat Kane, 'We have the (soft) power', *Scotsman*, 25 February 2014.

43. James MacMillan, 'God preserve us from washed-up celebs and preening 'artists' telling us how to vote', *Daily Telegraph*, 3 May 2011,
http://blogs.telegraph.co.uk/culture/jmacmillan/100053259/god-preserve-us-from-washed-up-celebs-and-preening-artists-telling-us-how-to-vote

44. Allan Massie, 'Kane's depressing view of democracy', *Scotsman*, 13 August 2014.

45. Italics inserted by the author.

46. Alan Bissett, 'The writers Alex Salmond is courting now will hold him to account', *Guardian*, 14 July 2013.

47. Interview with Denise Mina, 18 March 2015.

48. Alex Massie, 'Where's the art, National Collective?' *Scotsman*, 14 March 2015,
http://www.scotsman.com/lifestyle/arts/news/alex-massie-where-s-the-art-national-collective-1-3718728

49. Martyn McLaughlin, 'William McIlvanney impressed by independence hope', *Scotland on Sunday*, 22 February 2015

50. Mike Small, 'Writer's Bloc', *Bella Caledonia*, 20 July 2014,
http://bellacaledonia.org.uk/2014/07/20/writers-bloc-2/

51. Small, 'Writer's Bloc'.

52. Small, 'Writer's Bloc'.

53. Hugh Andrew, 'Amazon jobs come at a high price for Scotland', *Scotsman*, 8 December 2011,.

54. Ben Child, 'Scottish government funding for Brave "harmed rest of country's film industry"', *Guardian*, 27 November 2013; Brian Ferguson, 'Public funding of Brave hurt Scots film industry', *Scotsman*, 26 November 2013.

55. Alan Bissett, 'The writers Alex Salmond'.

56. Neal Ascherson, 'Scottish Independence is Inevitable', *New York Times*, 18 July 2014.

57. Val McDermid, 'Away with the fearties', *Guardian*, 22 August 2014.

58. Phil Miller, 'Interview: Vicky Featherstone, National Theatre of Scotland', *Herald*, 17 December 2012.

59. Brian Ferguson, 'John Byrne insists Gray is wrong', *Scotsman*, 20 December 2012.

60. 'Unionists condemn poet's call for "social audit"', *Courier*, 19 December 2012.

61. Deborah Orr, 'Scotland should not be wasting time on blaming the English any more', *Guardian*, 21 December 2014.

62. Brian Ferguson, 'Author Alasdair Gray denies anti-English claims', *Scotsman*, 13 August 2014.

63. Brian Ferguson, 'John Byrne says modern Scots artists don't work', *Scotsman*, 13 June 2014.

64. Brian Groom, 'Scottish vote: false votes and "fascism"', *Financial Times*, 9 June 2014.

65. Jenny Hjul, 'Are Scottish artists too afraid to say No?, *Daily Telegraph* 12 June 2014, http://blogs.telegraph.co.uk/news/jennyhjul/100276048/are-scottish-artists-too-afraid-to-say-no/

66. Hjul, "Are Scottish artists'.

67. Claire MacMillan, 'Scottish composers and the referendum – nationalism and patriotism do not necessarily go hand in hand', *The Gramophone*, 8 September 2014.

68. Interview with Eddie McGuire, 5 April 2015.

69. Billy Bragg, 'Exclusive: Scottish nationalism and British nationalism aren't the same', *Guardian*, 16 September 2014.

70. Phil Miller, 'Denise Mina: I'm voting No...indy is a conceptual mistake', *Herald*, 17 September 2014.

71. Interview with Denise Mina, 18 March 2015.

72. Interview with Denise Mina, 18 March 2015.

73. Interview with Denise Mina, 18 March 2015.

74. Ewan Morrison, 'I've Decided to Vote Yes by Ewan Morrison', *Bella Caledonia*, 5 July 2014, http://bellacaledonia.org.uk/2014/07/05/ive-decided-to-vote-yes-by-ewan-morrison/

75. Ewan Morrison, 'YES: Why I Joined Yes and Why I Changed to No', Wake Up Scotland [2014], https://wakeupscotland.wordpress.com/2014/09/15/ewan-morrison-yes-why-i-joined-yes-and-why-i-changed-to-no/ (accessed 24 September 2014).

76. Morrison, 'YES: Why I Joined Yes'.

77. Morrison, 'YES: Why I Joined Yes'.

78. Morrison, 'YES: Why I Joined Yes'.

79. C.J. Sansom, 'Scottish independence: saying no will arrest rise of populist nationalism', *Guardian*, 15 September 2014, http://www.theguardian.com/commentisfree/2014/sep/15/scottish-independence-populist-nationalism-cj-sansom

80. Sansom, 'Scottish independence'.

81. C.J. Sansom, *Dominion*, London: Mantle, 2012, p.p.590-93..

82. Sansom, *Dominion*, p. 591.

83. 'Edinburgh Writer C.J. Sansom enters Independence debate', *Daily Record*, 23 April 2014.

84. 'Edinburgh Writer C.J. Sansom'.

85. Brian Wilson, 'Time for independent experts in Scotland', *Scotsman*, 17 October 2015.

86. Ken Walton, 'Would SSO survive Scottish independence?', *Scotsman*, 11 August 2014.

87. See James MacMillan, 'I had not thought about it like that before', in Tom Devine (ed), *Scotland's Shame*, Edinburgh Mainstream, 1999, p.p.13-24.

88. Letter from James MacMillan 28 March 2015.

89. Interview with Stuart Kelly, 16 March 2015.

90. Letter from James MacMillan 28 March 2015.

91. Brian Ferguson, 'Fringe comics 'afraid' to tell referendum jokes', *Scotsman*, 7 June 2014.

92. Tom Peterkin, Stand up comedian Susan Calman faced a barrage of abuse', *Scotsman*, 2 May 2013.

93. *Daily Record*, 30 June 2014.

94. Bissett, 'How Scottish Theatre', online letter from 'Lit Grrrl', 3 April 2015.

95. Chris Deerin, 'Why does the Scottish independence movement produce such bad art', 13 August 2014 (originally published in the *Daily Mail*), https://medium.com/@chrisdeerin/why-does-the-scottish-independence-movement-produce-such-bad-art-3cab8e4e6753

96. Magnus Linklater, 'Bill Paterson: '"It's never felt so Scottish"', *Times* (Scottish edition), 19 September 2015.

97. Massie 'Where's the art'.

98. Interview with Stuart Kelly, 16 March 2015.

99. O'Hagan, 'Beast of a Nation'.

100. Stanley Baxter: 'Canny' Scots will vote No in September', *Herald*, 24 June 2014.

101. Mike Wade, 'Schama laments 'tribalism' that could destroy Britain', *Times*, 24 June 2014.

102. 'Scottish separatism? I blame that dreadful Braveheart film', *Daily Telegraph*, 24 June 2014.

103. BBC Newsnight, 8 September 2014.

104. Tom Devine, 'How history turned against Tory-voting Scotland', Guardian, 14 September 2014.

105. Alf Young, 'Professor Sir Tom Devine: A Riposte', *Wake Up Scotland*, 15 September 2014, https://wakeupscotland.wordpress.com/2014/09/15/alf-young-professor-sir-tom-devine-a-riposte/

106. Billy Kay, 'Scottish independence essay: Yes to a richer future', *Scotsman*, 29 July 2014.

107. Michael Ignatieff, 'A secessionist lust for power that tears lives asunder', *Financial Times*, 27 June 2014.

108. *Independent*, 2 February 2013, http://www.independent.co.uk/news/uk/this-britain/scottish-power-irvine-welsh-makes-an-impassioned-personal-plea-for-an-independent-scotland-8473639.html

109. Richard Pine, *The Disappointed Bridge: Ireland and the Post-colonial World*, Cambridge: Cambridge Scholars Publishing, 2014, p. 535.

110. Interview, 5 April 2015.

111. See the review of this book in *Scottish Affairs*, Vol 24, no 3, 2015, p.p. 232-34.

112. Irvine Welsh, *A Decent Ride*, London: Jonathan Cape, 2015.

CHAPTER 7: SCOTTISH NATIONALISM AND THE WORLD

The devolution settlement of 1999 made foreign policy a Westminster prerogative. But the SNP periodically grabs headlines by pursuing its own foreign policy and from May 2015, Alex Salmond has been the party's foreign affairs spokesman at Westminster.

However, it is possible to view the party's focus on the international stage as a gigantic bluff. Throughout its 72-year-existence, the SNP has not exhibited much curiosity about the world beyond Britain. Escaping from England's orbit has obviously been a primary objective. Serious planning for independence has rarely been such a pressing concern for the leadership. Accordingly, it doesn't feel compelled to study the experience of places which previously launched themselves as new states. The party is surprisingly ignorant about conditions in places like Scandinavia whose 20th century advances it believes Scotland is capable of emulating. Alex Salmond, the longest-serving SNP leader, travelled abroad but often it was to up-and-coming countries whose prestige might rub off on Scotland's government through some kind of indirect association. He was careful not to raise any human rights issues (such as expressing concern to China over Tibet) but he has criticised Western powers, or organizations which they influence such as NATO, if their actions display a trace of the arrogance and aggression which the SNP feel has shaped London's attitude to Scotland for much of history. Accordingly, it is not surprising that the SNP is one of the political forces which gives vocal backing to the nationalism of Palestinians that is ranged against Israel.

Scotland Emerges But World Leaders Draw Back

Those who wondered what the first really well-known SNP politician, the Glasgow lawyer Winnie Ewing, meant when she boldly declared, 'Stop the world, Scotland wants to get on', may already have an answer '.[1] She uttered this bold cry just after being responsible for the SNP's first decisive electoral breakthrough in 1967. For some decades, it could have been assumed that, once on the global escalator, Scotland would be a social democratic, pro-Western and essentially moderate voice in world affairs. Common interests and the ties of history and kinship would be underscored. There would be no attempt to uproot British symbols and other cultural markers and instead a cultural symbiosis would be encouraged. Independent Scotland's early rulers would be likely to ensure that relations between the new independent state and the remainder of the United Kingdom would be close and amicable.

But after Alex Salmond took the reins of power in 1990, it soon transpired that this was a premature judgment. He boldly promoted an edgy, disputatious and even self-righteous Scotland that was prepared to re-define its international role. After winning in 2007, he seemed to be more comfortable with countries and leaders who had challenged Western domination in various ways. There were few inhibitions about noisily challenging British interests even if the practical gain for Scotland was slight. It grew increasingly unlikely that a Scotland dominated by Salmond and like-minded Scots would wish to align with Britain and America on critical issues as indeed most of the countries in north-west Europe had done for a long time. By the time Salmond stepped down as leader in 2015 having left his indelible mark on Scottish affairs, it no longer seemed outlandish to think that Scotland might align itself on foreign and defence issues very differently than it had done as part of the United Kingdom.

The most significant straw in the wind was the Megrahi affair which erupted suddenly in 2009. It involved a collision not with London but with Washington. It did not matter that the USA had been a magnet for Scottish migrants over centuries or that, arguably, its intervention in the Second World War had prevented Scotland (as part of Britain) from falling under the sway of a frightening continental tyranny.

The Nationalists have, by now, gained plenty of experience in defying Britain and challenging its international approach to issues as diverse as upholding NATO as a nuclear defence alliance and opposing armed action against the Serbian regime of Slobodan Milošević in 1999 when it was seeking to expel most Albanians from the disputed province of Kosovo.

A Nationalist-inclined Scotland hoped to create a different world in which there was less meddling and armed intervention especially by major western countries. Hard nationalists in ideological terms saw their country as having been a prime victim of British imperial might stretching over centuries. A country already possessing clear vestiges of nationhood suffered at the hands of English rulers like Edward I, Henry VIII and in the 18th century from the Duke of Cumberland who earned the sobriquet 'Butcher' for the way he quelled the 1745 rebellion. The fact that numerous Scots had a conspicuous role in the 18th century British slave trade and that two of them Dr William Jardine and Sir James Matheson sparked a war with China when its rulers tried to restrict the trade of opium, is usually lightly passed over.

Scotland's potential to be an awkward and potentially disruptive state began to be more widely appreciated in 2014. During the referendum of that year, Salmond reacted with undisguised irritation when at least one foreign leader pronounced on Scotland's future in ways he didn't like. This was the then Prime Minister of Australia, Tony Abbott. In August 2014, he prefaced his remarks on the imminent referendum by saying: 'What the Scots do is a matter for the Scots and not for a moment do I presume to tell Scottish voters which way they should vote'. But he was prepared to be forthright and went on to say that he believed 'an independent Scotland would not be in the best interests of the international community'.[2] He expressed his belief that 'the people who would like to see the break-up of the United Kingdom are not the friends of justice, not the friends of freedom, and that the countries that would cheer at the prospect of the break-up with the United Kingdom are not the countries whose company one would like to keep'.[3] In response Alex Salmond declared that the referendum was a 'model of democratic conduct' and Mr Abbott's comments were 'offensive to the Scottish people... Who is Mr Abbott to lecture Scots on freedom and justice?'.[4]

Australia is an anti-model for the SNP. The country still wishes to maintain organic ties with Britain. This was shown decisively in 1999 when 55 per cent of Australians rejected a republic and backed the continuing role of the monarchy in Australian government and law. Each of Australia's six states rejected the republican plan. The only place which didn't was the Australian Capital Territory at Canberra; home to the political class and its media and bureaucratic ancillaries, it backed a republic by a clear two-thirds.

In 1999, brash pundits, celebrities and gurus of various kinds helped to turn the tide against their own republican cause by their often patronising manner. Similar types wish to re-engineer the Scottish psyche so that the country can be an exemplar in terms of global left-wing radicalism and unrealistic and costly social experiments at home. They predominated in Salmond's campaign and have put plenty off. But many contemporary Scots may lack the independence of spirit and dislike of authoritarianism which defined emerging Australia after it was settled in 1788. These are characteristics which it has never quite lost.

Salmond suggested that Abbott had been urged to speak out at the behest of David Cameron and British officials. It is unlikely that Abbot had any need of such prompting. He is likely to see the threat that an adventurer like Salmond poses to already frayed Western democratic unity. I doubt if, like Cameron, he would have allowed a 3-year referendum campaign to ensue and denied a vote on 18 September 2014 to Scots living in other parts of the UK.

The SNP needed to be more diplomatic when the Chinese authorities made plain (albeit more diplomatically than Abbott had done) their unhappiness about the break-up of Britain. When questioned on Scotland's independence referendum during a trip to Britain in June 2014, Premier Li Keqiang said he wanted to see a 'united United Kingdom'.[5] 'I believe that the United Kingdom can stay at the forefront in leading the world's growth and development and also continue to play an important and even bigger role for regional stability and global peace,' Li said.

A journalist later asked the Scottish minister for Culture Fiona Hyslop 'if she thinks, given the premier's remarks, Beijing feels threatened by the referendum'. 'Wearing a stony expression', she contented herself with saying that 'I think he was being diplomatically polite to his [British] hosts'.[6]

But Beijing might well have had cause to fear 'the demonstration effect' of a British break-up. It has faced worsening secessionist unrest in the autonomous region of Sinkiang, formerly Eastern Turkistan. It had been brought under Chinese rule only due to costly and protracted Chinese military efforts in the 18th century, the same period when Scotland was united with the rest of Britain, albeit in a far more peaceable manner.

In many other parts of the world the eruption of a territorial nationalism is seen as unsettling in an island long viewed as a model of continuity and stability on a fractured planet. During the referendum years, as Salmond and his colleagues made political nationalism palatable for huge numbers of previously indifferent Scots, the world remained largely numb to, or even suspicious, of the SNP's aims and outlook.

The SNP was unable to line up any currently active world political figures to give even tepid endorsement to its plans. It was probably not for a lack of trying. In 2010, only days before announcing his plans for a separate Scottish state, Alex Salmond had 'anxiously' pleaded with a British Embassy to secure him a high-profile meeting with the French Prime Minister François Fillon. Such talks would have buttressed his claim to be a world statesman in his own right, carving out his own foreign policy separate to that of the UK. But, despite repeated attempts, Mr Fillon's office told the embassy he did not have time for such an encounter. The SNP leader did not disclose the snub, instead issuing a press release stating: 'Scotland's Auld Alliance with France represents a strong, enduring bond.'[7]

Earlier, Salmond had solicited support from world figures to support his 2009 decision to release, on compassionate grounds, the man convicted in a Scottish court of the Lockerbie bombing, Britain's biggest ever mass murder. Documents secured under freedom of information law found that both Nelson Mandela and Archbishop Desmond Tutu complied but hardly anyone else did. Mary Robinson, the former Irish President, refused. It had previously been disclosed that Salmond's officials drafted a statement for the US tycoon Donald Trump, saying he hoped the decision would 'break the cycle of violence around the world' and urging critics not to 'ever demean' Scotland. But he refused to go ahead.[8]

As interest in the referendum drama mounted, top-level backing for Scottish secession remained virtually impossible to detect. Philip Stephens wrote in the *Financial Times* under the headline 'The world is saying No to Scottish separation':

'I have not heard a single soul from Washington or Delhi, Brussels or Beijing suggest separation could be good for Scotland or Britain. "God forbid!" said a puzzled Sushma Swaraj, India's foreign minister, when told this week that Scotland may indeed opt for separation'. 'Travel beyond Britain's shores and the persistent question you hear is the simplest one. Why? How can one of the world's most successful multinational states contemplate such a wilful act of self-harm'.[9]

The SNP has never shown any inhibitions about proclaiming itself a party of nationalism. This concept is still seen as tarnished by the behaviour of ruling ultra-nationalists in inter-war Europe above all in Italy and Germany. Except perhaps in Spain where the main party in the Basque region is known as the Basque Nationalist party (PNV), elsewhere in Europe it would usually be seen as liability to give nationalism such prominence in a party's title. In Eastern Europe after 1989, aggressively nationalist parties preferred to emphasise 'National Unity' or 'Radicalism' in their titles and, in the Romania of the early 1990s, I was even told by anti-minority political figures that they were not 'nationalist'.

Perhaps the Scottish Nationalists are so un-preoccupied about their name because in Britain, nationalism has rarely (until now) had the unsettling overtones it had acquired on the continent by the mid-20th century. It may be an unconscious acknowledgement by Scottish separatists that they are operating in the relatively calmer British environment. Or, alternatively, it may be an example of the party's self-referential character: its name is increasingly familiar and effective at home and therefore nothing else matters, certainly not any doubtful associations with darker moments of European history.

But undoubtedly in many other parts of the world the eruption of a territorial nationalism is seen as unsettling in an island long regarded as a model of continuity and stability. During the referendum years, Alex Salmond and his colleagues succeeded in making political nationalism palatable for huge numbers of previously doubting Scots, but the world has remained largely numb to, or even suspicious of the SNP's aims and outlook.

Self-interest is a big part of the reason. Most states are ethnically mixed in the composition of their population. There can be few of them that have not faced a challenge to the shape of their borders since the advent of modern nationalism. Plenty within the EU are wary about new states being carved from within existing borders. The latest was Kosovo in 2008. A hard-core of EU states refuse to recognise it. Perhaps it is no coincidence that several of them, Spain, Romania and Bosnia Herzegovina, are grappling with secessionist tendencies of greater or lesser intensity. All the 28 member-states of the EU would have to give their approval for Scotland joining. Lord Kerr of Kinlochard who was head of the diplomatic service from 1997 to 2002, has written that: 'Of course, the arguments for respecting the democratic will of the Scots would be strong; but so, in some EU capitals, might be the desire to demonstrate to domestic secessionists that the road to independent EU membership could be long and winding.'[10]

For several years, Britain's economic performance has enabled it to stand apart from the crisis-ridden Eurozone, comprising 19 of the EU's 28 members. There is bound to be not only puzzlement but also apprehension if it turns out that a relatively successful country like Britain is not immune from powerful centrifugal forces. If Britain, a nuclear power, member of the UN Security Council, a hub of world communications, and the planet's 6th largest economy, succumbs to Balkanisation, then just which countries are really immune from disintegration.

A breakaway push from Scotland might have been viewed differently if it had occurred in the 1980s. There was no doubt that then, the quantity of oil in Scottish waters was capable of giving Scotland's small population a high standard of living. At the same time, Britain was in a bit of a mess. It was clearly internally divided, there was a seemingly never-ending conflict in Northern Ireland, as well as acute and recurrent problems with industrial relations. The era of decolonisation from parts of Africa and Asia was still fresh in many minds. Yet Scots overwhelmingly shrunk from leaving Britain at that time and were prepared to endure even the highly unpopular government of Margaret Thatcher. It suggests that the long-term approach of many Scots to independence has not been shaped by economic considerations but by fluctuating collective emotions and indeed the world is struggling to discern what lies at their root.

An American journalist Neil Irwin (whose name suggests that he may be of Scottish extraction), wrestled with this difficulty as he tried to explain the mood in Scotland to the readership of the *New York Times* on the eve of the 2014 referendum:

'If you had told someone in 2012 that in just two years the eurozone would remain bonded together but the United Kingdom might not, they would have thought you insane. But here we are.

What's all the more remarkable about this possible secession is that major, specific grievances over public policy between Scotland and the rest of Britain are hard to identify. This isn't like the Southern chunk of the United States seceding in 1860 because it was committed to slavery and the North was against it. ...

The economic and geopolitical advantages of being a larger country offer some advantages that a small country cannot match. It's no accident that the United States is the richest country in the world, creator of some of the most meaningful technological advances of the last century; it is not for nothing that Europeans who speak different languages and have different cultures have tried to emulate it with the E.U. In big countries, businesses can get all the benefits of scale, selling within giant markets that all use the same currency with the same legal system. In geopolitics, large countries can strike hard bargains to get access to one another's markets, while trouncing smaller rivals at the negotiating table.

And big countries tend to be more resilient to shocks. Imagine how much economic trouble the Republic of Louisiana would have been in after Hurricane Katrina or the Independent Nation of New York City after the Sept. 11, 2001, attacks'.

Irwin concluded that it was emotion and sentiment rather than any pragmatic cost- benefit analysis which explained the momentum behind separation in 2014: 'Many Scots feel as if they have more to gain from governing alongside people who look like them and talk like them than they have to lose from no longer being part of a bigger, more powerful nation. A video posted by the pro-independence campaign captures a bit of this. Amid soft-focus images of beautiful Scottish landscapes and charming-looking Scots going about their day, a woman holding flowers says: "Independence. It's what we all want in our lives. So why shouldn't our country be independent too?'[11]

From 2015, with its 56 MPs in the British House of Commons, the SNP will have a platform to try and convince the world that far from being outlandish, independence for Scotland is the normal end-point in the journey of an ancient nation with a newly-discovered sense of pride. It will be by no means out of character if Alex Salmond decides to use Westminster as an arena to argue that globalisation has not curtailed the relevance of small states. It has ample facilities to entertain high-profile guests and hold eye-catching stunts and public events that keep the Scottish question in the limelight. In the aftermath of a victory for pro-independence forces in the Spanish region of Catalonia on 27 September 2015 (one that failed to win an absolute majority of the electorate) the SNP even made a daring claim. The Spanish and Catalan authorities were informed that it was prepared to 'mediate and assist' using its experience in the recent 'consensual' Scottish referendum.[12] The cheeky demarche assumes that an event which had no lack of street level intimidation will somehow be regarded as 'consensual' and that the SNP will be viewed as a genuinely disinterested party rather than one primarily motivated by its own internal agenda, namely to create a precedent in Spain that will hasten the break-up of the United Kingdom.

Populists are Everywhere

It might be viewed as the stuff of a political fantasy novel for the best-known figure in an anti-British political movement to behave in this way. The novelist Tom Sharpe could have provided much mirth and fury by inventing a character like Alex Salmond. Figures ready to tweak the tail of the British Lion have emerged periodically in British political history from the Irish nationalist Charles Stewart Parnell in the 1880s to Malta's Dom Mintoff in the 1970s.

When Mintoff died aged 96 in 2012, the headline over his obituary in one British paper read: 'Pugnacious Prime Minister of Malta who fought for liberation from British colonial rule'. This 'clever and quarrelsome, driven and cussed' politician as Prime Minister in the mid-1950s at first desired 'a total merger with Britain that would see Maltese MPs at Westminster and full, unrestricted British citizenship for every inhabitant of the island'.[13] Independent from 1964 but still using the British pound and with the armed forces under British control, Mintoff, back in power from 1971, opted for bold nationalist self-assertion. He exploited his island's strategic geographic position to obtain financial inducements from China and the Soviet Union which alarmed Britain and NATO. He visited Colonel Gaddafi's Libya half a dozen times in his first two years in office. In 1974, Malta threw off a century and a half of allegiance to the crown to become a republic within the Commonwealth. By 1979, the last British troops had been withdrawn but Mintoff's squabbles with Britain sporadically erupted as when the British press was banned from Malta in retaliation for what he deemed its slanted coverage.

Given the degree to which Alex Salmond has promoted a confrontational relationship with London, it is not at all far-fetched to see an even more turbulent contest between a nationalist Scotland and not only London but the rest of the West in the time ahead. It is also quite possible that at the close of Salmond's life, obituaries will appear in the London media similar to this one in the *Independent*:

'His foes were only too happy to see the back of a man they regarded as a scheming bully with totalitarian tendencies. His allies as well often found Mintoff quite maddening: impatient, self-centred, and domineering.

But indubitably he was a patriot, who more than any other individual, and largely by the force of his own personality, was responsible for the independent Malta of today'.[14]

Mintoff was an iconoclast only really able to turn (thankfully briefly) to his bizarre neighbour Gaddafi. But Salmond is far more representative of world politics where populists who seek to appeal to the mass of voters through emotion rather than reason and by identifying internal and external foes, have become plentiful. Unruly politicians, seeking to probe and push back Western influence have far more opportunities to cause mayhem. The late Hugo Chavez in Venezuela and Tayip Erdogan in Turkey are just the best-known serial rule-breakers who have presided over significant middle-level countries. They smashed down powerful ruling establishments, pursued adversarial, rather than prudent policies, separated 'the moral masses from unethical elites' while building up personal systems of wealth and power which often dwarfed the privileges of those whom they had toppled.[15] They also looked for illiberal allies across the world in order to make it hard for the West to move against them if their actions became too disruptive.

It is not hard at all to envisage Salmond (or a successor) moving in this direction. He has successfully depicted himself as the champion of a moral Scottish citizenry against an unaccountable landed elite, and a Labour ruling party that prefers to bend the knee to London rather than stand up for Scotland. He has sought allies not among other unfree nations or European minorities but among bigger states often flush with economic resources and who wish to pursue a path separate from, and sometimes in collision with, the West. He enjoys the advantage that his foes at the top of UK politics seem complacent and battle-weary by comparison. Scandals at the top of British political life such as the one involving the deputy head of the House of Lords, John Sewel, who was forced to quit on July 2015 after pictures appeared in the press of him allegedly snorting cocaine while consorting with prostitutes, make his disruptive role all the easier.[16] Populists like Salmond are no longer viewed as exotic or faintly sinister but ultimately parochial figures; they enjoy world notice, and access to resources which fuel their populist cause, and are capable of causing headaches especially for defensive Western leaderships.

Populist parties makes the EU nervous. Too many shocks and upsets have occurred as a result of movements like Jörg haider Freedom Party in Austria, the Lega Nord and the Five Star movement in Italy, the Party for Freedom (VVD) of Geert Wilders in the Netherlands, and, above all, Syriza in Greece, challenging the EU's direction of travel. The SNP may insist that it is Europhile and not Eurosceptic but this was also the original position of Viktor Orbán's Fidesz movement. Prime Minister of Hungary from 1998 to 2002 and again from 2010 onwards, Orbán's political career began when his country was still a communist 'People's Democracy'. He led what was then a liberal anti-communist youth movement and acquired fame for publically protesting past repressive action by the Soviet Union in Hungary and challenging the right of the Soviet Union to direct his country's affairs from behind the scenes. But today Orbán admits to being an advocate of an 'illiberal democracy' and in September 2014 he froze gas deliveries to Ukraine as the country could not afford to run the risk of losing its own Russian gas supplies.[17] He has combined what have sometimes been seen as expressions of Hungarian chauvinism with a readiness to endorse some but not all aspects of the world view of Russia's President Vladimir Putin. Outside Scotland, there is perhaps no other European country where genuinely competitive elections take place, but in which a single party holds such complete sway.

Salmond himself has gone on record in 2014 to describe Putin as 'an effective politician' who 'had restored a substantial part of Russian pride and that must be a good thing.'[18] The interviews in which these remarks were made occurred on the eve of Russia's seizure of Crimea. But a search for any subsequent distancing by Salmond from his cordial stance towards Putin has yielded up no results. So it would not be unreasonable for some EU decision-makers to assume that as a full member of the EU, a nationalist-led Scotland might prove a disruptive actor especially upon realising the capacity of Brussels to interfere in Scottish affairs far more than London previously did.

For the EU Scottish Nationalism is Still Nationalism

The growing tendency of the EU institutions to suborne the sovereignty of its national members, has disillusioned one of the SNP's most prominent figures. Jim Sillars, who started out in politics as a Labour MP (first elected in 1970) was the architect of the SNP's 'Independence in Europe' policy which has shaped its stance towards the EU since 1988. He persuaded a party which had previously believed that EU membership would merely swap British rule for EU control, that embracing the European integration project could speed up the acquisition of Scottish independence. A Scotland which had cut loose from the rest of the UK would be far from isolated in the world. As a full EU member-state, it would wield influence in an entity that at that time was emerging as one of the world's crucial power centres. With English increasingly the dominant language in EU business, Scotland could even leapfrog ahead of other countries, its talented decision-makers exercising the kind of influence in Brussels which in times past they had exercised in London. But Sillars recanted as the EU, in his eyes, turned into an unrepresentative behemoth.

Like Mintoff of Malta, he has switched from being ready to subsume his country's identity in a wider political union, to asserting a robust nationalism that should not be checked by centralising forces from wherever they came. He has complained about the 'centralising treaties' of Amsterdam, Nice and above all Lisbon which have given the EU 'state status' in that it can sign international treaties and agreements as would any other sovereign.'[19] This was not the EU that he had championed back in 1988 when he had glimpsed a cooperative alliance of nations whose members could still exercise veto power if the European Commission advanced proposals that seriously damaged any of their interests. By 2015, he was seriously urging the party to re-think its whole position on the EU. As an alternative, he proposed that Scotland link up with the European Free Trade Association (EFTA), a group of four countries that are part of the EU's single market but do not sign-up to all their treaties and tariffs. Sillars enjoys respect in SNP ranks for his campaigning prowess in 2014, but his call for the party to consider other options has fallen on deaf ears. 'Nowhere have I found a critique of an EU where the right of the state to veto has almost disappeared… 'Rightly or wrongly, the SNP seems to give the impression that the EU is "good" full stop,' Sillars ruefully observes.[20]

Alex Salmond continues to be conspicuously pro-EU, perhaps being principally concerned about the leverage it could give Scotland's rulers on the world stage and less bothered than Sillars about the curbs on what policies a Scottish government could follow on home soil. But Salmond's own pragmatic Europhilia has not deterred him from opposing the 1999 EU-NATO intervention in Kosovo and he falsely claimed in 2012 that advice had been received indicating that there were no impediments for Scotland's early admission as an independent state.[21]

It is not unreasonable to judge that the EU's attraction has essentially been a tactical one for the SNP; the powerful magnetic role which it exercised across much of Europe for over fifty years suggested that upon leaving Britain, Scotland would not face an awkward transition. Instead, it would join a dynamic entity that enjoyed status and legitimacy and had enabled countries emerging from tyranny in different parts of Europe to find a new path to respectability and modernisation.

But the SNP struggles to promote the European cause in quite the same way that Liberal Democrat politicians have often done in Britain. Occasional florid claims have been made that Scotland, in partnership with others, is capable of demonstrating 'the soft power' which the EU for a long time wielded in the European neighbourhood. But the calamitous economic crisis in the single currency area comprising 19 out of 28 EU members, and the failure of the EU to restrain Russian offensive moves in Ukraine or deter pressure on the Baltic states (EU members since 2005), has exposed the limits of EU power.

Perhaps understandably the EU mood has become cautious especially about any territorial change that would involve its own core members. On 12 September 2012, José Manuel Barroso, the president of the European Commission from 2004 to 2014, was widely condemned by SNP supporters when, upon being asked directly about Scottish secession on the BBC's World at One programme, he stated that he would not speculate about possible secessions before going on to say that: 'A new state, if it wants to join the European Union, has to apply to become a member like any state ... and the other states have to give their consent'.[22] In an interview on the BBC's 'Andrew Marr show' in February 2014, Barroso said it would be 'extremely difficult' for an independent Scotland to join the EU, which the SNP's deputy leader, John Swinney described as 'pretty preposterous'.[23]

The SNP's argument is that since Scotland is already subject to EU law, membership should be automatic and it had some influential backers such as Sir David Edward, who used to sit as a British judge on the European Court of Justice. The SNP has insisted also that, if Scotland were thrown out of the EU, England would be too. But the pro-independence journalist Iain MacWhirter observed that 'the EU spokespeople do not appear to be saying that either, and seem to accept that the UK minus Scotland would still be a member state'.[24]

Barroso was written off by plenty in the SNP as a transitory Portuguese figure, perhaps even a stooge of the British government and certainly unlikely to have become the EU's top bureaucrat but for the backing of Tony Blair back in 2004. But there was no criticism from Barroso's colleagues or from other member states in the wake of his rather blunt interventions. The prospect of Britain disintegrating may have been too alarming a thought at a time when plenty of troubles were piling up for the EU. Indeed, in 2015, when the UK government announced there would shortly be a referendum on the country's membership of the EU, it might have been expected that in parts of the EU power structure, the reaction might have been good riddance: if you are unhappy with current arrangements, then just walk straight out the exit and there is no need to look behind you.

But instead, there was no shortage of expressions of concern from leading EU players desperate to stave off fresh destabilisation. Britain had played a balancing role, especially as Franco-German cooperation, the axis around which the EU has evolved, delivered less and less for the EU project after 2008.

It was a more pragmatic and less ideological member, one which complained about bureaucratic overload but often had a far better record in implementing EU directives than other countries which proclaimed their European orientation. Ambrose Evans-Pritchard, a well-connected journalist was even arguing in mid-2015 that: 'Germany has opened the door to a grand bargain and possible treaty changes to prevent Britain pulling out of the European Union, a risk deemed calamitous for German interests and for the long-term stability of the EU'.

He quoted Wolfgang Schäuble, the influential German finance minister as saying: 'We have a huge interest in the UK remaining a strong and engaged member'. According to the journalist, Schäuble was determined to find some way to combine its own drive for deep reforms of the EU system with Britain's particular demands. 'We will try to move in this direction, possibly through agreements that would later be incorporated into treaty changes. There is a big margin of manoeuvre', the German minister was quoted as saying.[25]

Among its European partners, no shock of any kind was desired from Britain whether it be abrupt departure from the EU or the break-up of the country. The SNP, however, was unmoved; the EU link continues to be one of the primary means for it to put Britain behind it and venture into international affairs as a sovereign state. So far it only matters to a fringe in the SNP that the EU will constrain Scotland's freedom of action given the sovereignty it has extracted from individual members. Whether sickly, quarrelsome or else dynamic and achievement-orientated, the current state of the EU doesn't seem to interest the SNP overmuch. Holyrood has yet to hear a compelling debate on EU matters in which SNP parliamentarians genuinely explore what future model of integration suits Scotland's needs best. Instead, boiler-plate speeches are often the order of the day. In summary, the EU is largely a propaganda prop for the SNP.

Scandinavian Fantasies

So too is a part of the continent which for long has been a world brand denoting progress, civilized conduct, and human innovation in taming a challenging environment – Scandinavia.

Norway, 200 hundred miles north-east of Scotland is, on many measures, the most successful country in the world. It has consistently ranked first (ahead of Switzerland and Australia) in the UN's Human Development Index, which measures quality of life, literacy, and longevity. Alex Salmond used to regularly proclaim that Scotland was poised to enter the Scandinavian 'arc of prosperity' if it had the good sense to pull away from the rest of Britain.[26] He and his party identified with the big state, multiculturalism, neutrality and with pro-environmental policies that seemed to rule the roost in Europe's high north. But even as Scotland made world headlines over many months in 2014, nobody of any note in Norway, Denmark and Sweden urged Scotland to open a southern extension of Scandinavia. At $500 billion and $560 billion respectively, the economies of Norway and Sweden are more than twice the size of Scotland's.[27] Besides, the social democratic, open door, and state-led model for Scandinavian society extolled by the SNP had become increasingly obsolete by the start of the 21st century.

Scotland's major banks would have collapsed in 2008 but for a rescue mounted by the British government which continued to generously fund the country's experiment in devolution. In Sweden during the 1990s, there were a series of financial shocks that actually saw leading banks collapse and interest rates rise to 500 per cent. Instead of intensifying state paternalism, Sweden slashed a forest of regulations and embraced competition. Government spending fell from a massive 67 per cent of GDP in 1993 to 49 per cent in 2014. Sweden's top rate of tax has been slashed by 27 percentage points since 1983 while taxes on property, gifts, wealth and inheritance were abolished.[28] In Denmark, parents can use state money to send their children to private schools and then top it up with their own money. Private companies run a quarter of Sweden's primary health care practices and some of its leading hospitals. Sweden has one of the liveliest start-up scenes in Europe. It also has the second-largest venture capital industry as a proportion of GDP after the United Kingdom.

Thanks to its oil wealth, Norway has remained wedded to socialist economics for somewhat longer. But, by 2014, its vision, like that of the rest of Scandinavia, had grown much closer to Mrs Thatcher's vision of an entrepreneurial society than to the egalitarian paradise of Olof Palme, Sweden's last notable left-wing Prime Minister. The Norwegian welfare-state was also being opened up to welfare entrepreneurs. It is private companies that are selling Norway's oil extraction skills across the world.[29]

In 2010 Salmond rhapsodized about how 'Norway has breezed through recession more successfully than any other country in Europe'. But he failed to be candid and show that it was partly by embracing economic approaches which he and his party regard as heresy.[30] The SNP's economic vision for Scotland remains that of a state–managed society in which entrepreneurs are given a subordinate role. Norway's sovereign wealth fund (valued at about £508 billion), is often invoked as an ideal. But Norway could easily have spent its oil wealth on welfare or prestige infrastructural projects. The SNP's readiness to keep open an airport like Prestwick, lacking customers but near the birthplace of Nicola Sturgeon, and to promote expensive green energy projects, suggests that it would have quite possibly spent an equivalent windfall on electoral bribes or ideological hobby-horses.

Parts of Scandinavia are unfortunately moving closer to Scotland due to the rise of communal tensions of the kind which stalked heavily populated parts of that country for several hundred years. Unlike the 19th century rural Irish immigrants to Scotland, immigrants from north and east Africa and mainly Muslim in culture and faith, were welcomed to Scandinavia, mainly for altruistic reasons, and the newcomers received similar or greater levels of assistance from the state already given to indigenous citizens. But many have failed to assimilate and tense enclaves have sprung up which have given cities like Malmo in western Sweden, a reputation for intolerance (especially towards Jews).[31] Six days of rioting in Sweden in May 2013 and the February 2015 attack on a free speech event at a Copenhagen cafe leading to the death of a documentary film-maker, Finn Norgaard are the kinds of events which, unfortunately, are starting to define a socially fractured Scandinavia for the rest of the world.[32]

The kind of right-of-centre parties which the SNP at times seems happy to banish from Scotland, have been flourishing in all the Scandinavian countries (as well as Finland) during the early 21st century. Nordic Horizons is a think-tank set up by the journalist Lesley Riddoch, one of the most high-profile independence advocates in Scotland, in order to increase awareness of Scandinavia at home, but increasingly what it is having to cover is the electoral success of parties which would be dismissed as reactionary, xenophobic (and probably only really belonging in England). Riddoch dutifully enlisted a contributor to explain how the vote for the right-wing Sweden Democrats doubled in the 2014 general election to make it the third main party.[33] At the time of writing, Nordic Horizons has yet to comment on the Danish elections of June 2015. The political television drama, *Borgen,* set in Denmark had popularised the image of a progressive country where a woman who was often compared to Scotland's Nicola Sturgeon, played a commanding role in national politics. But the result saw the defeat of Denmark's Social Democrat Prime Minister Helle Thorning-Schmidt and the rise of the populist Danish People's party which captured 21.0 per cent of the vote. It has stayed out of government but one of its founders Pia Kjaersgaard is now Speaker of the Danish parliament.

Scottish radicals dreaming of a Nordic-style transformation for their country claim they share a sense of social justice and solidarity with their Nordic neighbours. But the main comparisons, at least historically, are a propensity for the men to drink, people to leave their homelands in large numbers, and Protestantism to exercise a long-term religious hold. Until communal tensions undermined social cohesion in Denmark and Sweden, there was considerable unity and internal peace. Political and economic polarisation were not noteworthy features of Scandinavia as instability periodically rocked other parts of Europe. In the countryside, there were numerous small landed proprietors not the polarised model in Scotland of an aristocratic elite and landless labourers or tenant farmers leading an often precarious existence. Scandinavia industrialised later and at a slower pace than Scotland. Labour relations were better otherwise it would have been very hard for Sweden to establish the number of engineering companies of world rank that it still has. Scotland has now lost nearly all of its heavy industry and a sombre atmosphere can prevail in what used to be busy industrial centres.

The SNP rarely entertains comparisons which show that Scotland economically has more in common with the north of England and post-industrial parts of France and Germany than with much of Scandinavia. Nor does it appear to want to catch up with changing geo-political realities. In 2011, on the basis of projections which suggested that that the ice cap covering Greenland, and perhaps even the North Pole itself, was melting, Angus Robertson MP called for Scotland to become involved in northern diplomatic, security and environmental initiatives. 'Norway, Denmark, Russia, Canada and the United States have all developed specific policy priorities for the High North and Arctic' and Scotland simply mustn't be left behind was his view. He rightly identified ensuring 'stability in the region, which necessitates ecological, economic, diplomatic and defence cooperation and understanding'.[34] But reports of the pace of global warming appear to have been exaggerated and soon it was Russian belligerence which was increasingly troubling all the Scandinavian countries and Finland. Sweden in 2014 and 2015 grew increasingly apprehensive about incursions into its airspace by Russian jets and also reports that Russian submarines entered its largely undefended territorial waters with impunity.[35] In 2015, faced with similar concerns, Finland sent out letters to 900,000 male citizens reminding them that military conscription still applied and to be prepared for the call-up in the event of an emergency.[36]

The Finnish military was looking towards joining NATO according to the same report and in famously neutral Sweden, there was a sharp rise in support for joining NATO, up from 17 per cent in 2012 to 31 per cent in 2014.[37] Denmark, a founder-member of NATO had been warned by the Russian ambassador to Denmark in 2015 that his country would aim nuclear missiles at Danish warships if his country joined NATO's missile defence system.[38]

The mood in SNP-dominated Scotland was completely at variance with the one of anxiety in Scandinavia where governments and citizens were suddenly confronted with challenges to their peace and security which they had not faced even at the height of the Cold War. Many in the SNP remained hostile to NATO and a prominent figure like Jim Sillars argued a year after Russia's seizure of Crimea that the SNP was wrong to have 'an uncritical position' on the EU's role in what he described as 'the Ukrainian civil war'. He complained about the decision of Humza Yousaf MSP, External Affairs Minister, to write 'an article in which he pledged full Scottish support for the EU line on sanctions against Russia. This article implicitly accepted that the EU had no fault in the matter of Ukrainian-Russian relations, was devoid of knowledge in respect of long standing Russian security policy, and the role the EU and Nato have played in undermining that policy', Sillars wrote.[39]

In Scandinavia, it is only in far-left circles that imperialist aggression is seen as largely emanating from the West while Russian actions are better understood in terms of self-defence. The current secretary-general of NATO, Jens Stoltenberg used to head the Norwegian Labour Party. His predecessor Anders Fogh Rasmussen was a Dane who belonged to the Venstre (Liberal) party (both men having been Prime Ministers of their respective countries). If Scandinavian countries wish to have strong ties with their maritime neighbour across the Norwegian and North seas, the evidence is strong that they view an undivided Britain as their logical partner.

Norwegian Political scientist Oivind Bratberg told the BBC's Alan Little: 'Norwegians are very fond of the idea of Britain. They look back at the war with loyalty towards London, where our government and our royal family were located. It's very difficult to conceive of Scotland as detached from the UK'.[40]

An ex-Australian Prime Minister Malcolm Fraser and Ireland's Pat Cox, a former head of the European Parliament both backed Scottish independence but no prominent Scandinavian in politics past or present did so. In June 2014 Carl Bildt the Swedish foreign minister, equated Scottish independence with the 'Balkanisation of the British Isles'. He warned that it could set off 'unforeseen chain reactions' and stated that 'it is not something we are looking forward to'.[41] Bildt had been a UN envoy in the Balkans as well as serving as Sweden's Prime Minister but Alex Salmond did not hesitate to brand his intervention as 'insulting' and 'very foolish'.[42]

While serving in the Balkans, Bildt might have encountered not a few Alex Salmonds, personable local notables with an easy charm but a slipperiness when it came to being tied down to honouring any undertakings entered into and a capacity to become belligerent if their aims in the ethnic political field were challenged. But he would have found it virtually impossible to identify a politician as colourful and confrontational as the Scottish leader in the entire 20th century history of the various Scandinavian countries.

The Scandinavian consensus appears to be that there is still pressing need for a strong and undivided Britain, especially in times of uncertainty challenging the previous geo-political stability of northern Europe. In 2011, when Angus Robertson, the SNP's then spokesman on foreign affairs said that one of the first things an independent Scotland would do would be to apply to join the Nordic Council, a steering group of Nordic countries, its head was diplomatically silent.[43]

The wooing of Scandinavia appears to be based less on concrete interests and associations and more on exaggerated assumptions and clichés that seem to melt away on closer examination. At the time of writing the closest political soul-mate for the SNP is not to be found in any part of Scandinavia but in England where huge enthusiasm has been generated for Jeremy Corbyn's bid to become leader of the Labour Party. The rise of 66-year-old Corbyn after 32 years of obscurity in the British Parliament except when backing extremist causes, is likely to puzzle many Scandinavians. Writing in the communist *Morning Star* newspaper in 2014, he berated the 'enormous expansion of Nato into a global force' and urged a 'serious debate about Britain's overall defence and foreign policy' (including the nuclear deterrent) as 'Nato membership has brought us enormous levels of military expenditure and... involved us in countless conflicts.' He would not 'condone Russian behaviour or expansion in Ukraine but he said 'it is not unprovoked'.[44] Corbyn's rise has been hailed by at least one prominent Independence campaigner Cat Boyd in the pro-SNP, *National*.[45] But as long as he doesn't become Prime Minister, Nordic policy-makers are likely to be more concerned by the potential impact of the separatist ambitions of the SNP on their own neighbourhood, that is when they think of Scotland at all.

Ireland: from anti-Model to Model and Back

Parts of Scotland's east coast and, above all, the Northern Isles may have a strong Scandinavian imprint. But, arguably, much of Scotland's west coast is more Irish than Scandinavian in influence. Ireland is Scotland's nearest maritime neighbour. It was an Irish tribe the Scoti who gave the country its modern name. 16th century Scots established a colony in the adjacent Irish province of Ulster: some of its inhabitants moved on to North America and helped establish, and build up, the United States. Many of those that remained were later caught up in a searing territorial conflict in the last decades of the 20th century.

Scottish Nationalists have only been absorbed with Ireland for a short few years, roughly the 1998-2008 decade. At that time, Ireland was the lead-model for how a once poor country could flourish under EU tutelage. In 1998, when Jacques Santer, then President of the European Commission, addressed Irish parliamentarians, he noted how 'it is rare to find any period of such profound transformation which has been as successfully managed as here in Ireland'.[46]

The economic breakthrough which began around 1988 was admiringly dubbed the Celtic Tiger for emulating Asian countries in attracting prestigious companies through which rapid export-led growth boomed. North American firms which dominated the new investors and the Irish economy would do far more business with Britain and the USA than with its continental EU partners for many years to come. It was no small achievement for Ireland to build a pharmaceutical, medical and software industry far from Europe's geographic core.[47]

Understandably, Alex Salmond was eager to link the political fortunes of the SNP to the prowess of the 'Celtic Tiger'. In 2008 he insisted, in a lecture that he gave in Dublin, that where Ireland led, Scotland would soon follow: 'Scotland looks out to an Arc of Prosperity around us. Ireland, Iceland, Norway, Finland and Denmark. All small independent nations. All stable, secure and prosperous. Of all these nations, no example is more impressive and inspiring than Ireland. And none is more relevant to the decisions that Scotland faces today'.[48] Ian Bell, a pro-independence columnist in the *Herald*, warned Salmond of the dangers of 'unthinking imitation'. He advised 'Best stick to Norway, for now'.[49] This was prudent advice from a journalist proud to be related to the Edinburgh-born James Connolly, a participant in the founding act of independent Ireland, the Dublin Easter Rising of 1916.

The hubris of many in the political and economic elite that had emerged from this event, had led the state and private firms to pour enormous funding into the property sector. Indeed, by 2008 it emerged that the Irish banking sector had lent three times the country's income in often reckless transactions. When this asset bubble collapsed not long after Salmond's speech, the Irish Government made a colossal misjudgement and decided to guarantee the assets and liabilities of the massively over-extended banking sector. In the years ahead, having bought toxic bank assets, the state sold off many of its own physical assets. By 2012, Ireland was well on the way to losing the equivalent of €41bn, the amount of receipts it had received from the EU budget over the entire period from 1973 to 2009.[50]

Ireland was promptly dropped by the SNP as a viable counter-model to a London-led Britain. There are stirrings of renewed SNP interest as the Irish economy slowly emerges from its 7-year depression. But during the dark post-2008 era of heavy emigration and the steep decline of much of the domestic economy, Ireland returned to being the obstacle that made at least some Scots nervous about Salmond's intention to plunge the country into the unknown. For it was hard to disguise that during the first 70 years of the post-British state, independence had far from been a success. This was primarily not due to the partition of the island of Ireland (which cannot have helped the state's prospects) but instead to glaring policy errors by the nationalist elite in Dublin that did not begin to be reversed until the 1960s. Unimaginative economic nationalism was tried and reluctantly dropped but only after over a million people had emigrated (mainly to England, ironically the home of 'the conquering Saxon foe').

Ireland is widely seen as a pioneer in resisting aggressive British power. But it is possible to argue that Anglophobia is of far lesser intensity there than in Scotland even before its mass conversion to nationalism. English journalists covering the 1916-23 troubles in Ireland did not encounter the hostility that sometimes lay in wait for them on the Scottish referendum trail in 2014.[51] England had long been an economic lifeline however reactionary its political approach to Ireland could be. Irishmen had served in the British army for hundreds of years. They had built the infrastructure of an industrialising Britain. In the 1940s and 1950s hundreds of thousands of young people offered nationalist indoctrination in Irish classrooms, came to England in search of work; they found some prejudice but, more importantly, countless economic opportunities denied to them back home. From the 1960s onwards, the Irish in Britain became prominent in a range of professions ranging from financial services to the media.

The period of the troubles in Ulster, from 1969 to 1994 was when the Irish rose in a lot of the English professions. The IRA was planting bombs in English cities.

The backlash was restrained and British visitors to Ireland were rarely received with coolness or hostility. By contrast, there have been anecdotal stories of English visitors being treated in a graceless way while holidaying in post-2012 Scotland (and one former Labour cabinet minister in a Blair government whom I talked to in May 2015 mentioned that in her English North-East constituency, there was a growing reluctance to make the relatively short trip to Scotland because of the uncertainty of the welcome).

Hostility to British symbols, such as the decision to name Glasgow's newest hospital after Queen Elizabeth II, would suggest there are many newly-embittered Scots. But for nearly all of the period since 1707, London (unlike in Ireland) actively refrained from intervening in Scottish affairs. The country was largely self-managed by the Kirk and later the Scottish middle-class until waves of post-war social reform produced increasing centralisation from London. Similarly, in the 1980s, Thatcher's pro-market approach to policy-making, leading to privatisation of state utilities and the poll tax, was pushed ahead by a state machine which she acquired control over, sparking huge and enduring resentment in Scotland.

One reader contributing a comment to a Lesley Riddoch article on Scandinavia, put it this way:

'Scottish hatred of England is really hatred of Thatcherism. It is possible to love England, but it is impossible for anyone of sensibility to love Thatcherism, that acme of selfishness and pettiness and short-sightedness.

When England plumped for Thatcherism it was a fateful betrayal of its own soul, as when the Germans voted Nazi.

After this, there was no way back to being the kindly and noble spirit it had once had'.[52]

The cruder forms of Anglophobia are often to be found on the Scottish far-left which has enjoyed success in escaping from the political wilderness by depicting Thatcherism as the default English position towards Scotland. One detailed survey in 2015 showed that nearly 16 per cent of Scots possessed far-left views in politics compared with just under 10 per cent in England. Perhaps a strong impetus is provided by those Irish-minded Scots who remain an influential demographic in the parts of west-central Scotland where their ancestors settled at various stages of Scotland's industrial era. My own were part of this immigrant wave and, intermittently, during a 32-year academic career, I have analysed the mental make-up of this sub-national category of people in Scottish life. A rebel culture, defined by veneration for Irish nationalist heroes, and given solid expression through the existence of Celtic football club, has emerged from the shadows as anti-British views have gone mainstream in Scotland. Ireland is viewed as a pure and mystical land populated by heroes, very much the same fantasy which a certain proportion of Afro-Caribbeans who were Rastafarians used to project towards Ethiopia. Since Ireland is bathed in such a romantic haze, it is usually pointless to draw attention to the state-building failures of the independence era. During the current crisis, Ireland's arguably harsh treatment at the hands of EU decision-makers which has prompted a vast exodus of its younger citizens is of no relevance not least because Britain has had no incriminating role in this episode. So it is in vain for an author like Edinburgh-born Kevin Toolis to urge restive Scots (whether or not Hibernian in ancestry) to look over their shoulders at the Irish experience. Writing in the *Financial Times* in 2014, he pointed out that 'a nationalist state has carved itself out of the UK before. It was a disaster.... For all his bluster and his mesmerising appeal, Mr Salmond is merely re-enacting the same empty farce in the would-be Scottish Free State'.[53]

The anti-British rejectionism which proved so useful for the SNP in storming previously 'No Go' areas for it on Clydeside in 2014-15, has few echoes in Ireland itself outside parts of Belfast or (London)Derry, the site of the Bloody Sunday shootings of unarmed civilians in 1972 which left 13 dead. Irish intellectuals, belonging to the liberal left, have usually disdained what they see as atavistic expressions of nationalism. They have tended to be wary or hostile to Sinn Fein not just when it was the political wing of the IRA but, later, as it moved to carve out a power-base in Irish politics. But several well-known Irish commentators have enthusiastically embraced Scottish nationalism, seeing it as a case apart.

Fintan O'Toole is perhaps the best-known one. He manages to overlook the anti-British dimension lurking at the base of SNP support, particularly in west-central Scotland. Writing one day before the 2014 referendum, he saw the Yes side as 'a civic movement for independence', committed to equality and greater political accountability. The unsettling climate which made many pro-British Scots fearful about declaring their allegiances in public, was never mentioned.[54] Several months earlier, he claimed that 'the language of tribal nationalism is starkly unspoken. For an issue of such moment, the debate has been remarkably civilised and thoughtful'.[55] And one year later, he was claiming that:

'Scotland is much better placed than Ireland was to avoid the pitfalls that can follow independence, such as a focus on nationalism rather than the ability to better determine policy goals.

...It's coming to this question at a time when a great deal of the stupidity is gone and therefore you can take a decision on independence in a way that allows you to avoid having to learn the hard way what those stupidities were'.[56]

Yet by then with the collapse in the price of oil leading to a £10 billion shortfall in public funding, there was no admission from O'Toole that doubt might exist about the economic sustainability of an independent Scotland.

In 2015, he was still exhilarated by the vigour of democratic engagement despite the pro-government mobs which had forced Labour campaigners and speakers to run for cover just months earlier. He refused to recognize what Kevin Toolis (unlike him, rather sympathetic to Irish Republicanism in the past), had woken up to:

[a]'referendum debate [that] has collapsed into a slanging match where the best lack conviction and the worst are full of passionate intensity....
Mr Salmond would no doubt like to be remembered for leading his people into the promised land. In his hubris, he is leading Scotland into the sterile wilderness and the chains of another empty nationalism'.[57]

O'Toole was careful in his journalism in Scotland to usually overlook Alex Salmond. His myopic approach to stirring events beyond Ireland's shores is not dissimilar to that of Irish commentators in the 1930s who extolled the bold new times associated with experiments in European politics that cast aside fusty parliamentarism, in the process conveniently overlooking the Blackshirts, castor oil, and strong-arm methods of rule. These were usually conservatives of a pro-clerical disposition. But it is commentators ostensibly on the left who have shown the greatest readiness to bestow respectability on political movements whose intentions and deeds often reveal that they deserve very little such indulgence.

It was hard to avoid thinking of the SNP in 2015 when reading this unflattering assessment of Sinn Fein by a British official involved in the negotiations that culminated in the treaty that established independent Ireland in 1921: 'The greatest weakness of the Sinn Fein government', he wrote 'is that it is almost void of any admission to the world or themselves that they can either think what is wrong or do what is wrong. That is exactly what the Greek writers meant by 'hubris'; the frame of mind which, on their theory, the gods instill into people whom they have marked for destruction'.[58]

The Fine Gael party successors of the Irish revolutionaries who have been in charge of Ireland since 2011 have remained tight-lipped about turbulence in Scotland even though a partition of Britain is likely to be challenging for Ireland. But Ruaridh Quinn, the Minister of Education from 2011 to 2014, belonging to the Irish Labour Party, which stood aside from the post-1916 Irish revolution, broke his silence in 2014. He declared that due to the existence of secessionist movements in Spain and Belgium, it was 'highly probable' their parliaments would vote against Scotland joining the EU. He also predicted that the country would have to adopt the Euro as the price for gaining full EU membership after a pro-independence vote.[59]

Economic ties have grown between Scotland and Ireland which is now Scotland's eighth largest export market. Some 6000 Scottish jobs are directly dependent on

Irish companies. So have diplomatic ties according to Pat Bourne, Ireland's consul general to Scotland: 'Over the past 20 years [Scotland and Ireland] have become much closer. It's the Good Friday Agreement, the cross-island institutions, devolution'.[60] The upbeat views of Peter Geoghegan, an industrious Irish journalist based in Scotland, may help to define the outlook of middle-class opinion in Dublin towards Scottish events. But even he has been troubled by the slowness of a the SNP government to clean-up a centralized police force after a series of damaging revelations about negligence, snooping on journalists, and arming officers contrary to regulations. Tarnished public servants enjoying political favour are impervious to pressure to stand down from civil society.[61]

Ireland experienced decades of stifling and inefficient rule in which ruling politicians and favoured state officials were able to defy normal political conventions and behave in a sometimes arbitrary fashion. The reluctance of some Dublin-based commentators to highlight to Scots some of the pitfalls of Ireland's independence experience just increases the likelihood that cronyism and patronage politics may be a big part of any Scottish experiment in the politics of sovereignty.

America: the SNP's Passive Aggressive Stance

It is inevitable that in Ireland, a country where the radical left has usually been far from power, there are restless pundits keen to extol Scottish separatism due to the apparently progressive movement driving it forward. But in the United States, it is very hard to find prominent figures keen to endorse Scottish Nationalism. The USA arguably possesses a public culture inherited from Britain. The political union may have been severed by the American Revolution of 1776-83 but a recognisable Anglo-American culture influenced by common law, Christianity, a shared language, and often similar approaches to economics and commerce, bound the two countries together for centuries into the future.[62] While it is not outlandish for an Irish public figure to embrace Scottish independence, this appears to be an offbeat or bizarre step to be taken by Americans unless they are unhappy with the country's own mores and direction and see Scotland as offering an advanced European model for change.

Counter-cultural Americans who feel that their country should decisively move in a social democratic direction have always been prominent, especially in higher education and parts of the media. But only one, so far, has enthusiastically backed the SNP. This is 73-year-old Joseph Stiglitz, a Nobel laureate for economics. He has been a tireless critic of what he sees as America's role as the world's economic policeman. He sits on the SNP government's Council of Economic advisers. Unsurprisingly for some, he endorses several controversial economic moves by the SNP. Thus, he backed Salmond's much criticised plan to keep sterling as Scotland's currency in the event of independence which in many eyes exposed the lack of serious preparation for what followed any departure from Britain.[63] Stiglitz also defended the SNP's threat to walk away from UK government debt if London refused to share the pound and the Bank of England, saying it would be a 'legitimate position', because there had to be a fair division of assets and liabilities.[64] He also figured among well-known US economists who, in 2015, urged a strategy of defiance on the radical left Greek government of Alexis Tsipras as it confronted the EU and the IMF over the scale of Greece's debt. He was among those criticised by local economists for trying to lead the country into a disastrous confrontation which would leave the Greek economy in shreds and the country possibly outside the EU.[65]

As an advocate of the retreat of American economic power, it is perhaps unsurprising that Stiglitz has chiefly been an adviser to populists, first to the Papandreou dynasty in Greece of Andreas and George.[66] In 2005, when it was already obvious to many how damaging the senior Papendreous's stint as Prime Minister for much of the 1980s, had been to the Greek economy, Stiglitz addressed the well endowed Andreas G. Papandreou Foundation on the subject of 'Rich and Poor in the international economic system'. In February 2010, three months before Greece took a bailout from the EU and the IMF to avert a financial default, he publicly stated: 'There's clearly no risk of default. I'm very confident about it'.[67] But in the case of Argentina, he argued that the country had no choice but to default on its debt and he has served as a paid expert for the Peronist government of Christina Kirchner. His involvement with this populist administration has extended to backing an appeal in an American court against a ruling that Argentina was required to pay $1.3 billion in a dispute over unpaid bonds.[68]

It is entirely in character for Salmond to reach out to a publicity-conscious and high earning economist like Stiglitz prepared to endorse movements that advocate sweeping aside conventional responses to global economic problems. But acquiring such a figure as his best-known international adviser is unlikely to impress policy-makers in Washington.

There are other radical US economists who are dismayed by the superficiality of the SNP's economic plans. The best-known is Paul Krugman. He described Salmond's currency-sharing plan as 'deeply-muddle-headed', believing that one 'lesson of the euro crisis, surely, is that sharing a common currency without having a shared federal government is very dangerous'.[69]

In North America, it's necessary to look to the once-restive Canadian province of Quebec to identify an explicit political ally of the SNP. This is the Parti Québécois (PQ). Salmond once described this separatist force in Canada as his favourite nationalist party. The PQ used to be a skilful cultivator of ethnic discontent and Quebec has acquired certain aspects of sovereignty that the SNP longs to possess. The legislature is called the National Assembly; its taxpayers file two tax returns; Quebec has observer status at the United Nations, and has seven delegates-general pursuing Quebec's interests all over the world (including in Mexico City and Munich but not in Edinburgh).[70]

The PQ first took charge of the federal province's government in 1976; as in Scotland, it benefited from the rise of secularism (in Quebec's case toppling the Catholic Church as the dominant force in the province). Quebec almost voted to break away from the rest of Canada in a referendum on sovereignty held in 1995. But it is now difficult to persuade young people especially of the merits of going it alone. The bureaucratic and crony-ridden mini-state created by the PQ is not an attractive model.[71] Its inability to attract skilled immigrants and investment means that Quebec's share of Canada's population and economic wealth has fallen sharply during the PQ's ascendancy.

The PQ is dominated by lawyers and by figures who have made careers in the state bureaucracy. Pauline Marois, Prime Minister from 2012 to 2014 , played a vital role in expanding the role of the state in the health, social welfare and education sectors during the heyday of its power in the final quarter of the 20th century. But the PQ has always been better-known for its aggressive language policy designed to reverse the tide of Englishness. In 1977 Bill 101, the Charter of the French language was passed into law. It resolved 'to make French the language of Government and the Law, as well as the normal and everyday language of work, instruction, commerce and business'. Major businesses needed to ensure that product descriptions and advertising were in French.

The PQ eventually ran out of steam because it was unable to match its heady dose of identity policies with practical economic and social ones that could enable it to keep up with other parts of Canada. Out of office from 2003 to 2012; it embraced even more direct language militancy in order to shore up the core ethnic vote. While electioneering in 2012, Pauline Marois stated that people who did not pass a French test would be prohibited from running for public office or contributing to political parties. She retreated only after an outcry. But the PQ intended to forbid ethnic French speakers (*Québécois de souche*) as well as immigrants and their descendants, from attending English language junior colleges.[72]

During her brief tenure as Prime Minister in 2012-13, Pauline Marois visited Scotland and met with Salmond but he was careful not to be seen in public with her: 'there was no joint press conference, no communiqué nor a grand dinner at his official residence, Bute House'.[73] Mainly thanks to PQ policies, there was a flight of industry to the benefit of cities like Toronto. It would hardly assist the separatist cause if at the height of the referendum season, the SNP leader consorted with a political soul-mate whose pursuit of identity politics had led to such damage. No less than 800,000 Anglophone speakers have departed Quebec in the last fifty years. Many of these are bound to have been people of Scottish descent. It is possible to see them as casualties of vindictive nationalism. Not surprisingly, the SNP ignores Scottish-heritage Scots who endorse a British culture and it is likely that their numbers will be swelled as Scottish residents squeezed by the SNP's ideological policies quit Scotland in growing numbers.

The percentage of French speakers in Canada fell from just under 30 percent up to the 1970s to 22 per cent in 2012.[74] To bolster the population size, PQ governments encouraged emigration from other Francophone countries. It turned out that most of the new Quebecois were likely to be from poor countries like Haiti (the only other notable French-speaking country in the Americas) or from formerly French-ruled North Africa. Eventually, Quebec began to experience some of the tensions which have flared up in West European countries where a liberal secular society co-exists uneasily with the pious, male-dominated and rural values of some of the newcomers. But in the 2012 election, the PQ opportunistically tried to disassociate itself from its own poorly worked-out immigration policy. In a so-called charter of secularism, Marois proposed to ban the display of all religious dress or symbols (except the crucifix) by anyone who works for the government.[75]

The PQ was also ready to promote a two-tier citizenship model. Under it, civil and political rights would be distributed according to a person's grasp of the French language. It may have crept back to office in 2012 with 31.9 percent of the vote but, by then the party may well have reached the logical end-point arising from a noisy promotion of ethnic and linguistic difference that has largely benefited an elite enjoying well-paid state jobs. Quebec had become stuck with a nationalism possessing no positive vision for society. Instead there is a readiness to generate low-level conflict to enable the political machine to benefit materially from office. Scotland doesn't have a language question but the SNP's direction of travel is much the same – towards a constant absorption with constitutional arrangements and identity politics and where contrasts with the rest of the United Kingdom are deliberately underscored and celebrated.

Canada had been governed from 2006 to 2015 by self-confident Conservatives under Stephen Harper, an arguably more skilful Unionist than his British counterpart David Cameron. The PQ is struggling to remain relevant but it has taken nearly fifty years for many Quebecois to see through demagogic nationalism.

Turning to the United States, it is difficult to find any reference-point which would enable a connection with Scottish Nationalism to be affirmed. Arthur Donaldson, leader of the SNP in the 1960s, lived in America after the First World War and found no interest among Americans born in Scotland or of Scottish descent in the cause of independence which he felt so passionately about. Demagogic politicians threatening to overturn American conventions with a populist platform have been remarkably thin on the ground there compared with the Europe of the 1930s or the early 21st century. There are far more opportunities for mavericks given the federal system with mini-governments in each of the 50 states but the only serious regional populist challenge was that of Huey Long, governor of and later Senator for, the state of Louisiana until his assassination in 1935. Donald Trump, who has shaken up the early stages of the fight for the US Republican party nomination, is more of a brash exhibitionist without a proper movement behind him.

The strong influence of an independent middle-class, often unencumbered by obsessions with class or status, has usually guaranteed underlying stability in American politics.[76] Calamitous episodes in national history such as the 1861-65 Civil War and the Great Depression from 1929 to the mid-1930s, raised doubts about the viability of the USA. But the country has known social mobility and improving living standards for much of its existence, and belatedly these have been within reach for black Americans also over the last half-century as well as immigrants now from all over the world.

In 2008, while speaking at the University of Virginia, in his first US visit as Scotland's First Minister, Alex Salmond contended that Scotland's 14th century struggle for independence had influenced the American revolution nearly 500 years later.[77] In 2013, speaking this time at Princeton University, Salmond was prepared to endorse the popular myth that the Declaration of Independence was somehow modelled on the so-called Declaration of Arbroath of 1320 (to the disappointment of a Scottish academic in the audience highly knowledgeable about American history).[78]

It is normal for a movement seeking wider legitimation like the SNP to claim that medieval resistance to foreign occupation of its country might somehow have been a significant influence on the American revolution. What has come down in history as Scotland's war of independence undoubtedly possessed national characteristics but it also had many of the hallmarks of a brutal and uninhibited power-struggle between members of an Anglo-Norman-Scottish elite. Robert the Bruce, seen as a towering figure in Scottish history had lands in both England and Scotland. He was among the numerous Scottish nobles who had paid homage to England's King Edward I after the defeat and execution in 1305 of William Wallace, someone far more consistent in his opposition to English rule. It is now unfashionable to claim that Bruce mounted resistance to English rule primarily to further his own personal ambitions to wield power in Scotland. But if this was a primary motive for him, he would have been no different from countless other strong-willed nobles whose hunger for territory has sometimes been posthumously reframed as the first blow in modern national liberation struggles.[79]

The 1320 Declaration of Arbroath describes the Scots as 'a holy people' but who still destroyed the Picts, and it contains the stirring words that 'We fight not for glory, nor riches, nor honours but for freedom'. Salmond informed his Virginia audience in 2008 that it was possibly the most important document in Scotland's entire history. But the heady proclamation was made while King Robert was mounting devastating attacks on the north of England and largely neglecting Scotland's internal development.

Nobles in Scotland enjoyed sweeping privileges and exercised often much tighter control on the lives of common folk than their English counterparts did. The rapid decline of English feudalism and the growth not only of a middle-class but a peasantry with legal rights protected under Common Law, made late medieval England a more advanced kingdom than Scotland. The northern realm could be described as a typical European country with a pronounced aristocratic culture. Patterns of subordination and command made life intolerable for many and (along with poor land) encouraged emigration first to continental Europe and, from the 17th century, to the colonies of the New World.

It was probably less a deep sense of history and more a vague expression of goodwill towards Scotland as a central part of the British motherland, which may explain why, on 4 April 2008, President George W. Bush signed a Presidential Proclamation making the anniversary of the Declaration of Arbroath, 6 April, National Tartan Day in the USA. The 1776 rebellion of American settlers against clumsy and increasingly arbitrary rule from London could, at a certain distance, be seen as emulating the earlier medieval revolt in Scotland. But it could also be viewed as the start of a war that was fought 'by British Americans against a German King for British ideals'.[80] These were the words of Virginia-born Nancy Astor, the first-ever woman MP to take her seat in the House of Commons. According to Daniel Hannan, the resolutions of the rebellious colonists Continental Congress are 'a protracted complaint about the violations of traditional British liberties'.[81] The Declaration of Independence was a reformulation of the principle which had animated English moderates in their struggle against the Stuart dynasty, culminating in the revolution of 1688. Some of the clauses of England's 1689 Bill of Rights were copied without amendment into the American Constitution.

An intensified sense of British national identity arguably lay behind the American Revolution. Edmund Burke in 1775 drew out the connection in a speech on the need for conciliation between colonists and the home country:

'The colonists emigrated from you when this part of your character [love of free-dom] was most predominant; and they took this bias and direction the moment they parted from your hands. They are therefore not only devoted to liberty, but to liberty according to English ideas, and on English principles'.[82]

Perhaps a seminal influence on the outlook of American revolutionary leaders like Thomas Jefferson and Benjamin Franklin was the pragmatic thought of the 18th century Scottish Enlightenment. It was associated with philosophers, economists and historians like David Hume, Adam Smith and Adam Ferguson who placed the welfare of individuals and the stability of society at the centre of their ideas. By con-trast, the lawyers and intellectuals who prepared the way for the French revolution believed that millenarian ideas could take society in a fundamentally better direc-tion. The French revolution only had a small number of adherents in Scotland. Its appeal slumped after the slaughter of members of the aristocracy and then bloody infighting among the radicals themselves brought withering condemnation from Burke in particular. Scotland produced only a few adherents. One of them was the lawyer Thomas Muir sentenced by a Scottish court in 1793 to transportation to Australia after being involved in an abortive uprising against the British state that also involved the United Irishmen.

On the occasion of the 250th anniversary of Muir's birth, on 24 August 2015, Alex Salmond delivered a speech extolling his memory. It was another clue, if any were needed, that it was the radical Jacobin tradition of toppling established authori-ty and not the pragmatism of 18th century Scottish philosophers and economists which animates the SNP.

In 2009, rather to their bewilderment, US decision-makers and public opinion found that the Scottish government had carried out a decision which hurt many American citizens whose political representatives would have been among those who just one year earlier had enthusiastically voted for a Friends of Scotland caucus to be formed in the US Congress. On 20 August of that year, the Scottish Justice minister Kenny MacAskill announced the release, on compassionate grounds, of Abdelbaset al-Megrahi convicted for blowing up a Pan Am jet carrying 259 people, 180 of whom had been US citizens. On 21 December 1989, a device had detonated, bringing down the plane while it was over the Scottish town of Lockerbie. Megrahi, a Libyan national, was convicted in a Scottish court of the terrorist act and MacAs-kill decided to release him on compassionate grounds after he was diagnosed with advanced terminal cancer. In a press conference he gave on the day this happened, the world's media were told that the action was rooted in 'the values, beliefs and common humanity that defines us as Scots'.[83]

On closer inspection it was made in collusion with the Brown government at

Westminster which was keen to regularise ties with Colonel Gaddafi mainly for commercial reasons. And in order to expedite the release of Megrahi, the Scottish government ensured that there were only cursory medical checks carried out on the prisoner who, far from being at death's door lived for another 44 months.[84]

US secretary of State Hillary Clinton had expressed her concern in two phone conversations with MacAskill about the release of someone guilty of such a grave crime in the absence of any substantial evidence about his innocence. Four days before the release, the director of the FBI, Robert S Mueller III wrote to the Scottish politician in terms which had rarely been used by a senior US official towards a friendly country.[85] But nobody in the SNP broke ranks, and the party was unmoved by the anger of US policy-makers and relatives of those killed, MacAskill stating that Scotland should not be 'forced into debasing its values'.[86]

Most Scots continue to have a positive outlook towards the USA and the SNP's standing in the polls slumped for over a year. Polls showed that a clear majority of people in Scotland were unhappy about the release of Megrahi. But numerous figures from the arts, media and entertainment industries which the SNP relied upon to expand its influence in society, stepped forward to hail the action. Their mood was perhaps best summed up by the journalist Lesley Riddoch who congratulated the SNP for not 'kow-towing to the world's most powerful nation'.[87]

The SNP lacks the solidarity movement for Scotland in grassroots America which Irish Republicans could rely on. It is unable to influence voting outcomes as Irish-Americans could do. So a prudent leadership might have concluded that it would need all the friends it could get among US policy-makers if Scotland was to jump free from Britain on acceptable terms and be accepted into the community of nation-states. Yet it could not resist baiting the USA over such an emotive issue, knowing the damage that was bound to be done to bilateral relations. The signs are that it was playing to the gallery at home. In 2009, it still only led a minority government. It knew that examples of overbearing and arrogant American behaviour rankled with politically restive Scots who had yet to embrace the party. Memories remained fresh of US foreign policy opposed to apparently progressive movements during the Cold War. But in Scotland's 15 universities and in the media, there was usually less willingness to recall a different side to trans-Atlantic relations; to the undoubted fact that much of American intervention in both world wars had a disinterested character and that after 1945, without the presence of US forces in central Europe, there would have been little to stop Stalin or his successors occupying all of Germany and reaching the English Channel.

Scotland possesses in full the schizophrenic attitude towards the United States that has been commonplace in different parts of Europe for a long time. Sigmund

Freud called America 'a mistake, a gigantic mistake'. George Bernard Shaw had earlier quipped that 'an asylum for the sane would be empty in America'.[88] Fearing its unruly democracy, many Europeans had supported the slave-holding states of the Confederacy during the Civil War of the 1860s. At least in and around Scotland's main city, Glasgow, the abolitionist cause linked with President Abraham Lincoln and the Union was more popular. Later, American popular culture was adored by the inhabitants of this overcrowded industrial city. From the 1920s to the 1960s, it was almost second to none anywhere in the world for the number of cinemas showing Hollywood products and dance halls with the latest musical craze from the New World. Yet it was also Glasgow where the students of the city's main university, in 2014, overwhelmingly elected as their honorary rector Edward Snowden. A year earlier, this former US National Security Agency contractor had fled to Russia after releasing tens of thousands of classified documents which included the personal details of individuals in repressive countries who had been prepared to cooperate with the US authorities

What can perhaps be best described as the SNP's passive-aggressive stance towards the USA continued after the party's major win in the 2011 Scottish election. Visits to the USA by top figures, (Salmond included) resumed as if there had been no unpleasantness in 2009. In 2012 party members narrowly agreed to stay in NATO while remaining opposed to the continuation of a nuclear base at Faslane or allowing ships docked in, or navigating Scottish waters, to carry nuclear weapons.

Defence Offers Insight into SNP's Global Outlook

Faslane was carefully chosen in the 1960s, offering deep-water access for the navy's submarines directly into the Irish Sea and the North Atlantic. In 1961 the US established a base nearby at Holy Loch, used for Polaris and Poseidon nuclear submarines. It closed in 1992 when it appeared that super-power tensions were likely to abate for the long duration. But even before tensions with Russia revived spectacularly after 2010, the USA was keen for Britain to maintain and renew the Trident nuclear deterrent. If Britain were ever to adopt a non-nuclear defence policy, France would be the only European nuclear ally the USA could rely on (and at the height of the Cold War under de Gaulle it had been a far from reliable partner).

In her speeches on the subject, Nicola Sturgeon often uses terms such as 'obscenity', 'morally unjustifiable' and 'economically indefensible' to slam Trident.[89] Within days of its knock-out win in the UK general election of May 2015, the SNP was championing the cause of a 25-year-old Royal navy submariner William McNeilly who went absent without leave in that month after claiming there were safety risks to servicemen and the public due to military negligence. The party centred a debate in the House of Commons around the issue on 27 May but the next day the ministry of defence released a detailed statement, refuting all but one of the submariner's claims. Investigations into his claim that E-cigarettes were being used at sea continued and he was discharged from the service soon afterwards.[90]

The nuclear base on the Clyde fuelled the anger of many new SNP members and it is quite possible that if the issue of NATO membership was put to a conference vote in the future, the SNP would vote to shun NATO. However, at least in 2013, there is evidence that the views of the Scottish public were more moderate. A detailed poll carried out by Lord Ashcroft revealed that 51 per cent of Scots wanted a replacement for Trident, while only 34 per cent would give up nuclear weapons.[91]

After Sturgeon addressed an anti-Trident rally in Glasgow in May 2015, the journalist Chris Deerin pungently summed up the outlook of those Scots who inhabited the real world rather than an idealistic one where it was assumed that nuclear weapons could be disinvented and rogue powers hoping to acquire them, could be trusted:

'I spent some time looking at the photos posted online from George Square, where people had gathered with banners proclaiming "Bairns Not Bombs" and "Welfare Not Warfare". My first thought, perhaps uncharitably, was that they appeared a well-fed bunch and that this would be a good time for an enterprising burglar to visit the mansions of Glasgow's impeccably liberal West End. My second thought was that I, too, prefer bairns and welfare to bombs and warfare, as indeed does everyone I know, regardless of political disposition. And my final thought, as the saintly hordes marched and chanted and tweeted and cheerily posed for selfies and were addressed by the First Minister as if she were campaigning to be president of Glasgow Caledonian student union, was how remote Scotland's political and civic culture has grown from any semblance of mature engagement with the world—the real one, that is, as opposed to the one it dreamily wishes existed.[...]

Naturally, this is not the case made by the 'pro-bairn' protestors. Rather, they would see us unilaterally disarm in order to make a bold international statement, and to free up money to be spent on 'welfare'.[92]

US policy-makers seem to have only woken up to the SNP's threat to banish nuclear weapons from a sovereign Scotland fully under its control in early 2015 as polls showed the party heading towards its landslide victory that spring. David Cameron was on an official visit to Washington then and Sir Christopher Meyer, British ambassador to the US from 1997 to 2003 issued a blunt public warning that the much-vaunted 'special relationship' was 'hanging by a thread' in part due to events in Scotland that seemed quite outlandish to Americans who thought themselves well-informed about Britain. He wrote:

'The prospect of the "Yes" vote prevailing in the referendum on Scottish independence shook Washington to the core. Had the SNP won and forced the closure of the Faslane nuclear submarine base, it would have been a severe blow to American and Nato interests just when the alliance needs to be on its mettle to deter Putin's revanchist ambitions. And American diplomats do not think the danger of Scottish independence has gone away'.[93] The US consulate in Edinburgh continued to be a backwater though, staffed by a junior official from the US State Department.

In 2014, a prescient warning had been issued by a Washington-based analyst Andrew Apostolou that 'NATO could find itself paralysed in a crisis by such a difficult member'. The SNP had already spelled out that in an 'independent Scotland's military power only be used 'in accordance with the principles of the U.N. Charter; properly agreed by the Scottish Government [and] approved by the Scottish Parliament'.[94] These assertions were contained in the Scottish government's 2013 White Paper on Independence which condemned Trident as an affront to basic decency'.[95] But the SNP cannot be unaware that nuclear weapons are the very bedrock of the Nato alliance. As the *Daily Telegraph*'s foreign affairs editor David Blair wrote: 'In the final analysis, the security of every Nato member is guaranteed by the US nuclear arsenal…If you think that reliance on Trident is immoral, then it cannot be right to stay in a military alliance that, well, relies on Trident'.

Blair made the shrewd observation in a 2014 article that nuclear weapons may not be what the SNP chiefly objects to 'but rather hostility to sovereignty being violated by outside powers'.[96]

The SNP displays the stock nationalist attitude about needing to demonstrate that it is the undisputed master in its own house at least on symbolic issues. Instinctive sympathy has been shown when other countries have had their sovereignty interfered with by Western powers. When NATO fought its only war in Kosovo in 1999 (without UN approval), Salmond called it 'an action of dubious legality,but above all one of unpardonable folly'.[97]

The removal of the nuclear deterrence from Faslane and the building of a costly replacement base elsewhere on the island would prove extremely disruptive for NATO at a time of mounting pressure from the Arctic Circle to the Mediterranean. The SNP has tried to allay concern by pointing out that its objective is to create Nordic-style military forces for Scotland. But the party rarely acknowledges that 'NATO's northern members shelter under the alliance's nuclear umbrella. They also supplement their small militaries with U.S. defence capabilities'.[98] So perhaps not many Nordic decision-makers are likely to be thrilled to see a new independent nation, claiming to be part of southern Scandinavia but ready to place the region in potential harm by adopting such a cavalier attitude to vital security issues.

Denmark, Norway and Iceland also draw upon Washington and London's extensive intelligence-gathering apparatus. In contrast, Scottish nationalists want to break away from the U.K.'s security agencies. David Blair has written that 'an independent Scotland wouldn't be a member of the "Five Eyes," the unique intelligence-sharing agreement linking Australia, Canada, New Zealand, the U.K. and the U.S. The Five Eyes accord is built on trust, which Scotland will lose the moment it leaves the arrangement'.[99]

Enemies of NATO's capability might be happy to see a quarrelsome Scotland inside the Atlantic alliance, continually raising procedural points, rather than being an outright neutral country. Steve Forbes, an American publishing executive and twice a candidate for the nomination of the Republican Party for President, is probably the best-known US citizen to publicly express serious concern about the impact of Scottish independence on the wider world.

In a British press article days before the referendum, he paraphrased his concerns by stating that:

'My grandfather emigrated from Scotland over 100 years ago. I was brought up imbibing all the romantic and glorious history of Robert the Bruce and the spider, the heroic battle of Bannockburn, and the thrilling adventures of Bonnie Prince Charlie'. But he warned that the break-up of Britain was likely to worsen the security situation in Europe as well as contribute to political instability in different parts of the continent:

' We are in one of those dangerous periods of history when things can go terribly wrong. The break-up of Great Britain would encourage all the forces of chaos, terrorism and aggression and set a terrible precedent....

Vladimir Putin would use the break-up to give legitimacy to his efforts to hive off the eastern part of Ukraine.... Russia is economically weak, but Putin has Bonapartist ambitions that will eventually be turned on Poland'.[100]

In a speech to the Brookings Institute in Washington on 7 April 2014, Lord George Robertson, a Scottish politician who had been Secretary-General of NATO from 1999 to 2003, amplified many of these fears.

He argued that:

'The loudest cheers for the breakup of Britain would be from our adversaries and our enemies.

For the second military power in the West to shatter this year would be cataclysmic in geostrategic terms.

If the United Kingdom was to face a split at this, of all times, and find itself embroiled for several years in a torrid, complex, difficult and debilitating divorce, it would rob the West of a serious partner just when solidity and cool nerves are vital. Nobody should underestimate the effect all of that would have on existing global balances...'[101]

Israel/ Palestine Also Exemplifies SNP Worldview

On 24 July 2015, as I passed by on an errand, I discovered that the World under-21 Lacrosse championships were being held at the University of Edinburgh's Peffermill sports grounds in the south of the city. Their visibility was not due to the cheers of spectators but to the abundance of Palestinian flags on lampposts stretched along Peffermill Road and the knot of demonstrators at the entrance to the sports ground. Pro-Palestinian (or more accurately anti-Israel) protests were hardly new in Edinburgh. Arguably, the city boasted the most vocal and militant group anywhere in Western Europe demanding an international boycott of Israel from sports to diplomacy - the Scottish Palestine Solidarity Campaign (SPSC).[102]

What was astounding was the noise level coming from the high-powered megaphones held by activists: it seemed absolutely surreal in a quiet Edinburgh suburb. In the residential houses opposite the venue, people were emerging from their homes looking disorientated and far from happy at the bedlam occurring at a time in the morning when many would have only just got up. A senior police officer 'to whom I spoke appeared not very comfortable either but he emphasised that the demonstrators had the right to be there and make their protest even if it was an extremely noisy one. How the police responded would depend in part on the level of complaints they were receiving. Although it was only the second day of a week-long event, complaints were starting to come in especially from disconsolate locals.

Once again Scotland's capital had shown itself to be a global hot spot for protesters determined to brand Israel as an apartheid state. In past years, concerts by top orchestras from Israel had been disrupted and supermarkets stocking goods from Israel picketed. Far from being an embarrassment to the SNP government, its top officials have made common cause with some of these protesters. The Salmond government displayed nonchalance in the summer of 2014 when the only Israeli feature at the Edinburgh Festival, a Hip Hop theatre production from the Incubator Theatre of Jerusalem, was unable to perform at the festival. There was light policing, and the performance was abandoned after one airing thanks in no small measure to demonstrators being able to block the entry point. As a ticket-holder who had not succeeded in gaining entry, I thought that those in operational charge of 'Police Scotland' were, at best, amateurish and forgetful about citizens' elementary rights. At worst, they may have been accessories in the curtailment of free speech.[103]

Arik Eshet, the company's artistic director, afterwards expressed his astonishment at the police stance and about being left in the lurch by the festival bureaucrats. In an affluent, supremely middle-class city with academic, media, ecclesiastical and cultural elites, the only people who offered gestures of sympathy to him and his cast were other performers.[104] Leading cultural figures have no qualms about endorsing such near-mob actions. Among the fifty intellectuals who issued a statement saying that the play must not go ahead were Scotland's official national poet (or 'maker'), Liz Lochhead, and the well-known novelist Alasdair Gray.[105]

The SNP's reaction to Al Q'aida's attacks in America on 9/11 was an early indication of its outlook on Middle East matters. Michael Russell, the SNP's education spokesman, called for 'clear proof of the guilt of Osama Bin Laden' which had 'to be laid at the bar of world opinion and be seen to be conclusive'.[106]

The SNP has been engaged in something of a Dutch auction with its Labour rival to derive advantage from Middle Eastern woes: between 2011 and 2014, there had been fifty Members' Motions in the Scottish Parliament relating to Israel, out of a total of 260 that relate to world issues. In August 2014, a debate was held on the violence in Gaza in which no member was ready to show understanding of the reasons why Israel had to respond with firmness in the face of rocket attacks from Hamas-controlled Gaza directed at civilians. In boilerplate speeches, virtually no mention was made of the Yezidi, Kurdish, Christian, and Shi'a minorities who had been enduring terrifying levels of violence at the hands of the Islamist militants of ISIL following its seizure of much of Iraq.

The SNP government issued double the number of statements during the six week-long conflict in Gaza in 2014 than it had during the previous three years of conflict in Syria. Alex Salmond was an early supporter of an arms embargo on Israel while in 2010, he called for economic sanctions terming Israel's interception of the Mavi Marmara, the ship attempting to break the blockade of Gaza, 'an atrocity on the high seas' even after Israeli soldiers had been attacked by pro-Hamas militants from Turkey claiming to be 'aid workers'.

In August 2014, Nicola Sturgeon was the lead speaker at 'a Stop the War coalition Women for Gaza' rally in Glasgow at which it would have been hard to avoid encountering SPSC activists. One of her fellow speakers was the Respect party candidate, Yvonne Ridley, who had days earlier called for a 'Zionist-free Scotland'.[107] Her colleague in this far-left party, the British MP George Galloway (a Scot from Dundee), had caused shock when a YouTube video surfaced in which he declared that the city where he was an MP, Bradford, should boycott Israeli goods, academics and even tourists.[108]

The SNP appears unworried by the impact on the Scottish Jewish community of making common cause with militants on the Palestinian issue whose methods of agitation are often radical. On 10 August 2014, the Scottish Council of Jewish Communities (SCoJeC) issued a statement, observing that 'the disproportionate obsession with Israel in Scottish public life... has itself made many Jewish people very uncomfortable, whatever their views on the current conflict.'[109] It claimed that the tense atmosphere was adversely affecting everyday community relations. Scotland historically had frowned upon anti-Semitism, but the new situation reflected the mounting insecurity felt by European Jews from Manchester to Berlin.

In the first week of August, SCoJeC had received around 25 reports relating to at least 12 separate anti-Semitic incidents, almost as many as in the whole of 2013. Those reported to the police ranged from threatening phone calls, emails, and graffiti on synagogues to two cases of incitement to break criminal law. Friction has also been reported in workplaces, outside school gates and on university campuses. Scotland's Jewish community had shrunk to around 5,000 in 2014 , having been as high as 80,000 in 1950.[110]

In remarks perhaps directed in particular at Scotland's government, Scotland's Jewish Council pointed out that 'Anti-Semitism does not consist only in personal abuse of individual Jews; it includes the application of different rules to Jewish people, institutions—and to the only Jewish country.' By this stage, even London's *Guardian* newspaper, long a critic of Israel, was expressing alarm about where things were heading. It referred to the worst outbreaks of anti-Semitism seen in Europe since the 1930s and pointed out that most Jews feel bound up with Israel, even if that relationship is 'one of doubt and anxiety': 'To demand that Jews surrender that connection is to tell Jews how they might—and how they might not—live as Jews. Such demands have an ugly history.'[111]

Israel with its prowess in developing new industries and showing dynamism and flair on the economic front is not a country that the SNP government feels Scotland needs to learn much or anything from. Humza Yousaf, a Scot of Pakistani origin who, aged 27, was appointed minister for external relations in 2012, is a frequent visitor to the Middle East where his mission is to foster bilateral links with wealthy states in the region. But neither he nor Salmond nor Sturgeon have visited Israel.

With just over 7 million people, Israel has the highest density of economic start-ups in the world–3,850, or one for every 1,844 Israelis. It has lost out on billions in other opportunities because of boycotts on Israeli goods, occasional warfare and the constant threat of terrorism. These drawbacks are only partly compensated for by the nearly $3 billion in foreign aid that Israel receives annually from the U.S.[112]

From 1993 to 2014, real GDP increased fourfold in Israel, and real GDP per capita rose by 250 percent. A country which had virtually zero industry at its birth is now far more industrialised than Scotland. Would-be Scottish state-builders could learn from certain Israeli traits conducive to entrepreneurship, especially in the technological field. They include risk taking, a positive attitude toward failure and an inclination to question authority.[113] By now there is growing evidence that if independence is acquired by the SNP, the party will be more preoccupied with forging alliances which enable a nationalist elite to bask in the global limelight than in carrying out painstaking and unglamorous investigations about how to revive technological innovation and entrepreneurship in a country that long ago now used to be known as a workshop of the industrial world.

Conclusion

The SNP is not really preoccupied by the rest of the world. Its external relations strategy operates at the level of winning over elites in countries which might smooth its path to independence. It tends to steer clear of minority nationalism in continental Europe because it is viewed as inferior to the nationalism of reputedly one of Europe's oldest countries. By rushing to offer its services as a mediator in an *internal* dispute between the Madrid government and Catalan separatists in September 2015, the SNP displayed its narcissistic approach to international relations rather well.

Neither is the SNP keen to seek out new ideas from elsewhere that can be applied to make independence a success. Under Alex Salmond, there is a preference for wooing thinkers and publicists prominent in academia and the media who are prepared to defend the actions of small countries challenging bigger forces even when the former behave in quixotic and impractical ways. There is a remarkable lack of interest in the exploits of Scots who contributed to building flourishing political, economic and social institutions in places ranging from Canada to Hong Kong. Perhaps these Scots disqualified themselves by showing a commitment to an Anglosphere where strong attachments remained to Britain, the USA or the British Commonwealth. More preferred as a model is Quebec where nationalists ran a patronage state in which its backers chiefly prospered as the province fell behind the rest of Canada in many key respects. Today, the mistakes and excesses of the Quebec separatists have backfired on them. But the SNP is reluctant to draw attention to a soulmate's failings and instead it endorses movements and countries seen as resisting imperialism and the remnants of colonialism.

The cause of the Palestinians is a major preoccupation which helps to give the SNP a certain visibility because there is no other international one which is quite so fashionable. Israel is largely shunned despite the lessons in practical nation-building which it might offer Scotland. In the face of American disbelief, the SNP government released the Libyan national found guilty in a Scottish court of carrying out the worst terrorist action on British soil. The 2009 event was infused with Scottish moralism but a trade-off appears to have been made with the British government.

Salmond's courtship of governments in the Middle East and South and East Asia appears to spring from similar calculations. But the SNP has been rebuffed by China and India when the Scottish government needed their backing most, during the 2014 referendum. Meanwhile, it promotes Scotland as a mini-Scandinavia irrespective of the fact that Scandinavian opinion much prefers Britain to stay united, especially at a time of growing international tension.

Scotland has an identity in the wider world that many countries of a similar size lack. But the world is simply not drawn to the upsurge of Scottish identity politics. The EU remains as wary as ever of outspoken nationalism and the bellicose features of the Yes campaign at street level in 2014 will not have assisted the SNP's reputation. The USA is bound to be underwhelmed by Scottish Nationalism. Too many vocal supporters of the party see challenging America as confirmation of their progressivism. Salmond probably feels at home in this folksy larger than life country but too often he behaves towards America in the same way as an opportunistic suitor hoping to separate an elderly matron of some of her wealth. His approach towards America is insincere and ultimately incoherent.

There are no well-positioned international advocates other than the economist Joseph Stiglitz and the press baron Rupert Murdoch who largely confines his advocacy to his Scottish (and not global) media titles. Perhaps the world is simply jaded because there have been waves of small-scale nationalism in times past which have not always left it a more settled place. The noisy, intrusive and sometimes altogether bombastic nature of this assertive nationalism may repel far more global onlookers than it attracts.

I once compared Alex Salmond with a bumptious squire forever dragging his rather plain daughter around the royal courts of Europe in search of a husband who would transform the family's status: 'For 18th-century Vienna, Hanover or Naples substitute Qatar, Beijing and any Scandinavian capital you care to name: Alex is banging at the door proclaiming that no more is fair Scotland to be viewed as a mere province but as a proud nation about to enter into its inheritance.'[114] Spurts of energy to boost the SNP's global profile are normal. They are what an ambitious nationalist party does to capture the attention of influential global actors. If Scotland does succeed in joining the club of nation-states, embassies will be opened and a seat at the United Nations provided. It remains to be seen though, what benefits Scots will enjoy from being part of a state whose economic means dictate that its diplomatic footprint will be tiny compared with that of Britain's right now. Diplomatic assistance will be needed as much as ever since it is unlikely the exodus of Scots looking for economic fulfilment elsewhere will cease upon the coming of independence. The experience of countries like Ireland would suggest that independence will greatly augment the Scottish Diaspora.

But unwary Scots may find that the liberation era contains very little for them: ruling nationalists may be far more absorbed with promoting the territory and the credentials of the elite in charge of the new country as well as the backers upon whom they relied to break free of Britain. It would not be the first time that nationalists showed themselves far more infatuated with asserting the identity of a territory on the world stage rather than the interest and welfare of the people inhabiting it.

Neighbours who previously relied upon Britain as an anchor of stability in northwest Europe may also be discomfited by the abrupt emergence of a new country which, in order to survive economically, may seek new alliances that upset the regional power-balance. There is nothing to suggest that SNP politicians who would run a post-British Scotland are of a superior calibre to those of other newly-independent small nations who behaved in just such an opportunistic way when they emerged from the remains of post-World War I empires. The world therefore may have some cause to remain very pensive about the emergence of Scottish Nationalism, but a self-referential movement like the SNP is unlikely to be unduly troubled by the numbness of the world towards it.

Notes for Chapter 7

1. BBC News, 'Profile: Scottish National Party', 5 April 2010, http://news.bbc.co.uk/1/hi/uk_politics/election_2010/scotland/8583067.stm.
2. 'Australian PM: Indy Scotland would not be in world's best interest', *Herald*, 16 August 2014, http://www.heraldscotland.com/politics/referendum-news/australian-pm-indy-scotland-would-not-be-in-worlds-best-interests.1408170886
3. 'Scots independence a bad idea, says Australian PM', *Times*, 16 August 2014, http://www.thetimes.co.uk/tto/news/politics/article4178043.ece
4. 'Alex Salmond is not impressed', *Huffington Post*, 16 August 2014, http://www.huffingtonpost.co.uk/2014/08/16/scottish-independence-alex-salmond-australia_n_5684184.html
5. 'Chinese Premier calls for a "united" UK', BBC news, 17 June 2014, http://www.bbc.co.uk/news/uk-scotland-scotland-politics-27894257
6. Mark O'Neill, 'Courting the dragon: How Scotland is seeking to woo China', *South China Morning Post*, 7 September 2014.
7. Simon Johnson, 'Alex Salmond begged leading world figures to support Lockerbie decision', *Daily Telegraph*, 7 December 2012, http://www.telegraph.co.uk/news/uknews/scotland/9730915/Alex-Salmond-begged-leading-world-figures-to-support-Lockerbie-decision.html

8. Johnson, 'Alex Salmond begged'.

9. Philip Stephens, 'The world is saying No to Scottish separation', *Financial Times*, 12 September 2014.

10. John Kerr, 'The EU and an independent Scotland Written', *Centre for European Reform*, 23 July 2014.

11. Neil Irwin, 'Why Does Scotland Want Independence. Its Culture V Economics', *New York Times*, 13 September 2014.

12. David Leask, 'SNP offers to mediate in Catalonia power crisis', *Herald*, 29 September 2015.

13. Obituary, 'Dom Mintoff', *Independent*, 23 August 2012.

14. Ibid.

15. Takis S Pappas 'Carry on Sisyphus: short answers on Greece's post-electoral politics', *Open Democracy*, 26 January 2015.

16. BBC News, 26 July 2015, http://www.bbc.co.uk/news/uk-politics-33667676

17. *Guardian*, 26 September 2014, http://www.theguardian.com/world/2014/sep/26/hungary-suspends-gas-supplies-ukraine-pressure-moscow

18. Severin Carrell, 'Alex Salmond defends Vladimir Putin remarks', *Guardian*, 30 April 2014, http://www.theguardian.com/politics/2014/apr/30/alex-salmond-vladimir-putin-remarks

19. Ben Wray, 'Jim Sillars renews calls for SNP to re-think Europe following Greek deal', *Common Space*, 27February 2015, http://commonspace.scot

20. Wray, 'Jim Sillars'.

21. Kiran Stacey, 'Salmond mired in row over EU membership', *Financial Times*, 25 October 2010, http://www.ft.com/cms/s/0/d4485894-1eb2-11e2-bebc-00144feabdc0.html#axzz3iuHyioZI

22. *Guardian*, 12 September 2012, http://www.theguardian.com/politics/2012/sep/12/barroso-doubt-scotland-eu-membership

23. BBC News, 16 February 2014, http://www.bbc.co.uk/news/uk-scotland-scotland-politics-26215963

24. Iain MacWhirter 'EU has done nothing to help independence vote', *Herald*, 13 September 2012

25. Ambrose Evans-Pritchard 'Grand bargain emerging on Europe as Germany adjusts to Cameron victory', *Daily Telegraph*, 21 May 2015, <http://www.telegraph.co.uk/finance/11621737/Grand-bargain-emerging-on-Europe-as-Germany-adjusts-to-Cameron-victory.html#disqus_thread>

26. 'First Minister Alex Salmond at Trinity College Dublin', 13 February 2008, http://www.gov.scot/News/Speeches/Speeches/First-Minister/dublin

27. David Blair, 'If Britain breaks up the rest of the world will think we have taken leave of our senses', *Daily Telegraph*, 5 September 2014, http://blogs.telegraph.co.uk/news/

davidblair/100285373/scottish-independence-if-britain-breaks-up-the-rest-of-the-world-would-think-weve-taken-leave-of-our-senses/4927236990_48abbe8790/

28. Adrian Wooldridge, "Nordic model a fantasy", *Scotsman,* 13 August 2014, http://www.scotsman.com/news/scottish-independnce-essay-nordic-model-a-fantasy-1-3507354#comments-area>

29. Wooldridge, 'Nordic model'.

30. Linn Kristen Klausen, 'An Independent Scotland to become a Nordic country', *Foreign Affairs Review,* 8 May 2014. http://foreignaffairsreview.co.uk/2014/05/independence-scotland-nordic/

31. Michael Stothard, 'Shooting highlights Sweden's social tensions, *Financial Times,* 20 April 2012, http://www.ft.com/cms/s/0/899b0e9e-7ef9-11e1-a26e-00144feab49a.html#axzz3ic1talqL

32. 'Sweden's blazing riots', *Economist,* 1 June 2013, http://www.economist.com/news/europe/21578725-scandinavian-idyll-disrupted-arson-and-unrest-blazing-surprise; Iain MacWhirter, 'Lessons from our Nordic Cousins', *Herald,* 18 June 2015.

33. http://www.nordichorizons.org/swedish-elections-kristina-lemon-notes-and-audio.html

34. Angus Robertson: 'High time to join our friends in the North and face the Arctic challenge', *Scotsman,* 29 November 2011.

35. 'Sweden is fighting intruders naked', *Politico,* 1 June 2015, http://www.politico.eu/article/sweden-is-fighting-intruders-naked/

36. 'Finnish military preparing 900,000 reservists', *Newsweek,* 28 April 2015, http://europe.newsweek.com/finish-military-preparing-900000-reservists-crisis-situation-326712

37. http://www.thelocal.se/20150520/nearly-one-third-of-swedes-want-to-join-nato

38. 'Russia threatened to aim nuclear missiles at Danish warships', *Reuters,* 22 March 2015, http://www.reuters.com/article/2015/03/22/us-denmark-russia-idUSKBN0MI0ML20150322

39. Ben Wray, 'Jim Sillars renews calls for SNP to re-think Europe following Greek deal', *Commonspace,* 27 February 2015, https://commonspace.scot/articles/531/jim-sillars-renews-calls-for-snp-to-re-think-europe-following-greek-deal

40. Allan Little, 'Would the Scandinavians want Scotland', *Guardian,* 26 January 2014, http://www.theguardian.com/uk-news/shortcuts/2014/jan/26/would-scandinavians-want-scotland

41. 'Scottish independence: Carl Bildt says Yes vote 'profound' for UK and EU', *BBC News,* 4 June 2014, http://www.bbc.co.uk/news/uk-scotland-scotland-politics-27696769

42. *Herald,* 10 June 2014. http://www.heraldscotland.com/news/13164705.Alex_Salmond_slams_very_foolish_Swedish_Foreign_Minister_Bildt/

43. Wooldridge, 'Nordic model'.

44. Gary Kent, *Window on Westminster,* 8 May 2015.
http://rudaw.net/english/opinion/05082015

45. Cat Boyd, 'Corbyn may be best thing to happen for generations', *National,* 4 August 2015.

46. Ray MacSharry, and Padraic White, T*he Making of the Celtic Tiger: the Inside story of Ireland's boom economy,* (Cork: Mercier Press, 2000), p. 154.

47. Tom Gallagher, *Europe's Path to Crisis,* Manchester: Manchester University Press, 2014, p. 94.

48. Shuggy's Blog, 'Ireland and the Case for Scottish Independence', 21 November 2010, http://modies.blogspot.co.uk/2010/11/on-ireland-and-case-for-scottish.html

49. Ibid.

50. Colm McCarthy, 'Sarkozy's grandstanding on our corporation tax misses the point', *Sunday Independent* (Dublin), 16 January 2011.

51. See Maurice Walsh, *The News from Ireland: Foreign Journalists and the Irish Revolution,* London: IB Tauris, 2011.

52. Lesley Riddoch, 'Look north, Scotland', *Guardian,* 5 December 2011

53. Kevin Toolis, 'Scots should recall the poverty of the Irish Free State', *Financial Times,* 2 May 2014.

54. Fintan O'Toole, 'Scottish referendum: Musings of a reluctant nationalist', *Irish Times,* 17 September 2014.

55. Fintan O'Toole, Scotland's vote is not about Braveheart. It's about democracy', *Guardian,* 4 August 2015.

56. Peter Geoghegan, 'Fintan O'Toole on referenda', *National,* 1 June 2015.

57. Toolis, 'Scots should recall'.

58. Ronan Fanning, 'Lowry may yet act as the catalyst to coalition divide', *Irish Times,* 7 April 2013

59. Ben Riley-Smith, 'Spain and Belgium "would veto an independent Scotland in EU"', *Daily Telegraph,* 25 August 2014,
http://www.telegraph.co.uk/news/uknews/scottish-independence/11054187/Spain-and-Belgium-would-veto-an-independent-Scotlands-EU-membership.html#disqus_thread>

60. Peter Geoghegan, 'Irish Ayes: A new chapter is opening up in Scottish-Irish relations', *National,* 22 June 2015.

61. https://twitter.com/peterkgeoghegan/status/627828191005179904 [accessed 16 August 2015]

62. See Russell Kirk, *America's British Culture,* New Brunswick: Transaction Publishers, 1994 edition.

63. Mure Dickie, 'Stiglitz endorses SNP's currency plan', *Financial Times,* 25 August 2013

64. *Daily Telegraph,* 26 August 2014;

http://www.telegraph.co.uk/news/uknews/scottish-independence/11058138/London-is-bluffing-over-currency-union-claims-Salmond-adviser.html

65. Yannis Palaiologo, 'Beware of American econ professors'! *Politico* EU, 11 August 2015, http://www.politico.eu/article/tsipras-greee-creditors-euro-high-profile-us-economists/>

66. Joseph Stiglitz, 'America is on the wrong side of history', *Guardian*, 6 August 2015, http://www.theguardian.com/business/2015/aug/06/joseph-stiglitz-america-wrong-side-of-history

67. Eliana Johnson, 'Joseph Stiglitz's Curious "Outside Activities"', *National Review Online*, 16 May 2014.

68. Johnson, 'Joseph Stiglitz's Curious'.

69. Paul Krugman, 'Scots Wha Hae', *New York Times*, 24 February 2014, http://krugman.blogs.nytimes.com/2014/02/24/scots-wha-hae/?_php=true&_type=blogs&_r=0

70. Tom Gallagher, 'Nationalists recoil from militant Quebec parallel', *The Commentator*, 7 September 2012. http://www.thecommentator.com/article/1622/scottish_nationalists_recoil_from_militant_quebec_parallel

71. Graeme Hamilton, 'What is happening in Canada?': Country's reputation with investors could take hit over Quebec corruption scandal', *National Post*, 13 June 2013, http://news.nationalpost.com/news/canada/canadian-politics/what-is-happening-in-canada-countrys-reputation-with-investors-could-take-hit-over-quebec-corruption-scandal

72. Gallagher, 'Nationalists recoil'.

73. *Guardian*, 8 February 2013, http://www.theguardian.com/politics/scottish-independence-blog/2013/feb/08/alexsalmond-quebec-canada

74. Robert Bothwell 'Quebec sleeps. Or does it'? *The Star*, 3 January 2012.

75. Celine Cooper, 'PQ's vision may not be Quebecers', *Montreal Gazette* 28 August 2012.

76. See John Harmon McElroy, *American Beliefs: What keeps a big country and a diverse people united?* Chicago: Ivan R. Dee, 1999.

77. http://www.gov.scot/News/Speeches/Speeches/First-Minister/Virginia(accessed 16 August 2015).

78. Andrew Hook, 'Alex Salmond, Sally Magnusson, and 'The Wealth of Nations', *Scottish Review*, 25 April 2013

79. See Colm McNamee, *Robert Bruce: Our Most Valiant Prince, King and Lord*, Edinburgh: Birlinn, 2011 ed, p.p. 72-122; also, by the same author, *The Wars of the Bruces in Scotland, England and Ireland 1306-1328*, Edinburgh: John Donald, 2006 ed.p.p. 84-85, 95-99.

80. Daniel Hannan 'Why Britons should celebrate the American Declaration of Independence', *Daily Telegraph*, 4 July 2013

81. Hannan 'Why Britons should celebrate'.

82. Quoted in Hannan 'Why Britons should celebrate'

83. 'Lockerbie bomber freed from jail', BBC News, 20 August 2009, http://news.bbc.co.uk/1/hi/scotland/south_of_scotland/8197370.stm

84. Editorial, 'The more we learn the worse it gets', Sunday Telegraph, 6 September 2009.

85. Letter from FBI director Robert S. Mueller III to Scottish Minister Kenny MacAskill, 22 August 2009, https://www.fbi.gov/news/pressrel/press-releases/letter-from-fbi-director-robert-s.-mueller-iii-to-scottish-minister-kenny-macaskill

86. Evening Standard (London), 26 August 2009.

87. Lesley Riddoch, 'Megrahi release an independent step', Guardian, 22 August 2009.

88. Tom Gallagher, 'America is all around us', Scottish Review, 12 May 2010, http://www.scottishreview.net/TGallagher202.html.

89. Torcuil Crichton ' SNP shapes up for battle royale over Trident', Westminster blog, 28 May 2015, http://whitehall1212.blogspot.co.uk/

90. Libby Brooks, 'Awol sailor's Trident safety fears unfounded, says defence secretary', Guardian, 28 May 2015.

91. Lord Ashcroft 'Trident: The SNP shoots the messenger', Lord Ashcroft Polls, 13 May 2013 http://lordashcroftpolls.com/2013/05/trident-the-snp-shoots-the-messenger/

92. Chris Deerin, 'Back the Bomb: Thanks to Trident, we can be massively smug and safe', 'Back the Bomb', https://medium.com/@chrisdeerin (originally published in the Scottish Daily Mail).

93. Sir Christopher Meyer 'Our special relationship hangs by a thread', Daily Telegraph, 15 January 2015, http://www.telegraph.co.uk/news/politics/11345045/Our-special-relationship-hangs-by-a-thread.html#disqus_thread

94. Andrew Apostolou, 'Scotland Isn't Ready for the International Stage', Wall Street Journal, 15 September 2014.

95. Scotland's Future, Chapter 6, International Relations and Defence, Edinburgh: Scottish Government, 2013. http://www.gov.scot/Publications/2013/11/9348/10

96. David Blair, 'Scottish independence: if Britain breaks up, the rest of the world would think we've taken leave of our senses', Daily Telegraph, 5 September 2014, http://blogs.telegraph.co.uk/news/davidblair/100285373/scottish-independence-if-britain-breaks-up-the-rest-of-the-world-would-think-weve-taken-leave-of-our-senses/4927236990_48abbe8790/

97. BBC news, 29 March 1999, http://news.bbc.co.uk/1/hi/uk_politics/307225.stm

98. Blair, 'Scottish independence'.

99. Blair, 'Scottish independence'.

100. Steve Forbes, 'Scotland will never be a big player on the world stage', Daily Telegraph, 17 September 2014, <http://www.telegraph.co.uk/news/uknews/scottish-independence/11099498/Scotland-will-never-be-a-big-player-on-the-world-

101. http://www.brookings.edu/blogs/brookings-now/posts/2014/04/lord-george-robert-son-forces-of-darkness-love-scottish-split-from-united-kingdom

102. 'What is going on in the Scottish Palestine Solidarity Campaign?' *Harry's Place,* 14 March 2008, http://hurryupharry.org/2008/03/14/what-is-going-on-in-the-scottish-palestine-solidarity-campaign/

103. Tom Gallagher, 'Edinburgh a sad symbol of anti-Israeli intolerance', *American Interest,* 19 August 2014. http://www.the-american-interest.com/2014/08/19/edinburgh-a-sad-symbol-of-anti-israeli-intolerance/

104. Tom Gallagher, 'Is cowardly Edinburgh fit for a global arts festival', *The Commentator,* 12 August 2014, http://www.thecommentator.com/article/5158/is_cowardly_edinburgh_fit_for_a_global_arts_festival

105. Phil Miller, 'Artists call for fringe show from Israel to be cancelled', *Herald,* 18 July 2014,http://www.heraldscotland.com/news/home-news/artists-call-for-fringe-show-from-israel-to-be-cancelled; 'Edinburgh a Sad Symbol'.

106. Robert Philpot, 'SNP may force Labour to take tougher line on Israel', *Jewish chronicle*, 8 April 2015, http://news.bbc.co.uk/1/hi/in_depth/uk_politics/2001/conferences_2001/snp/1552415.stm.

107. Philpot, 'SNP may force Labour'.

108. 'Left-Wing-MP Galloway Declares Town Of Bradford Israel-Free Zone', *Breitbart,* 7 August 2014, http://www.breitbart.com/Breitbart-London/2014/08/07/Left-Wing-MP-Galloway-Declares-Town-Of-Bradford-Israel-Free-Zone>

109. Gallagher, 'Edinburgh a sad symbol'.

110. Gallagher, 'Edinburgh a sad symbol'.

111. 'Editorial', *Guardian,* 8 August 2014. http://www.theguardian.com/commentis-free/2014/aug/08/guardian-view-gaza-rise-antisemitism.

112. Maureen Farrell, 'Israel As Incubator', *Forbes,* 10 November 2009.

113. Michael Tanner, 'Israel's Culture of Entrepreneurship and Success', *Realclearpolitics,* 5 August 2013, www.realclearpolitics.com/articles/2012/08/05/israels_culture_of_entrepreneurship_and_success_115008.html 5 August 2012

114. Tom Gallagher, 'The danger of letting the police decide what is offensive', *Scottish Review,* 21 December 2011, http://www.scottishreview.net/TomGallagher211.shtml

CONCLUSION: UNENLIGHTENED TIMES IN SCOTLAND AND BEYOND

This book has examined the reasons for the dramatic rise in fortunes of a separatist party in the northern third of Britain. It has probed and profiled a party that is among the best in the world at campaigning and using the very latest techniques of online persuasion to get its pro-independence message across. With seemingly capable leaders the Scottish National Party now thrives after years in the doldrums. But it is increasingly clear that it is not simply the prowess of the SNP that is responsible for the mass appeal of political separatism (nor the mediocrity of many of its opponents). In government for eight years, the SNP's administration of Scotland has been a poor quality one. Important policy areas like education, health and policing have slipped into crisis. However insistent it is on having a second referendum so that Scots deliver the 'correct' verdict on independence it has neglected making any real plans for a post-British future. It is clear that many in the SNP wish to rely on continued British goodwill in the form of a currency union or financial subsidies, rather than concentrate on the tasks of building a completely new state.

The rhetoric of the SNP may be that of independence but in practice the party prefers to have a dependency relationship with both the rest of the UK (and also the EU). It is a Jekyll and Hyde relationship in which London and England (the dominant partner of the 308-year union) are accused of numerous sins and slights against Scotland. But in practice the Nationalists are reluctant to let go and make a completely fresh start. They have done well electorally by building a factory of grievances or a politics of resentment against southern Britain. The party's less enlightened spirits have not hesitated to tap into a strain of Anglophobia that has long been found within Scottish popular culture. But over 60 per cent of Scotland's exports are destined for the rest of the UK. It lacks a separate economic profile. It has no credible plans to replace British state employers upon whom the prosperity of a string of Scottish towns depend. Much of the service sector which maintains once bustling and industrial Glasgow, still Scotland's largest city, would struggle to remain viable.

But it was Glasgow which Alex Salmond dubbed as 'Freedom City' in 2014 because of its newly acquired fidelity to the nationalist cause. Numerous Glaswegians now like the disobedient spirit of the SNP. A segment of its citizens have always been unruly and volatile. This turbulence finally played out in the political arena with dramatic results. Glasgow was one of four electoral districts in Scotland which voted in favour of independence in the 2014 referendum. The Yes side's campaign played to the rebellious streak of the place and its appetite for risk-taking. This derring-do had hitherto been reflected in alarming statistics for health and mortality due to the readiness of many inhabitants to eat, drink and smoke in reckless ways.

Away from Clydeside, Scots long had a reputation for being more cautious and conventional in their approach to life. Edinburgh, Scotland's capital, just an hour away by train has always been a more measured and introspective place. And following the referendum there seemed to be good grounds for caution.

Oil is Scotland's one major natural source of energy. But due to the slump in the world price, revenues are now only a fraction of what the SNP's 2014 blueprint for independence stated would be needed to pay the state's bills. In May 2014, a few months before the referendum the Scottish government said that revenues for the next five years would range between £15.8 billion and £38.7 billion. In June 2015, revising those projections, it conceded that they would be between £2.4 billion and £10.8 billion. The economics journalist David Smith has written: 'Taking the midpoint of those ranges, and the mid-point of the latest range looks generous given the oil price, the post-referendum [funding] projection is less than a quarter of what it was'.[1] In 2014, 'more was spent on UK offshore oil and gas operations than was earned on production'. Exploration is at its lowest since the 1970s. 65,000 jobs have been lost in the North Sea in the twenty months up to September 2015.[2]

Many voters on average incomes with a mortgage to pay, private sector rent to pay, or employed by outside firms, or else the British state, might therefore have had cause to ponder about their livelihoods as a British general election swiftly approached. But it was actually an issueless contest. Who best stood up for Scotland was the only thing that seemed to count and the SNP swept nearly all parts of the country with the claim that it would be the nation's champion in the territorial duel with London.

After seventy years of wandering in the political desert, the SNP made an enormous discovery about the mood and outlook of the Scots in 2014 and 2015. The loyalty of a great many could easily be won and kept by remaining vague and tight-lipped about the party's plans for the future. Instead a cacophony of noisy indignation about the alleged role of Scotland's island partner England in holding the country back, detached people from their former relaxed or non-existent views on constitutional questions and turned countless numbers into militant separatists. Without the agitational tools of social media it would have been difficult to accomplish this exercise in mass persuasion.

The genius of nationalism lies in its mobilisation for political ends of emotions that people feel as more authentic, less negotiable than the ones which normally shape ordinary politics. But it should be noted that cultural shifts, separate from the political movement, have encouraged restiveness and even a mutinous feeling towards Britain. This is the case even for perhaps large numbers of Scots who began adulthood with some degree of attachment for Britain.

Much of society has become more hedonistic and excitable as absorption in civic and community endeavours faded. The rise of the dissatisfied and egotistical citizen ready to endorse a political party whose leaders also have a self-absorbed and basically populist profile, had been predicted by the Spanish philosopher José Ortega y Gasset in the 1920s. In *The Revolt of the Masses* published in 1929, he warned that society's vital energies would be sapped thanks to dumbed down citizens surrendering their fate to an interventionist state where populists held sway.

Scotland was then a politically placid, (perhaps even stagnant) part of a British state that had remained almost completely free from inter-war fascism and it is unlikely that Ortega would have looked there for corroboration of his ideas. But by the early 21st century, several of the main bulwarks of underlying stability were fast disappearing. Civic associations were in retreat and the state assumed an ever-larger role in people's lives, fuelling expectations and offering a platform for militant groups determined to strengthen their influence over state and society even further. Religious observance, rather high in European terms until the 1970s, was plummeting. Marriage was becoming a casualty of growing individual non-conformity. Casual relationships would increasingly be the norm especially among lower-income citizens who flocked to the SNP in 2015. It was surely not unusual for a casual and short-term approach to personal life to spill over into politics.

So, to answer the question posed in the opening paragraph, profound changes in society making it more volatile and attuned to radical solutions for political issues may well help to explain the sheer velocity of the SNP surge. But it should not be forgotten that the SNP is far from being the only such anti-system political force in Europe, offering an exciting outlet for restive and often economically under-active people who had grown contemptuous of established political institutions.

Elsewhere, anti-system political forces have emerged from social movements that reach out to young people in particular. With youth unemployment standing at 25 per cent in the 19 EU countries which use the Euro as their currency by 2015 and at a staggering 55. 5 per cent in Spain and 58.3 per cent in Greece, there was a new class which radicals were able to reach out to. This was the *precariat,* often well-educated young people who are frozen out of the labour market and whose expectations of leading the kind of normal personal and professional life previous generations had taken for granted, have been cruelly dashed. Against the background of a protracted economic crisis in much of the Eurozone, parties that promise to dissolve the post-war truce between capital and labour and proceed with a radical redistribution of wealth, have surged in several countries.

In Britain, social and economic conditions are far less stark than in much of the Eurozone. The youth unemployment figure was 14.1 per cent in mid-2015. In Scotland youth unemployment had fallen to reach 14%, the lowest total there since April-June 2008. London, Edinburgh and other UK cities are a magnet for young Europeans elsewhere seeking work at different pay levels. But Jeremy Corbyn, the new leader of the British Labour Party is hoping to make young people frozen out of the housing market due to excessive house prices and rents, one of the engines for a far-left drive to be at the centre of political power in Britain.

However impractical the core economic plans of a Corbyn-led Labour Party, Podemos in Spain or Syriza in Greece are, they and other previously fringe elements have shown themselves to be adept, sophisticated even, at acquiring power. This is a trait which the radical left shares with the SNP and may help to explain why an alliance between the two was able to operate during the referendum years. While Marxist and especially Trotskyite demands for a state-controlled economic order are just as unrealistic as they were when pursued by their predecessors over the past century, these forces have managed to spread their influence across important branches of national life, even more successfully in academia, teaching and parts of the media than in the trade-union field.

The SNP never displayed similar prowess but its impatience to shape state broad-casting around what it sees as Scottish norms shows its desire to fill up strategic spaces. In government, it has established tight control over the civil service, increasingly over numerous non-governmental bodies delivering services and offering advice to the state, as well as over society itself. The energy which the SNP has not displayed in planning for an independent future, has instead been ploughed into micro-managing the lives of citizens by a range of intrusive measures.

Far from being an anachronism in a globalising age, the SNP is a very contemporary political force. Parties which represent the class, occupational, religious or secular interest and outlooks of their voting base are on the defensive and increasingly in retreat. Society has become more fragmented and fluid. It is identity politics which increasingly motivate voters in an age of anxiety over immigration, corporate global power or other forms of remote control felt to marginalise and dis-empower citizens. Parties able to offer seemingly fresh narratives based around mobilising identity are very much in vogue. It may well be that, in their turn, parties in the beleaguered centre of European politics will regroup around defence of a *cosmopolitan* identity.

Privatised existences, exemplified by addiction to online technology, have made people increasingly self-absorbed. Their own feelings often count for more than group loyalties stemming from locality, family, workplace or faith community. The genius of the SNP (with movements elsewhere probably likely to follow) is to give such passive and unfulfilled individualism a collective outlet. The SNP has successfully emerged as a surrogate family at the national level. But its message is not one of solidarity, restraint, and long-term cooperation in order to build a better Scotland. Very often it is rather bellicose, emphasising partisanship, sometimes along territorial lines. In Glasgow, social conflict in some poorer areas once involved gangs feuding over territory. The SNP has shown particular flair in harnessing social tensions in this unruly city which used to play out in religious strife and neighbourhood factionalism, channelling them instead into politics.

So the SNP is currently in a position much-coveted by populist parties. It has become a conduit for emotions that are often negative ones but which place few demands on the leadership to work hard to deliver effective policies. As he attempts to board a plane leaving London, its former leader can pretend to be the captain of the 'Spaceship Enterprise' of *Star Trek* science fiction fame without too many people asking if he may have taken leave of his senses.[3] Nationalists can be more self-indulgent and wayward than other politicians because nationalism so often manages to persuade lots of voters to suspend their critical faculties. But sooner or later, the SNP may have to confront certain glaring inconsistencies.

There is the fact that an independent Scotland, so bound up economically with the rest of the UK, is likely to enjoy little real economic self-determination. Moreover, austerity on a scale far greater than what was seen in the dark night of 1980s Thatcherism may be necessary if a future Scottish government is to run anything like a balanced budget. These warnings are dismissed as Unionism's 'Project Fear' but Alex Bell, who wrote the first draft of the 2013 White Paper and still a convinced nationalist, has gone much further. He wrote on 16 November 2015: 'The interests of the SNP and the interests of independence have diverged. Independence needs facts and planning. The leadership fear those facts will rip the party apart. The SNP is growing comfortable in its role as the 'Scotland' party within a lop-sided UK, while pretending it is still fighting for independence to keep the party together'.

'The SNP's model of independence', Bell wrote in the same article, 'is broken beyond repair....'

'The campaign towards the 2014 vote, and the economic information since, has kicked the old model to death'.

'The idea that you could have a Scotland with high public spending, low taxes, a stable economy and reasonable government debt was wishful a year ago - now it is deluded.'[4]

The fact that such a large portion of the electorate is impervious to these kind of soundly-based concerns may be an indication of how unready a lot of Scots are to shoulder any post-independence burdens but how keen is their appetite for conflict for its own sake.

Those who worry about a world that is sliding towards ever greater discord and fragmentation should take a closer look at Scotland. It is in the vanguard of what may possibly be seen as a new epoch of turbulence arising in some of the most stable countries on the planet. Impatience with conventional rules of political behaviour and contempt for often floundering elites as they seek to uphold them, are now widespread across much of the West. Perhaps this mutinous mood was last seen in the 1920s and 1930s when the old political order in most of mainland Europe was fatally undermined by the catastrophe of the First World War and a string of related economic and political misfortunes.

It is far too glib to assume that contemporary populist movements are linear descendents of inter-war authoritarian movements. For one thing, it is not economic desperation or mass trauma arising from participation in conflict that is spurring them. But there is a sense that authority is inauthentic, shallow and even illegitimate. Political forces supposed to represent citizens, channel their interests and exercise a prudent sway over government affairs, appear increasingly incompetent or else negligent in exercising the core functions of democratic government. The need for a radical reset is a cry which has adherents in the left, centre and right of politics, among contrasting different social groups and among people with a regional or sub-national identity hitherto disinclined to challenge state boundaries.

This new culture of smouldering revolt has given a tremendous boost to causes that have been tried and discarded in the past as impractical, exactly like Scottish nationalism. It has proven a springtime for unruly and egotistical politicians who were often derided and certainly overlooked in more settled times. Now these outspoken and irreverent tribunes have a mass audience among the discontented. They have few solutions for major problems. But nor are they pressed to provide them. Solutions imply that people are thinking of the long-term, of their own children's prospects or of how their community or nation may fare. But many voters are now self-referential and present-orientated. It is how they feel today which preoccupies them. Their distress is often not economic at all but instead emotional. In politics, they search for alternatives that can fill the spiritual void in the lives of many.

Highly adaptable, nationalism has once again found an outlet in a fresh historical epoch of discontent. This book suggests that the flimsiness of the nationalist political offer, in the case of Scotland, is bound sooner or later to lead to disappointment and rejection. What is desperately needed is a new conversation about politics in Scotland. It has to be one that confronts the real problems of the country rather than alibis ranging from foodbanks to the alleged iniquities of the Westminster Parliament. Moreover a political relaunch must judge politicians and other aspirants for high office on their personal suitability to deliver policies that make a real difference to people's lives rather than give them a temporary emotive boost based on patriotic sentiment. Wanted are politicians who can engage with people on a serious basis, help restore a long-term perspective, and be seen as people bound up with the needs of local communities which have elected them.

But at the present time, the politicians who prevail are those who essentially patronise voters with patriotic but hollow rhetoric, who offer emotional quick-fixes based on an uncosted misty independence, and who increasingly treat their constituencies like absentee estates which can be overlooked because they are engaged on far more important patriotic work than mere community service. Often they are active on social media while in quite a few cases they have absolutely no hesitation about blocking their own constituents when they pose awkward questions to them in on-line communications. But as Labour's sole Scottish MP Ian Murray remarked on 9 November 2015, 'many SNP MPs, MSPs and candidates regularly retweet, reference and follow', Wings over Scotland.[5] He made this observation a few hours after Stuart Campbell had tweeted his followers: 'I hope an aeroplane delivering dirty needles to an incinerator crashes onto Ian Murray tonight'.[6] The MP observed: 'What has politics come to'?

Obviously, newly influential voices find it self-liberating to systematically release and foster hatreds. Shortly after his threat to Murray, Campbell continued: 'I swear from this day on I will do everything in my power to wipe Labour and the Tories from the face of Scotland. Just playing till now'.[7] 355 people had given their approval by daybreak on 10 November. Despite Nicola Sturgeon showing occasional flashes of insight about how potentially ruinous such polarising rhetoric could be for Scotland and despite the arguments in his *Wee Blue Book* having been systematically taken apart by the businessman Kevin Hague, Campbell remains a hero for many thousands of Scots.[8]

Scotland has to choose the path it wishes to go down. If it wishes to continue endorsing populists, a few of whom are very careful not to overlook their own financial affairs as they perform as tribunes of the people, the country will change its character and be seen as different by the rest of the world. Its national political life is likely to increasingly resemble Third World countries whose politics revolve around shrill nationalism and directing resentment at foreign centres which are convenient alibis for internal political failings. Not only will the country become hopelessly divided in the process (perhaps far worse so than in the polarised 2013-15 period) but it will be placed on a collision course with the rest of the island it has been united with for over three hundred years. There is barely concealed frustration among some cybernats about their lack of success in provoking an English backlash against Scottish demands. The contempt, shading into hatred, towards Scotland's partners in the Union has so far not been reciprocated elsewhere in Britain.

There was bemusement among commentators about the House of Commons vote on 9 November to grant Scotland greatly increased economic powers. From now on nearly half of the Scottish parliament's budget will no longer come from the UK treasury but will be raised from Scottish taxpayers. Among territorially devolved states, perhaps only Switzerland and Canada now enjoy greater devolution. But the SNP reacted as if it had been mugged by its British partners. Pete Wishart MP claimed 'we have been shown gross disrespect' in a debate marked by frequent noisy interruptions from him and his colleagues when Conservative and Labour MPs spoke.[9]

Much unavoidable damage will be caused if the flames of a northern revolt succeed in setting alight a once unified British House. It is a long-established entity associated with violence, injustice, and hypocrisy. But far more positively it has also created rules for managing a disorderly world, played a central role in halting at least one tyranny that threatened to plunge the world into darkness, and been a pioneer of social reform and political pluralism at home. A majority of Scots may decide eventually to sever their links with such a state exactly at the point when its responsible and virtuous features easily transcend its negative ones. But there are few signs that what is likely to follow the British epoch would easily replicate the sense of personal security and freedom that, for so long, made Britain known across the world as a safe and peaceable country.

The SNP has no model for self-rule and is reluctant to encourage internal debate about what could follow Britain. It is one of a number of ostensibly radical causes worldwide which trade on negation. It attacks a system which it depicts as unjust, interfering and illegitimate but has nothing to put in its place. Scottish nationalism is part of a wider category of movements which has exploited the rootlessness of people in an unsettled secular and materialist society to plant the flag of revolt. It has found fertile ground in Scotland for reasons I have tried to explain in the book. But it has few if any answers for concrete problems that affect citizens. In governing it is preoccupied with erecting barriers shutting off Scotland from the rest of the UK while making sure that there is still a financial lifeline from London to keep its quasi-separatist experiment afloat. Invariably, when forced by world events such as the Paris killings of 13 November to briefly lift its gaze from parochial concerns, it loudly proclaims the need for a *minimalist* response. The SNP's 'safety strategy' as articulated by Pat Kane, one of nationalism's intellectual gurus, a week earlier, is to endlessly signal to 'the frustrated and alienated of this planet' our 'good intent'.[10]

Perhaps the world has outgrown countries like Britain and the values that have been associated with it in recent times. Time may soon tell. The outcome of the current duel between separatists and unionists will not only decide the fate of Britain but also have a major impact beyond its shores due to what happens in Britain being noticed and sometimes emulated in many other places. Not all nationalists in Scotland are, by any means, spurred on primarily by an urge to repudiate and demolish a Union state which they have grown weary of. Eventually, they might feel just as big a loss as those attached to Britain if the future falls far short of their expectations. At the time of writing, autumn 2015, Nicola Sturgeon's government has been beset by events which show just how remarkably ill-prepared the nationalists are to be the architects of a new state nation. They suggest that the political giants supposedly leading Scotland towards a bright new dawn may really just be Lilliputians with a bold line in rhetoric. The lack of critical scrutiny shown towards Scotland's 'change' party has allowed self-serving behaviour, gross inefficiency in government, and the suspension of checks and balances to flourish. If independence is handed on a plate by a delirious population to a party which struggles to carry out everyday tasks of governance, it is a devastating indictment on Scotland and it will be hard to avoid the verdict that it now has little interest in counting itself among the countries which seek to be forces for moderation and even good in the world.

Notes for Conclusion

1. David Smith, 'The Great Escape: how Scotland Dodged a Bullet', *EconomicsUK*.Com, 12 September 2015, http://www.economicsuk.com/blog/002120.html
2. Douglas Fraser, 'Oil sector "has lost 65,000 jobs"', *BBC News,* 9 September 2015.
3. 'Alex Salmond barred from BA flight after booking as Star trek captain', *Press Association,* 4 October 2015.
4. Alex Bell, 'SNP Independence is dead – start again or shut up', Rattle, 16 November 2015, http://rattle.scot/snp-independence-is-dead-start-again-or-shut-up
5. Ian Murray on Twitter, 9 November 2015.
6. Wings over Scotland on Twitter, 9 November 2015.
7. Wings over Scotland on Twitter, 9 November 2015.
8. See Kevin Hague, 'Wings and His Wee Blue Book of Errors', *Chokkablog,* 25 October 2015, http://chokkablog.blogspot.co.uk/2015/10/wings-and-his-wee-blue-book-of-errors.html
9. 'Scotland Bill (Programme 2), Hansard, column 46, 9 November 2015.
10. *The National,* 7 November 2015.

INDEX

Abbreviations:
N = Nationalism
Sc = Scotland

INDEX

Morgan, Edwin (poet) 248
Morrison, Ewan (writer) 263-4
Morton, Tom (broadcaster) 261
Motherwell 91, 260
Mueller III, Robert S. (FBI chief) 309
Muir, Edwin (Scottish writer) 246-7
Muir, Thomas (18th century radical) 96, 308
Mullin, Roger (SNP MP 2015-) 95, 154
Mundell, David (MP 2005-) 201
Munro, Bill (pro-Union businessman) 232
Murdoch, Sir Rupert (media tycoon and SNP supporter) 45, 55, 92, 159,218, 225, 318
Murphy, Jim (MP 1997-2015) 89, 92, 130, 137, 152, 161, 165,171-5
Murray, Andy (tennis player) 208
Murray, Craig (SNP member and former diplomat) 85-6, 87-8, 167-8
Murray, Ian (MP 2010-) 168, 180, 332
Murrell, Peter (SNP official) 76-7, 194-5
Muslims, Scottish 92-3

Nairn, Tom, (political writer) 60
National, the 89, 334
National Collective 51, 80-1, 252-5, 257, 260, 261, 270, 274, 275
National Health Service (NHS) see Health service
Nationalism (general) 32-5
Neil, Andrew (broadcasting journalist) 176, 217
Neil, Alex (MSP 1999-) 107, n.104
Neill, A.S. (educationalist) 246
Nelson, Fraser (journalist) 134-5
New Zealand 19, 98, 312, 313
Nicolson, John (MP 2015-) 96
Noelle-Neumann, Elisabeth (political scientist) 37
Noon, Stephen (SNP strategist) 79-80, 82-3, 84
North Atlantic treaty Organization (NATO) 60, 88, 111, 280-1, 287, 290-1, 296, 300
Norgaard, Finn (slain film director) 293
Northern Ireland 42, 98, 125, 127, 263, 285
North Korea 19
Norway 130, 292-3, 295

Obama, Barack (US President) 4, 83
O'Brien, Cardinal Keith (Scottish RC prelate) 91
O'Brien, Neil (journalist) 50
Office of Budget Responsibility (OBR) 158
O'Hagan, Andrew (novelist) 250-1, 270
O'Hara, Brendan (MP 2015-) 48, 87
Oil (Scotland), 5, 26, 28, 40-1, , 43-4, 46, 57, 75, 113, 119, 120-1, 133, 135, 157-8, 160, 170, 175, 201, 228, 233, 293, 300-01, 327
Orange Order 91, 136
Orbán, Viktor (Hungarian politician) 288-9
Orr, Deborah (journalist) 260
Ortega y Gasset, José (political thinker) 5, 62, 157, 254-5, 328
Osborne, George (Conservative politician) 50, 114-15, 118, 179
O'Toole, Fintan (Irish journalist and author) 300-1

Paisley 46, 70, 163, 227,
Palestine, see Israel-Palestine
Palme, Olof (Swedish politician) 293
Papandreou, Andreas (Greek politician) 55, 303
Pappis, Takis (political scientist) 55
Parnell, C.S. (Irish nationalist) 206
Paterson, Bill (actor) 269
Paterson, Lindsay (political scientist) 124
Paterson, Niall (journalist) 167
Payne, Alison (public policy expert) 162
Pennington, Hugh (scientist and pro-Union voice) 121
Perry, Alex (journalist) 206-7, 213
Peronism 303
Peru 107, 244
Poland 244
Police 127-8, 196, 223-4
Political culture, adversarial 167, 206, authoritarian features 89-90, independence surges and 6, 28, religious dimension 98, rent-seeking 98-100, SNP activists outlook 28-9, state domination 99-100, world comparisons 287-9
Populism 7, 20, 28, 44-5, 54, 55-6, 100-1, 287-9 see also Alex SalmondPower, Wil-

INDEX

INDEX